23.00

AMERICAN WOMEN
images and realities

AMERICAN WOMEN
Images and Realities

Advisory Editors
ANNETTE K. BAXTER
LEON STEIN

A Note About This Volume

As a teen-ager, Caroline Wells Healy Dall (1822-1912) participated in Margaret Fuller's weekly transcendental "conversations" in Boston. But it was the mission work of the Rev. Joseph Tuckerman that drew her to Boston's slums, where for five years she operated a nursery for children of working women. Left with two children by a husband whose church mission to India lasted 31 years, she became a vigorous champion of women's rights. In this book she traces cultural traditions and religious influences that have blocked woman's entry into the professions, attacking especially the hypocritical charity which restricted woman's freedom to learn and to work.

THE COLLEGE, THE MARKET,

AND

THE COURT;

OR,

WOMAN'S RELATION TO EDUCATION, LABOR,
AND LAW

By CAROLINE H. DALL

ARNO PRESS
A New York Times Company
New York • 1972

Reprint Edition 1972 by Arno Press Inc.

Reprinted from a copy in The Princeton
University Library

American Women: Images and Realities
ISBN for complete set: 0-405-04445-3
See last pages of this volume for titles.

Manufactured in the United States of America

- - - - - - - - - - - -

Library of Congress Cataloging in Publication Data

Dall, Caroline Wells (Healey) 1822-1912.
   The college, the market, and the court.

   (American women: images and realities)
   1. Education of women. 2. Woman--Legal status,
laws, etc. 3. Woman--Employment. I. Title.
II. Series.
HQ1423.D22   1972   301.41'2   72-2596
ISBN 0-405-04453-4

THE COLLEGE, THE MARKET,

AND

THE COURT;

OR,

WOMAN'S RELATION TO EDUCATION, LABOR, AND LAW.

By CAROLINE H. DALL

AUTHOR OF "HISTORICAL SKETCHES," "SUNSHINE," "THE LIFE OF DR. ZAKRZEWSKA," ETC.

"Let this be copied out,
And keep it safe for our remembrance.
Return the precedent to these lords again." — KING JOHN.

"How canst thou make me thy friend who in nothing am like thee?
Thy life and dwelling are under the waters; but my way of living
Is to eat all that man does!" — BATRACHOMYOMACHIA.

BOSTON:
LEE AND SHEPARD.
1867.

Entered according to Act of Congress, in the year 1867, by
LEE AND SHEPARD,
In the Clerk's Office of the District Court of the District of Massachusetts.

CAMBRIDGE:
STEREOTYPED AND PRINTED BY JOHN WILSON AND SON.

TO

LUCRETIA MOTT,

FOR MORE THAN FIFTY YEARS A PREACHER AND REFORMER; SPOTLESS ALIKE IN ALL PUBLIC AND PRIVATE RELATIONS; WHOSE CHILDREN'S GRANDCHILDREN RISE UP TO CALL HER BLESSED;

This Book is Dedicated,

SINCE SHE IS THE BEST EXAMPLE THAT I KNOW OF WHAT ALL WOMEN MAY AND SHOULD BECOME.

"A woman
Leading with sober pace an armed man,
All bossed in gold, and thus the superscription:
'I, Justice, bring this injured exile back
To claim his portion in his father's hall.'"
SEVEN AGAINST THEBES.

A PREFACE

TO BE READ AFTER THE BOOK.

WHEN, some years ago, I delivered nine lectures upon the Condition of Woman, I had no intention of printing them until time had matured my judgments and justified my conclusions. Peculiar circumstances afterwards induced me to modify this decision. The first course of lectures, now printed as "The College," had proved unexpectedly popular, and was many times repeated. At its close, I announced the second course upon Labor, involving the subject of Prostitution as the result of Low Wages; and a very unexpected opposition ensued. My files can still show the large number of letters I received, beseeching me not to touch this subject; and private intercession followed, on the part of those I hold wisest and most dear, to the same effect. Why I did not yield to all the clamor, I cannot tell, — except that I was not working for myself nor *of* myself.

I thought it, however, necessary to take unusual precautions to prevent these lectures from being misunderstood. I wrote private notes, enclosing tickets, to almost all the leading clergymen, asking that they would attend them as a personal favor to myself. I believe I did not allude to the efforts which had been made to silence me, except when I wrote to those who had joined in the outcry. In that case, I demanded the attendance as an act of justice. These notes were kindly responded to; and grateful tears started to my eyes, when I found on the seats before me white-haired men, who set aside their prejudices for my sake. Whatever might have been thought before, the delivery of the lectures silenced all objections. They were fully attended and frequently repeated; and I followed the delivery by the printing of this particular course, in order that misunderstandings should not have time to establish themselves. The book was well received, both at home and abroad. Letters came to me from the far shores of India and Africa, thanking me for its publication. The first edition was sold at once; and I should have reprinted the book, but that I did not wish to re-issue these lectures in an isolated form. I wanted them reprinted, if at all, in their proper place, subordinated to my main thought.

I smile a little as I look back. The remonstrances upon my file, dated less than ten years ago, would now be earnestly repudiated by the dear friends who wrote them.

After the delivery of the third course, upon Law, local reasons decided the publication of that book. Many efforts were being made in the different States to change laws; and it was thought that the lectures would give necessary information.

Of the first course, nothing has ever been printed in this country. The second lecture was printed, by a sympathizing friend in England, as a tract, and widely circulated. Part of it was reprinted with approbation in the " Englishwoman's Journal." The whole of this course is now given to American readers in its proper connection, in which it is hoped, that its bearing upon the later lectures will be seen, and a new significance given to its suggestions. The history of these volumes seems to make it necessary to reprint the original Prefaces in connection with the lectures on Labor and Law.

In 1856, I conceived the thought of twelve lectures, to be written concerning Woman; to embrace, in four series of three each, all that I felt moved to say in relation to her interests. No one knew better than myself that they would be only "twelve baskets of fragments gathered up;" but I could not distrust the Divine Love which still feeds the multitudes, who wander in the desert, with " five loaves and two small fishes."

In the first three of these lectures, I stated woman's claim to a civil position, and asked that power should be given her, under a professedly republican government, to protect herself. In them I thus stated the argument on which I should proceed: " The right to education — that is, the right to the education or drawing-out of all the faculties God has given — *involves* the right to a choice of vocation; that is, the right to a choice of the end to which those faculties shall be trained. The choice of vocation necessarily *involves* the protection of that vocation, — the right to decide how far legislative action shall control it; in one word, the right to the elective franchise."

Proceeding upon this formula, I delivered, in 1858, a course of lectures stating "Woman's Claim to Education;" and this season I have condensed my thoughts upon the freedom of vocations into the three following lectures. There are still to be completed three lectures on "Woman's Civil Disabilities." I should prefer to unite the twelve lectures in a single publication; but reasons of imperative force have induced me to hurry the printing of these " Essays on Labor." Neither Education nor Civil Disability can dispute the public interest with this subject. No one can know better than myself upon what wide information, what thorough mental discipline, all considerations in regard to it should be based. I have tried to keep my work within the compass of my ability, and, without seeking rigid exactness of detail, to apply common sense and right reason to problems which beset every woman's path. At the very threshold of my work, I confronted a painful task. Before I could press the necessity of exertion, before I could plead that labor might be honored in the public eye, I felt that I must show some cause for the terrible earnestness with which I was moved; and I could only do it by facing boldly the question of "Death or Dishonor?"

"Why not leave it to be understood?" some persons may object. "Why not leave such work to man?" the public may continue.

In answer to the first question, I would say, that very few women have much knowledge of this "perishing class," except those actually engaged in ministering to its despair; and that the information I have given is drawn from wholly reliable sources, as the reader may see, but can be obtained only by hours — nay, days and weeks — of painful and exhausting study. Very gladly have I saved my audience that necessity: greatly have I abbreviated whatever I have quoted. But I *meant* to drive home the reality of that wretchedness: I *wanted* the women to whom I spoke to feel for those "in bonds as bound with them;" and to understand, that to save their own children, male and female, they must be willing to save the children of others. It will be observed, that I have said very little in regard to this class in the city of Boston; very little, also, that was definite in regard to our slop-shops. The deficiency is intentional. I would not have one woman feel that I had betrayed her confidence, nor one employer that I had singled him out as a victim; and it is almost impossible to speak on such subjects without finding the application made to one's hand. I may say, in general, that a very wide local experience sustains the arguments which I have based on published statistics.

It was also my earnest desire to prepare one article on this subject that might be put into the hands of both sexes; that might be opened to the young, and read in the family circle, without thrilling the reader with any emotion less sacred than religious pity. This cannot be true of the reports of any Moral Reform Society; for in them it is needful to print details so gross in character as to be fit reading for none but well-principled persons of mature age. It is not true of such a work as Dr. Sanger's; for his historical retrospect furnishes every possible excuse to the vices of youth, and is open to question on every page.

From the highest sources in this community — from the lips of distinguished clergymen, scholars, and men of the world — I have had every private assurance, that, in this respect, I have not failed.

It would be unjust not to state, that two powerful causes co-operate, in the city of Boston, with low wages, to cause the ruin of women; I mean the love of dress, and a morbid disgust at labor.

The love of dress was a motive which obviously had no natural relation to my subject. A disinclination to work, my readers may think, it was proper I should have treated; but it is the natural reflection of a state of things, in the upper classes, which would be a much fitter subject of rebuke.

So long as a lady will allow her guest to stand

exposed to snow and rain, rather than turn the handle of the door which she happens to be passing; so long as neither bread nor water can be passed at table, except at the omnipresent waiter's convenience, — servants will naturally think that there is something degrading and repulsive in work. This reform must begin in the higher classes.

But, if this subject must be treated at all, why should it not be left to men? Can women deal with it abstractly and fairly? The answer is simple. In physics, no scientific observations are reliable, so long as they proceed from one quarter alone; many observers must report, and their observations must be compared, before we can have a trustworthy result. So it is in social science. Men have been dealing with this great evil, unassisted, for thousands of years. By their own confession, it is as unapproachable and obstinate as ever. Conquered by its perpetual re-appearance, they have come to treat it as an "institution" to be "managed;" not an evil to be abolished, or a blasphemy to be hushed. But these lectures are not written for atheists. The speculative sceptic has retreated before the broad sunlight of modern civilization: only two classes of atheists remain, — men of science, who fancy that they have lost sight of the Creator in his works, and talk of the human soul as the most noble result of material forces; and people of fashion, who live "without God in the world." Why man should ever investigate the material universe without a tender and reverent, nay, a growing dependence on "the dear heart of God," we will not pause to inquire. The child does not let go his father's hand when he first comprehends the abundance of his resources. Neither the fountains of God's beauty, nor the perplexities of his nicely ordered law, loosen man's loving grasp. He clings all the closer in his joy, because he knows Him better. But why should not the denizens of the fashionable world be atheists? When I go among them, and listen to their heartless fooleries; when I see them absorbed by the vain nothings of their coterie, rapt in endless consultations about times and seasons, devoid of any real enjoyment, hopeless of noble occupation, with the days all empty and the nights all dark, — then I, too, shiver with doubt, and am ready to say in my heart, "There is no God." We can never believe in any spiritual reality of which our own souls do not receive some faint reflex. These people must do the will of the Father, before they can believe in his love. I do not write for them, but for thoughtful men and women, who rejoice in God's presence, deny the permanence of evil institutions, and are anxious to share with others the inheritance that belongs to the "child of the kingdom," — for those who have faith to remove mountains, and courage to confess the faith. For them I shall not have spoken too plainly.

Shortly after these essays were written, — in June, 1859, — I received from London Mrs. Jameson's "Letter to Lord John Russell;" and I cannot refrain from expressing the deep emotion with which I read what she had written to him upon the same subject. Well may she wear the silver hairs of her sixty years like a crown, if, only through their sanction, she may speak such noble words. But —

"Earnest purposes do age us fast;"

and many a true-hearted woman, far younger in years, would gladly bear witness with her.

I would not write, if I could, an "exhaustive" treatise. All I ask for my work is, that it should be "suggestive." With that purpose, I have worked out my schemes, in the last lecture, far enough to provoke objection, to stimulate the spirit of adventure, to show how easily the "work" may wait upon the "will." May the "Opening of the Gates" be near at hand!

It remains only to acknowledge my indebtedness to some English and American friends: and first to the "Englishwoman's Journal;" not merely for its own excellent articles, but for references and suggestions, most valuable when followed out. The story of the young straw-braider was drawn from its pages; and, disappointed in the arrival of original material from Paris, long expected, I have been compelled to depend upon it largely for my sketch of Félicie de Fauveau. To one of its editors, Miss B. R. Parkes, and to Madame Bodichon in London, as well as to the Rev. Mr. Higginson, I am under pleasant private obligations. I must rest content to seem largely indebted to the "Edinburgh Review," of April 1859, for condensing the results of the census. My materials were collected and arranged, when the article on " Female Industry" reached me; and the differences in treatment were so few, that I at once drew my pen through whatever was not sanctioned by its authority. The ladies who first directed my attention to the Waltham watch-factory, and to the inventors of artificial marble in France, will see from these few words that I am not forgetful.

BOSTON, November, 1859.

There seems, at first sight, a certain presumption in offering to an American public, at this moment, any book which does not treat of the great interests which convulse and perplex the United States. But experience has shown, that neither the individual nor the national mind can remain continually upon the rack; and both author and publisher have thought that a book upon a serious subject, popular in form and low in price, would find perhaps a more hearty welcome, under present circumstances, than in those prosperous days, when romances and poems, travels and biographies, were scattered over every table by the score.

"Woman's Right to Labor" owed its warm welcome, not to any power or skill in its author, but to the impatient interest of philanthropists in every thing relating to that subject. It remains to be seen, whether as large a portion of the public and the press are prepared to treat with candid consideration the subject of Law.

Both these volumes have been given to the world in their detached form, that they might receive the benefit of general criticism; that errors, inaccuracies, or misapprehensions, might be perceived and rectified before they took a permanent position as part of a larger work. All criticism, therefore, which is *honestly intended*, will be received with patience and gratitude; but a great deal falls to the lot of the author which cannot come under this head.

If we are told that a "wider acquaintance with the history" of a certain era will modify our views, it is natural to expect that an honest critic will show *where* the acquaintance fails, and how the views should be modified. When we are told that certain scientific illustrations, "though true in the main, are not accurate in detail," we may reasonably hope to see at least *one* error pointed out. When neither of these things is done, we sweep such remarks aside, as alike unprofitable to us and our readers.

A wide and generous sympathy in my aims has given me, thus far, all that I could desire of encouragement and appreciation; and this appreciation has come, in several instances, from a "household of faith" far removed from my own, and has been mingled in such cases with an outspoken regret, that one who "wrote so well, and felt so warmly," should not acknowledge on her pages the debt woman owes to Christianity, and unfurl an evangelical banner

b

above a Christ-like work. Because such friends have spoken tenderly, I answer them respectfully; because I never saw any church-door so narrow that I could not pass through it, nor so wide that it would open to all God's glory, I answer them without fear.

And, first, I believe in God, as the tender Father of all; as one who cares for the least of his children, and does not turn from the greatest; as one whose eye marks the smallest inequalities of happiness or condition, and holds them in a memory which does not fail. I believe in Christ as his authorized Teacher, anointed to reveal the fulness of God's love through his own life of practical good-will. I do not expect him to be superseded or set aside; and I do expect, that in proportion as men grow wiser, humbler, and sweeter, their eyes will open only the more widely to the great miracle of his spotless life, to the heavenly nature of his so simple teachings. And, next, I believe in my own work, — the elevation of woman through education, which is development; through labor, which is salvation; through legal rights, which are only freedom to develop and save, — as part of the mission of Jesus on the earth, authorized by him, inspired of God, and sure of fulfilment as any portion of his law. If at any time I have lost sight of this in expression, it is because I have thought it impossible that the purpose and character of my work should be mistaken. I am a slow and patient worker, — patient, because one may well be patient, if God can; and therefore no disappointment, no lack of appreciation, could sour or disturb me.

If I have justified the publication of this essay at the present moment, it may be thought that I shall not be able to justify the principal presumption; namely, that of a woman who undertakes to write upon law.

Such a treatise as this would be valueless, in my eyes, if it were written by a man. It is a woman's judgment in matters that concern women that the world demands, before any radical change can be made. To understand the laws under which I must live, no recondite learning, no broad scholarship, no professional study, can be fitly required. Common intelligence and common sense are all that society has any right to claim of me. Because most women shrink from criticising this law, I have criticised it.

Very recently, the "London Quarterly" said, in speaking of the republication of John Austin's work, that "English jurisprudence would be indebted for one of its highest aids to the reverential affection of a wife, and the patient industry of a refined and intelligent woman;" and Mrs. Austin defends her undertaking on this very ground, — that, if she had not superintended the work, *no one else would.* If John Austin's firm and penetrating intellect could not hold a score of persons about his lecturer's desk, and if it found its fit appreciation only in the grave, a conscientious woman need not shrink from any branch of his great subject, only because her audience will be small.

In one of his lectures upon Art, John Ruskin says : —

"Every leaf we have seen, connects its work with the entire and accumulated result of the work of its predecessors. Dying, it leaves its own small but well-labored thread ; adding, if imperceptibly, yet essentially, to the strength, from root to crest, of the trunk on which it has lived, and fitting that trunk for better service to the next year's foliage."

Let these words, printed on my titlepage, show the modesty of my aim, and the conscientious steadfastness of my purpose. As the leaf is to the tree, so is the individual to society. Tear away a single leaf from the towering crest, and the trunk does not seem to suffer: nevertheless, one small thread withers, one channel dries up, one source of beauty and use fails; and, from that moment, a certain sidewise tendency marks the growth.

To compact carefully one "well-labored thread," is all that I have sought to do, — to write a little book, that women might be won to read, as conscientiously as if it were a heavy tome, to be endlessly consulted by the bench.

In writing these three lectures, I feel quite sure that I must have made use of many significant expressions borrowed from those who have broken the way for me. For many years an extemporaneous lecturer on this and kindred topics, I have so wrought certain modes of expression into the fabric of my thought, that I do not *know* where to put my quotation-marks.

To Mrs. Hugo Reed, for instance, I know I must be under great obligations; and I can only hope, that she will trust me with her thoughts and words as generously as I desire to trust all my readers with mine. It is little matter who does the work, so that it be done; but I owe to one author, in particular, something like an explanation.

A few days before the third of these lectures was delivered in Boston (that is, before Jan. 23, 1861), a gentleman from Paris brought me from Madame d'Héricourt a book called "La Femme Affranchie," an answer to Michelet, Proudhon, Girardin, and Comte, which its author kindly desired I should translate for the American market. Unable to comply with her request, some weeks elapsed before I opened the book. I was struck with the energy, self-possession, and rapidity with which she seized the various points of the subject, with the thoroughness of her assault, and the temper of her argument. I did not sympathize in all her methods or conclusions; but I was interested to observe, that, in what I had then written and publicly spoken of the relations between suffrage and humanity, I had, in several instances, used her very words, or she had used mine. I did not alter my manuscript; but, with better times, we may hope for a translation of her spirited volumes, and the public will then do justice to her precedence.

I have been anxious to have positive proof of my conjecture in regard to the authorship of the " Lawe's Resolution of the Rights of Women;" but persevering endeavors in England, in several directions, have only left the matter as it stands in the text. It would be very interesting to know something of the private history of the man who wrote that book.

In the first of the following lectures, I have ventured a rhetorical allusion to the blue-laws of Connecticut. Since it went to press, I have seen it stated, on high authority, that any American writer who should " profess to believe in the existence of the blue-laws of New Haven would simply proclaim himself a dunce;" and the " Saturday Review" has been handled without gloves for taking this existence for granted.

I never supposed that the term "blue" applied to the color of the paper on which such laws were printed, any more than I supposed "blue Presbyterianism" referred to the color of the presbyters' gowns. I supposed it was the outgrowth of a popular sarcasm, descriptive, not of a "veritable code," nor of a "practical code unpublished," but of such portions of the general code as were repugnant to common sense, and the genial nature of man. This I still think will be found to be the case; and it is certainly to Connecticut divines and Connecticut newspapers that we owe the popular impression.

It was in the forty-sixth year of the independence of the United States that S. Andrus & Co., of Hartford, published a volume purporting to be a compendium of early judicial proceedings in Connecticut, and especially of that portion of the proceedings of the Colony of New Haven commonly called the "blue-laws." Charles A. Ingersoll, Esq., testified to the correctness of these copies of the ancient record.

As I quote this title wholly from memory, I am unable to say whether the colony ever fined a bishop for kissing his own wife on Sunday; but I have read more than once of such fines; and, if no laws remain unrepealed on the Connecticut statute-book quite as absurd in their spirit and general tendency, there are many on those of Massachusetts and New Hampshire: so I shall let my rhetorical flourish stand.

To my English friends, to Mr. Herndon of Illinois, Mr. Higginson, and Samuel F. Haven, Esq., of Worcester, I owe my usual acknowledgments for books lent, and service proffered, with a generosity and graceful readiness cheering to remember.

Nor will I omit, in what may be a last opportunity, to bear faithful testimony to the assistance rendered, in all my studies of this sort, by my friend, Mr. John Patton, of Montreal. No single person has helped me so much, so wisely, or so well.

In order to secure technical accuracy, my manuscript and proofs have been subjected to the revision of my friend, the Hon. Samuel E. Sewall. The principal alteration which Mr. Sewall has made, has been the substitution of the word "suffrage" for that of "franchise;" which latter I used in the Continental fashion. I prefer it to "suffrage," because it seems to have a broader signification; but I yield it to his suggestion.

I would gladly have dedicated this volume to the memory of the late John W. Browne, whose pure purpose and eminent gifts made me rejoice, while he was living, to call him friend. As, however, he never read the whole of the manuscript, I have given it a dedication " to the friends of forsaken women," which no one, who knew him well, will fail to perceive includes him.

BOSTON, Sept. 1, 1861.

CAROLINE H. DALL.

70, WARREN AVENUE,
    BOSTON, January, 1867.

CONTENTS.

THE COLLEGE.

I.

THE CHRISTIAN DEMAND AND THE PUBLIC OPINION.

Original Proposition. Objections to Republicanism. No Retrograde Steps Possible. The Educational Rights of Women. A Share of Opportunities the only Effectual Way. Both Sexes need the Oversight of Women. Men need the Needle. Sydney Smith to Lady Holland. The Education not Won till its Privileges are attained. Kapnist and the Normal School. Low Wages. An Illustration. The Social Position of the Teacher. The Spirit of Caste. Increase of Salaries. Is it Real or Nominal? What is the Standard of Education? Niebuhr to Madame Hensler. Cousin and Madame de Sablé. Examples of To-day do not Cheer. Opinion of the Druses.. Charles Lamb on Letitia Landon. Coventry Patmore. Mrs. Jameson on the English Deficiency. Standard of Italy. 500,000 Women in England. Dr. Gooch's Appeal. Opposition to first School of Design. Note on Miss Garrett. B. L. Bodichon on Jessie Meriton White and Medical Colleges. Need of a Medical Society. John Adams on his Wife. Why has not the Standard advanced? Alice Holliday in Egypt. Hekekyan Effendi speaking for the Massachusetts Board of Education. Madame Luce in Algiers. Her Workshop Discontinued. The

xxvi   CONTENTS.

Advance shown in such Lives. Mrs. Griffith. Janet Taylor.
Miss Martineau. "Aurora Leigh." Maria Mitchell. Oread Institute. New-York Schools. Vassar College. Michigan University.
Duty of Literary Men and Women to invigorate Public Opinion.
What *is* Public Opinion? Mary Patton. . . . . . pp. 1-48.

II.

HOW PUBLIC OPINION IS MADE.

Existing Opinion. Proverbs. The Novel kept Faith with the Classics. Social Customs. Newspapers. All form this Opinion. Individual Influence must stem the United Current. The Classics. Aristophanes. Iscomachus. Euripides. College Slang. St. John. Margaret Fuller on her "Beloved Greeks." Buckle. From Greece to Rome. Ovid. No Need to end Classical Study. Rather sanctify it. Perversions of History in the Classical Spirit. Hypatia. Aspasia. Society in the Time of Louis XIV. and Charles II. Lady Morgan on Alfred de Vigny. Rousseau. Dr. Day, Dr. Gregory, and Dr. Fordyce. Margaret Fuller. Association of Ideas. Fanny Wright. Captain Wallis and the Queen of Otaheite. Peru and the Formosa Isles. African Customs. Mrs. Kirkland on the Strong Box. Sir John Bowring on Marriage. Mrs. Barbauld. The Newspapers. Impure Habits. . . . . . . pp. 49-82.

III.

THE MEANING OF THE LIVES THAT HAVE MODIFIED PUBLIC OPINION.

Mary Wollstonecraft and the Literature of the Eighteenth Century. "Rights of Woman." "Not Empire, but Equality." Dr. Channing on Mrs. Wollstonecraft. Her Unhappy Home. Fanny Blood. Breaks up her School. Saves the French Crew. Provides for her Brothers and Sisters. Translations. Answer to Burke. Fuseli. Paris. Imlay. Helen Maria Williams. Happiness. Deserted in

CONTENTS. xxvii

Eighteen Months. Attempted Suicide. Goes to Norway. Final Separation. Marries Godwin. Birth of Mrs. Shelley. Death of Mary. Her Husband's Testimony. No Fair Statement recorded. Strength of Prejudice against her. A Republican and a Unitarian. The Judgment of her own Time upon her. The Right of Society to pass Judgment. Mr. Day and Maria Edgeworth. Lady Morgan. Always True to Freedom. Harriet Martineau. Thorough Work. Mrs. Jameson. Her Bravery and Truth. Woman's Rights Testimony. Mrs. Gaskell. Fredrika Bremer. The Brownings. "Aurora Leigh." Charlotte Bronté. "I Care for Myself." Our Abdiel. Margaret Fuller as a Person. "Woman in the Nineteenth Century." "Truth-teller and Truth-compeller." Rebuke to Harriet Martineau. Emerson's Misapprehension. Florence Nightingale. Santa Paula. Mary Patton. Miss Muloch libels Women. The Popular Idea of Love. Woman's Entire Self-possession. Carlyle and Count Zinzendorf. Who refuses Strength must miss Beauty. The Best Brains make the Best Housekeepers. The Affections of the Woman prompt and dignify the Labors of the Scholar. . . . . pp. 83–130.

THE MARKET.

I.

DEATH OR DISHONOR.

The Attar of Cashmere. Moral Force must change the Results of History. Statement of Subject. Death or Dishonor the Practical Question. An Honorable Independence the Way of Safety. The Forcing Pump and Siphon. Women must Work for Pay. Success the Best Argument. Competition in Rural Districts. Duchâtelet. Miss Craig. "Edinburgh Review." Dressmakers and Sir James Clarke. Lace-makers. Manchester Mantle-maker. 7,850 Ruined

CONTENTS.

Women in New York. Society Responsible for this Evil. Governesses. Mr. Mayhew to the "Morning Chronicle." The Minister's Daughter. The Power of a Divine Love. Noble Natures among the Fallen. The Glasgow Case. 1,680 Reformed French Women. The Straw-braider. Have Women Strength to Labor? Marie de Lamourous. The Young Laborer to be Protected by Social Influences. Women Hard Workers from the Beginning. China. Hindostan, Bombay Ghauts. Australia. Africa. Greece. Bertha of the Transjurane. Tyrolese Escort of Women. Germany. Montenegro. Holland. France. Widow Brulow. Nelly Giles. Ignacia Riso. Factory Labor in France. Sale of Wives at Derby and Dudley. Women in the Coal-mines. Pinmakers. Anna Gurney. Honduras. American Indians. Santa Cruz. Ohio and Pennsylvania. New York. Women of Lawrence. Ship "Grotto." Thomas Garratt concerning Sarah Ann Scofield. That all Men support all Women, an Absurd Fiction. . pp. 131–177.

II.

VERIFY YOUR CREDENTIALS.

Want of Employment lowers the Whole Moral Tone. Vigorous Women do not Ask what they shall Do. Idleness the Curse of Heaven. Organized Opposition on Man's Part. Mr. Bennett and the Watchmakers. Ribbon Looms at Coventry. The School at Marlborough House. Miss Spencer. Painting Crockery. Printing in America. Pennsylvania Medical Society, 1859. Want of Respect for Labor. Census of the United Kingdom. Agriculture. Mining. Fishing. Servants, &c. Reporters. Bright Festival. Metal Workers. Gillott's Pens. Jewelry. Screw-making. Button-making. Paper and Card Making. Engravers, Printers, &c., &c. The Lower Classes need the Brains of the Upper. Labor in the United States. Nantucket. Pennsylvania. Dr. Franklin's Sister-in-law. Mrs. Hillman. Mrs. Johnson. Martha B. Curtis. Ann Bent. Scientific Pursuits not Open. Clerks under Government. Census.

CONTENTS. xxix

Waltham Watch Factory. Dentists. School Committees. Postmistresses. Olive Rose. Semi-professions and Artists. Shoemaking in Lynn. Condition of the Poor dependent on the Action of the Rich. Happy Homes the Growth of Active Lives. The Pine and Ænemone. Emily Plater. " Verify your Credentials." Encouragement from Men; Faithfulness from Women. The Sorbonne. Madame Sirault. That Career fated which Woman may not share. Influence of the Sexes on each other. Baron Toermer and Félicie de Fauveau. . . . . pp. 178–220.

III.

"THE OPENING OF THE GATES."

The Drowning of Daughters. Teachers of Elocution and the Languages. Inspectors. Physicians. Dr. Heidenreich. Wood Carving. Properzia dei Rossi. Swiss Work. Elizabetta Sirani. Engravers. Barbers. Candied Fruit for Christmas. Pickles. Fruit Sauces. Dishmops. Gymnastics. Female Assistants in Jails, Prisons, Workhouses, not to be had till Public Opinion honors Labor. Florence Nightingale an Example. Parish Ministers. Deaconesses. Marian of the Seven Dials. Reading Aloud to the Perishing Classes. St. Pancras. Mrs. Wightman. A Training School. A Public Laundry and Bleaching Ground. Ready-made Clothing. An Assistance to our Practical Charity. Knitting Factory. Ornamental Work to be Avoided. Occupation for the Young Ladies at the West End. Mrs. Ellen Woodlock and her Industrial Schools. She takes Eighty Paupers out of the Poorhouse. Mr. Buckle's Position to be Questioned. Mistaken Moral Effort a Harm to Society. Want of Connection between the Employer and the Employed. People who want "a Chance Lift." Defects in our Present Intelligence-Offices. A Labor Exchange. The Argument Restated. Will you tread out the Nettles? The Drosera. Purposes the Blossoms of the Human Heart. . . . . pp. 221–261.

CONTENTS.

THE COURT.

I.

THE ORIENTAL ESTIMATE AND THE FRENCH LAW.

The Seat of the Law the Bosom of God? Of what Law? Legal Restrictions constantly Outgrown. The Laws which relate to Woman. Vishnu Sarma: the Hindoo Wife must use the Dialect of the Slave. Ancient Chinese Writer. Köhl on Turkish Husbands. Convent to lock up Ladies. The Island of Cœlebes. The Garrows in the North-east of India. The Muhar. Military Tribe of Nairs in Malabar. Later Proverbs; used by the Satirists. The Four Points to Consider. Discussion of Marriage and Divorce to be Deferred. The Public Opinion which has educated Woman, and her Approximation to it. Woman under Roman Law. Absence of well-tested Cotemporaneous Evidence. Theodora. French Law. Bonaparte's Opinion. The Estimate of a Double Character. Condition of the Peasant-woman. Need of Love in the Upper Classes. Business-freedom. George Sand. Rosa Bonheur, and the Claimants for Civil Rights. The Dotal founded on Roman Law; the Communal founded on German. Dotal Law rejected throughout Europe. Protection means Subordination. As a "Public Merchant," Woman becomes a French Citizen. Position contradictory: not allowed to rule the Household, which is called her Sphere. Civil Position. No Right of Promotion. Laws of Louisiana. Estimate of Woman under the "Code Napoléon:" tends to lower her Wages. List of Employments. The Needle-women of Paris. . . . . pp. 263–286.

II.

THE ENGLISH COMMON LAW.

It contains All to which we have any Need to Object. Literature. "The Lawe's Resolution of Woman's Rights." Inquiries as to its

Matters to be Discussed. The Duke of York's Trial. John Stuart Mill's Opinion. Dedication of his Essay on Liberty. Women of Upsal. On Juries. Miss Shedden. Russell on Female Evidence. Fate of the "Bulwarks of the English Constitution." Power of Women not Disputed while it was dependent on Property. It should depend on Humanity. Louis XIV. and the Fish-women. Pauline Roland and Madame Moniot. Men borrow the Suffrages of Women. Saxon Witas. Abbess Hilda. Council at Benconceld. King Edgar's Charter. Abbesses in Parliament. Peeresses in Parliament. East-India Stockholders. Stockholders in Banks. Association for the Promotion of Social Science. Mrs. Mill's Article. Florence Nightingale's Evidence. Petition to Parliament, and its Signers. The New Divorce Bill. Buckle's Lecture. Canadian Changes. Inconsistencies. Canadian Women as Voters. Pitcairn's Island . . . . pp. 287–341.

III.

THE UNITED-STATES LAW, AND SOME THOUGHTS ON HUMAN RIGHTS.

Condition of Women in Republics. Helvetia. Kent on the Law's Estimate. "The Man's Notion." Property-laws, and Natural Obligations of Husband and Wife. The Law's Indulgence. Marriage and Divorce in the Different States. Variety of the Laws. "Cruelty." What have the Woman's-Rights Party done? — changed the Law in nineteen States. The Law of Illinois. Rhode Island on Property. Vermont. Connecticut. New Hampshire. Massachusetts, and what remains to be done. Maine. Ohio. Judge Graham's Decision. Mrs. Dorr's Claim. New-York Property-bill of 1860, and its Supplement. Relief to 5,000 Women. Mrs. Stanton before the Legislature. The Right of Suffrage in New Jersey. Wisconsin. Michigan. Ohio. Kansas. Connecticut. Kentucky in Reference to Suffrage. A Woman's Right to Life, Liberty, and the Pursuit of Happiness. Mrs. John Adams

CONTENTS. xxxi

Author. Probability points to Sir John Doderidge. The Law, for Single Women, of Inheritance. Offices Open. Right to Vote, and Lady Packington. Sheriff of Westmoreland. Lady Rous. Henry VIII. and Lady Anne Berkeley. As Constable, and Overseer of the Poor. Female Voter in Nova Scotia. Law relating to Seduction: its Profanity. The French Law, as summed up by Legouvé. Woman's Opinion of this Law. Objections. Laws concerning Married Women. Impossibility of Divorce, from Hopeless Insanity. Instances where *Men* have taken the Law into their own Hands. Impossibility of Woman's ever doing this. Marriage of a Minor. A Wife loses *all* her Rights. Satire in a London Court. Truth of this. Consequent Unwillingness of the Honest Poor to Marry, and of Single Women of Rank to relinquish Power. Freedwomen at the South. The Descendant of Morgan the Buccaneer. Need of Equity. May make a Will by Permission. Nutriment of Infants. The Law resists Maternal Influence, and denies Natural Authority. Word not binding. Gifts Illegal. Indictments in the Husband's Name. Divorces: only Three ever granted to Women. The Widow recovers her Clothes and Jewels, but need not bury her Husband. Christian on Suffrage. Moderate Correction. Property-laws. The Hon. Mrs. Norton. Hungarian Freedom. Right to Vote. Experience in America. Parisian Milliner. "Union is Robbery." The Heiress. Longevity of the Wife. Woman discouraged from Labor by the Influence of the Laws of Property. Sexual Legislation thoroughly Immoral. Man's Adultery even a more Serious Evil than Woman's, so far as State Morals and Interests are concerned. Canton Glarus. "Courts have never gone that Length." Debate on the New Divorce Bill. Man's Fidelity considered an Imbecility. The Compliments of the Law. The Husband's Vigilance. Duplicity the Natural Result of Slavery. The Right of Suffrage. Objections Answered. The Abstract Right and the Practical Question. Suffrage to be limited by Education, not Money nor Sex. The "Sad Sisterhood." Woman has never had a Representative. Her Suffrage would put an End to Three Classes of Laws. Harris *vs.* Butler. Delicate and Hannah Corbin understood its Worthlessness. Richard Henry Lee on a Woman's Security. "Woman's Rights,"—a Phrase we all Hate: identical with "Human Rights,"—a Phrase we all Honor. Reception of Woman in the Lyceum. Labor to be honored through Woman. Trade to become a *Fine Art*. Property-holders must have Political Power. Mr. Phillips on Suffrage. The Lowell Mill. Dr. Hunt's Protests. Mean Men. Woman's Duty to the State a Moral Duty. Woman's Right to *Man* as Counsellor and Friend. The Constitution of the Family. The Historical Development of the Question. Mary Astell in the Seventeenth Century. Mary Wollstonecraft in the Eighteenth, and the Customs of Australia. Responses to her Appeal. Margaret Fuller in the Nineteenth. The great Lawsuit in 1844. Convention at Seneca Falls in 1848. National Association in 1850. Profane Inanity. Chinese Women. Does Power belong to Humanity or to Property? Mahomet, and the Right to Rule. Wendell Phillips and the Venetian Catechism. . . . . pp. 342–374.

TEN YEARS.

EDUCATION.—Absence of Discussion Wise. American Association for the Promotion of Social Science. Lectures from the Lowell Institute. Ripley College. Howard University. Professor Baldwin at Berea. St. Lawrence University, N.Y. Lombard University, Ill. Oberlin. List of Colleges it has Organized. Lane Seminary. President Finney. Ladies' Library. Ladies' Hall. Miss Fanny Jackson. A Confession. Antioch. Way thither. Yellow Springs. The Glen. Matins. Necessities. Changes in Buildings, Books, &c. Missionary Work. The Professors. The Brigadier-General. Literary Societies. A Southern Refugee. Vassar College. Lawrence University, Kansas. Letter from Miss Chapin. A Professor Elected. Michigan University. Miss Nightingale's Training-School for Nurses, Liverpool. Schools in Calcutta. Deaconesses. Kaiserworth. Strasburg. Basle. St. Loup. Geneva. Faubourg St. Antoine. Passevant Hospital. Bishop Kerfoot's Schools. . . . . pp. 377–429.

MEDICAL EDUCATION.—New-York Medical Society. Medical Society in London. Hospital of the Maternity in Paris. Miss Garrett and Apothecaries' Hall. Dr. Zakrzewska and the Medical Society. Medical Lectures at Harvard. Women and the Cossacks. Women and the Algerines. Women in India. Cause of Cholera. Success of Female Physicians. Dr. Ross. A Medical College Needed. New-England Hospital. . . . . pp. 429–434.

PULPIT.—Amélie von Braum. Mamsell Berg. Rev. Olympia Brown. Mrs. Jenkins. Mrs. Booth. Mrs. Timmins. Ann Rexford. Nancy Gove Cram. Abigail H. Roberts. Mrs. Hedges. The Church at Amsterdam, and its Deaconesses. Resolution at Syracuse. Delegates to Local Conferences. Mrs. Dall. Counsel to Women who desire to preach. . . . . pp. 434–447.

ART SCHOOLS.—Lowell Institute. Cooper Institute. Miss Roundtree and Miss Curtis. Coloring Photographs. Mrs. Elizabeth Murray and the London Society of Female Artists. . . . pp. 447–449.

LABOR.—Statistics of Eight-hour Movement. Factory Labor in England. Foreign Society for Employment of Women. Mending Schools. A Barber. Public Clerks. Fanny Paine. Musical Careers. Charlotte Hill. Williston Button-factory. Madam Clarke. A Capitalist. Mr. Thayer's Lodging-house for Girls. Young Women's Christian Association. Lodging-house in New York. Miss Hill's Ruskin Lodging-houses in London. Female Printers. A Notary Public. . . . . pp. 450–468.

LAW.—Married Women in New York. Right of an Ordained Woman to Marry in Massachusetts. School Committees. Richmond. Are a Woman's Clothes her own? State of Missouri. College. Where shall a Woman's Children go to Church? Francis Jackson's Will. Conference at Leipsic. Petition to enable Widows, Potter's County, Pa. Women as Bank Directors. . . . . . . pp. 468–472.

SUFFRAGE. — Kansas. Missouri in Congress. The Speaker of the House. Mercantile Library in Philadelphia. Voting in New Jersey. Mr. Parker at Perth Amboy. A Petition to Kentucky. Equal-Rights Association, Petitions, &c. George Thompson's Objections. John Stuart Mill and the Franchise. English Petition a Model. To be sustained by Able Men. Mrs. Bodichon's Pamphlets. Women Ejected. Austria. Swedish Reform Bill. Italian Law. The Hungarian Diet. . . . . . pp. 472–486.

CIVIL PROGRESS. — Australia. Moravia. Dublin. Aisne. Bergères. Need of a Newspaper. . . . . pp. 486–488.

OBITUARIES, &c. — Merian. Baring. Farnham. Lemonnier. Dr. Barry. Mrs. Severn Newton. . . . . pp. 488–491.

The Ballot will secure All Things. A Glimpse of the Wide West. Vassar and Miss Lyman. Oberlin and Mrs. Dascomb. Dr. Glass. Female Lecturers. Business Capacity of Women. The Ice in Fox River, Ill. Cholera at Elgin. Quincy High School. Coloring Photographs at the Cooper Institute. Conclusion. pp. 491–499.

THE COLLEGE;

OR,

WOMAN'S RELATION TO EDUCATION.

IN THREE LECTURES.

I. — The Christian Demand and the Public Opinion.
II. — How Public Opinion is made.
III. — The Meaning of the Lives that have modified it.

Now press the clarion on thy woman's lip,
(Love's holy kiss shall still keep consecrate,)
And breathe the fine, keen breath along the brass,
And blow all class-walls level as Jericho's
Past Jordan. . . . The world's old;
But the old world waits the hour to be renewed.
        AURORA LEIGH.

Two of far nobler shape, erect and tall, —
Godlike erect, with native honor clad
In naked majesty, — *seemed lords of all:*
And worthy seemed; for in their looks divine
The image of their glorious Maker shone, —
Truth, wisdom, sanctitude severe and pure;
Whence true authority in men.
        MILTON.

THE COLLEGE.

I.

THE CHRISTIAN DEMAND AND THE PUBLIC OPINION.

> "Since I am coming to that holy room,
>   Where, with the choir of saints for evermore,
> I shall be made thy music; as I come,
> I tune the instrument here at the door,
> And what I must do then, think here before."
>
>   MACDONALD.

TO propose an essay on education requires no little courage; for the term has covered, with its broad mantle, every thing that is stupid, perverse, and oppressive in literature. We will not tax ourselves, however, to consider exact theories, or suggest formal dissertations. In these lectures, let us take all the liberties of conversation; pass, in brief review, a wide range of subjects; comment lightly, not thoroughly, upon them; and trust to quick sympathies and intelligent apprehension to follow out any really useful suggestions that may be made.

Some time since, we laid down this proposition: "A man's right to education — that is, to the education or drawing-out of all the faculties God has given him — involves the right to a choice of vocation;

that is, to a choice of the end to which those faculties shall be trained. The choice of vocation involves the right and the duty of protecting that vocation; that is, the right of deciding how far it shall be taxed, in how many ways legislative action shall be allowed to control it; in one word, the right to the elective franchise."

This statement we made in the broadest way; applying it to the present condition of women, and intending to show, that, the moment society conceded the right to education, it conceded the whole question, unless this logic could be disputed.

Men of high standing have been found to question a position seemingly so impregnable, but only on the ground that republicanism is itself a failure, and that it is quite time that Massachusetts should insist upon a property qualification for voters.

In this State, so remarkable for its intelligence and mechanical skill, — a State which has sent regiment after regiment to the battle-field, armed by the college, rather than the court, — in this State, one somewhat eminent voice has been heard to whisper, that *men* have not this right to education; that the lower classes in this country are fatally injured by the advantages offered them; that they would be happier, more contented, and more useful, if left to take their chance, or compelled to pay for the reading and writing which their employers, in some kinds, might require.

We need not be sorry that these objections are so stated. They are a fair sample of all the objections that obtain against the legal emancipation of *woman*, an emancipation which Christ himself intended and prophesied, — speaking always of his kingdom as one in which no distinctions of sex should either be needed or recognized. Push any objector to the wall, and he will be compelled to shift his attitude. He says nothing more about women, but shields himself under the old autocratic pretension, that man, collectively taken, has *no* right to life, liberty, or the pursuit of happiness; that republicanism itself is a failure.

Our hearts need not sink in view of this assertion, apparently sustained by a civil war that fixes the suspicious eyes of autocratic Europe in sullen suspense. A republic, whose foundations were laid in usurpation, could not expect to stand, till it had, with its own right arm, struck off its "feet of clay." It is not freedom which fails, but slavery.

The course of the world is not retrograde. Massachusetts will not call a convention to insist upon a property qualification for voters, neither will she close her schoolhouses, nor forswear her ancient faith. The time shall yet come when she shall free herself from reproach, and fulfil the prophetic promise of her republicanism, by generous endowment for her women, and the open recognition of their citizenship.

It is not our purpose, however, to dwell upon facilities of school education. More conservative speakers will plead, eloquently as we could wish, in that behalf; and suggestions on other topics need to be made.

We have already said, that the educational rights of women are simply those of all human beings, — namely, " the right to be taught all common branches of learning, a sufficient use. of the needle, and any higher branches, for which they shall evince either taste or inclination ; the right to have colleges, schools of law, theology, and medicine open to them ; the right of access to all scientific and literary collections, to anatomical preparations, historical records, and rare manuscripts."

And we do not make this claim with any particular theory as to woman's powers or possibilities. She may be equal to man, or inferior to him. She may fail in rhetoric, and succeed in mathematics. She may be able to bear fewer hours of study. She may insist on more protracted labor. What we claim is, that no one knows, as yet, what women are, or what they can do, — least of all, those who have been wedded for years to that low standard of womanly achievement, which classical study tends to sustain. Because we do not know, because experiment is necessary, we claim that all educational institutions should be kept open for her; that she should be encouraged to avail herself of these, according to her own inclination; and that, so far as possible, she should pursue her studies, and test her powers, in company with man. We do not wish her to follow *any* dictation; not ours, nor another's. We ask for her a freedom she has never yet had. There is, between the sexes, a law of incessant, reciprocal action, of which God avails himself in the constitution of the family, when he permits brothers and sisters to nestle about one hearth-stone. Its ministration is essential to the best educational results. Our own educational institutions should rest upon this divine basis. In educating the sexes together under fatherly and motherly supervision,* we avail ourselves of the highest example; and the result will be a simplicity, modesty, and purity of character, not so easy to attain when general abstinence from each other's society makes the occasions of re-union a period of harmful excitement. Out of it would come a quick perception of mutual proprieties, delicate attention to manly and womanly habits, refinement of feeling, grace of manner, and a thoroughly symmetrical development. If the objections which are urged against this — the divine fashion of training men and women to the duties of life — were well founded, they would have been felt long ago in those district schools, attended by both sexes, which are the

---

* This does not mean the supervision of father and mother, but that into colleges, universities, medical schools, and whatever educational institutions may be named, the controlling and protecting influence of both sexes should be carried. I believe that every university should have a cultivated and elegant woman (not necessarily the *wife* of any of its officers), whose duty it should be to preside over its social life, and offer such allurements to virtuous pleasure that gambling-houses and worse shall lose their present fascinations. If young men could associate with virtuous and lovely women, under suitable sanction, in their college life, they would not, in general, go out of it in search of the vicious and unlovely. No one who lives within three miles of a large university need doubt the meaning of this paragraph. An age and a religious faith which discards the cloister, should discard a cloisteral fashion, wherever it exists.

pride of New England. The classes recently opened by the Lowell Institute, under the control of the Institute of Technology, are an effort in the right direction, for which we cannot be too grateful. Heretofore, every attempt to give advanced instruction to women has failed. Did a woman select the most accomplished instructor of men, and pay him the highest fee, she could not secure thorough tuition. He taught her without conscience in the higher branches; for he took it upon himself to assume that she would never put them to practical use. He treated her desire for such instruction as a caprice, though she might have shown her appreciation by the distinct bias of her life. We claim for women a share of the opportunities offered to men, because we believe that they will never be thoroughly taught until they are taught at the same time and in the same classes.

The most mischievous errors are perpetuated by drawing masculine and feminine lines in theory at the outset. The God-given impulse of sex, if left in complete freedom, will establish, in time, certain distinctions for itself; but these distinctions should never be pressed on any individual soul. Whether man or woman, each should be left free to choose its own methods of development. We pause, therefore, to show, that, when we spoke of a certain use of the needle as a matter to be taught to both sexes, we did so by no inadvertence. The use of the sewing machine is even now common to both;

but men, as well as women, should be taught to use their fingers for common purposes skilfully. Personal contact with the pauperism of large cities has sent this conviction home to many practical minds.

The rough tippets, mittens, and socks imported into the British Colonies, are the work of the Welsh farmers and the Shetland fishermen during the long tempestuous winter nights. In writing to Lady Holland, Sidney Smith pens some pleasant words on this subject.

"I wish I could sew," he says. "I believe one reason why women are so much more cheerful than men is because they can work, and so vary their employments. Lady —— used to teach her boys carpet-work. All men ought to learn to sew."

All men! and so might the cares of many women be lightened. Let us candidly confess our own indebtedness to the needle. How many hours of sorrow has it softened, how many bitter irritations calmed, how many confused thoughts reduced to order, how many life-plans sketched in purple!

Let us pass over that portion of our statement which hints at vocation, and confine ourselves, for the present, to that part of it which looks to an unrestricted mental culture. Nowhere is this systematically denied to women. It is quite common to hear people say, "There is no need to press that subject. Education in New England is free to women. In Bangor, Portsmouth, Newburyport, and Boston, they are better Latin scholars than the men. Nothing can set this stream back: turn and labor elsewhere."

We have shown to how very small an extent this statement is true. If it were true of the mere means of education, education itself is not won for woman, till it brings to her precisely the same blessings that it bears to the feet of man; till it gives her honor, respect, and bread; till position becomes the rightful inheritance of capacity, and social influence follows a knowledge of mathematics and the languages. Our deficiency in the last stages of the culture offered to our women made a strong impression on a late Russian traveller.

"Is that the best you can do?" said Mr. Kapnist, when he came out of the Mason-street Normal School for Girls. "It is very poor. In Russia, we should do better. At Cambridge, you have eminent men in every kind, — Agassiz, Gray, Peirce. Why do they not lecture to these women? In Russia, they would go everywhere, — speak to both sexes. At a certain age, recitation is the very poorest way of imparting knowledge."

To all adult minds, lectures convey instruction more happily than recitation; and, when men and women are taught together, the lecture system is valuable, because it permits the mind to appropriate its own nutriment, and does not oppress the faculties with uncongenial food.

To those who are familiar with the whole question, no theme is more painful than that of the inadequate compensation and depressed position of the female teacher. There is no need to harp on ‚this discordant string. Let us strike its key-note in a single story.

A year ago, in one of the most beautiful towns of this neighborhood, separated by a grassy common, shaded with drooping elms, rose two ample buildings, dedicated to the same purpose. They were the High Schools for the two sexes.

They were taught by two persons, admirably fitted for their work. The man, uncommonly happy in imparting instruction, was yet deficient in mathematics, and considered by competent judges inferior to the woman.

She was an orphan, with a young sister dependent upon her for instruction and support. She had been graduated with the highest honors at one of the State Normal Schools. She was delicate and beautiful; not in the least "strong-minded." Neither spectacles upon her nose, nor wooden soles to her boots, appealed to the popular indignation. All who knew her loved her; and the man whom we have named was not ashamed to receive instruction from her in geometry and algebra. The two schools were equal in numbers. The man was a bachelor, subject to no claim beyond his own necessity. What did common sense and right reason demand, but that these two persons should be treated alike by society, prudential committees, and so on? You shall hear what was the fact. The man was engaged at a salary of fifteen hundred dollars. The wealthiest class in the community intrusted its sons to his charge without question. Single, he was made much of in society, invited to parties, and had his own corner at many a tea-table, which he brightened with his pleasant jokes. He soon came to be a person in the town, — had his vote, was valued accordingly; went to church, was put upon committees, had a great deal to do with calling the new minister, and so, out of school, had pleasant and varied occupation, which saved his soul from racking to death over the ruts of the Latin grammar. Would we have it otherwise? Was it not all right? Certainly it was, and our friend deserved it; deserved, too, that when the second year was half over, and there were rumors that a distant city had secured his services, the committee should raise his salary two hundred and fifty dollars, and so keep him for themselves. But let us look at the reverse of the picture. The woman, burdened with the care of a younger sister, greatly this man's superior in mathematics and possibly in other things, was engaged at six hundred dollars. It was not customary for the wealthy families in that neighborhood to trust their girls to the tender mercies of a public school; so she had a class of pupils less elegant in manner, of more ordinary mental training, and every way more difficult to control. Still they were disciplined, and learned to love their teacher. A few of the parents called upon her, and she was occasionally invited to their homes. But these homes were not congenial to her tastes or habits. There was no intellectual stimulus derived from them to brighten her life. They offered neither pictures, statues, books, nor the results of travel, to her delicate and yearning appreciation. She talked, for the most part, of her pupils and their work; and the strain of her vocation, always heavier on woman than on man, wore more and more upon her soul. Society, as such, offered her no welcome.*

---

* " Society offered her no welcome." I am very well aware that this statement, taken with what I shall elsewhere indicate, will be considered an exaggeration; but, with a somewhat wide and varied experience of the United States and of Canada, I maintain it to be true. I am not to say what is true in the eyes of others, but what is true in my own. "What!" some one will exclaim, " education not a passport to social honor! Where was there ever a country where the teacher was respected as she is in New England?" Theoretically, this is true; and I have known a few instances in New England, in which teachers of private schools, of good family, successful in acquiring wealth (not necessarily through their schools), kept an eminent social position. Men generally keep a fair position; women, rarely. To test the truth of this, let me press the question. To whom do we all, to whom does the Commonwealth, owe a sacred debt, if not to the teachers of the primary and the grammar schools? Among these women, I have found some of the most delicate, high-bred, and cultivated women whom I have ever known of the same age. Let any one who sees them collected on public occasions glance at them, and judge; but, in cities at least, these women are never in society. Their meagre salaries prevent them from dressing as ladies must be dressed for a large company. For the same reason, their boarding-places are obscure and lonely. The middle class of artisans, &c., who send their children to the public schools, seek no intercourse with those whose refinement seems to isolate them; the upper class look down upon them very kindly, but never think of inviting them to meet distinguished people, of showing them rare books or pictures, of stimulating their worn-out faculties in any way. Why do we not make these teachers our first care? Should we not be more than repaid — if pay we must have — by the cheer and comfort added to the schoolroom in which our children are to be taught? I have tried the experiment of bringing these tired souls into contact with those who ought to refresh

She was nothing to the town. She hired her seat, and went to church. She had no vote, was never on a parish committee, had only one chance to change her position. That was to remove to a more con-

---

them. It does marvellously well, until the crucial question is asked, "Who is she?" If I answer, "The teacher of a primary school," what a change of countenance, what a fading of the cordial smile, what passive indifference! and this, in cases where, in refinement and delicacy of manner, the young lady might pass unchallenged anywhere. But let the subject of my experiment be a girl of genius; with such cultivation only as a Normal School could add to the education of a country home; deficient still in the minor graces of deportment; too energetic and adventurous, perhaps, to be elegant; and *who* will take a motherly interest in her, draw her within the charmed circle where she shall learn to carry herself with reserve and dignity, and to veil her flashing powers, that they may warm where they have hitherto consumed?

No: I do not exaggerate. I believe we are all concerned to know in what sort of homes, under what influences, with what helps to health and happiness, these lonely and isolated girls pass the hours when they are not engaged in teaching. It concerns us, in the first place, of course, because theirs are the direct influences which mould our children; but I scorn that argument. It concerns us far more because they are the children of the same Father, engaged in the most trying of human vocations, and entitled as women, especially as unprotected women, to the sympathy of all mothers.

Some years ago, a lady not yet out of her teens, and suddenly reduced in fortune, went to Virginia to teach. She had letters from persons of distinction, who had known her in her early home. The letters were delivered; but there the matter ended. But she was one of those persons who make a place for themselves; and, after the neighborhood grew proud of her, she was called down one day to meet the wife of a lieutenant in the navy, to whom one of her letters had been addressed. "I am sorry I have not called before," apologized the visitor; "but there are so many of *these teachers!*" She had no time to say more: the young girl's cheek kindled. "Madam," said she, springing to her feet, "I desire no attention from you which would not under any circumstances be accorded to your daughter's teacher;" and she left the room. It is a matter of small importance, that, in this case, the young teacher was soon placed in a position in which her good-will became important to the lieutenant's wife.

"This," you will say, "was at the South. It grew out of that spirit of 'caste' which died with slavery." Is it indeed dead? Is there no spirit of caste in Massachusetts?

genial neighborhood, at a lower salary; but she thought of her young sister, and refused. If the committee heard of it, they did not offer to increase her salary. They were men incapable of appreciating her rare and modest culture. There was a tendency to consumption in her frame. Had she been happy, she might have resisted it for years, perhaps for ever; but with the restless pining at her heart, that mental and moral marasmus, the physical disease soon showed itself. In the commencement of the third year of her teaching, she began to cough; and, in less than three months from the day when she heard her last class, she lay in an early but not unhonored grave. The deep affection of her classmates in the Normal School had always followed her; and one who chanced to hear of her illness brightened its rapid decline. This woman, herself prematurely old, in consequence of twelve years of labor on the Red River of Louisiana, the only place open to her, where her abilities were appreciated to the extent of twelve hundred dollars a year, and would enable her to support a widowed mother, — this woman, with her now-scanty purse, supplied the invalid with fresh flowers and sweet pictures; and, when her heavy eye grew weary of gazing, gently closed it in the sleep of death, scattered rare and fragrant blossoms over her unconscious form, and followed it to the grave. Those flowers! brought daily to her teacher's-desk by a friendly or loving hand, they might have fed a craving heart, and saved a precious life.

It is no new story. You have heard it many times. Do not reply in the stale maxims of political economy. Do not say that woman's labor is cheaper than man's, because it is more abundant. Unskilled labor, we will grant you, is more abundant; but such labor as is here offered must always be rare and valuable. To the applicants who came to fill her vacant place the committee said, " We do not expect to find another capable as she was. We have only to select one that *will do*." Yet they had not been ashamed to use that capacity without paying for it! Only ignorance and prejudice and custom stood in the way of its appreciation; only the want of that respect which a citizen can always command was at the bottom of her social isolation. She never complained; but we complain for her, sadly conscious, that, until men themselves perceive what is fit, the remonstrances of women will be fruitless. One such word as that spoken by the Hon. Joseph White at Framingham, in July, 1864, is worth more than all that women can say. Nevertheless, we women have our duty. It is to convince and stimulate men. Be on the watch, then, for such women; and claim for them their place and remuneration. Help society to understand its duty, to be frank and honorable. And if certain services are worth, as in this case, seventeen hundred and fifty dollars a year, pay for equal services, *by whomsoever rendered*, an equal sum.

Since I first began to speak upon this subject, a very great change has taken place: women are put in places which require higher culture and greater administrative capacity. They are also paid better wages: these wages are not yet in fair proportion to what are paid to men for the same work; and the shameful argument is still used, that we employ women, chiefly because men will not work for the same price. The Roxbury High School, the Shurtleff Grammar School in Chelsea, the Normal School at St. Louis, and the Normal School at Framingham, are now under the charge of women. In the list of teachers from the Oswego School, we find four who are paid one thousand dollars a year, and eleven who are paid seven hundred dollars. Our daily press is very well satisfied with this; but, since 1860, what portion of a decent living will seven hundred dollars provide to a cultivated woman? When the salaries of the St. Louis teachers were raised in 1866, the principal was obliged to express her indignation before her salary was raised to its present sum of two thousand dollars. Had she been a man, she would certainly have had as much as the principal of the High School; namely, twenty-seven hundred and fifty dollars. A graduate of Antioch College, assisting in the High School at St. Louis, has twelve hundred dollars, where a man would have seventeen hundred dollars. Miss Brackett's own assistants in the Normal School have eleven hundred dollars.

The appointment of Miss Johnson to the head of the Normal School at Framingham will open the way to a similar change in many quarters, if what

Governor Bullock has not disdained to call the "policy of Massachusetts" is consistently carried out. I do not know what salary is offered to Miss Johnson; but, if it were equal to that of the man who preceded her, would not the newspapers have told us? The comparative value of these salaries is not shown by the figures. It depends on the prices of gold, and of food and provisions, each year. It cannot be half as great as an inexperienced person would think.

There is a great want of female teachers of Latin and French. School committees assure me, that proficients in language would be certain of good pay in our high schools. For the most part, women prefer to devote themselves to mathematics. I used to say, with a smile, in the Western States, that all the women could read the "Mécanique Céleste;" but they found Cæsar and Télémaque equally uninteresting. Later, Colonel Higginson bears witness to the impossibility of getting good classical teachers.

It is a common idea, that the standard of education is higher now than it was thirty years ago. It may be doubted. More things are taught in schools, — ologies, isms, and the like; but the most thorough teachers are not the most popular, and it may be questioned, whether in the best minds on the Continent, in England, or this country, so great progress has been made as has been generally claimed. There is much more liberality in regard to the general question, but no more in regard to the ideal standard.

In one of Niebuhr's letters to Madame Hensler,

he says, in speaking of Klopstock: "The character of the women is a remarkable feature of the time of Klopstock's youth. The cultivation of the mind was carried incomparably farther with them than with nearly all the young women of our days; and this we should scarcely have expected to find in the cotemporaries of our grandmothers. It was not, therefore, the influence of our native literature; for that first rose into being along with, and under the influence of, the love inspired by these charming maidens. For some time after the Thirty Years' War, the ladies of Germany, particularly those of the middle classes, were excessively coarse and uneducated. This wonderful alteration must have taken place, therefore, during eighty years, — between 1660 and 1740; though we are quite ignorant how and when it began."

Passing over to France, we encounter the reputation of Madame de Sablé; a woman, let me remark, for the benefit of those who are afraid that the march of education will deprive them of their dinners, as celebrated for her exquisite cooking and delicate confections as she was for her literary ability. In speaking of her, Cousin says: "All the literature of maxims and thoughts, including those of La Rochefoucauld, grew up in the *salon* of a lovely woman withdrawn into a convent. Having no earthly pleasure but that of reliving her life, she knew how to impart her own taste to society, in which she met by chance an accomplished wit, whom she contrived to turn into a great writer." He is speaking of the early part of the seventeenth century; and, in spite of the notorious dissipation of the period, many gifted and many virtuous women crowded her *salon*,— the Princess Palatine, the Princesses of Condé, de Conti, de Longueville, and Schomberg, Anna de Rohan, and Mademoiselle herself. There the gentlemen carried the pages they wrote at home, and not only bore with, but accepted, the criticisms of the women. They had no compensation but their praises, unless, like La Rochefoucauld, they were cunning enough to demand a carrot pottage or some preserved plums in exchange for a page of literature. In England, it is not necessary to avail ourselves of an exceptional education, like that of Lady Jane Grey. Remembering the noble culture of Elizabeth Tudor and Mary Stuart, of the sturdy women of the Commonwealth, we might surely expect a greater progress in the national idea. But, if its average could be found, neither the wife of John Hampden nor Lady Russell would accept it. It would seem that our standard advances, if at all, by a series of Hugh Miller's parabolic curves. What we find, depends upon the point at which we happen to test the eccentric arc; and, when we enter the nineteenth century, we are forced to take refuge in analogy, and ask, "If the ancient Egyptians *ever* mastered the Copernican idea, why should Galileo be imprisoned to-day for insisting that the sun does not move round the earth?" The stimulating examples of noble and educated women, which now present themselves, do not cheer us as they should, while they remain exceptions. In making what Dickens would call an "indiscriminate and incontinent" excursion, into the regions of female thought and literature, we find its atmosphere in a somewhat unventilated condition, and are reminded of an opinion of the Druses which does not seem to have been wholly impertinent, that " literature is a mean and contemptible occupation, *fit only for women.*" Twenty years ago, when ties of an almost filial tenderness linked us to the household of the late Judge Cranch, we have often followed him, unrecognized, of a Saturday afternoon, when, returning from the bench, he climbed Capitol Hill, one hand grasping the handle of some colored washerwoman's basket, or slinging her heavy bundle over his shoulder on a stick. The dear remembrance, sustained by all the sweet and delicate courtesies of his private life, has always lain side by side in our mind with that exquisite Essay of Elia to which he first directed our attention, in which a noble reverence to woman is inculcated, and we are taught to judge every man's respect for the sex by his demeanor towards its humblest representative. Yet, if Judge Cranch never swerved from his gracious dignity, Charles Lamb did. Woman had not gained, in his life-time, such a hold upon her intellectual rights, that a dinner company dared chide him, when he said of Letitia Landon, " If she belonged to me, I would lock her up, and feed her on bread and water, till she gave up writing poetry. A female poet, or female author of any kind, ranks below an actress, *I* think."

We do not quote these words so much against Lamb himself, — for the lips of Mary Lamb's brother must have been thick with wine, when, with " stammering, insufficient sound," he included her in so sweeping a reprobation, — but to indicate the nature of that public opinion which is even now dwarfing the ideals of the best men; to show how little reliance is to be placed on the standard of the most generous, when a remark like this, uttered in a large literary circle, passes without criticism, and is recorded without conscious mortification, — recorded, too, by the father of that Coventry Patmore, who has known how to offer us, in later times, sugar-plums of his own *coloring*—let us add of his own *poisoning* also — under the alluring names of " betrothals " and " espousals." How far the *facts* are from the ideal standard, Mrs. Jameson, in a lecture lately delivered, will help us to show.

" With all our schools," she says, " of all denominations, it remains an astounding fact, that *one-half* of the women who annually become *wives*, in this England of ours, cannot sign their names in the parish register; and that this amount of ignorance in the lower classes is accompanied with an amount of ill-health, despondency, inaptitude, and uselessness in the so-called educated classes, which, taken together, prove that our boasted appliances are to a great extent failures."

The ancient standard of Italy was very high, even in the fifteenth century, if we consider only the literary skill or mathematical culture frequently desired and attained; but Anna Maria Mozzoni may con-congratulate herself on having given a moral and social impetus to it, which it has never before received. Her wise, considerate, philosophical suggestions will meet the cordial welcome of all right-minded women. If followed out, they will create nobler women than Tambroni or Laura Veratti.*

There was no institution in England for the proper training of sick nurses, when Florence Nightingale went to Kaiserworth, a small town near Düsseldorf, on the Rhine, to prepare herself to take charge of the Female Sanitorium. In Great Britain, at this moment, the excess of the female population over the male amounts to five hundred thousand souls; and from all directions we hear the cry, that *men* need educated assistants. What is the country doing to answer this cry, to educate her five hundred thousand women? In 1825 Dr. Gooch made a noble appeal to the English public, in behalf of educating women to be nurses; but there was no response. When the first school of design was started, a petition was drawn up and *signed*, praying that women might not be taught, at the expense of the Government, arts which would interfere with the employment of men, and "take the bread out of *their* mouths"!

---

* Un Passo Avanti nella Cultura Femminile Fesi e Progetto di Anna Maria Mozzoni Mitano. 1866.

Here was an absurd interference with the right of *feeding*, on the part of these petitioners! As if women did not want bread as well as men; and being, according to authority, the less intelligent and weaker sex, one would suppose that to help them to find it might be a part of that protection to which the Government stands pledged, and for which their property is taxed.

"But," says Mrs. Jameson, "if a petition were drawn up, and handed to medical men, praying that women should not be trained as nurses, nor taught the laws of health, I am afraid there are well-intentioned men, who would, at the time, be induced to sign it; but I believe that twenty, nay, even ten years hence, they would look back upon their signatures with as much disgust and amazement as is now excited by the attempt to explode and sneer down the school at Marlborough House."

Another noble English woman, Mrs. Barbara Leigh Bodichon, in a recent pamphlet called "Woman and Work," gives us the correspondence between Jessie Meriton White and the various medical schools to which she applied for admission. This lady had for several years had charge of two little lame children, one of them her own nephew. The latter, on account of some structural defect, had broken his leg sixteen times. Once, when suitable attendance was not to be had, his aunt set and splintered it herself. The physician who examined it advised her to apply for instruction. She applied to fourteen medical institutions in the city of London, asking sometimes for *private* anatomical instruction. The correspondence with four colleges in the year 1856 is given, — from the St. George's, the Royal College of Surgeons, St. Bartholomew's Hospital, and the University of London. It amply bears out her assertion, that she was nowhere met with solid objections, or with sensible and logical replies. Sometimes she was told of the *indelicacy* of her request! The University of London, which was legally bound by its charter to receive her, treated her as coolly as the rest; and in no case was any individual regret expressed for the official decision.

Indelicacy, forsooth! Where can we find it, if not in the impure nature which raises the objection, and the low manner of thinking in general society which consents to receive it? May not the mother, who receives her naked new-born child from the hand of God, fitly ask to understand the liabilities of its little frame? May not the wife, called in seasons of sickness to the most delicate and trying duties, modestly ask for that thorough culture which alone can make those duties easy? And who make this objection? Men who go shuddering and half-drunken into the dissecting room, to scatter vile jests above that prostrate temple of the Holy Ghost! Men who see nothing in the exquisite development of God's creation, but the reflection of their own obscene lives! Students who know no better way to steel their courage to the use of the scalpel than to play at foot-ball on the college green with a human skull, holding its dignity to the level of their own honor!*

The best hope that Jessie Meriton White has for England is, that some of the most distinguished professors shall consent in time to take classes of female students.

The office of the physician is as holy as that of the priest: formerly they were one; now, at least, the physician should be priest-like. Irreverence and impurity should be banished from medical ranks. The science of medicine stands in great need of the intuitive genius of woman. In pursuing it, she will need the steady caution of man. In this country and in France, earnest and devoted students of both sexes have stood in the dissecting room to the benefit of both. So let them continue to stand, till the spirit is known by its fruits. An impure man is no better than an impure woman; but impurity among men may be concealed. Let it come between the two sexes, and it will be brought at once into antagonism with society, and will meet its true desert. The objection reveals the secrets of the medical college, and is the strongest argument ever offered for the medical education of women.

If women are to practise as physicians, some means should be taken to protect society against those who are imperfectly educated. *What a degree means* will

---

* I would gladly expunge the bitter reproof of these lines; but they record a fact which occurred at a medical school, where such an application was made, and must stand as history.

always be doubtful, until men and women receive their degrees in the same way and from the same hands. America stands greatly in need of this protection. Crowds of unauthorized, half-educated women, some of whom have not been ashamed to cross the Atlantic, and have attracted such sympathy abroad as only a different class of students deserve, are thronging the valley of the Mississippi, as well as haunting with their empirical pretensions the purlieus of the seaboard cities. If men had received properly trained women into their colleges and medical societies, this would not have happened. Cannot such physicians as Dr. Zakrzewska, Dr. Blackwell, Dr. Sewall, Dr. Tyng, and Dr. Ross of Milwaukie, unite to organize a Woman's Medical Society, with an examining board whose diploma shall attest the character of the member? Dr. Storer's admirable pamphlet entitled "Why not?" points out an evil, which will never be remedied by thrusting empirical women into the positions now held by unscrupulous men.*

---

* The three parts of this book have been made to conform to the census and statistics of the year 1850. To bring them up to the year 1860 would require a repetition of all the labor originally devoted to the question. That would be unwise if it were possible, for it could not alter the bearing of any statements; and it is not possible, because we have now no certain values in America. I had from the first intended to indicate in notes any important changes that had taken place in this decade. I had earnestly hoped to be able to contradict here the statements in the text in regard to medical opportunities for women, and the proper training of sick nurses, in England. But my English correspondents assure me that I have no occasion to change any thing; that the facts remain substantially what they were when my manuscript was written.

"But," says some watchful woman, "has not Miss Garrett taken her de-

And what have we to say of our own country? Has the American standard reached a safe altitude, or must we admit that it has the same limitations? A popular width of view we have certainly gained in the last half-century; but have we made secure progress in the right direction? Some eighty years ago, John Adams wrote of his wife, " This lady was more beautiful than Lady Russell, had a brighter genius, more information, and more refined taste, and was at least her equal in virtues of the heart, in fortitude and firmness of character, in resignation to

---

gree from Apothecaries' Hall? and have not a few women at least been trained as sick nurses?"

There is still no *institution* for the training of sick nurses, as the text asserts. Some few have been trained in hospitals and the like, on conditions of service, or to supply the need of such institutions themselves. How does the matter stand with Miss Garrett? The press has made the most of her success: it lies with us to exhibit the naked truth. After applying in vain to the various medical colleges, Miss Garrett went to Apothecaries' Hall. Here they refused her; but she looked up their charter. She found the word indicating to whom degrees should be granted indeterminate, with no character of sex attached to it. Lawyers told her the hall must grant her a degree, or surrender its charter. She was wealthy, and in earnest. She pushed her advantage. "The Apothecaries' Hall" prescribed certain courses of instruction to be pursued and certified before the degree could be granted. These she pursued in private, paying the most exorbitant rates for her instruction. In one instance, for a course of lectures, to which a man's fee would have been *five* guineas, she paid *fifty;* and I am credibly informed that the round cost of these preparatory steps must have amounted to two thousand pounds. All honor to Miss Garrett! Should her genius as a physician equal her energy and her wealth, she may gain something for the cause she has espoused, by the honor and consideration she will win for her sex. Apart from this, it will be seen, she has gained nothing. Bribery is not possible to ordinary mortals; and the conditions of the degree, in the present state of public feeling, would make it wholly impracticable.

The case, as it has been stated to us, is an exemplification, on a gigantic scale, of all that we complain of; and proves our statement, that women have not won an education for themselves, till they win with it its legitimate re-the will of Heaven, and in all the virtues and graces of the Christian life. Like Lady Russell, she never discouraged her husband from running all hazards for the salvation of his country's liberties; she was willing to share with me, and that her children should share with us both, in all the dangerous consequences we had to hazard."

Will America ever offer to the world a nobler picture? Is it at this moment above or below our average ideal? " With such a mother," said John Quincy Adams, in Boston, less than twenty years ago, " with

---

sults. For their opportunities as things now stand, all over the world, women pay a premium on the terms offered to men. Let them take these opportunities as tools, and try to win their bread with them, and the wages offered are, as a rule, a large discount on those offered to men. Political economy has nothing to do with the exceptional cases in which this is most evident, — only the common, habitual idea, that the wages of women must be kept down; and that, to do it, the value of superior labor must not be recognized, as in the case of the female teacher quoted in the text.

In the Report of St. Mary's Dispensary for Women and Children, in Marylebone, I find Miss Elizabeth Garrett mentioned as the General Medical Attendant. The Devonshire-square Nursing Institute, established, I think, by Mrs. Fry, twenty years ago, sends out nurses on the request of clergymen. Several sisters give their whole time to it.

King's College pays one thousand pounds annually for nurses to St. John's Home.

St. Thomas's Hospital, where nurses are being trained by the Nightingale fund, rejected fifty applications in six months.

The excitement in England has had a wholesome effect upon colonial action. The East-Indian Government has lately given Lady Canning twenty thousand rupees, to assist in building a home for the Calcutta Nurses' Institute; and a movement is making in India to educate native women as physicians. See, in the Appendix, the account of Miss Nightingale's School for Nurses in Liverpool.

Since the above was written, in January, 1867, three ladies have taken their degrees at Apothecaries' Hall, having passed a good examination, in Euclid, arithmetic, English history, and Latin. The *cost* of these degrees has not transpired.

such a mother, it has been the perpetual instruction of my life to love and reverence the female sex; but I have been taught also — and the lesson is still more deeply impressed — I have been taught *not* to flatter them." Noble words! Gentlemen to whom it falls to deliver annually Normal-school addresses would do well to take a lesson from them. They would wince a little, could they hear the criticisms of the indignant girls upon their actual advice and praise. How would these men have liked it, if at fifteen they had been addressed as fathers of an unborn generation, whose especial duty it was to adapt themselves to this sphere? And why should men complain, that women look to marriage, and marriage only, as salvation, if the whole tenor of their own influence is used to emphasize it as woman's "manifest destiny"? " Are there not *two* married, and where is the one?" What propriety is there in assuming, in advance, that the sphere which married life opens has a stronger hold on one sex than the other?

We have said enough to show, that in Germany, France, England, and America, the ideal standard of education was sufficiently high over a century ago. Why has not such actual progress been made as might have been expected?

Because *public opinion* has constantly thwarted the ideal growth. Educated women have, for the most part, wanted courage to do what is right, unless sustained by men. In education, for the duties of which they are acknowledged to be superior, they have never insisted on the changes they knew to be necessary, but have uniformly succumbed to the masculine idea. Shall we blame them? Is a conflict in the heart of a family a pleasant thing? Certainly, the hand which the magnanimous sympathy of men has set free cannot cast the first stone. The slowness and faithlessness of men too often paralyzes the best efforts of women. The faith which Isabella showed Columbus, would be, at this moment, a grateful return from them. Charles Lamb has shown us how valueless to the working woman the support of delicate sentiment may be. The ringing of the glasses round a table dulled his exquisite ear to the fine spheral harmonies it had once caught. He broke, in an after-dinner tilt, the very lance with which he had pierced to the heart of the enemy's shield. If the ideal standard makes no headway against public opinion, what encouragement to our hopes does common life offer?

As exquisite beauty of water, hill, and dale lies hidden in many a country hamlet, unheeded by the guide-book, unsuspected by the traveller on the turnpike road; so, in society, self-sacrifice, noble daring, and saintly perseverance, nestle behind the prominent failure. We find them everywhere, except where we should most naturally look for them.

There is in England a Society for the Promotion of Female Education in the East. It undertakes to do *abroad* precisely the work that its individual members refuse to assist the community to do at home. Consequently, their printed schemes read like satires on their individual convictions. In the year 1835, Miss Alice Holliday called the attention of this society to the condition of women in Egypt and Abyssinia. She asked their sanction to her attempt to educate the women of Egypt, with an ultimate view to those of Abyssinia, whose condition chiefly interested her. She had pursued a severe course of study, unfriended and alone, before she asked this help. She had studied the severe sciences, the antiquities and customs of the countries themselves, and the Arabic and Coptic languages. She was fortunate also in stirring the enthusiasm of a certain Miss Rogers, who, unable to teach, was yet willing to accompany her friend, and devote her fortune to their mutual support. As these ladies wanted no money from the society they consulted, they were received as agents without difficulty, and reached Alexandria in the autumn of 1836. At this time Miss Holliday wrote: " The condition of the Coptic women is truly lamentable. Their abodes are like the filthiest holes in London; yet their persons are decked out in the most costly apparel. I have seen ladies sitting at their latticed windows, their heads and necks adorned with pearls and diamonds of the highest value, their bodies covered with the richest silks and velvets, while the room they occupied was the most disgusting scene you can imagine. Smoking and sleeping occupy their time. Female schools have never had an existence, and the prejudice against them is very strong."

We can recall the argument used in those Eastern lands, and the answer which civilization offered. "I am afraid to teach my women," said the Turk: "they are already crafty and impure. To gather them into public places is to offer a premium on immodesty, and a temptation to misconduct." The Christian answered proudly, "We can trust our women; yes, even in Paris and London."

Soon after their arrival, Miss Rogers died; but her friend was not discouraged. In the following March, an officer of state, Hekekyan Effendi, came to inquire whether she would take charge of the royal women, one hundred in number, and the nearest relatives of the sovereign. Much depended, it was thought, upon the co-operation of the oldest daughter, Nas-lee Hanoom; and it was His Highness's desire that the heads of the family should be formed into a committee to extend female schools. See how this Mohammedan officer writes to Miss Holliday.

"You have no doubt read much about hareems," he says, "yet little, I fear, that resembles the truth. We pay great respect to women and aged persons, whatever may be our own rank. Our children, however, are uneducated, in the European sense of the term. Besides being illiterate, they know nothing of domestic economy; and, in the middling and lower classes of the community, this ignorance is so profound as to endanger, by its dire consequences, domestic health, peace, and prosperity. This want is the first cause of slavery and its concomitant vices.

In seconding the illustrious efforts of Mehemet Ali, I have been able to trace our debasement as a nation to *no other cause* than the want of a useful and efficient moral education for our women. In giving to them enlightened education, we shall be striking at the root of the evils that afflict us; we shall diminish the dangers and misfortunes which proceed from ignorance and idleness. Habits of industry, cleanliness, order, and economy, by increasing happiness, make us morally better, and will secure that moral training to our children which no subsequent effort is sufficient to replace."

So true is it that the value of words is comparative, that all this might have been written by some Secretary of the Board of Education in Massachusetts. The arguments of the Turk and Effendi are very familiar to us. Modern civilized society shuts women out of schools to protect their modesty. Modern professors tell us how much they respect women, and value material training, at the very moment when they bar the gates of life against her. On the 27th of March, 1838, Miss Holliday went in state to the hareem. She was preceded by the two janissaries attached to the English Consulate, bearing their silver wands of office, and accompanied by the wife of Hekekyan. In the ante-room they were regaled with coffee out of golden cups set with diamonds. Young Georgian girls of great beauty brought sherbet and massive pipes with amber mouth-pieces. They were then introduced to the Princess Nas-lee, a little woman about forty, simply dressed; and, before the interview ended, Alice had promised to spend four hours of every day in the hareem. She began with instruction that tended to civilize daily life; and boxes of embroidery and baby-clothes, made for patterns in England, excited the first lively interest. She declined all invitations to take up her abode in the hareem, although promised entire liberty. She was *humble*, and, as a consequence, *wise*. She did not expect great results, or look for much enthusiasm, in the hareem.

In August, she writes: " My visits have been attended with the most cheering success. I am received and honored with every possible distinction; but, added to my school, it is a great fatigue." Her character in every way sustained the effect of her teaching. She was offered thirty pounds a month for her attendance at the hareem, but thought ten pounds sufficient, and would accept no more. In October, a box of presents was received from England. When Hekekyan was invited to look into this box, he seized upon some scientific plates sent to the young princess. "Ah!" said he, "these are the things we need." The Pacha was captivated, in his turn, by an orrery, and a model of the Thames Tunnel. The hareem sent back a similar box, and Nas-lee herself worked a scarf for the queen. Miss Holliday was soon ordered to translate some of her books into Turkish; and her princesses wrote touching letters to their English friends. Soon after, we find this indefatigable woman teaching English, French, drawing, and writing, in the hareem of a late Governor of Cairo. Education must begin with languages; for Egypt has no literature to offer to her children. In 1840 Victoria sent to the hareem a portrait of herself, which was carried in procession and hung with proper honors by the side of that of the pacha. Very soon came an Egyptian Society for the Promotion of Female Education. Scientific instruments and books were ordered. An infant school began with one hundred and fifty children. The hareem demanded another teacher, and Mrs. Lieder was sent out. In 1844 a male school was formed, and European teachers imported. The young girls, who had begun with needle-work eight years before, were now studying Turkish, Persian, and Arabic, geography, arithmetic, and drawing. "What a change," writes Alice in 1846, — "what a change within the last ten years! When I came to Egypt, there was not a woman who could read; and now some hundreds have not only the power, but the best books. Year after year, I have been permitted to see the growth of a new civilization. What a change has come over the royal family since I first entered it! The desire for trifles is preparing the way for our noblest gifts; and a fatal blow has been struck at the whole system of hareems." It would be pleasant to trace this devoted woman farther, to know whether she still lives, and if she has reached the Abyssinian plains. In this humble way began the great educational movement in Egypt, which gave strength and vitality to Mehemet Ali's best-considered plans, which has sent scores of young princes to Paris, and will eventually change the face of the whole land.

Alice Holliday succeeded, because the "sinews of war"—namely, the "purse-strings"—were in her own hands. Very similar in spirit was the enterprise of Madame Luce in Algiers, of which Madame Bodichon has given an interesting account. Madame Luce went to Algiers, soon after the conquest, about 1834, and was probably a teacher in the family of one of the resident functionaries. In 1845, nearly nine years after Alice had begun her Egyptian labors, Madame Luce was a widow, with very little money to devote to the work on which she had set her heart; namely, a school to civilize the women of Algiers. Government was already beginning to instruct the men; but the Mohammedan dread of proselytism stood in their way. The women were in the worst state,— closely veiled, taught no manual arts, having no skill in housekeeping even, — for the simple life of a warm climate, the scanty furniture, give no scope for such skill. To wash their linen, to clamber over the roofs to make calls, to offer coffee and receive it, to dress very splendidly at times, very untidily always, was the synopsis of their lives. They did not know their own ages, yet were liable to be sold in marriage at the age of ten. Upon such material, and at such a time,—when the value of a Moorish woman was estimated, like that of a cow, *by her weight*,— Madame Luce undertook to work. She had a Christian courage in her heart, which might put many a man to shame.

While laying her plans, she had perfected herself in the native tongue, and now commenced a campaign among the families of her acquaintance, coaxing them to trust their little girls to her for three or four hours a day, that they might be taught to read and write French, and also to sew neatly. Her presents, her philanthropic tact, her solemn promise not to interfere in matters of religion, won for her, at length, four little girls, whom she took to her own hired house without a moment's delay. As the rumor of her success spread, one child after another dropped in, till she had more than thirty. Finding the experiment answer beyond her hopes, she was compelled to demand assistance of the local government. Men have no faith in quixotic undertakings. As might have been expected, they complimented Madame Luce upon her energy, saw no use in educating Moorish women, and declined to assist her. She waited, in breathless suspense, till the day on which the Council were to meet, bribing the parents, clothing the children, and pursuing her noble work. " Surely," she thought, " they *will* devise some plan;" but the twilight of the 30th of December closed in, and they had not even alluded to her school. On the 1st of January, 1846, it was closed. Nine hundred miles from Paris, without the modern conveniences of transport, what do you suppose this woman did? Could she give up? She scorned an offer of personal remuneration made by a few gentlemen, and told them that what she wanted was adequate support for a national work. She pawned her plate, her jewels, even a gold thimble, and set off for Paris, where she arrived early in February, and sent in her report to the Minister of War. She went in person from deputy to deputy, detailing her plans. Poor Madame Luce! her success was not quite so speedy as Alice Holliday's, whose schools had doubtless stimulated her efforts. Everywhere she had to combat the scepticism, the indifference, the inertia, of worldly men. There was no Miss Rogers, with a kind heart and a long purse, to help her on her way. Nor did Madame Luce desire that there should be. She knew that individual efforts of such a kind can never last long; and she was determined to make the government adopt and become responsible for her work. Then it would outlive her. Then it might redeem the nation. At last, daylight began to dawn. The government gave her three thousand francs for her journey, and eleven hundred more on account of some claim of her deceased husband. They urged her return to Algiers, and promised still farther support. So perseveringly had she wrought, that, early in June, she was able to re-open her school, amid the rejoicings of parents and children. It was seven months before the government contrived to put the school on a better foundation. During this time, her pupils constantly increased, and she was put to the greatest straits to keep it together. The Curé of Algiers gave her a little money and a great deal of sympathy. The Count Guyot, high in office, helped her from his own purse. When she was entirely destitute, she would send one of her negresses to him, and he would send her enough for the day. On one occasion, he sent a small bag of money, left by the Duc de Nemours for the benefit of a journal which had ceased to exist. She found in this two hundred francs, which she received as a direct gift from Heaven. Thus she got along from hand to mouth. She engaged an Arab mistress, who was remarkably cultivated, to assist her, and to train the children in her own faith. Pledged as she was not to instruct them in Christianity, she had the sense to see, what few would have admitted, that such instruction was not only necessary, but desirable. It gave them the knowledge of one God, and made clear distinctions between right and wrong. At last, in January, 1847, the school was formally adopted, and received its first visit of inspection. The gentlemen were received by thirty-two pupils, and the Arab mistress *unveiled;* a great triumph of common sense, if we consider how short a time the school had been opened. Since that time, the work has steadily prospered. In 1858 it numbered one hundred and twenty pupils, between the ages of four and eighteen. The practical wisdom of Madame Luce led her to establish a workshop, where the older pupils learned the value of their labor, and earned a good deal of money. They had always a week's work in advance, when the wise, slow government put an end to it, whether to save the thirty-five pounds a year, which the salary of its superintendent cost, or to prevent competition with the nunneries, Madame Luce has never known. *She* thought it the best part of her plan, — far better than teaching the girls to turn a French phrase neatly for the satisfaction of inspectors. The government are now beginning to understand her value. They have established a second school in Algiers, and several in the provinces. The results are not miraculous, but they plant new germs of moral power and thought in every family circle which they touch. Such names as those of Alice Holliday and Madame Luce have a great value. These women and their labors are permeated by the Christian idea of self-surrender. The preponderance of this idea in these examples distinguishes them above women of the past, whether German *exaltadas*, brilliant adventurers amid the perils of the Froude, or witty loiterers in the *salon* of Madame de Sablé.

La Rochefoucauld, who was proud of Mademoiselle and her princesses, would only have sneered at Madame Luce; nor would Lady Russell, nor Mrs. John Adams, have followed Alice to Egypt cheerfully. Nor do these two women belong to the army of saints and martyrs. A religious devotee has in her a mistaken enthusiasm, and goes *away from* the world. These women are doing the work of saints and martyrs with a far higher appreciation of God's providence, of the uses of this world, and with all the hindrances that fall to the lot of simple human beings. It is not our intention to multiply such instances here: they belong, rather, to the illustrations of individual power. We must not forget, however, the existence, in England, of that circle of women, of whom Mrs. Bodichon, Mrs. Hugo Reid, Mrs. Browning, Mrs. Fox, Mrs. Jameson, and Bessie Raynor Parkes, are honorable examples. We have such lives as those of Mrs. Gaskell and Miss Evans; the scientific reputation not alone of Mrs. Somerville, but of Mrs. Griffith, to whose masculine power of research English marine botany may be said to owe its existence, and who still survives, at an advanced age, to see that knowledge becomes popular, in her cheerful and honored decline, which she pursued, for many a year, unassisted and alone. We have Mrs. Janet Taylor, one of the best and most popular teachers of navigation and nautical mathematics in all England. Her classes have been celebrated and numerously attended by men who have been long at sea, as well as by youths preparing for the merchant service; and, still farther, we have in cultivated circles, to balance the old prejudice, an encouraging liberality. A review, published in the Westminster, after the issue of Miss Martineau's pamphlet on the future government of India, shows conclusively that any woman who will do *good* work may feel sure of honest appreciation. If she does poor work, she will only the more provoke the enemy. Nothing could have been more ambitious than Miss Martineau's theme; but, when she showed herself well qualified to handle it, no one had any disposition to consider the choice unwomanly. Such criticisms are the exponents of the century's experience. They betray the unconscious drift of the public mind. A book is modest by the side of a pamphlet. The former may wait its day: the latter aspires to immediate influence, if it does any thing, — must mould the hour. It was once the chosen weapon of Milton and Bolingbroke, later of Ward and Brougham. Is it nothing, that a woman of advanced years, writing from an invalid's chamber, feels herself competent to wield it? Was it nothing, when, by her tracts on political economy, she gave an impulse to the middle classes of her native land, for which busy political men could not find time?

Is it not Godwin who says that "human nature is better read in romance than history"? Every actual life falls short of its ideal; but a poem dares demand some approximation to its standard from the whole world. In this way, "Aurora Leigh," into which Mrs. Browning confesses she has thrown her whole heart, is a wonderful indication of human thought and feeling. In this country, there are many significant signs of progress. The name of Maria Mitchell in astronomy; of the women engaged in the Coast Survey; of the professors at Antioch, Vassar, and Oberlin, — are familiarly known, and have their own power. Only lately, a Nashua factory-girl takes the highest honors at the Oread Institute; and its principal is willing to put her and two other graduates into competition with any three college graduates in New England for examination according to the curriculum. When she finished the education she had first earned the money to procure, she left her Worcester home, and, with quiet right-mindedness, went back to Nashua to labor for an indigent family. As she tends her loom on the Jackson Corporation, she will have leisure to investigate her *right* to these acquisitions.

In support of this " exception," the superintendent of the New-York City Schools, long ago, reported, that its female schools, whether by merit of teachers or pupils or both, are of a much higher grade than the male schools. Eighteen girls'-schools are superior, in average attainment, to the very best boys'-school. He goes on to speak of the rapidity with which women acquire knowledge, in terms which remind us of Margaret Fuller, when she remarks of Dr. Channing, that it was not very pleasant to read to him; "for," said she, "he takes in subjects more deliberately than is conceivable to us feminine people, with our habits of ducking, diving, or flying for truth." In speaking of her classes at Vassar College, Miss Mitchell says (1865): "I have a class of seventeen pupils, between the ages of sixteen and twenty-two. They come to me for fifty minutes every day. I allow them great freedom in questioning, and I am puzzled by them daily. They show more mathematical ability, and more originality of thought, than I had expected. I doubt whether young men would show as deep an interest. Are there seventeen students in Harvard College who take mathematical astronomy, do you think?"

At the session of the Michigan Legislature, held in

1857-8, petitions were received, asking that women might be permitted to enjoy all the advantages of the State University. The committee to whom the subject was referred, took counsel with the older colleges at the East, whose whole spirit and method is as much opposed to such an idea as that of Oxford. The result was, that they reported against any change for the present,—a report the more to be regretted, as Ann Arbor has a broader University foundation than any institution within the limits of the United States. The University has lately petitioned for a larger endowment, and again an effort has been made to secure its advantages for women; Theodore Tilton pleading before the committee in their behalf, in February, 1867. We know of twenty-seven colleges in the United States, open to men and women, of which Oberlin was the noble pioneer.*

The highest culture has been claimed for women: it has been shown, that, for two centuries, the ideal of such a culture has existed, but has been depressed by an erroneous public opinion. There has, however, been a steady growth in the right direction, which entitles us to ask for a "revised and corrected" public opinion. The influence of mental culture is a small thing by the side of that insinuating atmospheric power and the customs of society which it controls. All educated men and women, all liberal souls, therefore, should do their utmost to invigorate public opin-

---

* See Appendix.

ion. To allow no weakness to escape us, to challenge every falsehood as it passes, to brave every insinuation and sneer, is what duty demands. Can you not bear to be called "women's-rights women"? To whom has the name ever been agreeable? Society gives the lie to your purest instincts, and you bear it. It calls the truths you accept hard names, and you are dumb. It throws stones, and you shrink behind some ragged social fence, leaving a few weak women to stand the assault alone.

What influence has the highest literary character of America, at this moment, on the popular idea of women? "How much is there that we may not say *aloud*," wrote Niebuhr to Savigny, "for fear of being stoned by the stupid *good* people!" and upon this principle the thinkers of our society act; not a word escaping from their guarded homes to cheer the more exposed workers.

Prescott stabbed Philip II. to the heart without a qualm. Ticknor could give a life to the romance of old Spain. Froude has defended Henry VIII. Our best poets sing verses that enslave, since the song of beauty echoes always among tropical delights. "Barbara Frietchie" alone has been written for us. When George Curtis blows his clarion, a courtly throng come at the call. We yield with the rest to the charm of the lips on which Attic bees once clustered. What honor do we pay the fair proportions of the simple truth?

How can we settle questions of right and wrong for

remote periods, without knowing the faces of either in the street to-day? How shall any one honor Margaret of Parma, and pity poor crazy Joan in Spain, and have no heart for the heroism of Mary Patton? How unravel with patient study the *tracasseries* of Elizabeth Tudor and Mary Stuart, yet ignore the complications of the life he himself lives?

When Mary Patton had carried her ship round Cape Horn, — standing in a parlor where the air was close, though the breezes that entered at its open casement swept the Common as they came, a woman told, with newly kindled enthusiasm, the story of that wonderful voyage. She gave her, in warm words, her wifely and womanly due. " She saved the ship, God bless her!" she said as she concluded; and another voice, that once was sweet, responded, " More shame to her!"

"' More shame to her!'" repeated the first speaker, as if she had been struck a sudden blow; and turning quickly towards the girl, beautiful, well educated, carefully reared, who, in the fulness of her twenty summers, found time for church-going, for clothing the poor, for elegant study, for every thing but sympathy, — " More shame!" she repeated : " What! for saving life and property?" — " Better that they should all have gone to the bottom," returned her friend, " than that one woman should step out of her sphere!" Ah! the Infinite Father knows how to educate the public opinion that we need. Now and then he lifts a woman, as he did Mary Patton, against her will out of her ordinary routine; and, while all the world gaze at her with tender sympathy, they half accept the coming future.

Does it sadden you, that we should repeat such words? They did not shock the ears on which they fell; they met no farther rebuke than one astonished question. Yet what did they represent? Not the public opinion of Mary Patton. The New-York underwriters, when they voted her a thousand dollars, were a fit gauge of that. It was the public opinion of the "right of vocation" that the young girl unconsciously betrayed. Harsh words die on our lips, as we think, "This girl's life is aimless. *She* would gladly do some noble work, but society does not help her. She lacks courage to stand alone, and envies the very woman she decries."

"Public opinion is of slow growth," you retort: "do not charge its corruptions on the people of to-day."

The people of to-day are responsible for any corruptions which they do not reject.

We have seen that the standard of womanly education does not lead where it should, because controlled by a public opinion which demands too little. It becomes us here to investigate the origin of that public opinion, and to ask the meaning of the lives which have been lived in its despite.

II.

HOW PUBLIC OPINION IS MADE.

> "A governed thought, thinking no thought but good,
> Makes crowded houses, holy solitude."
> *Sanscrit Book of Good Counsels.*

THE existing public opinion with regard to woman has been formed by the influence of heathen ages and institutions, kept up by a mistaken study of the classics, — a study so pursued, that Athens and Rome, Aristophanes and Juvenal, are more responsible for the popular views of woman, and for the popular mistakes in regard to man's position toward her, than any thing that has been written later.

This influence pervades all history; and so the study of history becomes, in its turn, the source of still greater and more specious error, except to a few rare and original minds, whose eccentricities have been pardoned to their genius, but who have never influenced the world to the extent that they have been influenced by it.

The adages or proverbs of all nations are the outgrowths of their first attempts at civilization. They began at a time which knew neither letter-paper nor the printing-press; and they perpetuate the rudest ideas, such as are every way degrading to womanly virtue. The influence of general literature is impelled by the mingled current. For many centuries, it was the outgrowth of male minds only, of such as had been drilled for seven years at least into all the heathenisms of which we speak.

Women, when they first began to work, followed the masculine idea, shared the masculine culture. As a portion of general literature, the novel, as the most popular, exerts the widest sway. No educational influence in this country compares with it; even that of the pulpit looks trivial beside it. There are thousands whom that influence never reaches; hardly one who cannot beg or buy a newspaper, with its story by some " Sylvanus Cobb."

From the first splash of the Atlantic on a Massachusetts beach to the farthest cañon which the weary footsteps of the Mormon women at this moment press; from the shell-bound coast of Florida, hung with garlands of orange and lime, to the cold, green waters of Lake Superior, in their fretted chalice of copper and gold, — the novel holds its way. On the railroad, at the depot, in the Irish hut, in the Indian lodge, on the steamer and the canal-boat, in the Fifth-avenue palace, and the Five-Points den of infamy, its shabby livery betrays the work that it is doing.

Until very lately, it has kept faith with history and the classics; but it is passing more and more into the hands of women, — of late into the hands of noble and independent women; and there are signs which indicate that it may soon become a potent influence of redemption. It has thus far done infinite harm, by drawing false distinctions between the masculine and feminine elements of human nature, and perpetuating, through the influence of genius often *intensifying*, the educational power of a false theory of love.

Social customs follow in the train of literature; and sometimes in keeping with popular errors, but oftener in stern opposition to them, are the lives and labors of remarkable individuals of both sexes, — lives that show, if they show nothing else, how much the resolute endeavor of one noble heart may do towards making real and popular its own convictions.

The influence of newspapers sustains, of course, the general current derived from all these sources.

Public opinion, then, flows out of these streams, — out of classical literature, history, general reading, and the proverbial wisdom of all lands; out of social conventions, and customs and newspapers. These streams set one way. Only individual influences remain, to stem their united force.

We must treat of them more at length, and first of the classics. Until very lately, there were no proper helps to the study of Egyptian, Greek, or Roman mythology. It was studied by the letter, and made to have more or less meaning, according to the teacher who interpreted it. Lemprière had no room for moral deductions or symbolic indications; his columns read like a criminal report in the "New-York Herald." The Egyptian mythology was, doubtless, an older offshoot from the same stem. Many of its ceremonies, its symbols, and its idols, must be confused by the uninstructed mind with realities of the very lowest, perhaps we should not be far wrong if we said, of the most revolting stamp. The Greek classics, so far as I know them, present a singular mixture of influences; but, where woman is concerned, the lowest certainly preponderate. We should be sorry to lose Homer and Æschylus, Herodotus, Thucydides, and Xenophon, from our library; but of how many poets and dramatists, from the few fragments of Pindar and Anacreon down through the tragic poets, — down, very far down, indeed, to Aristophanes, — can we say as much?

There need be no doubt about Aristophanes. The world would be the purer, and all women grateful, if every copy of his works, and every coarse inference from them, could be swept out of existence to-morrow. When we find a *noble picture* in Xenophon, it had a noble original, like Panthea in Persia, as old perhaps as that fine saying in the Heetopades which all the younger Veds disown. When we find an *ignoble thought*, it seems to have been born out of his Greek experience. Transported by a fair ideal, Plato asks, in his "Republic," "Should not this sex, which we condemn to obscure duties, be destined to functions the most noble and elevated?" But it was only to take back the words in his "Timæus," and in the midst of a society that refused to let the wife sit at table with the husband, and whose young wives were not "tame" enough to speak to their husbands, if we may believe the words of Xenophon, until after months of marriage. When Iscomachus, the model of an Athenian husband, and the friend of Socrates, asked his wife if she knew whether he had married her for love, "I know nothing," she replied, "but to be faithful to you, and to learn what you teach." He responded by an exhortation on "*staying at home*," which has come down to posterity, and left her, with a kiss, for the saloon of Aspasia! Pindar and Anacreon, even when they find no better representatives than Dr. Wolcott and Tom Moore, still continue to crown the wine-cup, and impart a certain grace to unmanly orgies. A late French writer goes so far as to call Euripides "a woman-hater, who could not pardon Zeus for having made woman an indispensable agent in the preservation of the species." In his portraits of Iphigenia and Macaria, Euripides follows his conception of *heroic*, not human nature. They are demigoddesses; yet how are their white robes stained!

Iphigenia says, —

> "More than a thousand women is one man
> Worthy to see the light of day;"

a sentiment which has prevailed ever since.

> "Silence and a chaste reserve
> Is woman's genuine praise, and to remain
> Quiet within the house,"

proceeds Macaria, and still farther: —

> "Of prosperous future could I form
> One cheerful hope?
> A poor forsaken virgin who would deign
> To take in marriage? Who would wish for sons
> From one so wretched? Better, then, to die
> Than bear such undeservèd miseries!"

Here is the popular idea which curses society to-day, — no vocation possible to woman, if she may not be a wife, and bear children: and these are favorable specimens; they show the practical tendencies of the very best of Euripides. The heroic portions are like Miriam's song, and have nothing to do with us and our experiences.

In speaking of Aristophanes, I do not speak ignorantly. I know how much students consider themselves indebted to him for details of manners and customs, for political and social hints, for a sort of Dutch school of pen-painting.

But if a nation's life be so very vile, if crimes that we cannot name and do not understand be among its amusements, why permit the record to taint the mind and inflame the imagination of youth? Why put it with our own hands into the desks of those in no way prepared to use it? Would you have wit and humor? Sit down with Douglas Jerrold, or to the genial table spread by our Boston Autocrat, and you will have no relish left for the coarse fare of the Athenian. One of the most vulgar assaults ever made upon the movement to elevate woman in this country was made in a respectable quarterly by a Greek scholar. It was sustained by quotations from Aristophanes, and concluded by copious translations from one of his liveliest plays, offered as a specimen of the "riot and misrule" that we ambitious women were ready to inaugurate. Coarser words still our Greek scholar might have taken from the same source to illustrate his theory. He knew very well that the nineteenth century would bear hints, insinuations, sneers, any thing but plain speaking. We have limits: he observed them, and forbore. Women sometimes talk of Aristophanes as if they had read his plays with pleasure; a thing for which we can only account by supposing that they do not take the whole significance of what they read, — and this is often the case with men. But a college furnishes helps. The mysteries of the well-thumbed English key are translated afresh into what we may call "college slang," illustrated oftentimes by clever if vulgar caricatures, where a few significant lines tell in a moment what a pure mind would have pondered years without perceiving; and if, perchance, some modest woman finds her friend or lover at this work, society says only: " You should not have touched the young man's book. What harm for him to amuse himself? — only women should never find it out! Keep them pure, no matter what becomes of men. What business had you to know the meaning of those pencil marks?"

Even St. John does not hesitate to condemn Aristophanes.* " With an art in which Shakespeare was no mean proficient," he begins, " he opens up a more culpable source of interest in the frequent satire of vices condemned as commonly as they are practised. He unveils the mysteries of iniquity with a fearless

---

* Manners and Customs of Greece, vol. i. p. 337.

and by no means an unreluctant hand. He ventures fearlessly on themes which few before or since have touched, despising the stern condemnation of posterity. He evidently shared in the worst corruptions of his age, and, like many other satirists, availed himself joyfully of the mask of satire to entertain his own imagination with his own descriptions. No one, with the least clear-sightedness or candor, can fail to perceive the depraved moral character of Aristophanes. Only less filthy than Rabelais, his fancy runs riot among the moral jakes and common sewers of the world, over which, by consummate art and the matchless magic of his style, he contrives unhappily to breathe a fragrance which should never be found save where virtue is."

When I first took up my pen, knowing well that I should speak of Margaret Fuller's beloved Greeks in a tone somewhat different from hers, I did not know that I should have the sympathy of a single eminent scholar.

It was with no common pleasure, therefore, that, opening her Life at random, one day, I chanced upon these words from her own pen. She is speaking of a class of private pupils:—

"I have always thought all that was said about the anti-religious tendency of a classical education to be 'auld wives' tales.' But the puzzles (of my pupils) about Virgil's notions of heaven and virtue, and his gracefully described gods and goddesses, have led me to alter my opinions; and I suspect, from reminiscences of my own mental history, that, if all teachers do not think the same, it is from the want of an intimate knowledge of their pupils' minds. I really find it difficult to keep their *morale* steady, and am inclined to think many of my own sceptical sufferings are traceable to this source. I well remember what reflections arose in my childish mind from a comparison of the Hebrew history, where every moral obliquity is shown out with such *naïveté*, and the Greek history, full of sparkling deeds and brilliant sayings, and their gods and goddesses, the types of beauty and power, with the dazzling veil of flowery language and poetical imagery cast over their vices and failings." *

We may be permitted also to quote, from the competent pen of Buckle, the following words: —

"We have only to open the Greek literature," he says, in his lecture on "The Condition of Women," "to see with what airs of superiority, with what serene and lofty contempt, with what mocking and biting scorn, women were treated by that lively and ingenious people, who looked upon them *merely as toys.*"

Alas! we need no prophet to show that what pollutes the mind of youth and lover, by polluting the ideal of society, must soon pollute the mind of maiden and mistress. Is that a Christian country which permits this style of thinking? and how many

---

* Memoirs of S. M. Fuller, vol. i. p. 337.

men of the world accept the stainless virginity of Christ as the world's pattern of highest manliness?

Passing from Greece to Rome, you will see that even as we owe to Roman law, before the time of Justinian, almost all that is obnoxious in the English, retaining still the strange old Latin terms which were applied to our relations in a very barbarous state of society; so we owe to the time of Augustus, to the influence of satirists like Horace and Juvenal, almost all the wide-spread heresies in regard to human nature: if we had but time to look at it, we might say Calvinism among the rest.

The views of women are still lower. Cæsar and Cicero may be abstract nullities to our young student; but what can he learn from Ovid? It is not delicate to name the " Art of Love." In simple, honest truth, it is the same to read the Metamorphoses. You cannot ventilate a gross man's atmosphere; all the Betsy Trotwoods must toss their cushions on the lawn when he leaves the room. It is the old difference between " Don Juan " and " Childe Harold," only less. In the first, the unvarnished play of passion may disgust you until it instructs; in the second, you have the despairing misanthropy, the false philosophy, the devil in Gabriel's own garment, which is always fascinating to the young, morbid with the stimulus of growth, and which you might mistake for piety if you did not know it was born of the lassitude left by excess.

Latin mythology was but the corruption of the

older types. What was beauty once became here undisguised coarseness or worse. The gods who once endured sin now patronized and made money by it. These things are not without their influence. Above all, low images, witty slang, and sharp satire, have force beyond their own, when slowly studied out by the help of the lexicon. The women to whom I speak know this very well. They know that the Molière, the Dante, the Schiller, studied at school, are never forgotten. They smile to hear men call them hard to read: for them they glow with clear and significant meaning. Striking passages are indelibly impressed by associations of time or place or page, which can never be forgotten. *I would not put an end to classical study; I would only direct attention, through such remarks, to the dangers attendant on the present manner of study. Classical teachers should not be chosen for their learning alone. No Lord Chesterfield should teach manners, but some one whose daily "good morning" is precious. So no coarse, low-minded man should interpret Greek or Roman, but some noble soul, not indifferent to social progress, capable of discriminating, and of letting in a little Christian light upon those pagan times.* Where men and women are taught together, this thing settles itself; and this is a very strong argument for institutions like Antioch and Oberlin.

Then might the period passed at the Latin school and the college become of the greatest moral and intellectual use. Then would no graduating students run the risk of hearing from their favorite doctor of divinity, instead of sound scriptural exhortation, some doctrine whisked out of Epicurus, by a clever but unconscious *leger-de-plume*.

Do not tell us, O excellent man! that you have gone through all this training, and come out with your soul unstained. We look at you, and see a temperament cold as ice, passions and imagination that were never at a blood-heat since you were born, that never translated the cold paper image into the warm deed of your conscious mental life; and you shall not answer for us, nor for our children.

In leaving this branch of our subject to be more fitly pursued by others, we ought to add that mental purity is not enough insisted upon for either sex. It is only by the greatest faithfulness from the beginning in this respect that we become capable of "touching pitch" at a mature age, in a way to benefit either ourselves or the community. How desirable it is to keep the young eye steadily gazing at the light till it feels all that is lost in darkness, to keep the atmosphere serene and holy till the necessary conflicts of life begin! For such a dayspring to existence no price could be too high; and, if *desirable* to all, it is *essential* to those who inherit degrading tendencies.

We must speak now of history. For the most part, it has been written by men devoid of intentional injustice to the sex; but, when a man sits in a certain light, he is penetrated by its color, as the false shades in our omnibuses strike the fairest bloom black and blue. If the positive knowledge and Christian candor of the nineteenth century cannot compel Macaulay to confess that he has libelled the name of William Penn, what may be expected of the mistakes occasioned by the ignorance, the inadvertence, or the false theories of the past? Clearly that they also will remain uncorrected.

If men start with the idea that woman is an inferior being, incapable of wide interests, and created for their pleasure alone; if they enact laws and establish customs to sustain these views; if, for the most part, they shut her into hareems, consider her so dangerous that she may not walk the streets without a veil, — they will write history in accordance with such views, and, whatever may be the facts, they will be interpreted to suit them. They will dwell upon the lives which their theories explain: they will touch lightly or ignore those that puzzle them. We shall hear a great deal of Cleopatra and Messalina, of the mother of Nero and of Lucretia Borgia, of Catharine de Medicis and Marie Stuart, of the beautiful Gabrielle and Ninon de L'Enclos. They will tell us of bloody Mary, and that royal coquette, Elizabeth; and possibly of some saints and martyrs, not too grand in stature to wear the strait-jacket of their theories.

If they think that purity is required of woman alone, and all license permitted to man, they will value female chastity for the service it does poetry and the state, but never maidenhood devoted to noble uses and conscious of an immortal destiny.

Hypatia of Alexandria, noble and queenly, so queenly that those who did not understand, dared not libel her, — Hypatia, a woman of intellect so keen and grasping, that she would have been eminent in the nineteenth century, and may be met in the circles of some future sphere, erect and calm, by the side of our own Margaret Fuller, — she, who died a stainless virgin, torn in pieces by dogs, because she tried to shelter some wretched Jews from Christian wrath, and could even hold her Neo-Platonism a holier thing than that disgraced Christianity, — what do we know of her? Only the little which the letters of Synesius preserve, only the testimony borne by a few Christians, fathers of the Church *now*, but outlawed *then* by the popular grossness! Yet, a pure and fragrant waif from the dark ocean of that past, her name was permitted to float down to us, till Kingsley caught it, and, with the unscrupulousness of the advocate, *stained* it to serve his purpose.*

It would have been no matter, had not genius set its seal on the work, and so made it doubtful whether history has any Hypatia left. We must not fail to utter constant protest against such unfairness; and to assert again and again, that not a single weakness or folly attributed to Hypatia by the novelist — neither the worship of Venus Anadyomene nor the prospective marriage with the Roman governor, neither the superstitious fears, the ominous self-conceit, nor the half

---

* I have sustained this assertion in two articles on Hypatia, published in "Historical Sketches," 1855.

conscious personal ambition — is in the least sustained by the facts of history. She was pure and stainless: let us see to it that such memories are rescued.

And there is still another name, deeply wronged by the prejudice and party spirit of the past, which it is quite possible to redeem: I mean that of Aspasia. For many centuries, the very sound of it suggested an image of all womanly grace and genius, devoid of womanly virtue; the insight of a seer, the eloquence of an orator, but the voluptuousness of a courtesan. Very lately, the manly justice of Thirlwall and Grote, and the exquisite taste and imagination of Walter Savage Landor, have striven to repair the wrong. Her reputation fell a victim to the gross puns of Aristophanes, himself the hired mouth-piece of a political party that hated her, and whose misrepresentations were so contemptible in the eyes of Pericles, that he would not interfere to prevent them.

Would you have the history of that immortal marriage written truly?

Imagine the Greek ruler married, for some years, to a woman of the noblest Athenian blood, already the mother of two children, but one who, if irreproachable in conduct, was utterly incapable of taking in the scope of his plans, or sharing his lofty, adventurous thought. After years of weariness passed in her society, with no rest for his heart and no inspiration for his genius, there came to Athens a woman and a foreigner, in whom he found his peer, — a woman who gathered round her in a moment all that there was of free and noble in that world of poetry, statesmanship, and art. She was from the islands of the Archipelago, and, like the women of her country, walked the streets with her face unveiled.

Hardly had she come, before Socrates and Plato, and Anaxagoras the pure old man, became her frequent guests, and honored her with the name of friend. In such a society, Pericles saw that his own soul would grow; so sustained, he should be more for Athens and himself. He was no Christian to deny himself for the sake of that unhappy wife and children,— a wife whose discontent had already infected the state. The gods he knew — Zeus and Eros — smiled on the step he took. What if the laws of Athens forbade a legal marriage with a foreigner? Pericles was Athens; and what he respected, all men must honor. Aspasia had, so far as we know, a free maiden heart; and Pericles shows us in what light he regarded her, by divorcing his wife to consolidate their union, and subsequently forcing the courts to legitimate her child. Had he omitted these proofs of his own sincerity and her honor, not a voice would have been raised against either. What need to take these steps, if she were the woman Aristophanes would have us see?

This divorce created or strengthened the political opposition to Pericles. This opposition was headed by his two sons and their forsaken mother, joined by the pure Athenian blood to which theirs was akin, and gained all its strength and popularity from the wit and falsehood of Aristophanes and the players.

Follow the story as it goes, and see Aspasia, at last, summoned before the Areopagus. What are the charges against her? The very same that were preferred against her friends, Socrates and Anaxagoras. " She walks the streets unveiled, she sits at the table with men, she does not believe in the Greek gods, she talks about one sole Creator, she has original ideas about the motions of the sun and moon; *therefore* her society corrupts youth." Not a word about vice of any sort. Is it for abandoned women that the best men of any age are willing to entreat before a senate? The tears which Pericles shed then for Aspasia glitter like gems on the historic page.

When the plague came, his first thought was for her safety; and, after his death, her name shares the retirement of her widowed life. There was a rumor that she afterward married a rich grazier, whom she raised to eminence in the state. Not unlikely that such a rumor might grow in the minds of those who had not forgotten the great men *she* made, when they saw the success of Lysicles; but other authors assert that his wife was the Aspasia who was also known as a midwife in Athens.

It is a noble picture, it seems to me; and when we consider the prejudice of a Christian age and country, the mob that a Bloomer skirt will attract in our own cities, we need not wonder that slander followed an unveiled face in Athens.

What do we know of the women of the age of Augustus? — of the galaxy that spanned the sky of Louis XIV.?

Do you remember, as you read of those crowds of worthless women, what sort of public opinion educated them, — what sort of public opinion such histories tend to form? Do you ever ask any questions concerning the men of the same eras, — how they employed their time, and what part they took in those games of wanton folly? It is time that some one should: and I cannot help directing your attention to the significant fact, that while the word "mistress," applied to a woman, serves at once to mark her out for reprobation, there is no corresponding term, which, applied to man, produces the same effect; and this because the interests of the state are still paramount to the interests of the soul itself.

In speaking of the court of Charles II., Dr. William Alexander says, in 1799: "Its *tone* ruined all women: they were either adored as angels, or degraded to brute beasts. The satirists, who immediately arose, despised what they had themselves created, and gave the character to every line that has since been written concerning women," down to the verses of Churchill, and that often-quoted, well-remembered line of Pope, with which we need not soil our lips.

We may quote here a criticism upon the "Cinq-Mars" of Alfred de Vigny, taken from Lady Morgan's "France." You will find it especially interesting, because it bears on what has been suggested of the influence of history, and may be compared with a portion of one of Margaret Fuller's letters, in which she criticises the same work, and makes, in her own way, parallel reflections.

"I dipped also," says Lady Morgan, "into the 'Cinq-Mars' of Alfred de Vigny, a charming production. It gives the best course of practical politics, in its exposition of the miseries and vices incidental to the institutions of the middle ages. Behold Richelieu and Louis XIII. in the plenitude of their bad passions and unquestioned power, when —

'Torture interrogates and Pain replies.'

Behold, too, their victims, — Urbain, Grandier, De Thou, Cinq-Mars, and the long, heart-rending list of worth, genius, and innocence immolated. With such pictures in the hands of the youth of France, it is impossible they should retrograde. How different from the works of Louis XV.'s days, when the Marivaux, Crebillons, and Le Clos wrote for the especial corruption of that society from whose profligacy they borrowed their characters, incidents, and morals! Men would not now dare to name, in the presence of virtuous women, works which were once in the hands of every female of rank in France, — works which, like the novels of Richardson, had the seduction of innocence for their story, and witty libertinism and triumphant villany for their principal features.

"With such a literature, it was almost a miracle that one virtuous woman or one honest man was left in the country to create that revolution which was to purify its pestiferous atmosphere. Admirable for its genius, this work is still more so for its honesty."

In the praise given to this new literature is implied the censure passed upon the old. Of direct educational literature, we may say, that all writers, from Rousseau to Gregory, Fordyce, and the very latest in our own country, have exercised an enervating influence over public opinion, and helped to form the popular estimate of female ability. Rousseau's influence is still powerful. Let me quote from his "Emilius:" "Researches into abstract and speculative truths, the principles and axioms of science,— in short, every thing which tends to generalize ideas, — is out of the province of woman. All her ideas should be directed to the *study of men*. As to works of genius, they are beyond her capacity. She has not precision enough to succeed in accurate science; and physical knowledge belongs to those who are most active and most *inquisitive.*"

Alas for Mary Somerville, Janet Taylor, and Maria Mitchell, as well as for the popular idea that women are a *curious* sex! He goes on: "Woman should have the skill to incline *us* to do every thing which her sex will not enable her to do of herself. She should learn to penetrate the real sentiments of men, and should have the art to communicate those which are most agreeable to them, without *seeming to intend it.*"

This sounds somewhat barefaced; but it is the

model of all the advice which society is still giving. It is refreshing to catch the first gleam of something better from the author of "Sandford and Merton." "If women," says Mr. Day, "are in general feeble both in body and mind, it arises less from nature than from education. We encourage a vicious indolence and inactivity, which we falsely call delicacy. Instead of hardening their minds by the severer principles of reason and philosophy, we breed them to useless arts which terminate in vanity or sensuality. They are taught nothing but idle postures and foolish accomplishments." Dr. Gregory recommends dissimulation. Dr. Fordyce advises women to increase their power by reserve and coldness! When we hear of the educational restraints still exercised, of the innocent amusements forbidden, the compositions which may be written, but not read, lest the young girl might some time become the lecturer, — we cannot but feel that the step is not so very long from that time and country to this, and wonder at the folly which still refuses to trust the laws of God to a natural development. It is mortifying, too, to listen to the silly rhapsodies of Madame de Staël. "Though Rousseau has endeavored," she says, "to prevent women from interfering in public affairs, and acting a brilliant part in political life, yet, in speaking of them, how much has he done it to *their satisfaction!* If he wished to deprive them of some rights foreign to their sex, how has he for ever asserted for them all those to which it has a claim! What signifies it," she continues, "that his reason disputes with them for empire, while his heart is still devotedly theirs?"

What signifies it? It signifies a great deal. It signifies all the difference between life in a solitary seraglio, and life with God's world for an inheritance; all the difference between being the worn-out toy of one sensualist, and the inspiration of an unborn age; all the difference between the butterfly and the seraph, between the imprisoned nun and Longfellow's sweet St. Philomel. When we read these words, we thank Margaret Fuller for the very criticism which once moved a girlish ire. " De Staël's name," she wrote, " was not clear of offence; she could not forget the woman in the thought. Sentimental tears often dimmed her eagle glance." What a grateful contrast to all such sentimentalism do we find in Margaret's own sketch of the early life of Miranda!

" This child was early led to feel herself a child of the spirit. She took her place easily in the world of mind. A dignified sense of self-dependence was given as all her portion, and she found it a sure anchor. Her relations with others were fixed with equal security. With both men and women they were noble; affectionate without passion, intellectual without coldness. The world was free to her, and she lived freely in it. Outward adversity came, and inward conflict; but that self-respect had early been awakened, which must always lead at last to an outward security and an inward peace." Here is the great difficulty in the education of woman, to lead her to a point from which she shall naturally develop self-respect, and learn self-help. Old prejudices extinguish her as an individual, oblige her to renounce the inspiration in herself, and yield to all the weaknesses and wickednesses of man. Look at Chaucer's beau-ideal of a wife in the tale of Griselda, dwindled now into the patient Grissel of modern story. In her a woman is represented as perfect, because she ardently and constantly loved a monster who gained her by guile, and brutally abused her. Put the matter into plain English, and see if you would respect such a woman now. No: and therefore is it somewhat sad, that, in Tennyson's new Idyll, he must recreate this ideal in the Enid of Geraint; and that, out of four pictures of womanly love, only one seems human and natural, and that, the guilty love of Guinevère. The recently awakened interest in the position of woman is flooding the country with books relating to her and her sphere. They have, their *very titles* have, an immense educational influence. Let me direct your attention to one published in Boston by a leading house last winter, and entitled " Remarkable Women of Different Ages and Nations." Let us read the names of the thirteen women with whose lives it seeks to entertain the public: —

  Beatrice Cenci, the parricide.
  Charlotte Corday, the assassin.
  Joanna Southcote, the English prophetess.
  Jemima Wilkinson, the American prophetess.

Madame Ursinus, the poisoner.
Madame Göttfried, the poisoner.
Mademoiselle Clairon, the actress.
Harriet Mellon, the actress.
Madame Lenormand, the fortune-teller.
Angelica Kauffman, the artist.
Mary Baker, the impostor.
Pope Joan, the pontiff.
Joan of Arc, the warrior.

Look at the list! Assassins, parricides, and poisoners, fortune-tellers, and actresses! Let us hope they will always remain *remarkable!* In this list we have the name of one woman who never lived, and of four at least who in this country would owe all their celebrity to the police court; and this while history pants to be delivered of noble lives not known at all, like the women of the House of Montefeltro, or little known, like the pure and heroic wife of Condé, Clemence de Maillé. And by what black art, let us ask, are such names as Beatrice, and Charlotte Corday, sweet Joan of Arc, and dear Angelica Kauffman, a noble woman, whose happiness was wrecked upon a fiendish jest, juggled into this list? As well might you put Brutus who killed great Cæsar, and Lucretia of spotless fame, and Andrea del Sarto who loved a faithless wife, into the same category. Such association, however false, helps to educate the popular mind.

Of the power of adages, and that barbaric experience and civilization of which they are generally the exponent, we might write volumes; but the subject must be dismissed in this connection without a word. We must pass on to consider the force of social instincts and prejudices which underlie this general literature, and are as much stronger than it as the character of a man is stronger than his intellectual quality. A lecturer once said, " that the first prejudice which women have to encounter is one which exists before they are born, which leads fathers instinctively to look forward to the birth of sons, and to leave little room in their happy or ambitious schemes for the coming of a daughter." Not long since, a highly educated Englishman told me that this remark smote him to the heart. " I never expected to have any thing but a son," he declared; "and, when my little Minnie was born, I had made no preparation for her. I had neither a thought nor a scheme at her service."

Fanny Wright, in some essays published thirty years ago, says, " There are some parents who take one step in duty, and halt at the second. Our sons," they say, "will have to exercise political rights, and fill public offices. We must help them to whatever knowledge there is going, and make them as sharp-witted as their neighbors. As for our daughters, they can never be any thing; in fact, they are nothing. We give them to their mothers, who will take them to church and dancing-school, and, with the aid of fine clothes, fit them out for the market.

" But," she goes on to say, " let possibilities be what they will, no man has a *right* to calculate on them for his sons. He has only to consider them as human beings, and insure them a full development of all the faculties which belong to them as such. So, as respects his daughters, he has nothing to do with the injustice of law, nor the absurdities of society. His duty is plain, — to train them up as human beings, to seek for them, and with them, all just knowledge. Who among *men* contend best with the difficulties of life and society, — the strong-minded or the weak, the wise or the foolish? Who best control and mould opposing circumstances, — the educated or the ignorant? What is true of them is true of women also."

In the customs of nations, women find the most discouraging educational influences. While with us these customs all set one way, they are easily broken through by the untutored races, who still rely on the force of their primal instincts. When Captain Wallis went to see the Queen of Otaheite, a marsh which crossed the way proved a formidable obstacle to the puny Anglo-Saxon. No sooner did the queen perceive it, than, taking him up as if he were a meal-bag, she threw him over her shoulder, and strode along. Nobody smiled; even Captain Wallis does not appear to have felt mortified. These people were accustomed to the physical strength of their queen. It would be well if civilized nations could imitate them, far enough at least to remember, that wherever strength, whether mental or physical, is found, *there* it certainly belongs.

In Peru and the Formosa Isles, it is the women who choose their husbands, and not the men who choose their wives; and, from the moment of marriage, the man takes up his abode in his wife's family. Lord of creation in every other respect, he still owes to her whatever social standing and privileges he may possess. Such an exception is valueless, save that it shows us that sex does not absolutely, of itself, determine such customs.

The African kings are permitted to have many wives; but they respect the chastity of women, and require it. Dr. Livingstone tells us of an instance in which the royal succession finally lapsed upon a woman. Her counsellors forbade her to marry a single husband, telling her that it would create jealousies and divisions in the tribe. She must follow the royal custom. But pure womanly nature spoke louder than the counsellors. The poor queen renounced marriage altogether, and associated a half-brother in the government, upon whose children she settled the succession. Let this beautiful fact shame those coward souls who fear to trust to the instinctive purity of the sex.

He goes on to state, in a recent letter, that he has found nothing more remarkable, among the highly intelligent tribes of the Upper Sambesi, than the respect universally accorded to women.

" Many of the tribes are governed by a female chief. If you demand any thing of a man," remarks the intrepid explorer, " he replies, ' I will talk with my wife about it.' If the woman consents, your demand is granted. If she refuse, you will receive a negative reply. Women vote in all the public assemblies.

Among the Bushwanas and Kaffirs, the men swear by their fathers; but among the veritable Africans, occupying the centre of the continent, they always swear by their mother. If a young man falls in love with a maiden of another village, he leaves his own, and takes up his dwelling in hers. He is obliged to provide in part for the maintenance of his mother-in-law, and to assume a respectful attitude, a sort of semi-kneeling, in her presence. I was so much astonished at all these marks of respect for women, that I inquired of the Portuguese if such had always been the habit of the country. They assured me that such had always been the case."

If women were unwise managers of money, — a statement frequently made, but which we may safely deny, — it would be owing to the custom which has, through long ages, put the purse in the hands of "their master;" a custom so old, that to "husband" one's resources is a phrase which expresses man's pecuniary responsibility, and is always equivalent to locking one's money up. "It will be time enough," says Mrs. Kirkland, "to expect from woman a just economy when she is permitted to distribute a portion of the family resources. Witness those proud subscription-lists where one reads, 'Mr. B., twenty dollars;' and, just below, 'Mrs. B., ten dollars,'— which ten dollars Mrs. B. never saw, and would ask for in vain to distribute for her own pleasure."

And this custom has such educational force, that very liberal men refuse the smallest pecuniary independence to their wives to their very dying day. " The Turk does not lock up his wife with more care than the Christian his strong box. To that lock there is ever but one key, and that the master carries in his pocket. The case is not altered when the wife is about to close her weary eyes in death. She may have earned or inherited or saved the greater part of their common property, but without his consent she cannot bequeath a dollar." This passage reminds us of a criticism on the marriage service attributed to Sir John Bowring. This eccentric man considers it wicked from beginning to end. " Look at it," he says: "'with this ring I thee wed,' — that's sorcery; 'with my body I thee worship,' — that's idolatry; 'and with all my worldly goods I thee endow,' — that's a lie!"

It is the long customs of mankind which stand in the way of educating women to trades and professions. These matters are mainly in woman's own hands. One is glad to see in the English Parliament certain statements made in this connection, and others also in a London pamphlet on the nature of municipal government. In reply to the common argument that women ought not to enter certain vocations, because they would ultimately find themselves incompetent, it is stated, that, in all delicate handicrafts, men do the same. Thus, of those who learn to make watches and watchmakers' tools, not one-fifth continue in the trade; and, in the decoration of that delicate ware called Bohemian glass, by far the greater portion of apprentices give it up on account of natural unfitness.

It is the customs of society which sustain the prejudice against literary women. When Dr. Aikin published his " Miscellaneous Pieces," Fox met him in the street. " I particularly admire," said the orator, complimenting him, " your essay on Inconsistency." —" That," said Aikin, " is my sister's." — " Ah! well, I like that on Monastic Institutions." — " That is also hers," replied the honest man; and, in a tumult of confusion, Fox bowed himself away. Had public feeling been right, how gracefully he might have congratulated the brother on his sister's ability, how gladly might that brother have seen her excel himself! This sister was that Mrs. Barbauld who afterward did such womanly service, that we feel tempted to forgive the early fit of sentimentality which found vent in that rhymed nonsense, concluding, —

"Your best, your sweetest empire is to please."

The manners of men have their educational influence. The quiet turning-aside from women when matters of business, politics, or science are discussed; the common saying, " What have women to do with that? let them mind their knitting, or their house affairs;" the short answer when an interested question is asked, " You wouldn't understand it, if I told you," — all these depress and enervate, and, even if not *spoken*, the spirit of them animates all social life. " Men are suspicious," wrote Dr. Alexander in 1790, "that a rational education would open the eyes of women, and prompt them to assert the rights of which they have always been deprived." But education could not be withheld nor eyes closed for ever; therefore the time has come to claim these rights. The Sorbonne is already asked why it confers degrees upon women with one hand, while it quietly locks Margaret Fuller out of Arago's lecture-room with the other. Need we inquire what influence it would have upon society, if all literature and scientific opportunities, if all societies devoted to natural history and mathematics, if all colleges and public libraries the world over, were thrown open to woman?

In inferior circles, where no leading minds preside, it would be as it is now: there would be much idle prating, much foolish delay, much inconsequent discussion; but woman is quick to recognize genius, to listen when wisdom speaks. She chatters, to be sure, in the presence of fools; but, when earnest men come to know the value of her enthusiasm, they will never be willing to lose it. When the great door of the scholarly and scientific retreat is once thrown open, you will be surprised to see the crowd ready to enter; and, when the sexes kindle into intellectual life together, many a woman's coals will be modestly laid upon an honored altar, and the flames will rise all the higher because they have been so fed.

How can we estimate sufficiently the corrupting influence of the newspapers of the land?

We may hope your prejudices will defend woman

here, and you will acknowledge that the minds cannot be kept pure before whom their details are set. Let us go farther, and say that they cannot be kept pure, coming in contact as they do with minds among men that gloat over such records. God is just, and his compensations are terrible. If you do not spare the purity of the lowest in the land, you cannot save that of your wife and daughter. If you will not protect the vulgar against themselves, you cannot protect the refined against the vulgar. He is not a pure man, who, among his fellows, thinks a thought or utters a word he would blush to have his sister hear. She is not a pure woman, who, in the seclusion of her chamber, or gossip with her household, omits one of the proprieties which delicacy requires. She has no title to *our* respect, who is not secure in *her own*. How can we reach such a standard as this, if we invite pollution daily across our threshold, and call it harmless because it dresses in printer's ink? It is not enough that much of the obscenity is pure invention. The profit of the scandal overbalances the cost of the libel. The simplest item is turned to gross account. Even the intimation that the postmaster has placed a woman at the ladies' window in New York has to be coupled with the insinuation that she would have " done better at the gentlemen's." What business have you or I with details that concern only judge and jury? What good does it do society to quote high legal authority upon " flirtation," unless, indeed, we learn thereby to estimate aright the corrupting power of the first wrong step? Police reports, vulgar anecdotes, shocking accidents, and trivial gossip a child might be ashamed to repeat, make up the mass of our daily sheets. Happy is the editor who offers three columns of common sense daily to his readers. When, alas! shall we have a public willing to pay for common sense and pure reading alone?

A woman ought to turn like a flash of light from a foul page, a coarse and vulgar word. No wit should ever tempt her to read the one, or repeat the other; and what I say of woman, I *mean* of man. I have not two separate moral standards for the sexes.

Margaret Fuller speaks somewhere of certain habits of impure speech which she had heard attributed to ladies in a New-York hotel. What foundation that story had, we may never find; but all of us know some women before whom we keep the coldest reserve, and with whom we would never touch many a subject we should be willing to discuss with any pure-minded man. Ladies! Not all the gold of Pactolus, not all the beauty of Anadyomene, not all the wisdom of Minerva, could make such women *ladies!* We cannot redeem the poor denizens of Five Points till we have redeemed those of the Fifth Avenue.

Our own children must prattle oaths, if we will not hush the drunken brawler in the streets.

NOTE. — When this lecture was first delivered, in 1858, it excited more discussion than any "revolutionary notions" of which I have ever been suspected. Since then, the same ideas, as applied to other questions, have been expressed in various quarters. I think a thorough classical education necessary to a college bred man. As far as I have any opinions to express, they coincide with those recently uttered by John Stuart Mill at St. Andrew's.

I wish to sustain the remarks of the text by the following quotations:—

"Many things with the Greeks and Romans most venerable have not merely lost their sanctity in our eyes, but present contemptible and even ludicrous ideas to us. Hence, any allusion to them, or any expression of the feelings connected with them, or even a reference to the habits of thinking which those feelings have produced, must have an operation most unpropitious." — LORD BROUGHAM.

"The fictions constituting the epic poetry of Homer, Virgil, and their imitators, so far from being consonant with the taste and sense of modern readers, are, on the contrary, often annoying, from the absence of all moral or poetical justice."—"The gods who preside in this scenic exhibition are tainted with every vice which has since degraded their supposed subordinates of the human race. Cruelty, revenge, deceit, hatred, unrelenting rancor, and unbridled lust, are the qualities which call for approval in a generation professing to feel and practise virtues of an opposite nature. An exterminating war is undertaken for the sake of a vacillating adulteress, and its heroes quarrel implacably about the possession of their female slaves. Ulysses, on his return home, winds up the 'Odyssey' by a wholesale slaughter of his disorganized subjects, hangs up a dozen censurable females in a row, and puts Melanthius to a lingering death by gradual mutilation."—"In their social relations, the Greeks were licentious and exquisitely depraved. In their domestic habits, they were primitive, destitute, and uncleanly." — DR. JACOB BIGELOW.

These words represent the re-action of Christian morality against the abuses of classical study, to which I allude in my text. But let the classics be taught properly, and morality will have no complaint to make. We cannot understand the history of the world, without an intelligent investigation of its beginnings; but we should be carefully protected against assuming, as reasonable and proper, either the habits and opinions or the sarcasms of an extinct experience.

III.

THE MEANING OF THE LIVES THAT HAVE MODIFIED PUBLIC OPINION.

> "Speak! or I go no further.
> I need a goal, an aim. I cannot toil,
> *Because the steps are here;* in their ascent,
> Tell me THE END, or I sit still and weep."
> *Naturliche Tochter.*

WE have considered the controlling influence exercised by consolidated public opinion concerning women. We have asked from what sources this opinion was derived. We have now to consider some individual lives which have set it at defiance, and in that way done something towards its reconstruction.

Mary Wollstonecraft is chiefly known in this country as the wife of Godwin, and the author of a "Vindication of the Rights of Woman." This book is often accused of the most irreligious and libertine tendencies; and, for many years, her name stood in my own mind as the representative of an unfortunate woman of genius, unbalanced in character, and only to be remembered by the obstacles she had laid in the path of her sex. I turned instinctively from the idea I had somehow conceived of her; nor was it till a singular literary fact, the exponent of her individual power, arrested my attention, that I was tempted to take up the "Rights of Woman."

In making a rapid survey of English literature, to ascertain how many women had made a decisive mark upon it, and how many works had been published especially bearing upon woman's advancement, I at first experienced a bitter disappointment. Upon approaching the year 1800, however, I found a stream of literature rushing in, for which I could not account. It united many rivulets of thought and life. Some volumes were heavy and oppressive in a double sense; some were light as pamphlets; some consisted of translations from other languages; some were biographies; many were attempts at reconstruction on a rotten foundation; others, an attempt at the rebuilding of society from its very base. But these works all bore the same stamp, an impress powerful, but healthy. It seemed as if one thought had animated all these workers who had taken society by surprise; for the prejudice and bigotry they must have aroused had left no corresponding trace. The prefaces generally began, " On account of the interest lately excited," " The public mind seeming now to be interested;" and I read very few volumes before I discovered that the power which had aroused and interested was no other than Mary Wollstonecraft's " Rights of Woman."

These books ranged onward from 1790, and the force of the influence was not spent for twenty years. Among them, I recall, at this moment, Dr. Alexander's " History of Women" in two quarto volumes; Matilda Betham's " Biographical Dictionary," an *honest*, if not a valuable, attempt to supply a want still felt in English literature; and Cotton's translation of the mathematical works of Maria Agnesi. These were born of a common mother. I read the "Vindication," therefore, with persistent care; looking with fruitless question for the second and third volumes that were promised. Could this be the book which had been so abused for half a century? The American edition had been published before garbling became the fashion; but I took pains to collate it carefully with the English. It was all in vain. I found only a simple, determined, eloquent plea for a proper education for women, urged on social, moral, and religious grounds; an earnest protest against Rousseau and Dr. Gregory; and a demand that *men* should be subject to the same moral laws as women. Very revolutionary this! Reprint it, under modern sponsorship, and you would find it perhaps too heavy to read. It would only repeat what you all know, and you would miss the fanatical spice of our later speech. Yet this book was so much needed when it appeared, that it acted on the under-current of English thought and life like a subsoil plough, and brought all manner of abominations to the surface. The preface alone contains any allusion to woman's political rights. It is dedicated to Talleyrand, who, in publishing a pamphlet on national education, had admitted the inconsistency of debarring women from their exercise. From this preface, the *world* took fright, and *we* may judge in what manner she intended to follow up her plea for education. Let me quote a few passages. "I earnestly wish," she says, "to point out in what true dignity and human happiness consist. I wish to persuade women to acquire strength both of mind and body, and to convince them, that the soft phrases, 'susceptibility of heart,' 'delicacy of sentiment,' and 'refinement of taste,' are almost synonymous with epithets of weakness, and that those beings who are the objects of pity, and that kind of love which has been termed its sister, will soon become objects of contempt." — "An air of fashion is but a badge of slavery." — "It follows," she says farther on, "that women should either be shut up, like Eastern princesses, or educated in such a manner as to think and act for themselves." — "Suppose a woman trained to obedience, married to a sensible man, who directs her judgment, without permitting her to feel the servility of her position. She cannot ensure the life of her protector. He may die, and leave her at the head of a large family." — "It is not *empire*, but *equality*, woman should contend for. When women are sufficiently enlightened to discover their real interests, they will be very ready to resign all those prerogatives of love *which are not mutual* for the calm satisfactions of friendship and the tender confidence of habitual esteem. Before marriage, they will not assume any insolent airs, nor afterwards abjectly submit; but, endeavoring to act like reasonable creatures in both relations, they will not be tumbled from a throne to a stool."

This is the character of the whole book. It contains nothing more subversive of morality than these words. You cannot do better than read it, and receive, as I did, a lasting lesson on the folly of prejudice. As a work of art, it is irregular in method, and impulsive in execution; facts not to be wondered at, since it was written and printed in the brief space of six weeks. Dr. Channing once wrote of her: "I have lately read Mary Wollstonecraft's posthumous works. Her letters towards the close of the first volume are the best I ever read. They are superior to Sterne's. I consider her the greatest woman of the age. Her ' Rights of Woman' is a masculine performance, and ought to be studied by her sex; the sentiments are noble and generous."

What, then, was the character of the woman? Was it as strong and generous as the sentiments she advocated? Her life broke down some social barriers, and, though noble and heroic when viewed from within, looks hampered and unsatisfactory from the common stand-point. Godwin has erected an exquisite monument to her memory, in a sketch written soon after her decease. Mary Wollstonecraft was born near London in the year 1759. She came into an unhappy and uncongenial home. Her father was a passionate tyrant; her mother, compelled to submit to his caprice, became like every other slave, a tyrant where she had the power, and ruled her children with a rod of iron. By defending her mother from her husband's violence, Mary early extorted some degree of affection from the one, and respect from the other. Her father had some property, which he seems to have squandered by frequent changes of abode; and a day school at Beverley, in Yorkshire, gave her her principal advantages of education. An eccentric clergyman at Hoxton, named Clare, added some farther instruction. Under his roof, she formed an intimacy with Frances Blood, destined to influence her whole life. This girl was remarkably accomplished, and, at the age of eighteen, supported her father and mother and their family of younger children. She was delicately neat and proper in all she did; and her influence was of the greatest benefit to Mary, who had often desired to assist her family, but was deterred by the helpless condition of her mother. She now went as companion to a family at Bath, but soon relinquished the position, on account of her mother's serious illness. Mrs. Wollstonecraft was exacting and troublesome. Mary nursed her with devoted care, but, after her death, bade a final farewell to her father's roof. His affairs had become wretchedly involved; and, with Fanny Blood and her two sisters, she proceeded to open a day school. At first, she had looked upon Fanny as her superior, but her own force of character soon found its rightful position. The health of her friend broke down under her unnatural burden, and Mary's devotion to her for years was beautiful to see. Her marriage and removal to Lisbon, in a vain search for health, soon put this devotion to the test.

At this point, Mary Wollstonecraft's reputation was unsullied. She was an admirable manager, an efficient and successful teacher; yet, when Fannie became seriously ill, she did not hesitate to risk her only means of support, the prosperity of her school, to go to her. Her friend, Dr. Price, the Unitarian minister, and Mrs. Burgh, were annoyed at what they considered a quixotic devotion; but they supplied her with money, and she went. A few days closed in death an intimacy of more than ten years, which had been, until this time, Mary's tenderest interest in life. On her way home, her moral energy saved the lives of a French crew in a sailing vessel which she encountered, just about to founder. Her school had suffered by her absence; and the pressing necessities of Fanny's family, in which she still took an interest, induced her to have recourse to literature. The first ten pounds received from her " Thoughts on the Education of Daughters" went to their relief. Nothing can be sadder than to see a young girl placed as Mary Wollstonecraft now was, — compelled to fulfil the duties of a father and mother to younger brothers and sisters. The position is unnatural. Gratitude might be expected, but envy is more often felt. The personal advantages sought for their sakes, and not to be transferred except as a pecuniary profit, she is supposed to seek for her own. Affection partly yields, and enthusiasm does not replace it; while she is urged by necessities which make it difficult to bear the errors and intractabilities of those she is providing for. Still loving, and desiring to provide for her sisters, Mary thought it better to live apart from them, and accepted a temporary position as governess in Lord Kingsborough's family. When they left England, she went to Bristol, and published a novel, which, founded on her ten years of friendly devotion, took the highest rank as a work of sentiment. The next three years were spent in her own house, in London, in the active service of the publisher, Johnson. She translated from French, German, and Italian, wrote several books for children, and took a large share in the conduct of the "Analytical Review."

Her translation of Salzman's "Elements of Morality" led to an interesting correspondence with its author, who repaid the service, subsequently, by translating into German her "Rights of Woman." These occupations, if they did little towards the discipline of her powers, served to rouse her from the dejection into which the death of her friend had plunged her. Her earnings were now devoted to her own family. One sister she kept at Paris for two years to qualify her as a governess; another she placed as parlor-boarder at a London school. Her brother James she sent to Woolwich; afterward procuring for him a position in the navy, where he soon rose to be a lieutenant. Her favorite, Charles, she placed with a farmer for instruction; and then fitted him out for America, where he grew wealthy on the basis she provided. This brother must have left a large family in the State of New York. Her brothers and sisters thus established, she attempted to rescue a support for her father from his broken and confused fortunes. This proving impossible, he was supported by her own labor, until his death. The very great demands made upon her by such natural obligations did not prevent her from assuming others. She adopted for her own the child of a dead friend, the niece of John Hunter. Her brilliancy, her personal beauty, her unselfish devotion, could not fail to win for her many loving friends; and among them the French Revolution found her. The work which first gave her her proper literary rank was her answer to Burke's Reflections upon that movement. She wrote rapidly: her pamphlet was the first of the many that appeared, and obtained extraordinary success. The public applause warmed her, and her next production was her celebrated " Vindication of the Rights of Woman." The startling energy with which she exploded the system of gallantry, a miserable relic of the Stuart courts, roused the popular indignation. It was hard to reconcile the vigor of her rebuke to the tender sentiment which trembled through the book, and also to the impression produced by Mary herself, lovely in person, and, in the most engaging sense, feminine in her manners. Her intimacy with the historical painter, Fuseli, followed. He was a man of powerful genius and strong prejudices. His influence upon Mary, if it was sometimes refreshing, could not always have been beneficial. The reader of Haydon's Autobiography will remember this man. A wider knowledge of the world would have protected her from his influence: as it was, she pursued the intimacy with unsuspecting delight; for Fuseli was a contented husband, and his wife was her friend. She was now in her thirty-second year; she had arrived at a period when domestic happiness of some sort becomes essential to the strongest woman. The fullest-fruited laurel then withers before her eyes, if it has not taken root at her own hearth. At the close of the year 1792, Mary took refuge in Paris from the chagrin and restlessness which began to oppress her. Her years of toil had left her sad and lonely: she needed to rest for a little while in human affection. She could not even write to her own satisfaction; for her morbid fatigue led her to reproduce Fuseli's cynicism, and she dared not trust herself. She entered the best circles of Parisian society, and became intimate with the leaders of the Revolution. In four months after her arrival occurred the most untoward event of her life,— her marriage to a worthless American named Gilbert Imlay; a name rescued from oblivion only by his temporary attachment to her. I say her *marriage*, for Imlay offered himself in marriage, and was accepted as a husband; but, taking advantage of a custom not unusual at Paris in those disorderly times, Mary refused to consummate the legal forms. Mr. Imlay had no property. Mary had a large family to support; and she neither wished to become answerable for his debts, nor to make him responsible for hers. She took the name of Imlay; and, expecting to follow her brother to America, she obtained from our ambassador at Paris a certificate of American citizenship, to serve as a temporary protection. In order that you may comprehend the precise significance which this step had in that place and at that time, let me remind you, that Helen Maria Williams, her personal friend, and the ward of Dr. Rees of cyclopedic memory, was married in the same way to a Mr. Edwards, then in Paris. She was a well-known writer of that period; and we are still indebted to her for some of the best hymns sung in our churches, — among them, that well-known hymn, beginning, " While thee I seek, protecting Power." But her husband was worthy of the trust she had reposed in him, and she never turned a ready pen against the follies of society: so *her* character has never stood in the public stocks.

It will be impossible to consider Mary's attachment to Imlay in any degree rational, if we look only at her *character*, and keep out of sight her peculiar personal *history*.

The dawdling inefficiency and brutal temper of her father had disgusted her alike with " men of spirit " and " men of straw." In her husband, she saw, as she thought, a certain democratic manliness; and his daring speculations seemed to be inspired by courage and genius. The affections which had been roused by her admiring intercourse with Fuseli kindled gladly on this new shrine, where no social duty, nor stern sense of personal honor, contended against her warming fancy. For the first time in her life, she found herself happy; and happiness gave her back the beauty of early youth. She was playful, gentle, sympathetic. Her eyes had new brightness, her cheeks new color, and the bewitching tenderness of her smile fascinated the very women who approached her. She had been married eighteen months, her love braving all the trials that must have come, when Imlay left her for London. She had expected his quick return; but delay followed delay, and Mary passed a year with a new-born child, learning, by slow and painful degrees, that she had trusted this man beyond his worth. At last, he sent for her to London, where his misconduct affected her mind to such an extent, that she twice attempted her own life, and was rescued the second time with difficulty. As soon as she recovered from the fever which had induced delirium, her native strength told her what she ought to do. Imlay had business in Norway, which required a confidential and judicious agent. She determined to take this upon herself; and hoped, by absence and success, to regain the affection she had lost. The man was, in no sense, worthy of her. On her return, she tried, for the sake of their child, to remain in the same house with him. It was not possible; and, very soon, a final separation took place. It would have taken place long before, but that Imlay was a man who could not wholly escape from a fascination he had once felt. After he became involved in low connections, he could never re-enter her presence, without resuming, for the time, the sympathetic delicacy befitting her lover. During all this time, Mary had occupied herself with literary work. She never spoke of Imlay, and would allow no one to blame him in her presence. Conscious of her own upright intentions, it must have been no small mortification to find her insight and generosity baffled. She felt that she was herself to blame for having placed an impulsive man in a position to which he was wholly unequal. She was everywhere received and treated as a married woman, and lost none of the respect and affection she had well deserved. In April, 1797, she was married to Godwin, the author of " St. Leon;" and this marriage deprived her of two new friends, whom she held very dear. Godwin was so artless, that he imagined his wife's social position would be improved by an honorable marriage; but it obliged Mrs. Inchbald and Mrs. Siddons to admit that the nature of her marriage to Imlay allowed her to take her divorce into her own hands.

Wonderful inconsistency of society, which, having interpreted truly her upright nature through years of desertion, now condemned her, — whether for her first wrong step, for assuming her own divorce, or for loving a man of undoubted probity, who could tell? A short year of undisturbed happiness followed, when the birth of their only child — the late Mrs. Shelley — suddenly put an end to her life.

A beautiful memorial survives her, in these words

of her husband. "This light," he says, "was lent me for a very little while, and it is now extinguished for ever. The strength of Mary's mind lay in her intuition. In a robust and unwavering judgment of this sort, there is a kind of witchcraft. When it decides justly, it produces a responsive vibration in every ingenuous mind. In this sense, my oscillation and scepticism were often fixed by her boldness." I am very well aware how much courage is required of any woman who shall seem to defend Mary Godwin from the popular conception of her. I know that the woman should herself be spotless who would attempt to rectify that conception, yet two circumstances seem to compel explanation. In the first place, there is no question, that if the views of woman which are now beginning to move society originated with her scholarly, republican friend, Mrs. Catharine Macaulay, yet the fire and eloquence of Mary's own words were needed to give them currency. Society has been just so far as this, that it has identified her with the subject of "Woman's Rights;" and all of us who are carried forward by a momentum which she imparted, must desire to understand the nature of the impulse which controls us.

In the second place, Godwin's short Life of her has been long out of print, and has now become very rare; and I have not been able to find a single encyclopædia or biographical dictionary which gives the facts correctly. Turn to them, and you will find that Mary Wollstonecraft had a criminal but fruitless attachment for Fuseli; that she formed another, of *the same kind*, for an American, who deserted her. I brand these statements as malicious falsehoods, carelessly repeated now that they have been long exploded: and, as I write these statements, the tears rush to my eyes; for where are the descendants of the brothers and sisters whom she reared? where are the kindred of Fannie Blood and John Hunter, whose lives her generous efforts gladdened? Nay, might not one man of the drowning crew she forced the captain of her ship to rescue, speak a noble word in her behalf? I have narrated her life with some detail, for you must understand the facts upon which you pass judgment; and these details are many of them gathered from private sources.

To understand the strength of the prejudice against Mary Wollstonecraft, you should see that from all the autobiographies of the period her name is excluded; as if the friends of those who had been intimate with her while living, would not permit the association of names after death. I have said, that, until her marriage to Godwin, she kept her place in English society; and women of the most sensitive propriety, such as Mrs. Siddons and Mrs. Inchbald, admitted her to their intimacy. How, then, did such a prejudice grow up? It was probably forming in the popular mind while she was happy in the affection of her friends; and, the moment they found it conventionally needful to sacrifice her, the outbreak was unrestrained. In the first place, she was an ardent republican; a thing no less antagonistic to English feeling in her day, than we have seen it prove in ours. In the second, she was a Unitarian; and Unitarians were radicals in politics as well as in religion. In the third place, being a republican, and a resident of Paris in its troubled times, she was supposed to share the disorder of its morals; an impression which her attempted suicides no doubt confirmed.

We shall not share in this country in any prejudice which republicanism or Unitarianism excited. We are, I trust, ready to admit that an attempt at suicide could only come with delirium, for which she would be as free from responsibility as for a typhoid fever or an Asiatic cholera. What we have to do, then, is to understand her relation to the laws of marriage, and to see how far her second marriage can be justified. When she met Imlay at Paris, I do not think she had ever considered the social bearing of these laws, except so far as her mother's experience had pained her. That experience made her willing to do what other women about her were doing, with no bad result that she could see, to keep herself free from pecuniary entanglement. In one way, this was prudent; in an other way, it was extremely imprudent; and the imprudence touched a more vital point than the prudence: but that it was never considered criminal by wise and candid judges, that she was never compromised in any relation up to this, the intimacies we have recorded prove. Had she been a weak, *immoral* woman, she would have continued to live with

Imlay for her child's sake, but availing herself of the shelter of a connection from which she recoiled. At this moment, she wrote to her husband, " Your reputation shall not suffer. I shall never have a confidant. I am content with the approbation of my own mind; and, if there be a Searcher of hearts, mine will not be rejected." And again: " My child may have reason to blush for her mother's want of prudence; but she shall never despise me." These are not the words of a weak or irreligious woman. So far, then, all was well, except that society had no efficient outlawry for the man who had deserted her. She still occasionally met him, but bore the unexpected trial, when it came, with dignity and sweetness. When Godwin sought her in marriage, he knew, of course, that no legal ties bound her. Mary saw no harm in using the liberty that remained to her. " Why could she not have remained single?" said the world; but had the world been so just and kind to her, that we could expect her to resist the influence of a generous and courageous love? Had she lived in this country, and been divorced by the laws of Indiana, society would have been silent; but the real evil would have been the same.

" Never did there exist a woman," said her husband, " who might with less fear expose her actions, and call upon the universe to judge them." I believe this to be true so far as her own relations were concerned; and I believe, that, by her second marriage, she meant to exercise a right of protest against existing laws, which two of the most gifted children of the nineteenth century have exercised again in our own time with emphasis. It requires a philosophic mind to see the relation of the individual to the state: heroic, indeed, is the spirit which, perceiving it, braves the common expectation by a defiant life. On the other hand, it is by no prejudice that we demand this account of each person's private affairs. It is a demand born of an ill-defined, dimly entertained, but still a just idea of the relations of God, the family, and the state. I ought not to say so much, without adding that no one in this country can adequately judge of the pressure of the marriage laws as they still exist in England. What is resisted, is, in most instances, what no American woman would be expected to bear; but for England, as for this country, I rest in the confident hope that a right adjustment of woman's relation to society will change healthfully all existing legislation. Such legislation as that of Indiana does not seem to me an advance, although it may have been demanded by an *advancing* public sentiment.

I have said this honestly, with a tender pity in my heart, to clear the memory of a much-abused woman. Does any one ask me if I would justify the position in which she stood? I answer, frankly, No. We do not live to ourselves alone; and if we are ever tempted to take a step against the moral convictions of the world, believing that we can do as we will with our own, one would think the possibility that children may be born to inherit the obloquy we excite, without themselves deserving it, would be enough to deter any right-minded woman. No love or care, or abject self-sacrifice, can reconcile a child to the stain of illegitimacy. "What does the Lord thy God require of thee?"—"To do justly, love mercy, and walk humbly." It is not walking humbly to set up our own conception of fitness against the accumulated experience of mankind. Still farther: It is of very little importance what others may think of us, when we are acting conscientiously; but what we think of others, our own mood of mind towards God and man,—that is of the very greatest.

The influence of the "Vindication of the Rights of Woman" was greatly aided by the efforts of Mr. Day, and of Maria Edgeworth, whose literary career began about the time of its publication. Following closely upon these, and so nearly parallel in effort, and equal in varied ability, that we hardly know in what order to name them, are Lady Morgan, Harriet Martineau, and Mrs. Jameson. Sydney Morgan, sitting alone at the age of fourscore in her tiny house at Dublin, filled like a museum with the accumulation of her years of travel, projecting the publication of her last work, was lately, like Mrs. Somerville at Florence, a pensioner of Queen Victoria. But, from the hour of her first appearance as the author of the "Wild Irish Girl," she has exercised a generous womanly influence. Under the disguise of novels, books of travel, and the like, she has published an immense number of volumes, filled with information which may be a little too crowded for convenience, but always accurate, always original, and, for the most part, received from historic sources, in personal intercourse. Her warm hatred of tyranny made friends for her, wherever she went. When a young girl, she took up the cause of her own country with a vehemence which won the liberal party, and made her fashionable before she was approved. "The wild Irish girl" and her harp were essential to the success of every entertainment; and invitations lay two or three deep for every evening. She entered society with beauty, wit, and prestige. She might have done what she would. She chose to remain faithful to unpopular opinions. After her marriage to Sir Charles Morgan, they went, for economical reasons, to the Continent, where they eventually spent many years. In France, Lafayette, Ségur, Dénon, and L'Aguisseau were her intimate friends; and in the *salon* of the Princess de Salm she was always a welcome guest. In Germany, Flanders, and Italy, not only the liberal youth, but the learned eld, crowded her apartments, gave her minute information, and became devoted cicerones. The friendship of cardinals and princes did not dim her natural democracy of view; and her last words were as true to liberty as her first. Her works on France and Italy were proscribed in both countries; yet " Young France " and " Young Italy " contrived to obtain and read them. She came into fashion in Paris whenever the Bourbons went out;

and, when she dined with Rothschild, his famous cook acknowledged her friendship for the people in autographs of spun sugar! " We shall meet at the breakfast of the Austrian ambassador," said a Parisian fop, as he made his bow. " Not we," she laughed in answer: " it would be as much as his place is worth to ask me. " Wherever she went, and whatever she did, her ears were always open to a woman's name; and, with the most loyal interest, she gathered up every thing relating to their lives, their influence, and their disabilities. What she was told as gossip, was retained, studied out, and digested, before, with the piquancy of a French woman and the warmth of an Irish, it was given to the world. The first two volumes of her " History of Woman " do not touch a period of universal interest; but, had she been able to complete the work, it would have exhausted the subject. In the Béguine, she says: " Women meddle with politics as well as tent-stitch, and, like Madame de Maintenon, bring their work-bags to the Privy Council, and direct the affairs of Europe while they trace patterns for footstools. The influence of woman will ever be exercised directly or indirectly in all good or evil. It is a part of the scheme of nature. Give her, then, such light as she is capable of receiving. Educate her, whatever her station, for taking her part in society. Her ignorance has often made her interference fatal; her knowledge, never." The cordial sympathy of her husband has made Lady Morgan's life beautiful. His legal knowledge and antiquarian taste added their own charm to whatever she undertook.

How great and worthy is the literary position of Harriet Martineau, we all know. Its retro-actionary influence in favor of the ability and freedom of her sex is what we are to indicate here. For whatever immediate purpose she writes, her words bear indirectly on the widest womanly emancipation. May this remark stimulate your curiosity, and keep you on the alert for pregnant sentences! Such sentences tell more of the progress of human thought than some of us suspect: they indicate its natural, habitual poise. " Women especially," she writes, " should be allowed the free use of whatever strength their Maker has seen fit to give them. It is essential to the virtue of society, that they should be allowed the freest moral action, unfettered by ignorance, and unintimidated by authority; for it is an unquestioned and unquestionable fact, that, if women were not weak, men would not be wicked, and that, if women were bravely pure, there would be an end of the dastardly tyranny of licentiousness." This passage will have all the more power over observant readers, because it occurs unexpectedly, and marks the opportunity seized to speak a necessary if unwelcome truth.

What noble service Mrs. Jameson rendered in the field of art or letters did not leave her indifferent to the interests of her sex. She was placed in circumstances to make her see quickly and feel deeply all that relates to womanly position and development. An early martyr to the prejudices of society; married, I think at sixteen, to a man far beyond her own rank in life, who left her at the altar, — she bore the title of wife, and led the life of a celibate: but her first word for her sex was as strong and true as her last, while her own path lay between lines of living fire. Only lately did we hear of her as a lecturer and reformer; but, nearly thirty years ago, we might have cut from her pages the following words: "We are told openly by moralists and politicians, that it is for the general good of society, nay, an absolute necessity, that one-fifth part of the female sex should be condemned as the legitimate prey of the other, predoomed to die in reprobation in the streets, in hospitals, that the virtue of the rest may be preserved, and the pride and the passions of men both satisfied. But I have a bitter pleasure in thinking, that this most base and cruel conventional law is avenged upon those who made and uphold it; that here the sacrifice of a certain number of one sex to the permitted license of the other is no general good, but a general curse, a very ulcer in the bosom of society." Can you guess how brave and pure a woman was needed to write those words? All the indirect tendency of her works is in keeping with them; and we recognize the same voice, as she said in a later lecture: —

"When female nurses were to be sent to the Crimea, there was to be met the mockery of the light-minded, the atrocious innuendoes of the dissolute, the sneers of the ignorant, and the scepticism of the cold. I have seen men who deem it quite a natural and proper thing that women — *some women* at least — should lead the life of a courtesan, put on a look of offended propriety at the idea of a woman nursing a sick soldier. I have seen men — ay, and women too — who deem it a matter of course that our streets should be haunted by contagious vice, disgusted at the idea of women turning apothecaries and *hôpitalières*. And, worse than all, I have heard men — and women too — who acknowledge the gospel of Christ, who call themselves by his name, who believe in his mission of mercy, disputing about the exact shade of orthodoxy in a woman who had offered up every faculty of her being at the feet of the Redeemer."*

Remember that these words were spoken where they belonged, in the very heart of Belgravia, to the very people who deserved them, and respect the brave purity which compelled lips as well as pen to utterance. It would scarce be honest not to say, in this connection, that Mrs. Jameson took some pains, so long as she lived, to separate herself from the American Woman's-Rights party — a party, it may be, only represented to her by the vulgar pretension of travelling Bloomers. Some of us take comfort in remembering how much more easily the misrepresentations

---

* In allusion to the Unitarianism of Florence Nightingale.

of the press, or the intrusions of unfit subjects on womanly discussion, will float across the wide Atlantic, than our weightier works. When she said, in the same breath, concerning a decree of the French Consulate, " I confess, I should like to see a decree of *our* Parliament beginning with a recognition that women do exist as a part of the community, whose responsibilities are to be acknowledged, and whose capabilities are to be made available, not separately, but conjointly with those of men," we know that she worked for us and with us, and forgive the want of recognition in gratitude for the real service.

Mrs. Gaskell has perhaps done more than any woman of this century, not confessedly devoted to our cause, to elevate the condition of her sex, and disseminate liberal ideas as to their needs and culture. The first part of her career was one of those brilliant successes which startle us into surprise and admiration. It was checked midway by the publication of her life of Charlotte Brontë, the best and noblest of her works. Checked, because condemned in that instance without a hearing, she could never afterwards feel the elastic pleasure which was natural to her in composing and printing; and, for three long years afterwards, never touched her pen. I would not allude to this subject, if every notice of her, since her death, had not done so; repeating the old censure, as a matter of course. Here in America, we exculpate her. The public was wrong, in the first place, inasmuch as it has come to demand biography before biography is possible. The publisher was wrong, in the second; for he ought to have known, and could easily have ascertained, how plain a statement the English law would permit. The public was still further wrong, when it attributed misapprehension and carelessness to a woman whom it very well knew to be incapable of either. I, for one, shall never forgive nor forget the officious censure given by one who must have known that the legal apology tendered, in Mrs. Gaskell's absence, to protect her pecuniary interests, had the unfortunate effect to put her in a position where explanation and self-defence were alike impossible. Mrs. Gaskell had deserved the steady confidence of the public.

I have kept till the last the name of Fredrika Bremer, whose good fortune it was to secure lasting benefits to her sex. God sent to her early years dark trials and privations. Her father's tyrannical hand crushed all power and loveliness out of her life. At first, she rebelled against her sufferings; but, when he died in her girlhood, she was able to see that they lent strength to her efforts for her sex. It was the rumor of what we are doing in this country for women that first drew her hither. It is not the fashion for Miss Bremer's friends fully to recognize her position in this respect. I owe my own convictions on the subject of suffrage to the reflections she awakened. When I told her that my mind was undecided on this point, she showed her disappointment so plainly, that I was forced to reconsider the whole subject. Miss

Bremer did not hurry her work: she had a serene confidence that she should be permitted to finish what she had begun. She secured popularity by her cheerful humor, her genuine feeling, her true appreciation of men, and her insight into the conditions of family happiness, before she made any direct appeal against existing laws. Those who will read her novels thoughtfully, however, will see that she was, from the first, intent upon making such an effort possible. From the beginning, she pleaded for the social independence of wives; asked for them a separate purse; showed that woman could not even give her love freely, until she was independent of him to whom she owed it. To a just state of society, to noble family relations, entire freedom is essential.

Under her influence, females had been admitted to the Musical Academy. The directors of the Industrial School at Stockholm had attempted to form a class, and Professor Quarnstromm had opened his classes at the Academy of Fine Arts to women. Cheered by her sympathy, a female surgeon had sustained herself in Stockholm; and Bishop Argardh indorsed the darkest picture she had ever drawn, when he pleaded with the state to establish a girls'-school. It was at this juncture that Miss Bremer published "Hertha." This book was a direct blow aimed at the laws of Sweden concerning women. By this time, she had herself become, in Sweden, what we might fitly call a "crowned head." She was everywhere treated with distinction; and her sudden appearance in any place was greeted with the enthusiasm usually shown by such nations only to their princes. She said of her new book, " I have poured into it more of my heart and life than into any thing which I have ever written;" and verily she had her reward. She was at Rome, two years after, — in 1858, — when the glad news reached her, that King Oscar, at the opening of the Diet, had proposed a bill entitling women to hold independent property at the age of twenty-five. All Sweden had read the book which moved the heart of the king; and the assembled representatives rent the air with their acclamations.

In the following spring, the old University town of Upsala, where her friend Bergfalk occupies a chair, granted the *right of suffrage* to fifty women owning real estate, and to thirty-one doing business on their own account. The representative whom their votes went to elect was to sit in the House of Burgesses. Miss Bremer was not ashamed to shed happy tears when this news reached her. If she had ever reproached Providence with the bitter sorrow of her early years, she was penitent and grateful now. Then was fulfilled the prophecy which she had uttered, as she left our shores, " The nation which was first among Scandinavians to liberate its slaves, shall also be the first to emancipate its women."

This is not the place to unfold the delicate sheaths of meaning with which flower-like Robert Browning invests his thought; but the man who wrote the " Blot on the Scutcheon," and the exquisite sketch of "Pippa Passes," has done such justice to the sex, and so far helped the cause of right feeling and right thinking in respect to some of the most delicate problems that concern it, that we are compelled to speak of him gratefully. His marriage, too, is still fragrant; a full-fruited flower of promise to the world, which makes us see the best things possible, and believe that the time is coming when man and woman will not seldom stand before the altar as equal and individual, yet sacredly one. To Elizabeth Browning, to whom was given in her life that place of pre-eminence among women which Shakspere must always hold among men, we owe grateful thanks, for the scholarly achievement, the conscientious study, the womanly zeal, which distinguished all her work. When theology sometimes wrestled with poetry in her speech, we translated it into a freer tongue, and thanked her all the same. In "Aurora Leigh" she stabbed every conventional falsity to the heart, and held the ear tenaciously till she had delivered all her oracle.

"I read a score of books on womanhood,
To prove, if women do not think at all,
They may teach thinking, — books demonstrating
Their right of comprehending husband's talk,
When not too deep, and even of answering."

" I perceive
The headache is too noble for my sex:
You think the heartache would sound decenter."

" Such praise
As men give women, when they judge a book,
Not as mere *work*, but as mere *woman's work*,
Expressing the comparative respect,
Which means the absolute scorn."

The woman who wrote these words counsels us from her grave; and, taught by her, we do not hesitate to say, —

"Deal with us nobly, women though we be,
And honor us with truth, if not with praise."

Yet these were all to a certain extent indirect influences. Can I utter without trembling the two names which sit upon the thrones of female power in the Old World and the New? I mean Charlotte Brontë and Margaret Fuller. I wish I could confer a proper emphasis upon my words, when I say that the publication of "Jane Eyre" formed the chief era in the literature of women since that literature began. Into it was compressed all the feeling and experience of a very remarkable life, — feeling and experience entertained without the smallest sense of responsibility to the conventional world. The life of the author touched the restrictions of society, as the spheral curves touch the tangents which square them, so slightly as never to impair its wonderful individuality. Who would not seek a wife like Jane Eyre? Who does not rejoice in the smallest detail of that sparkling and varied courtship? Think of those words of Rochester, when, holding her with the grasp of a madman, he says, " Never was any thing at once so frail and so indomitable. A mere reed she feels in my hand. I could bend her with my finger and thumb. And what good would it do, if I bent, if I uptore, if I crushed her? Consider that eye; consider the wild, resolute, free thing looking out of it, defying me with more than courage, — with a stern triumph. Whatever I do with its cage, I cannot get at it, the savage beautiful creature! If I tear, if I rend the slight prison, my outrage will only set the captive free. Conqueror I might be of the house; but the inmate would escape to heaven, before I could call myself possessor of its clay dwelling-place. And it is you, spirit, with will and energy and virtue and purity, that I want, not alone your brittle frame."

And from what literature, of ancient or modern growth, shall we match Jane's answer, when passion presses, crying, " Who in the world cares for you? or who will be injured by what *you* do?"

" *I* care for *myself*," is the indomitable reply: " the more solitary, the more friendless, the more unsustained, I am, the more I will respect myself. I will keep the law given by God, sanctioned by man. I will hold by the principles received by me when I was sane, and not mad, as I am now. Laws and principles are not for the times when there is no temptation. They are for such moments as this, when body and soul rise in mutiny against their rigor. Stringent are they? Inviolate they shall be. If, at my individual convenience, I might break them, what would be their worth? They have a worth, so I have always believed; and, if I cannot believe it now, it is because I am insane, with my veins running fire, and my heart beating faster than I can count. Preconceived opinions, foregone determinations, are all

I have at this hour to stand by. *There* I plant my foot!"

Other women have been brave and pure, but this woman was an Abdiel. Never had she faltered in her life, never encountered a sham but to crush it. We did not know what freedom meant, till we had this book. Its advent was an era, not merely in the literature, but in the life, of woman. Its welcome, so profound, so stirring, betrayed the secrets of womanly nature. Do you remember how you sat and discussed this book, far into the night? — how you wondered whether man or woman wrote it? — how the women it enfranchised *looked* their scorn when you suggested the first possibility? — how your temper and feeling, and sense of justice, were roused by it? All this was because a life resolute and free poured itself out between those covers. A woman delicate, cleanly, quaint, secured the polished purity of every page. Will you start, if I ask you who ever stated the Woman's-Rights' argument with the serene force of the little lace-mender in the "Professor"? Do you not envy her and her husband the happy English home secured by their united labors? Ah! when she gave us later that exquisite miniature of her sister Emily which she called "Shirley," that noble bit of Rubens color which she named "Villette," the same flood of womanly thought and feeling poured through the prayer, — *the same flood*, though we no longer started as when we first heard society's signal gun, and saw her whole fleet hoist the flag of distress. Women ought to buy that old stone house upon the hillside, set in among the tombs, and framed in purple heather. The lives which began and ended there have hedged it in with laurels. Read this life and these works, and learn what fortunes hang upon a noble living. Read them, that you may learn how to cheer the world with what is natural and dignified, to do your Master's work, regardless of narrow criticism or still disdain. The host of imitators who stand about Charlotte Brontë's still-open grave are the best tribute to the power that went out from her, — a power tempered by the sweetest personal graces, by a housekeeping delicate and pure and tasteful, which never lets us dream of Jane in her school at Morton, of Shirley in her peach-room parlor, of the lace-mender at the professor's desk, or Lucy Snowe in the first class of Paul Emanuel, as otherwise than brilliant in cleanliness and order. I turn reluctantly from a life so well known, and now, thank God, beginning to be so well understood.

I do not treat of Margaret Fuller as a literary power; for, whatever may be her rank in this respect, she does not exert a tithe of the influence in this way, which attaches to the idea of her as a person, to *herself* as the centre of the radiant and shining group of women who were known as " Margaret's friends."

Her " Woman in the Nineteenth Century " is a scholarly, refined, and noble plea for the freedom of her sex. In point of ability, no book can be named with it, if we except that of Madame d'Héricourt.

It has an advantage over that of Mary Wollstonecraft, in being, so far as the author could make it, a *complete* statement; but it is written so much more from the stand-point of thought and feeling, that it has had a far more limited influence. There is not a word in the "Vindication" which the most simple might not read as he ran, and, reading, understand; but much of the "Nineteenth Century" depends upon a critical scholarship, and an evasive delicacy of sentiment and thought, which elude the common grasp. Precious passages have become axioms. "Let her be a sea-captain, if she will," has a power in both hemispheres; for it has been justified to learned and simple, by Captain Betsy, of the Scotch schooner, "Cleotus," and the sweet and noble woman who so lately carried an American ship round Cape Horn. The life of Margaret Fuller is in everybody's hands; but not even Boston *women* appreciate her personal influence. Who *else* could be expected to understand it? Her very existence was a stimulus to endeavor; and hundreds of women become practical "Exaltadas," because they saw the position she was permitted to hold. "I always know a Boston woman," said a rough German miner to me, beyond Lake Huron: "she always has Margaret Fuller's stamp upon her;" and I felt that his words were true. We have missed her sadly since she was taken from us. Ever memorable will be the "Life and Writings," which revive our memories better than they satisfy our demands. "It will be seen," she once wrote, "that my youth was not unfriended, since those great minds came to me in kindness." We have not been unfriended either, since she was permitted to come to us. If I were to characterize her in two words, it would be as " Truth-teller and Truth-compeller." She not only spoke what she thought, in her own way, let it be abrupt or gentle, but she compelled us to do the same. There was something in her presence which tore away all disguises: even unconscious pretension could not bear it. We were soon made to feel whether we had any right to our own thoughts. " What I especially admired in her," says Dr. Hedge, " was her intellectual sincerity. Her judgments took no bribe from her sex or sphere, nor from custom nor tradition nor caprice. She valued truth supremely, both for herself and others. The question with her was, not what *should* be believed, nor what *ought* to be true, but what is true. Her 'yes' and 'no' were never conventional; and she often amazed people by a cool and unsuspected dissent from the commonplaces of popular acceptation."

" Truth-teller and Truth-compeller," — the words seem to fall like the shadow of Omnipotence, a noble fillet for a woman's forehead. What a noble *character* that must have been, which inspired the remark made after her marriage: —

" Her life, since she went abroad, is wholly unknown to me; but I have an unshaken trust, that what Margaret did she can defend." An " unshaken trust," — such words are a challenge to all noble living. In great and small matters, we are told, she was a woman of her word, and so gave those who conversed with her the unspeakable comfort which flows from plaindealing. "I walk over burning ploughshares, and they sear my feet, yet nothing but truth will do," she says; and again, in a letter to a friend: "My own entire sincerity in every passage of life gives me a right to expect that I shall be met by no unmeaning phrases or attentions."

I enlarge upon this trait of character, for I think it Margaret's due. Everybody here knows her reputation as a scholar: few know her character as a woman. In beautiful keeping with this trait was her letter to Miss Martineau, after the publication of her book upon this country.

"When Jouffroy writes his lectures," she says, "I am not conversant with all his topics; but I can appreciate his lucid style and admirable method. When Webster speaks on the currency, I do not understand the subject; but I do understand his mode of treating it, and can see what a blaze of light flows from his torch. When Harriet Martineau writes about America, I often cannot test that rashness and inaccuracy of which I hear so much; but I can feel that they exist. A want of soundness and patient investigation is found throughout the book; and I cannot be happy in it, because it is not worthy of my friend.

"I have thought it right to say all this to you, since I feel it. I have shrunk from the effort, for I fear that

I must lose you. If your heart turn from me, I shall still love you; and I could no more have been happy in your friendship, if I had not spoken out."

What a noble pattern in that letter for us all! The electric power of her womanhood, which claimed the inmost being of every one with whom she came in contact, I can best express in the words of Emerson: —

"She had found out her own secret by early comparison, and knew what power to draw confidence, what necessity to lead in every circle, belonged of right to her. She had drawn to her every superior young man or woman she had ever met; and whole romances of life and love had been confided, counselled, thought, and lived through, in her cognizance and sympathy. She extorted the secret of life which cannot be told without setting heart and mind in a glow, and thus she had the best of those she saw. She lived in a superior circle; for people suppressed all their commonplaces in her presence. Her mood applied itself to the mood of her companion, point to point, in the most limber, sinuous, vital way, and drew out the most extraordinary narratives."

When we remember this wealth of sympathy and appreciation, is it not sad to hear her say, no one ever gave such invitation to her mind as to tempt her to a full confession? — that she felt a power to enrich her thought with such wealth and variety of embellishment as would no doubt be tedious to such as she conversed with?

A bitter reproach to us women, certainly. What better *could* we do than listen, while she embellished her thought with all wealth and variety possible? And I quote the saying, because hers are not the only noble lips which have a right to repeat it. Could we but be patient listeners! In that way, we might educate powers of expression, and become possessed of wealth of which we have very little idea. What does such a saying record, — her egotism or our selfishness, her insatiable demand or our bankruptcy? We may well confess to mortification when we read; but it is not felt for *her*. Very beautiful is the conception of this Memoir of Margaret, this triune testimony of independent minds. We should be more grateful for the analytical skill shown in Emerson's contribution, did it not bear witness to *power*, rather than *appreciation*. We see, though he could not, what Margaret missed in her friend. She could not exempt the finest thinker she knew from the customary tribute; but he could not pay her in current coin, — only in some native ore, which it cost her much to make available at need. Some time may *women* write the lives of women! Why not warm thy scalpel, O philosopher! out of regard to what was once tender, quivering, human flesh? Rumor and prejudice carried the news of Margaret's faults far enough while she was living: what we need now is to send on the same wave the most abundant and satisfying proof of her goodness and genius. When great men speak of her, they should speak grandly, and find for what vulgar natures *must* misconceive, the noble and generous interpretation. I do not mean that SHE would have shrunk from the boldest statement of the truth. It was in her to invite it. " She could say," says Emerson, " as if she were stating a scientific fact, in enumerating the merits of somebody, *he appreciates me;* " and he refers this saying to the "mountainous *me*" of hereditary organization, italicizing the offending monosyllable. But, in Margaret's mind, the emphasis lay quite as often on the word *appreciates;* and the statement was of a psychological fact, a superiority to vulgar prejudice, which laid some claim to her generous estimate in return. Ah! when those we love are gone for ever, their faults drop away, like the garment, which was of the earth, earthy; but to great and noble words, to heroic and womanly living, God has given a power of blessing far beyond the grave. We lost her at a moment when we could ill bear it, — when, instructed by the noble sympathies of Mazzini, softened by her own sweet and tender ministrations in Italian hospitals, revealed at length in loving beauty by a wife's and mother's experience, she might have come home the woman she had often made us dream of. We see the shadow of it all in that little picture which once hung on the walls of the Boston Athenæum; and, God willing, we shall yet encounter the glad reality beyond the reach of tempests, beyond the need of wreck, lifted into true deserving of so great a privilege on the broad ocean of an Infinite Love!

Florence Nightingale is no exception in the history of her sex, only a consummate flower of its daily bloom. Ever since the commencement of the Christian era, whole armies of women have devoted themselves, not for a few years only, like Florence Nightingale, but for their whole lives long, to the same painful duties, — women who organized their bands with an efficiency and thoroughness, felt to this very day, and which made them the competent instructors of Florence Nightingale in the Crimea. The holiest vocation fails to instruct the unprepared mind. The soil of the nineteenth century is fallow; but in the year 385 a saintly woman traversed those same Crimean shores. Of her it was written: —

"She was marvellous debonaire and piteous to them that were sicke and comforted them, and served them right humbly, and gave them largely to eat, such as they asked; but to herself she was hard in her sickness and scarce, for she refused to eat flesh, how well she gave it to others, and also to drink wine. She was oft by them that were sicke, and she laid the pillows aright and in point, and she rubbed their feet, and boiled water to wash them; and it seemed to her that the less she did to the sicke in service, so much the less service did she to God, and deserved the less mercy; therefore she was to them piteous, and nothing to herself."

The Church canonized this woman, who carried her own substance to the work in which the British Government sustained Florence Nightingale so many centuries later; but the public mind was not prepared, so the world has never rung to the name of Santa Paula.

Florence Nightingale's most heroic service lay in breaking open the storehouses at Scutari. It may have cost her very little, but at that moment the force of accumulated character made itself felt. An everlasting reproach to all cowards of circumlocution offices, the duty not a single commissioned officer had courage to assume has gently crowned the woman with the woven suffrages of the world.

The name of Mary Patton has with us also a true educational power. There was no obstacle nor vulgar prejudice which this heroic girl was not called to combat. Not twenty years old, with two little children clinging to her skirts, and the great primal sorrow of her sex overshadowing her afresh, with her husband bereft of reason, and neither nurse nor physician at hand, she kept the ship's reckoning, overpowered a mutinous mate, and carried her vessel triumphantly in to the destined port.

The author of "John Halifax" has so laid us under obligation by work faithfully done, that it seems worth while to indicate the inconsistencies which warp her "Thoughts about Women."

She speaks of the "Woman's-Rights movement" in this country, as if it were a movement to *force* women into a certain position, instead of an effort to set them *free*, to the end that they may ascertain whether they have any capacity for it. She sneers at letters and account-books kept by women; and we read her words in a country where women are widely and creditably established as book-keepers, and where they hold classes to instruct others in accounts! She tells us that more than one-half of English women are obliged to provide for themselves; and gives a noble example of two young women, who, on their father's death, continued to carry on a disagreeable business, to keep books, manage stock, and control agents. They sustained a delicate mother in ease, and never once compromised their womanhood. What became of the womanly unfitness for letters and accounts in that case? She speaks of the contemptible and unwomanly habit of beating down, and says that men are less prone to it than women. Who keeps the purse-strings of a family? Who condemn women to the practical ignorance which makes them too uncertain of values to turn at once from a manifest overcharge?

But, sadder still, this woman brings against her sex the two grave charges of common falsehood and disloyalty in friendship. We may pity her for a social experience which seems to her to justify the statement; but let us never repeat the libel. Let Margaret Fuller answer it, not only by a life of radiant truth, but by the words in which she speaks of the honor of which young hearts are capable, and the secret of her own young life voluntarily kept by forty girls.

In her chapter on "Lost Women," Miss Muloch

does grateful service when she draws attention to those who choose to dwell in the very gutters of idle gossip and filthy scandal, who soil their lips and tongues while they take selfishly faithful care of their reputations. This word needed to be spoken. Better for a woman, that she should be a cast-away in a city refuge, with a mind comparatively pure, than a woman in high society, capable of catching or uttertering the vile " double entendre," always on the lookout for a possible vulgarism, wringing decency out of human life as if it were only a wet napkin, and sceptical of the purity and innocence she has not yet found in her own heart.

In estimating the influences which modify public opinion concerning women, I am not willing to be silent concerning the popular idea of love. It is a common thing to hear it said, with a sort of sneer, that no *man* ever died for love, — as if it were a quite romantic and in nowise *dis*creditable thing that many women should!

Creditable and discreditable elements may enter into the assumed fact as it regards man; but if he does not die for love because he more thoroughly acknowledges his responsibility, keeping God in his right place *above*, and his own heart and its idols in their right place *below*, then we may drop the unwomanly sneer, and go and do likewise.

I shall have little hope for woman, till *she* learns to feel that to die for love is not so much a pitiful as a disgraceful thing; that it proves of itself that God was never to her what he should have been; that life had no aim so holy as the weak indulgence of a sentiment or a passion, or some generous longing for some duty God did not set before her; that all the world's work and society's ambition was hidden from her by a desire for personal happiness, spread like a film over her moral vision.

No better education do I claim for woman than her entire *self-possession*, the ultimate endowment of all the promise she carries in her nature. "The great law of culture," says Carlyle, "is, Let each become all that he was created capable of being; expand, if possible, to his full growth; and show himself in his own shape and stature, be they what they may." — "The excellent woman," writes the Hindoo in Calcutta, "is she who, if the father dies, can be father and provider to the household."

"Who," says Count Zinzendorf in Germany, — "who but my wife could have been alternately servant and mistress without affectation and without pride? Who could have maintained like her, in a democratic community, all outward and inward distinctions? Who, without a murmur, would have met such peril? Who could have raised such sums of money, and acquitted them on her own credit?"

To such women I think men will always offer generous help; and, even if they did not, there are props of God's own disposing. Let woman once reject the absurd notion that she was created for happiness, let her constitute herself instead a creator of it, let her accept with joy the fact that this is a working-day world; then she will no longer strive to escape from labor, discipline, or sorrow, but will gladly hail each in its turn as part of God's appointed teaching, a shadow crossing the sunshine to show that it is bright. Perhaps such a life is not easy, perhaps many feet must falter on such a path; but, indicating what I earnestly believe to be the will and way of God for us all, I earnestly entreat you to enter and walk therein. Some words written by John Ruskin upon Art seem to me to have such force in this connection as to make it justifiable to quote them.

Speaking of a painter who could only paint the fair and graceful in landscape, he says: —

"But such work had, nevertheless, its stern limitations, and marks of everlasting inferiority. Always soothing and pathetic, it could never be sublime, never freely nor entrancingly beautiful; for the man's narrow spirit could not cast itself freely into any scene. The calm cheerfulness which shrank from the shadow of the cypress and the distortion of the olive, could not enter into the brightness of the sky they pierced, nor the softness of the bloom they bore. For every sorrow that his heart turned from, he lost a consolation. For every fear which he dared not confront, he parted with a portion of his manliness. The unsceptred sweep of the storm-clouds, the fair freedom of glancing shower and flickering sunbeam, sunk into sweet rectitudes and decent formalisms; and, before eyes that refused to be dazzled or darkened, the hours of sunset wreathed their rays unheeded, and the mists of the Apennines spread their blue veils in vain."

Imagine these words written metaphorically of your own inner lives, and accept the lesson they convey. Be earnest to inherit the whole of human life. Insist on turning the golden shield, till you have, not merely the iron lining full in view, but whatsoever Medusa's head the Divine hand has traced thereon.

See how many women have excelled in literature and art, in philosophy and science, within the present century. Their literary contributions owe their popularity to intrinsic excellence: they have sought and found the light of day, without the pompous recommendations of institutions, or the forced encouragement of a clique. There is no limit to womanly attainment, other than the force of womanly desire. Bihéron, destined to become an anatomist, becomes one, whether the college of dissectors smile or frown. Wittembach, versed alike in the mysteries of ancient tongues and modern physics, becomes the counsellor of the wisest men of her time, without neglecting her pantry or her needle. There is no excuse for neglecting any home duty for the most desirable foreign pursuit. Let buttons and shirt-bosoms have their day, the lexicon or grammar its own also. Let the dinner-table be carefully spread; the food, not only well cooked, but gracefully laid, — before we seek the more precious nutriment of culture: and this, not so much because any one has a right to say it *shall* be so, as out of our own tender regard to the needs of others, and a desire, through every possible self-sacrifice, to make the common road easier, and turn recreant public opinion to its proper vent. Let a neatness as exquisite as womanly and as polished as that of Charlotte Brontë, pervade not only our homes, but consecrate our own personal appearance; then may we safely wear the livery of schools. It may be double-dyed in indigo; yet, with this accessory, no man will assert that it is unbecoming, no woman have need to comfort her own ignorance by an unsisterly sneer.

If God intends woman to walk side by side with man wherever he sees fit to go, the movement now beginning must materially develop civilization. Finer elements will be poured into the molten metal of society; and, when the next cast is taken, we shall see sharper edges, bolder reliefs, and a finer lining, than we have been wont. Nor shall we miss the gentler graces. The classical world bitterly mourned the young and gifted lecturer, Olympia Morata; but not with the broken-hearted agony of the husband whose strength and life she had always been. Clotilda Tambroni was crowned, not only with the laurels of a Greek professorship, but with modesty and every virtue.

It was the tender appreciation of the WOMEN of Bologna that erected a stately monument to Laura Veratti.

In England, a woman writes admirable tales to endow a bishopric in a distant land. In our country, it was a pleasant omen, that the woman who first made literature a profession was urged to it, neither by scholarly taste nor an eccentric ambition, but to fulfil a mother's duty to four orphan children. Her literary career is not yet closed; and, though not lofty in its range, has been steadily pursued, and deserves the regard which it has won.

The names of Sedgwick, Sigourney, Kirkland, and Child suggest womanly excellences first of all. Let us pay the debt we owe these women, by following hopefully in the paths they have opened, till we create a public opinion without reproach.

> "If I speak untenderly,
> This evening, my belovèd, pardon it;
> And comprehend me, that I loved you so,
> I set you on the level of my soul,
> And overwashed you with the bitter brine
> Of some habitual thoughts."

> "Alas! long-suffering and most patient God,
> Thou need'st be surelier God to bear with us,
> Than even to have made us! Belovèd, let us love so well,
> Our works shall still be better for our love,
> And still our love be sweeter for our work!"

THE MARKET;

OR,

WOMAN'S POSITION AS REGARDS WAGES AND WORK.

IN THREE LECTURES,

DELIVERED IN BOSTON, NOVEMBER, 1859.

  I. — DEATH OR DISHONOR.
  II. — VERIFY YOUR CREDENTIALS.
  III. — "THE OPENING OF THE GATES."

"And could he find
A woman, in her womanhood, as great
As he was in his manhood, then, he sang,
The *twain together* well might change the world."

"But he never mocks;
For mockery is the fume of little hearts."

"For, in those days,
No knight of Arthur's noblest dealt in scorn;
But if a man were halt or hunched, — in him,
By those whom God had made full-fed and tall,
Scorn was allowed, as *part* of his defect."
GUINEVERE, *in Idyls of the King.*

THE MARKET.

I.

DEATH OR DISHONOR.

"How high, beneficent, sternly inexorable, if forgotten, is the duty laid, not on women only, but on every creature, in regard to these particulars!" — T. CARLYLE.

THE delicate ladies on Beacon Street, who order their ices and creams flavored with vanilla or pear-juice, may not know that bituminous coal, rope-ends, and creosote, furnish a larger proportion of the piquant seasoning than the blossoming bean or the orchard-tree; but every man of science does.*

Already the chemist furnishes the attar of Cashmere from heaps of offal that lie rotting by the way. It is as if God forced man face to face with every repellent fact of nature, and said, "Slake thy thirst at this turbid fountain, child of the dust; or the

---

* "Now that we can produce artificially, and from waste and even noisome materials, the ethereal liquids to which the fragrance of the pear, the pineapple, and the melon are due, and can manufacture spirits of wine from coal-gas and oil of vitriol, we can scarcely be over-sanguine as to what we shall yet effect as competitors with living organisms in the production of certain compounds." — GEORGE WILSON'S *Life of Forbes*, p. 129.

purer streams of the hillside shall trickle for thee in vain."

Somewhat so, I am compelled to turn your eyes to the most repulsive side of human life. I do not do it willingly, but of a necessity; not because I like it, but because it is essential to the argument. May the contact prove, that the perfumed joy of later years has disguised itself, for both of us, in the rotting accumulations of our social life!

It rests with yourselves to decide. These lectures may be useless; they may fill your minds with painful details, open hideous vistas, and blind you to the tempting, heavenward ways which we love to see the young and beautiful pursue.

But, in such case, the responsibility is not mine. *I* would have you look on vice, that you may learn to loathe it; *I* would have you realize, that what a noble friend of ours has called the "perishing classes" are made of men and women like yourselves.

Bidding you trust, to a certain extent, to the truth of those terrible statistics that crush Thomas Henry Buckle in their grasp, I would still have you remember, that, beside the active laws of moral and material life, there is ever the living God immanent in the world; and that it is always for *you* to change the results of history, at any given era, according to the great first law, — none the less real because so often forgotten, — that this living God helps or hinders you as you will, and becomes, at any moment that you choose, an important element in each calculation.

The subject at present before us is "Woman's Claims to Labor."

These claims rest upon three points: —

First, The absolute necessity of bread.

Second, A natural ability, physical and psychical; and an attraction inherent in the ability.

Third, An absolute want of the moral nature.

Having treated these in turn, I propose to show you what practical opposition man offers to her advance; what fault lies in herself; how much more numerous are the occupations open than is generally supposed; and what social obstructions have prevented her taking advantage of them.

In this connection, I shall speak of those women who have opened a way for their sex; and shall offer to you certain plans of action, by which, it seems to me, the convenience and the happiness of the employer and the employed may be materially advanced, especially as regards our own city. Like a wise child, who from his fretful pillow takes the pill first, and the conserve afterwards, I shall open the most painful branch of my subject in this lecture, and turn from it as soon as the needed impression has been made.

I ask for woman, then, free, untrammelled access to all fields of labor; and I ask it, first, on the ground that she needs to be fed, and that the question which is at this moment before the great body of working women is "death or dishonor:" for lust is a better paymaster than the mill-owner or the tailor, and economy never yet shook hands with crime.

Do you object, that America is free from this alternative? I will prove you the contrary within a rod of your own doorstep.

Do you assert, that, if all avenues were thrown open, it would not increase the quantity of work; and that there would be more laborers in consequence, and lower wages for all?

Lower wages for *some*, I reply; but certainly higher wages for women; and they, too, would be raised to the rank of partners, and personal ill treatment would not follow those who had position and property before the law.

You offer them a high education in vain till you add to it the stimulus of a free career. In this lecture, I undertake to prove to you, that a large majority of women stand in such relations to their employers, that they are compelled to death or a life of shame. Why not choose death, then?

So I asked once of a woman thus pressed to the wall. "Ah, madam!" she answered, "I chose it long ago for myself; but what shall I do for my mother and child?"

The superior has a right to every advantage which he can honestly gain, as well as the inferior; but he has no right to increase any natural difference in his favor, if he believe it to exist, by laws or customs which cripple the inferior. If, as political economists tell us, it is chiefly by man, collectively taken, that the property of society is created; and if, on that very ground, man's interest has the first claim to consideration, — does it not follow, that every friend of woman will try to induce her to become a capitalist, and open to her, as her first path to safety, the way to honorable independence? And, in this connection, I must repeat what some of you have often heard me say, that a want of respect for labor, and a want of respect for woman, lies at the bottom of all our difficulties, low wages included.

I will not admit that the argument of the political economist has, as yet, any rightful connection with the price of woman's work. "The price of labor will always rise or fall," he says, "as the number of laborers is small or large; and it is because there are too many women for a few avenues of labor that the wages are so low." If man believes this, let him help us to open new avenues, and so reduce the number in any one. But I claim that he has increased the natural difference in his own favor, supposing that there be any such, by laws and customs which cripple woman; and that his own lust of gain stands in the way of her daily bread. Just so in hydraulics, men tell us, that water rises everywhere to the level of its source; but you may raise it a thousand feet higher by the aid of your forcing-pump, or drop it from a siphon a thousand feet below. And a forcing-pump and a siphon has man imposed upon the natural currents of labor. If, in my correspondence with employers last winter, one man told me with pride that he gave from eight to fifty cents for the making of pantaloons, including the heaviest doeskins, he *forgot* to tell me what he charged his customers for the same work. Ah! on those bills, so long unpaid, the eight cents sometimes rises to thirty, and the fifty cents *always* to a dollar or a dollar and twenty-five cents.

The most efficient help this class of work-women could receive would be the thorough adoption of the cash system, and the establishment of a large workshop in the *hands of women* consenting to moderate profits, and superintended by those whose position in society would win respect for labor. When I said, six months ago, that ten Beacon-street women, engaged in honorable work, would do more for this cause than all the female artists, all the speech-making and conventions, in the world, I was entirely in earnest.

It is pretty and lady-like, men think, to paint and chisel: philanthropic young ladies must work for nothing, like the angels. *Let* them, when they rise to angelic spheres; but, here and now, every woman who works for nothing helps to keep her sister's wages down, — helps to keep the question of death or dishonor perpetually before the women of the slop-shop.

Why? Because she helps to depress the estimate of woman's ability. What is persistently given for nothing is everywhere thought to be worth nothing. I throw open a door here for some stifled sufferer at the West End: let her open a clothing establishment, and employ her own sex; let her make money by it, and watch for the end. When an Employment Society or a Needle-woman's Friend becomes bankrupt in purse, it is bankrupt in morals and argument as well.

The wheels of the world move on the grooves of good management, of success. Set these once firmly underneath, and the outcry against our moral Fultons will be hushed.

In country villages and farming districts, there is a great deal of harmful competition with the girls of the slop-shops, which can never be ended until it is considered respectable for women openly to earn money. The stitching of wallets, hat-linings, and shoe-bindings, the more delicate labor on linen collars and shirt-bosoms, is carried on now not merely by so-called benevolent societies who want to build churches, lecture-rooms, and so on, but by rich farmers' wives, who keep or do not keep servants, in the long, summer afternoons and winter evenings, because it is work that can be done privately, and is sought to supply them with jewelry and dress. If they will not educate their minds by profitable reading, it is earnestly to be desired they should work, but openly, for money, and at such trades as naturally fall to their lot. Herb and fruit drying, distilling, preserving, pickling, market-gardening, may yet lay the foundations of ample fortune for many a woman. I have passed a summer amid lovely landscapes, where the women found neither fruit not vegetables for their table, but let the brown earth plead to them in vain; while they stitched, stitched, stitched the long hours away, every broken needle bearing witness against the broken lives of women who needed in distant cities, where they stood homeless and starving, the work their sisters pilfered, sitting at their ease beside the hearth-stone. Their ignorance was their excuse. Let it not be ours.

And, first, for a few general statements.

An indispensable requisite for what the Germans call a "bread study" is, that, for average talent, it should command moderate success. "Of all causes of prostitution in Paris," says Duchâtelet, "and probably in all great towns, none is so active as the want of work, or inadequate remuneration. What are the earnings of our laundresses, seamstresses, and milliners? Compare the price of labor with the price of dishonor, and you will cease to be surprised that women fall. Out of 5,183 prostitutes in Paris, I found that 2,696 had been driven to the streets by starvation; and 89, to feed starving parents or children. That is 300 over one-half of the whole number."

"It is well known," writes Miss Craig, in Edinburgh, "how brief is the career that our female criminals run. How they are recruited, it is not hard to guess in a country where there are fifty thousand women working for less than sixpence a day, and a hundred thousand for less than one shilling."

When, a few years ago, the "Edinburgh Review" collected the statistics of female labor, it found the wages about half what were paid to men. But no reason was assigned for this difference; only, one master gardener ventured to assert, that women ate less than men!

An advertisement in London for fifty dressmakers brought seven hundred applicants to the door of the warehouse; and, after long waiting, a police-officer brought the employer to explain why they could not all be hired. Sir James Clarke tells us, that the results of the inquiry into the condition of this class of women exceeded in horror those of the factory commission. Eighteen hours a day was the allotted time for work; and nothing but strong coffee enabled them to ply their needles. Fifteen hundred employers keep fifteen thousand girls. In driving times, they work all night. One girl testified that she had worked through the whole Sunday fifteen times in two years.

The lacemakers also work from twelve to twenty hours; and, in families where a peculiar " knack" is thought to be transmitted, children are put to this work from the age of two years. There is no regular time for food or sleep in certain stages of the manufacture; and many of these overworked women become vagrants.

A terrible letter from a Manchester mantle-maker was lately published, in which she pleads to be permitted to earn twopence an hour, when compelled to work overtime (that is, over twelve hours a day); and says, pitifully, that, if the present regulations go on, nothing but death can save her from dishonor.

A Persian traveller, who visited the bazaar in Soho, was greatly shocked when he found that all those young women were earning their own living; and plumed himself on the superior happiness of the women of his own country. What would he have said, could he have followed the clergyman's daughter, as we must do, from a happy home and fine sewing, down, through all the degradations of the slop-shop, to the very gutter?

But this is England.

Out of two thousand women who work for their daily bread in New York, five hundred and thirty-four receive a dollar a week. " How many men," asks Dr. Chapin, " would keep off death and conquer the Devil on such wages? One woman had to do it by making caps at two cents each! Think of this, women who like to buy things cheap: for, if the veil could be lifted from your eyes, *you* would see — the angels *do* see — on your gay, white dresses many a crimson stain;,and among the dewy flowers with which you wreathe your hair, the grass that grows on graves!"

Seven thousand eight hundred and fifty ruined women walk the streets of New York, — five hundred ordinary omnibus-loads. They are chiefly young women under twenty, and the average length of the lives they lead is just four years. Every four years, then, seven thousand eight hundred and fifty women are drawn from their homes, many of them from simple, rural hearths, to meet this fate. What drives them to it? The want of bread.

Last October, two vagrant women came before a a Liverpool court, who testified that they had been driven to evil courses by blows, and forced to support in idleness, by their vice, the father of one, and the husband of the other.

This statement shocks you: but poor pay strikes

as heavy a blow as a husband's right arm; and these seven thousand eight hundred and fifty women in New York supported hundreds of men in ease, before they dropped from the seamstress's chair to the curbstone and the gutter.*

Tait says that the permanent prostitution of any city bears a recognized numerical relation to its means of occupation. You ask for proof.

Out of two thousand cases in the city of New York, five hundred and twenty-five pleaded destitution as the cause.

One of the police-officers testified of one girl, " She struggled hard before she fell; living on bread and water, and sleeping in station-houses. In three years, I have known more than fifty such cases."

A young girl of seventeen was left with the care of a sick, crippled sister. They were left to touch the very brink of despair. A kindly, fair-faced woman brought work which saved them from death. More was promised, on conditions that you can guess; and the toils so skilfully woven, that the young and healthy longed for her sister's sickly face and broken limb to ward off her fate.

---

* What I mean here will be understood by a reference to Emile Souvestre's " Philosophe sous les Toits." In a pretty story of two women employed in a clasp-factory, he speaks of their low wages, and says, that, having worked for thirty years, they had seen ten masters grow wealthy and retire from business, without having changed, in any degree, their own position.

These claspmakers certainly supported these ten masters and their families in ease; and, wonderful to relate, these two did not fall.

An angel, clothed in white, sat on the sepulchre wherein their hopes were buried, all through that thirty years.

"When a whole day's work brings only a few pennies," said another to Dr. Sanger, "a smile will buy me a dinner."

Out of these two thousand women, one thousand eight hundred and eighty had been brought up "*to do nothing:*" but, of all the trades, dressmaking furnished the largest proportion; and yet you think you pay your dressmakers well!

Out of the two thousand, all but fifty-one had been religiously educated.

"It has been shown elsewhere," says Dr. Sanger, "that the public are responsible for this evil, because they persist in excluding women from many kinds of employment for which they are fitted, while for work that is open they receive inadequate compensation. The community are equally responsible for non-interference with openly acknowledged evils."

Thus far I have spoken of New York. I might speak to you of Philadelphia and Boston, and tell you of ruin wrought under my own eyes; of the daughter of a State-street merchant found in the gutters of Toronto years ago; of a daughter whom that wealthy father dared not deny, when I wrote to him, though he refused to furnish the bread that would have kept her from sin. I know how hard it is for a true and good man to open his eyes to the wickedness and misery near at hand. I have no desire to draw down upon myself the local wrath of small clothiers and petty officials. You know what wages are in England: let us go thither for our concluding facts.

There are five hundred thousand single women in England, and one out of every thirteen is a thing of shame; that is, there are thirty-eight thousand four hundred and sixty-one women of the town.

Almost none of these women are drawn from domestic service. Many were found in New York who had lived out for twenty-five cents a week, and from that dropped to moral death.

You know what to expect from the lot of English dressmakers, mantlemakers, and laceweavers; but does it not chill you with horror to think that the class of governesses and private teachers furnishes also a certain number?

There is in London a Governesses' Benevolent Institution. There were lately before its committee a hundred and twenty candidates for annuities of a hundred dollars a year. Ninety-nine were unmarried, eighty-three were literally penniless, all of them were over fifty years of age, and forty-nine of them were over sixty.

One woman had labored for twenty-six years, supporting a mother and five brothers and sisters, all of whom she had educated at her own expense; but she had not saved a penny. Three were ruined by attempting to sustain their fathers in business. Six had invalid sisters dependent upon them. These are the histories of pure, untarnished names: fancy for yourselves the tales told by dishonored lips. The labors of Mr. Mayhew among this forsaken class of women are probably familiar by name to you all.

To deepen the impression which I wish to make, I shall quote some of the evidence offered by him in his letters to the "Morning Chronicle," and close this branch of my subject. Eleven thousand women under twenty are employed in the slop-shops. If their own words do not touch you, mine, of course, will fail.

1st Case. — " I work from six, A.M., to ten, P.M. In the best weeks, I clear a dollar and fifty cents; but I only average seventy-five cents the year round. My mother is sixty-seven, and seldom gets a day's work. She scours pots for the publicans at thirty-seven cents a day, but is otherwise dependent upon me. I was a good girl when I first went to work, and struggled hard to keep pure; but I had not enough to eat. Then I took up with a young man, turned of twenty, who said he would make me his lawful wife; but I *hardly cared, so I could feed myself and mother.** Many young girls tempted me, — they were so happy with enough to eat and drink. Could I have honestly earned enough for food and clothes, I would never have gone wrong; no, never. I fought against it to the last. If I had been born a lady, it would *not have been hard to act like one.*"

2d Case. — " I earn seventy-five cents a week clear. My husband has been dead seven year, and I have buried three children. I was happy so long as he lived (here she hid her face in a rusty shawl, and burst into tears). I was always true to him, so help me

---

* This may strike some readers like the hardihood of willing vice; but it is only callousness, born of exposure to hopeless cold and hunger.

God! I was an honest woman up to the time my security* died. I swear it. I am glad my children are dead; for I could not feed them."

3d Case. — " I was an honest woman till my husband died. I can put my hand on my heart, and swear it. But I was penniless, and a baby to keep. The world has drove me about so. When I want clothes, I *must* go to the streets."

4th Case. — " I am the daughter of a minister of the gospel; and I pledge my word solemnly and sacredly, that it was the low price paid for my labor that drove me to sin. I could only make thirty-four cents a week at shirts, and should have starved but for the street. At last, I swore to myself that I would keep from it for my boy's sake. I had pawned my clothes, and slept in a shawl and petticoat under a butcher's shed. I was trying to get to the workhouse. I had had no food for two days. My baby's legs froze to my side, and I sank upon a doorstep. A lady found us, and would have fed us; but I could not eat. She rubbed the baby's legs with brandy. That night I got to the workhouse: but they would not take me in without an order; so I went back to sin for one month. It was the last. In my heart I hated it; my whole nature rebelled at it; and nobody but God

---

* When a woman wishes to get slop-work, she must find some friend, who will either deposit, or become responsible for, a sum equal to the value of the work she is permitted to carry home. This person is called her "security." The longer she works, the lower she falls; and, on the death of the "security," it is often impossible to replace him. The custom does not seem to be *general* in this country.

knows how I struggled to give it up. I pawned my only gown more than once."

Look at the frightful calmness of this story: "They would not admit me to the workhouse without an order; *so I went back to sin for one month.*" When this girl told her story to Mr. Mayhew, she had been eight years at service, honored by her employers. Her personal beauty was so great, and the whole story so romantic, that Mr. Mayhew could hardly believe that she had come to him of her own accord to save other women from the same fate; and he took a day's journey into the country to confirm the facts. Her employers spoke in high terms of her honesty, sobriety, industry, and modesty. For her child's sake, she begged him to conceal her name; and she told her story with her face hidden in her hands, sobbing so as scarcely to be understood, and the tears dropping through.

If you do not realize the commonness of these tragedies, may God help you! Some of you will assert that all this is necessary; that, in this age, a certain proportion of women must meet this fate; and wall me up with statistics.

I tell you to bring the battering-ram of a Divine Love to bear on that wall. You will find, then, that, just as much as it was decreed that such women should be, it was decreed that an infinite saving power should exist, and that you should help to make it available. You may make these statistics what you will, not in an hour or a day, but in *time*.

Some of you will assert that women capable of falling thus can hardly be worth saving. I *know* there is some wilful vice; I do not desire to blink the truth: but, among those whom ill-paid labor forces into sin, there are women nobler and more disinterested than many who remain pure. Look at the stories I have told you, — women working for their kindred; a young girl of seventeen ruined to find bread for a crippled sister. In New York, the thirty-seven women supporting infirm parents; twenty-nine providing for nephews and nieces; twenty-three, widows with the care of young children.

Those of you who have had personal experience of these women will not need me to tell you that *they* never pay low wages. The washerwomen and starchers whom they employ are always well paid and well treated. They give much in charity to save others, as they often say, from their fate, and doubtless in the secret hope that God will permit them thus to atone for their sin. A few years ago, three young girls lived together in Glasgow. One of them, the youngest and frailest, a girl whose story was like that of Mrs. Gaskell's "Ruth," had left a rural home for a dressmaker's workroom. She fell into a decline, and, in her frequent delirium, raved about the bleat of her father's sheep, the evening cow-bell, and the crowing of the cock. In her lucid moments, the thought that she must die in shame convulsed her with agony. The two remaining girls took counsel. "There is no hope for us," they said; "but perhaps God will forgive us if we save her. Let us send her into the country, and work for her till she dies." And so they did, adding to the reckless wear of their horrid life the toil of the needlewoman; but, believe me, they never forgot the dying smile of her they had saved. Did you or I ever make a sacrifice which would compare with that? It is painful for me to stand here, and present this subject; it is, perhaps, painful for you to listen: but, with such women among the ruined, only cowards, it seems to me, would refuse to risk all things to save them.*

---

* Those who are unaccustomed to this class of women will be inclined to think that the state of things represented in the text has long passed away. People who know nothing of the value of money talk a great deal about "increase of wages," and are apt to say that any honest woman can now get a living. Women's wages are at this moment of less value than they were before the war; and, to confirm the foregoing statements, I add here the statements of my friend Mrs. Corbin, which reach me as I go to press:—

"At a meeting of the Liberal Christian League, held at Rev. Robert Collyer's church, on Sunday evening, Feb. 3, a report was read by the Chairman of the Committee on Friendless Women, from which the following is an extract:—

Your Committee aimed [in visiting houses of ill-fame], in Chicago, to find out, as nearly as possible, the general facts concerning the lives of this class of women.

It was found that these women of pleasure, as they are called, instead of leading the idle and luxurious life which many imagine, are, in fact, the most steadily employed of any class in the community, and have the least available leisure. Your Committee have never yet visited a house of this kind, staying on the average half an hour, but they have found male visitors, either there when they entered, or coming in before they left; and this in the open day. Inquiries put to the women concerning their hours of leisure developed incidentally the fact, that it is only at certain times, on certain days, that they can get out; and then it must be strictly in the prosecution of their calling. The terms on which these women are kept, are usually a certain stipulated sum per week for room rent, and, over and above this, the half of their earnings; which makes it necessary for the keepers to have a constant eye upon the girls, to prevent their taking money outside. The number of men supporting these houses is, moreover, so much greater than the number of women supported therein, that every girl is kept in constant requisition, either at the house, or as a walking advertisement on the street and at public places.

Your Committee, before making these visits, were constantly assured that these

In France, where all women of this class are registered, Duchâtelet found 1,680 who had erased their names from the list, on the plea that they had found honest occupation. He traced them: 108 had become housekeepers; 864, seamstresses; 247, shopkeepers; and 461, domestics.

The Society for the Rescue of Young Women, in London, admitted two hundred members last year. It asks no questions of those who enter; and the wisdom of this is shown in the fact, that its subscription-list contains the names of sixty former inmates,

women preferred this way of life, and would scout the efforts of their own sex at reforming them. Your Committee take great pleasure in reporting, that, in every instance, they have found this charge *utterly unsustained*. Everywhere doors were freely opened to them; they were treated with as much politeness and cordiality as they have ever received in the most respectable houses; and the conversation was of the freest and most satisfactory character.

'Are you happy in this life?' was asked of a delicate girl in her teens, who had been seen, five minutes before, dancing and singing about a man in an adjoining apartment in the most wanton manner, — 'Are you happy in this life?'

Tears, sudden and sincere, with a look of indignant protest, filled her eyes, as she answered, —

'Think how we have to treat the men: that of itself is enough to prevent *any woman* from being happy.'

'But you do not always talk this way to men?' was the reply.

'Oh, no!' she said; 'I would never tell *a man* that. We always tell the men that we like this life, and would not live any other, if we could; but *women know*.'

Another voluntarily mentioned the intemperance with which they are universally and justly charged, as one of the hard necessities of their position. Women ought not to drink, she admitted; but they would die if they did not, or go mad with anguish and despair.

Your Committee feel, that, at the present stage of investigation, it may seem premature to speak of the causes of this terrible evil; this slavery, which their observation assures them is more degrading and horrible than any other upon the face of the earth: but two causes have met them so constantly face to face, that they cannot in justice refrain from mentioning them.

The first is the terribly prevalent and everywhere tolerated licentiousness of men. Your Committee believe it to be an admitted fact, that, if to-day every woman of abandoned life could suddenly be removed from the dens of this city and placed in a respectable position, it would not be six months before their places would be filled, from the ranks of women who are now virtuous; and they have no faith in any

whose subscriptions range from twenty-five cents to twenty dollars per annum.

A terrible account has lately been published of the straw-bonnet warehouses in London, by one who has worked in them. One single story will show you, how that *touch of truth*, which, far more than the touch of genius, makes the " whole world kin," revealed a noble human nature in the midst of what seemed utter depravity.

system of reform which does not strike effectual blows at this, the mainspring of the evil.

Over against this, the first great pillar of the institution, stands the almost equally colossal one of poverty, and the exclusion of women from the ordinary fields of labor.

' Here is what I work for,' said a fine, strong-looking woman, as she placed her hand on the head of a bright boy of two years. ' He is my child. I have him to support. There is no other way in which I could earn a comfortable subsistence for myself and him.'

Another, the keeper of a house of ill-fame, an intelligent, graceful, refined-looking woman, — a woman who would have been an ornament to any society, — said : —

' I was left suddenly poor, with my mother to support. I had never been used to work, and there seemed no work I could do that would support us both. The circumstances of my life seemed to force me into this way of living;' which meant, of course, that some man stood ready to offer her kindness, protection, support, every thing but marriage, and she accepted it. ' My mother, to-day, is as innocent of any knowledge of my way of life, as a saint in heaven. I live in daily terror and solicitude lest she should find it out, for it would kill her. I am going soon on a visit to her, and shall carry with me twelve hundred and fifty dollars, with which to secure her a home for life; so that, whatever happens to me. she will be provided for.'

In confirmation of this story, a hack came to the door while she was speaking, to carry her to the train she had previously indicated; which fact, together with her earnest and sincere manner, left no doubt in the minds of your Committee concerning the truthfulness of her story.

In regard to the series of meetings proposed to be inaugurated, your Committee are obliged for the present to report unfavorably, for the following reasons : —

The proposition was everywhere cordially met among the women. They readily agreed to the usefulness of the project, and mentioned only one objection, and that to time. 'Sunday,' was the invariable answer, 'is our busiest day. We could hardly get away at all on that day ; but we will try to do so.' Your Committee saw at once the blunder they had made in forgetting that Sunday is the leisure day of men ; and therefore went to the first appointed meeting, through a cold and blinding snowstorm, with little hope of success. They found the room already occupied by some six or eight street roughs, evidently waiting for what might transpire. They left the

One day, the worn-out women tried to compel a young, fresh worker to do less than she was able, or to secrete a portion of her braid, instead of making it up. They could not prevail. " Are you a Metherdis, miss?" asked one woman. " I'm not a thief," she replied gently. A big, bad woman stole her extra plait; but no one dared insult her. Once she fainted, and some one offered her gin; but the big, bad woman started forward: " Would you make her a devil like the rest of us?" she cried; " I'd sooner see her

room very soon, but took their station about the door, and remained there as long as the Committee did. Subsequent inquiries confirmed the impression, that they were sent there by some of the men who had been in the houses at the time of the visits, to break up the meetings, for which purpose, of course, only their presence would be necessary.

Beyond this determined opposition which would no doubt be encountered at the hands of the male supporters of the institution, your Committee see but one serious difficulty; and that is, the deep-rooted scepticism which prevail among the women concerning any general sentiment of Christian charity in their behalf They have so long been persecuted with unjust opprobrium, abandoned, outcast, left to live or die as they might, without one word of pity or encouragement, while the men who shared their sins, and were oftentimes the guiltier partners, were the honored and trusted associates of Christian women, pillars perhaps in Christian churches, that they have naturally come to feel, that the sympathy of one or two good women, however earnest and grateful it may be in itself, will be of little avail against the malignity of the whole banded world.

Still your Committee have seen nothing, so far, to discourage them in their efforts, but every thing to impress upon them the feeling of imperative duty in this direction.

(Signed) Mrs C. F. CORBIN, Chairman.

"The plan of action proposed by this Committee was to visit the women in a friendly, Christ-like spirit, inaugurate a series of meetings among them, organize efforts in the direction of saving their money, so that they might be able to take an independent position, with only such moral support as should be necessary to enable them to face the opposition of the world, and to direct their lavish free-heartedness into channels of benevolence toward the old and worn-out of their number. Pure and healthful pleasures would also be provided for them, good music, the reading of fine poems and interesting stories, and so a beginning made toward introducing principles of steadiness and sobriety into their now totally abandoned and desperate lives."

stabbed!" and she got her a cup of tea from her own "screw."* When they were kept late, this woman walked home with her, cautioning her against gin, against young men, especially the gentry, and bidding her not forget her prayers: "for," said she, "*you* know how; *I* was never teached." As she parted from her one night, she said, " I don't expect it's any use; but it would do no harm if you prayed *once* for me." Who will say that this woman was irreclaimable? And, in estimating the chances of saving a depraved woman, you should always remember, that, in nine cases out of twelve, she sold herself, not to vice, but to what seemed, at least, to her longing heart, like *love*. Put yourself in her place. Do not start: it will do you no harm. Think what it would be to slave soul and body, day after day, for a crust and a cup of cold water. Not so much would your failing body crave one nourishing meal, as the aching, human heart within you one tender look, one loving word. If, in your misery, you had kept some beauty; if you had known no gentler touch than a drunken father's blow or a mother's curse, — how strong would be the temptation when one above you pleaded for affection! See how like an angel of light this demon would descend! O my sisters! you have never read this story right. Such a woman is no monster, only a gentle-hearted creature, unsupported by God's law, unrestrained by self-control. Your scorn, the world's

---

* This expression, used in all such places to denote the food, tea, coffee, or gin, used by the overstrained girls, is terribly significant.

rejection, *may* make her what you think. Meanwhile, are you above temptation ? Does not conscience enforce my plea ?

" Some positions," says Legouvé, " attract by their ease; but it is work that purifies and fills existence. God permits hard trials; but he has appointed labor, and we forget them all. A serious comforter, it gives always more than it promises, and dries the bitterest tears. A pleasure unequalled in itself, it is the salt of all other pleasures.*

You have seen that a necessity to live demands of you new fields for woman to work in; and the question arises, Is she fit for these new duties? †

I consider the question of intellectual ability settled.

---

* I do not know that any person has ever practically carried out Legouvé's estimate of labor as a moral help, but Marie de Lamourous, the foundress of the House of Mercy at Bourdeaux. This was a refuge for ruined women, whom she trained to self-support. Some one offered her a sum sufficient to insure her family a comfortable living; but she wisely refused it. "No false pretences," she said: "if we are not compelled to labor, we shall not labor. An idle mind makes its own temptations. I can do nothing without work."

† When woman's power to work is called in question, men almost always remark, that she has shown no *inventive* genius whatever. Should a proper history of the arts ever be written, this will be found to be an entire mistake. Patentees are not always inventors; and many of these, after hopeless labor carried on for years, have owed a final success to some woman's power of adaptation. We need not, however, take refuge in general statement, nor in the traditional fact that she invented spindle, distaff, needle, and scissors. Any new-born barbarian, pressed by necessity, might accomplish so much. The most delicate and beautiful obstetrical instruments were invented by Madame Boivin. Madame Ducoudray invented the manikin; Madame Breton, the system of artificial nourishment for babes; Morandi and Biheron adapted wax to the purposes of medical illustration; and it was to the observations of Mademoiselle Biheron, recorded in wax, that Dr. Hunter owed the illustrations of his best work. He was her generous friend; but she preceded him seven years in this direction, and may possibly

The volumes of science, mathematics, general literature, &c., which women have given to the world, without sharing to the full the educational advantages of man, seem to promise that they shall outstrip him here, the moment they have a fair start. But I go farther, and state boldly, that women have, from the beginning, done the hardest and most unwholesome work of the world in all countries, whether civilized or uncivilized; and I am prepared to prove it. I do not mean that rocking the cradle and making bread is as hard work as any, but that women have always been doing man's work, and that all the outcry society makes against work for women is not to protect *women*, but a

---

have given him the right to use her observations as his own. Madame Rondet has, in the present century, invented a tube to be used in cases of restoration from asphyxia. It is easy to quote these cases from the history of medicine, because an honest French physician has taken pains to preserve them; but the following instances of inventive and mechanical power may be less known: —

In 1823, *the first patent of invention* was taken out in Paris by Madame Dutillet, for the formation of artificial marble. This was so successful a patent, that she sold it in 1824; and the purchaser renewed it, with still further improvements.

In 1836, Burrows, an Englishman, took out a patent for cement. Madame Bex, of Paris, found this cement a failure in damp places, and published a method of less limited application, in which bitumen was employed.

In 1840, Mrs. Marshall, once of Manchester, England, and now of Edinburgh, was struck with the idea, that the electric forces evolved by decaying animal and vegetable matter, acting upon calcareous substances, must have much to do with the natural formation of marble. In five years, by upwards of ten thousand experiments, she perfected an artificial marble, whose constituents and manufacture were entirely within control, and which could be made in hours or months, at the maker's volition. To this cement she gave the simple Italian name of *intonuca*. It is singular that she should so intuitively have seized this secret; for, under Madame Dutillet's patent, we are expressly informed that all vegetable matter must be removed from the

certain class called *ladies*. Now, I believe that work is good for ladies; so let us look at the truth. " Let it once be understood," says one of our English friends, " that the young business-woman is shielded by the social intercourse of those who are called ladies, and it would obviate many of those grave objections which deter parents from consenting that their children shall brave the world in shops and warehouses."

Most certainly it would; and to this point we must frequently return. Meanwhile, says Sydney Smith, " so long as girls and boys run about in the dirt, and trundle hoop together, they are both precisely alike;" and I shall proceed to show that large numbers have not only played but worked in the dirt together, and trundled hoop, not merely through our own lives, but ever since work and play began.

---

composition, if we would have the cement indestructible. The example is an interesting one; for the ten thousand disagreeable experiments show that one woman at least possessed the power of persistent application, of long-protracted labor, so often denied.

Starch first came into use in England in 1564. It was carried thither by a Mrs. Dinghen Vanden Plasse, of Flanders, who set up business as a professed starcher, and instructed others how to use the article for five pounds, and how to make it for twenty pounds.

Side-saddles for ladies first came into use in 1138. Anne, queen of Richard II., introduced these to the English ladies.

The braiding of straw in this country was first begun in Providence, in 1798, by Mrs. Betsey Baker, lately residing in Dedham, Mass. The first bonnet she made was of seven straws with bobbin let in like open-work, and lined with pink satin.

I had hoped to add to these names that of a peasant woman, who successfully drained a large estate in France after her own original fashion, and was sent from Paris to do the same in French Guiana for the government; but, although no phantom, she eludes my researches.

THE MARKET.

I shall speak first of Asiatic women; and I can afford to begin by quoting a Cochin-China proverb, to the effect that "a woman has nine lives, and bears a great deal of killing." I do not know anything else about the Cochin-China women; but this looks as if their lot were no exception to the general rule. The Chinese peasant-woman goes to the field with her male infant on her back, and ploughs, sows, and reaps, exposed to all the changes of the weather. When her husband is proved criminal, she must die as his accomplice; having, at least, strength enough to suffer. In Calcutta, women are the masons who keep the roof tight; and you may see them daily carrying their hods of cement, spreading it on the tops of houses, and flattening it with a wooden rammer like that with which our Irishmen pave the streets.

You have heard of the Bombay ghauts. Ghaut is a native word, which means "passage through;" and it is applied by the resident not only to the railway cut between the hills, but to the hills themselves. These are of volcanic origin, — a sort of trap. Formed beneath the water, the mass cooled as it was thrown up, and the sides do not slope much. "When I gained an elevation of two thousand feet," says my correspondent, "and looked back, I saw hills of all shapes and sizes thrown up, and ravines thousands of feet below, all looking like the dried bed of an ocean. The table-land on which I stood is two thousand five hundred feet above the level of the sea; and, as this is the elevation at Poonah, the railroad from Campoolu winds as it can along the sides of the mountains. There are twenty-five tunnels through the solid rock on this road, each half a mile long or more. There are piers of solid stone, with arches spanning forty feet, which rise a hundred above the valley. Part of the grade was formed by lowering men with ropes, to drill the holes for blasting, a thousand feet above the ravine. There are twenty thousand workmen employed; and one-third, or about seven thousand, of these are "— what do you think? In a country where no European man can labor, where the native rests until compelled by his conqueror to work, in the year 1859 behold seven thousand *women* laboring in the ghauts! Climbing, climbing, through the cloudless day, *women* carry baskets of stone and earth upon their heads, to creep to the edge of the ravines, and fill with these tedious contributions thousands of perpendicular feet; and the men who pay them, doubtless, talk to their daughters about *woman's* lack of physical strength!

In Australia, the woman carries the burdens which man's indolence refuses; and the deserts of Africa bear the same testimony in freedom that we glean from the witness of slavery. In the West-India Islands, the patient negress toils by the side of her mate, doing to the full as hard a day's work, though encumbered by the weight of a child upon her back; but she does not share, in the same way, his hours of rest. The customs of Africa still prevail, and she offers her husband's food and tobacco on her knees.

Nor does the poetry of ancient Greece show us the so-long vaunted delicacy of the sex. Homer's princesses beat linen on the rocks, and Andromache shares all the functions of the groom: —

> "For this, high fed in plenteous stalls ye stand,
> Served with pure wheat, and by a princess' hand;
> For this, my spouse, of great Actæon's line,
> So oft hath steeped the strengthening grain in wine!"

We have crossed the boundary line of Europe, without any change in the indications; and we may drop from Homer to the middle ages, or modern times, as well.

The traveller who gazes admiringly upon the vine-clad hills of the Jura, rising, terrace upon terrace, till the eye can scarce distinguish the limit between the work of man and the rock of ages which still crowns the summit, will learn with surprise that the mind which conceived of such stupendous labor, and the hand which held out honor and freedom as its reward, were a woman's.

Under a burning sun, or exposed to a bitter, glacial *bise*, the first cultivators, partly women, climbed slowly and painfully, by rocky ledges or crevices, along those dangerous slopes and beetling cliffs, where trees were to be hewn down and briers plucked up, raising by manual efforts alone the stone necessary for the steps and walls, and the deep tunnels for the safe passage of the torrents which vegetation now conceals. And among them, wherever her donkey's foot could find a way, went the woman who devised the work and bestowed the guerdon, with the distaff on her saddle, which gives her to this day the name of Bertha the spinner.

Yes, it was Bertha, of the Transjurane, who, about the middle of the tenth century, undertook this work; opened the old Roman roads; and, in defending her people against the Saracen hordes, first devised, it may be, the modern telegraph. A prolonged line from her Alps to the Jura is still set with the solid stone towers from which Bertha's sentinels warned each other.*

On the 13th of April, 1809, the French and Bavarian prisoners held by the Tyrolese at Steinach were marched to Schwatz, and thence to Salzburg, under an escort of women: and the prisoners, at least, felt sufficient confidence in the physical strength of the guard; for they made no attempt to escape.

"Not a year ago," writes Anna Johnson of Germany, "I saw a young girl standing up to her knees in a manure-heap, which she shovelled into a cart, and then drove to the field. She was hired to do this work at fourteen dollars a year. On the mountains, the women were carrying soil and manure to the vines in baskets, as Queen Bertha taught them nine centuries ago." A still less pleasant picture may be drawn from Köhl's "Reminiscences of Montenegro." "Down among the stones, on the banks of the Fuimera," he says, "some Cattaro women and girls were washing and scraping the entrails of the goats that the men had brought to market. There was one tall, slender,

---

* Historical Pictures of the Middle Ages, in Black and White.

handsome girl, dressed in a crimson petticoat, and jacket embroidered with gold, and her hair elegantly fastened with golden pins. A pair of richly wrought slippers lay on the stone beside her; and she laughed and talked merrily as she washed and scraped away. At last, she packed the whole into a tub, and lifted it on her gayly dressed head to carry home. The next day was Sunday; and I met her, radiant with beauty and gold embroidery, on her way to church. I often met these girls carrying on foot the baggage of the riding-parties."

In 1850, a clergyman of this city tells me that he saw women, wearing leathern breast-plates, harnessed to the canal-boats of the Low Countries, and doing the work of oxen.

In France, we find the same evidences of out-door work and physical ability. Galignani tells us, that, in consequence of the success of a certain Madame Isabelle in breaking horses for the Russian Army, the French minister of war lately authorized her to proceed officially before a commission of officers, with General Régnault de St. Jean d'Angely at their head, to break some horses for the cavalry. After twenty days, the animals were so completely broken, that the minister immediately entered into an arrangement with her to introduce her system into all the schools of cavalry in the empire, beginning with that of Saumur.

Marshal Baraguay d'Hilliers, at Nantes, recently made a distribution of St. Helena medals to the old soldiers of the empire. Among the number was a woman named Jeanne Louise Antonini, who had served ten years in the navy, and fifteen in the infantry, where she obtained the rank of non-commisioned officer in the seventieth regiment of the line. She received nine wounds while bravely fighting. "It is not the *coat* that makes the man," said our marshal when he gave the medal.

One of the great celebrities of the Invalides was buried, very lately, with great pomp. This "old invalid" was an individual of the softer sex, — the widow Brulow, — who entered the army, in 1792, as a soldier in the forty-second regiment of infantry, authorized to enlist, in spite of her sex, by General Casabianca. At Fort Gesco, she was promoted to the rank of sergeant, after being severely wounded in the encounter which took place. Perceiving that the troops were getting short of powder, she set out alone at midnight for Calvi, roused the women of that place to the number of sixty, and started them off for Gesco, laden with powder and ammunition, which enabled the little fort to hold out eight and forty hours longer, until relief came. A little after, at the siege of Calvi, the widow Brulow, while in charge of a gun, was so desperately wounded that she was forced to renounce her military career; and none other was open to her but the retirement of the Invalides, where she was admitted with the rank of sub-lieutenant. The present emperor, to whom the widow Brulow was introduced on his visit to the Invalides, presented her with the cross of the Legion of Honor and the medal of St. Helena; her comrades, by acclamation, having designated her as most worthy of the honor. By a decree, dated from the imperial headquarters, since our first edition was printed, we learn that the race of heroines is not extinct; for two other women, by that decree, obtained the military medal for their courage at the battle of Magenta.

There recently died, at Portsea, in England, a woman, ninety years of age, named Nelly Giles. She was one of the few surviving witnesses of the battle of the Nile; having been on board His Majesty's ship "Bellerophon," in the command of Captain Darby, and in all subsequent engagements under Nelson. During the action of the Nile, she was surrounded by heaps of slain and wounded; and she nursed the latter tenderly, undismayed by the horrors of the scene. Three days after the battle, she gave birth to a son.

The government, in consideration of her great attention to the sick and wounded, and of the assistance she gave the surgeons, awarded her a gratuity of seventeen pounds a year for her life.

A young patriot, named Francisco Riso, was killed on April 4, 1862, at Palermo, during a popular demonstration which took place before Garibaldi's arrival. On April 20, his father, Giovanni Riso, sixty years old, was shot by the Bourbon soldiers, without so much as the form of a trial. On the very day that Garibaldi entered Palermo, a young and beautiful nun,

Ignacia Riso, the sister and daughter of the two Risos named above, left the convent, and, amidst a shower of balls and grape-shot, — a cross in one hand, and a poignard in the other, — placed herself at the head of Garibaldi's column, crying, "Down with the Bourbons! Death to the tyrant! Vengeance!" She kept her place as long as the fighting lasted; and her courageous attitude electrified the volunteers. Ever since that day, the name of Ignacia Riso has been held sacred. When she passes in the street, the soldiers bow low, and bless her with the most profound respect. Garibaldi himself pays her great attention, and loves her as if she were his own daughter.

From instances like these, refreshing because they tell of self-imposed labor and eccentric character, we turn with less pleasure to the statistics of the factories. Here men have left to women not only the worst paid but the most unwholesome work of the respective mills.

Women, in France, are employed in the manufacture of cotton, silk, and wool. The cotton manufacture compels two processes which are very injurious, — the beating of the cotton, which brings on a distressing phthisis; and the preparation, or dressing, which needs a degree of heat not to be endured after mature age. Both these departments are filled by women paid at half-prices.

The woollen manufacture compels only one unwholesome process, — that of carding; but all the carders are women at half-wages.

In the silk factories, again, there are two unwholesome processes entirely carried on by women. The first is the drawing of the cocoons, where the hands must be kept constantly in boiling water, and the odor of the putrefying insects constantly fills the lungs; the second is carding the floss, the fine lint of which affects the bronchial tubes. Six out of every eight women so employed die in a few months. Healthy young girls from the mountains soon develop tubercular consumption; and, to complete the dreadful tale, they are kept upon the lowest wages; being paid only twenty cents where a man would earn sixty.*

The Anglo-Saxons, says the historian, "had not been long settled in England before the more savage of their traits were softened down. The wife continued to be regularly purchased by her husband, and the contract was considered a mere money bargain, long subsequent to the reign of Ethelbert." And why? Not because love was mercenary; but because woman was regarded, in the first place, as a beast of burden, a laborer. In the "Romany Rye," we are told that the sale of a wife with a halter round her neck is still a legal transaction in England. "It must be done in the cattle-market, as if she were a mare; all women being considered as mares by the old English law, and, indeed, called mares in certain counties where genuine old English law is still preserved."

---
* Ernest Legouvé.

Such a sale as this was recently completed at Worcester, and the agreement between the men was published in the " Worcester Chronicle."

" Thomas Middleton delivered up his wife Mary Middleton to Philip Rostins for one shilling and a quart of ale; and parted wholly and solely for life, never to trouble one another.

"Witness. (Signed)   THOMAS × MIDDLETON, his mark.
Witness.   MARY MIDDLETON, his wife.
Witness.   PHILIP × ROSTINS, his mark.
Witness.   S. H. STONE, Crown Inn, Friar St."

I have preserved the old expression *mare* in my quotation, to indicate, not the degradation to which women fell, but that it was as a beast of burden that men regarded her. Several cases of sales, such as is here referred to, have occurred within a few years; but this is the only certificate of transfer that I ever saw. I desire to direct your attention to the remarkable fact, that, of the three parties to it, the wife, who was sold, was the *only* one who could write her name. The men signed it by a mark.*
" A generation back," says Cobbett, " it was a common thing to see women, half naked, working like beasts, chained to carts, upon the common roads of England."

---

* While these papers were preparing for the press, the record of another such sale, in August, 1859, disgraced the English nation. Opposite the brewery, at Dudley, in Staffordshire, not many miles from Kidderminster and Birmingham, a man named Pensotte sold his wife, with a halter round her neck, for sixpence. He had previously dragged her — a three weeks' bride — three quarters of a mile in this state. It is intimated in this case, that she was not faithful; but it is the first time I ever saw such a charge

When Lord Ashley's Commission reported, in 1842, five thousand females were at work, more than a thousand feet below the soil, in the coal-mines of the north of England. These women were nearly naked, and drew trucks, in harness, on all-fours, like beasts of burden. You cannot have forgotten the remarkable description of such women in D'Israeli's novel of " The Sibyl."

" They come forth. The plain is covered with the swarming multitude : bands of stalwart men, broad-chested and muscular, wet with toil, and black as the children of the tropics ; troops of youth, alas ! of *both sexes*, though neither their raiment nor their language indicates the difference. All are clad in male attire, and oaths that men might shudder to hear issue from lips born to breathe words of sweetness. Yet these are to be, some *are*, the mothers of England! Can we wonder at the hideous coarseness of their language, when we remember the savage rudeness of their lives ? Naked to the waist, an iron chain fastened to a belt of leather runs between their legs, clad in canvas ; while, on hands and feet, an English girl, for twelve, sometimes for sixteen,

---

attached to such an account. Americans are anxious to understand this outrage. Is it possible that a government which forbids the sale of a negro cannot forbid the sale of a Saxon wife? What shadow of law sustains the custom? Is the woman supposed to be sold into wifehood or servitude? I have taken it for granted that the word "mare" shows that she is regarded as a beast of burden. It is impossible for the fairest and loftiest woman in England — nay, for Victoria herself — not to suffer, in some degree, from the public opinion which such transactions, ever so rarely occurring, tend to form.

hours a day, hauls and hurries tubs of coal along subterranean roads, dark, precipitous, and plashy." These women, *called* free, were the wretched slaves of capital. In the life of Stephenson, the railway engineer, you will find a further account of them, and may read the chilling answer given by a woman whom he asked if she had ever heard of Jesus, " that no such hand had ever worked in her shaft!" Let the proprietors of English mines remember! No such hand did ever work in those shafts, yet they called themselves Christian men! True as death were the words. If the *law* is now free of reproach, the *evil* has by no means ceased to exist: the Master still stands knocking.

" Children," wrote Lord Ashley, " are taken to work when only four years old, girls as well as boys. Dragging the coal carriages requires the whole strength of either sex. Young men and women, married women and married men, work together through the same number of hours, almost, sometimes quite, naked, constantly demoralizing each other. It stints their growth and cripples their limbs." In the east of Scotland, they still toil up steep ladders from the shafts.

If it were my purpose to show you moral degradation, you could hardly bear what I must say; but I desire only, at this moment, to show you these men and women *working*, as Sydney Smith would say, *in the dirt together*. In 1842, the Earl of Durham knew of this; and he and the set with whom he lived dared, doubtless, to whisper to the ladies in their halls, that women were not made to labor!

In the calico-mills, girls grind and mix the colors. They are called *teerers*. They begin at five years of age, and labor twelve hours a day, sometimes sixteen; and are kept late into the night to prepare for the following day.

In Sedgely and Warrington, the fate of the female pinmakers is no better. They begin at five years of age, and work from twelve to sixteen hours a day. If refractory, they are struck at Wiltenhall with strap, stick, hammer, or file, in spite of the delicacy of the sex. In Sedgely, more women are employed than men; but they do not fare any better: their bodies are seamed by blows given with bars of burning iron.

O my sisters! why has God sheltered *us* in quiet homes? What have we done to deserve a happier fate? Why were we not left to writhe beneath the blows of the smith, or the outrage of a market-sale?

Because God has laid down a responsibility by the side of every privilege, and requires us to labor not merely to set such women free, but to establish a freedom and security *by law*, — the law of custom as well as the law of courts, which we only possess through usurpation or indulgence.

I will not leave these English shores without alluding to the physical strength shown by that lovely paralytic, Anna Gurney. Deprived of the use of her limbs in very early life, she acquired the Latin, Greek, and Hebrew, and finally the Teutonic tongues, with a facility and thoroughness that her Anglo-Saxon translations show. Men might be excused if they sheltered from contact with the world this infirm creature, dependent upon artificial aid for every movement; but what did she choose for herself?

In 1825, after her mother's death, she went to live at Northrepps. At her own expense, she procured one of Manby's apparatus for saving the lives of seamen cast upon that dangerous coast; and, in cases of great urgency and peril, she caused herself to be carried down to the beach, and, from the sick chair which she wheeled over the sand, directed every movement for the rescue and recovery of the half-drowned men.

Look at the pictures! See that grimy, tangled woman in harness, straining, in full health, along the coal-shafts! See, nearer, this lovely cripple, the Quaker cap folded over her soft, brown hair, her soul erect and noble, doing the duty of a Grace Darling! The first labors like the brute beast, the victim of human misgovernment and heathenish ignorance; the last chooses for herself a conflict with the storm, and earns, with as full right as any brother, the meed of the world.

Let us pass over to America. The Caribs of Honduras are a hardy race, and do not share the prejudices of Massachusetts on the subject of labor. Each man has several wives. For each he clears a plantation and builds a house. In a year, she has every kind of breadstuff under cultivation; and hires creers, which she freights for Truxillo and Belize, her husband often commanding for her. If her agricultural labors prove too heavy, as a thrifty woman will sometimes make them, she hires her husband to work for her at two dollars a week.

So the Northern Indian glides nimbly through the woods; while the squaw carries on her unlucky back their common food and covering, or perhaps hauls the canoe across the portage. A Jesuit priest rebuked an Orinoco woman for infanticide. "I wish *my* mother had been brave enough to part with me!" was her reply. "Our husbands go to hunt; and we drag after them, one baby at the breast, another on our back. When we return, we cannot sleep, but must grind maize all night for their chica. Drunken, they beat us, or stamp us under foot; and, after twenty years of such labor, a young wife is brought home to abuse us and such children as we have not killed. What ought I to do?"

At Santa Cruz, Theodore Parker writes to Francis Jackson that men and women work together to repair the public highway; hoeing the earth into trays, and throwing it into a cart which they drag and push together.

In Ohio, last year, about thirty girls went from farm to farm, hoeing, ploughing, and the like, for sixty-two and a half cents a day. At Media, in Pennsylvania, two girls named Miller carry on a farm of three hundred acres; raising hay and grain, hiring labor, but working mostly themselves. These women are not ignorant: they at one time made meteorological observations for an association auxiliary to the Smithsonian Institute. But labor attracts them, as it would many women if they were not oppressed by public opinion.

"In New York," writes a late correspondent of the "Lily," "I saw women performing the most menial offices,—carrying parcels for grocers, and trunks for steamboats. They often sweep the crossings in muddy weather; and I once saw one carrying brick and mortar for a mason."

During the late terrible destruction of property at the Lawrence mills, the women, heroic in every department, did not excuse themselves from the severest labor. When, after hours of extreme exertion, the firemen, worn down and quite exhausted, called for help, a bevy of ladies, who were standing on the sidewalk in Canal Street, flew over to the engines, and, "manning" the brakes, worked the machine, amid the cheers of the firemen.

You know what bodily strength and nervous energy carried Mary Patton round Cape Horn. Well, on the 25th of June, 1858, the British ship "Grotto" left Cuba; and, on the second day, the yellow-fever broke out in the worst form. Seven days after, so many had died, that there remained only the captain, his wife, and two of the crew. Then the captain was taken ill; and, beside nursing him, the poor wife, who had already nursed officers and men, took her station at the wheel, and steered by his instructions for Sandy Hook. There the steam-tug "Huntress" found them, the heroic woman at the wheel, the husband at that moment struggling with death; and, when they reached New York, three out of eleven, one of them the suffering wife, survived to tell the tale, and show how a woman can work. So common are such instances becoming, that you have hardly heard the name of this Mrs. Nichols, for whom tender charity soon cared.

A mutiny on board the ship "Maria," of New York, was put down Nov. 10, 1860, by the energy and decision of the wife of the master, Captain Clark, who, with pistols in her hands, threatened to shoot one of the mutineers if he did not desist. He was cowed into submission; and, a signal being made to the revenue cutter, the mutineers were taken into custody. The mate would have been killed, but for the heroic woman's intrepidity.

But all such labor is the result of compulsion, — compulsion of barbarism, of slavery, of unfair competition, or dire disease. Let us close this branch of our subject with a picture homely but attractive. "According to thy request," writes a Quaker friend from Wilmington, Del., "I send thee some facts concerning Sarah Ann Scofield. Some fifteen years since, her father became very much involved in debt. He owed some ten or twelve hundred dollars; having lost largely by working for cotton and woollen mills.

His business was making spindles and fliers. His daughter, then just sixteen, proposed to go into her father's shop and assist him; she being the oldest of seven children. He accepted her offer, and told me himself, that, in twelve months, she could finish more work, and do it better, than any man he had ever trained for eighteen. She earned fifteen dollars a week at the rate he then paid other hands. Her father died. Her two oldest brothers learned the trade of her, and went away. She has now two younger sisters in apprenticeship, and a brother fourteen years of age, all working under her; turning, polishing, filing, and fitting all kinds of machinery. I went out to see her last week. She was then making water-rams to force streams into barns and houses. She is also beginning to make many kinds of carriage-axles. She is her own draughtsman, and occasionally does her own forging. To use her own words, 'What any man can do, I can but try at.' She has a steam-engine, every part of which she understands; and I know that her work gives entire satisfaction. When they have steady employment, they clear sixty dollars a week; and she says she would rather work at it for her bread, than at sewing for ten times the money. The truth is, it is a business she is fond of."

I have shown you that a very large number of women are compelled to self-support; that the old idea, that all men support all women, is an absurd fiction; and, if you require other evidence than mine, you may find it in the English courts, under the working of the new Divorce Bill. Nearly all the women who have applied for divorces have proved that the subsistence of the family depended upon them. Out of six million of British women over twenty-one years of age, one-half are industrial in their mode of life, and more than two millions are self-supporting in their industry like men. Put this fact fully before your eyes.

Driven to self-support, you have seen, also, that low wages and comparatively few and overcrowded avenues of labor compel women to vicious courses for their daily bread. The streets of Paris, London, Edinburgh, New York, and Boston, tell us the same painful story; and in glaring, crimson letters, rises everywhere the question, — " Death or dishonor ? " I have shown you that there is encouragement for moral effort, because these women escape from vice as fast as they find work to do. " Have they strength for the conflict," you ask, " or desire to enter such fields ? " Find your answer in what they have done from the earliest ages, with the foot of Confucius and Vishnu, of capital and interest, upon their necks. In the lovely lives of Bertha and Ann Gurney, and the powerful attraction of Sarah Scofield, you have found pleasanter pictures whereon to rest your eyes. Let no man taunt woman with inability to labor, till the coal-mines and the metal-works, the rotting cocoons and fuzzing-cards, give up their dead; till he shares with her, equally at least, the perils of manufactures and the press of the market. As partners, they must test and prove their comparative power.

We must next consider what need woman's moral nature has of work, and what sort of opposition man practically offers her.

II.

VERIFY YOUR CREDENTIALS.

> "This hurts most, this . . . that, after all, we are paid
> The worth of our work, perhaps."
>
> E. B. Browning.

IF low wages, by actually starving women and those dependent upon them, force many into vicious courses, so does the want of employment lower the whole moral tone, and destroy even the domestic efficiency of those whose minds seek variety and freedom. More than once have I been to insane asylums with young girls whom active and acceptable employment would have saved from mania; and scores of times have young women of fortune asked me, "What can you give me to do?"

And to this question there is, in the present state of the public mind, no possible answer. No woman of rank can find work, if she do not happen to be philanthropic, literary, or artistic in her taste, without braving the influence of home, or, what is next dearest, the social circle, and earning for herself a position so conspicuous as to be painful to the most energetic. The woman who is prepared for all this will not ask anybody what she is to do: she will take her work into her own hands, and do it.

That was a pleasant time in the history of the world, when every woman found, in spinning, weaving, and sewing, in the active labor of a small or the skilful management of a large household, full employment for time and thought, under the cheering shelter of a husband's or father's smile. That was a pleasant time also, when, in the middle English classes, women worked freely by a husband's side, with more regard to his interest than heed of the world's talk. But with the wide intellectual culture that America has been the first country in the world to offer to women, individual tastes and wishes must develop in single women; and all men who value the moral health of society must aid this development.

There is no greater enemy to body and soul than idleness, unless it be the absurd public sentiment which compels to idleness. Thousands and tens of thousands have fallen victims to it. The woman who will not labor, rich or honored though she be, bends her head to the inevitable curse of Heaven.

This curse works in failing health, fading beauty, broken temper, and weary days. Let her never fancy, that, being neither wife nor mother, she is exempt from the law: she cannot balance that decree of God by the foolish customs of society or the weak objections of her kindred. Never let her say she does not *need* to labor. Disease, depression, moral idiocy, or inertia, follow on an idle life. He who never rests has made woman in His image; and health, beauty, force, and influence follow on the steps of labor alone.

I shall not pursue this subject; for it is far easier for you to think it out, than to gather the facts I wish to bring before you. Read " Shirley," and let the saddest hours of Caroline Helstone's life bear witness for thousands who never find a vocation. Read the " Professor," and let its sweet stimulus kindle in you some appreciation of the joy which mutual labor can bring to a happy husband and wife.

Sad, indeed, then, is it when man himself represses a woman's longing for work, whether from false tenderness, from a dread of public opinion, a shrinking from her ultimate independence, or a small personal jealousy. That he does, in the aggregate and as an individual, so repress it, is unfortunately matter of history: it is no invention of an outraged inferior. I could offer you many private examples of this; but those that carry proofs of their reality with them will, I fear, seem very familiar. The first consists in the opposition shown to the attempt of Mr. Bennett to establish young women as watchmakers. Honorary Secretary to the Horological Department of the great Exhibition, he could not help observing the superiority of the Genevese watches, in cheapness and convenience of carriage. In England, watches are so dear that only the privileged classes can carry them. It would be for the interests of the manufacturers, of course, to be able to compete with the Swiss; but they were too short-sighted to see it. Finding that twenty thousand women and girls were employed in Switzerland in the manufacture of watches and watchmakers' tools, Mr. Bennett undertook to deliver a public lecture on the subject. It was interrupted by hisses, and broken up like a New-York convention. Three well-educated women then applied to him to be taught; but no Englishman could be found to take them. A Swiss, settled in London, did. They made more progress in six months than ordinary boys in six years; but they, as well as their teacher, were so cruelly persecuted, that it was found necessary to relinquish the attempt. My impression is, though I cannot find the account in print, that a further effort was made on a more extended scale, something like a school; and this was resisted by such combined effort on the part of the trade, that Mr. Bennett and his friends began to make a stir through the press. The "Edinburgh Review" mentions a watchmaker's wife who wished to work with her husband in his special department. Finding that it could not be done with the consent of the trade, she undertook, instead, the engraving of the brass work; but, though working in her own house, she was at last successful only under the plea that she had been regularly apprenticed by her father, also in the business. She persevered, and taught her two daughters; and so will many others.

Women in England must certainly make watches; and the time is not far distant when the men of Coventry will yield to this demand, as they have already yielded to others. A few years ago, winding silk, weaving ribbon, and pasting patterns of floss upon cards, excited the same opposition; but now thousands of women pursue these employments, and the men look on as quietly as the grazing cattle in the fields.

"The first steam factory in Coventry," says the "Edinburgh Review" for October, 1859, — "a very small factory, — was burned down during a quarrel about wages. Then there was an opposition to the employment of women at the looms. To this day, one of the lightest and easiest processes in the manufacture, which a child might manage, is engrossed by the men, under heavy penalties."

Fancy a strong man winding silk for a whole day, or sorting colors in floss! How has he ever degraded himself to such girls' work?

I need only remind you of the formal petition sent in at the time of the opening of the School of Design at Marlborough House, to entreat the Government not to instruct and aid women, lest the poor, helpless men should starve! A similar prejudice, much more active than any in America, prevents English women from qualifying themselves as physicians. Dr. Spencer, of Bristol, really educated his daughter as an accoucheuse; but the prejudice was so strong that she was not allowed to practise, and became a governess instead. The same prejudice kept the English Army suffering for months, while it delayed the departure of female nurses to the Crimea.

In Staffordshire, women are employed to paint crockery and china, which they can do with more taste and grace than men. It seems hardly credible, that the desire of the men to keep down their wages should deprive the females of the customary hand-rest; which would, of course, diminish the fatigue, and make the pencil-stroke more certain. I am happy to believe that not an employer in the United States would submit to this absurd demand; and the result of any such attempt on the part of workmen would probably be a general permission to leave. We are, in this country, much more free from the control of guilds and unions of various sorts than the people of England; yet the conduct of our printers furnishes a fair parallel to these foreign facts. Within a few years, there have been more than twenty strikes in printing-offices, consequent upon the employment of a few women; and the result has generally been an entire change of hands, masters in America not enduring dictation.

In August of 1854, the journeymen employed in the office of the "Philadelphia Daily Register" left the office, in high dudgeon, because the publisher had employed two women as type-setters in a separate office. They acted in conformity to a resolve of the Printers' Union, and were permitted to depart. But this was not all. Threats of personal violence followed all who sought the waiting work, and an attempt was made to cut the rope by which the forms are raised. The result would have been to break up the type, prevent the issue of the paper, and run the risk of endangering life. Complaints were lodged against the printers; and, after a hearing, they were each held to bail in six hundred dollars, to answer to the charge of conspiracy, at the Court of Quarter Sessions.

About the same time, a printer in the same establishment with the "Lily," but working on the "Home Visitor," refused to give some necessary instruction to a girl employed on the first paper. It was found that all the hands had signed an agreement never to work with or instruct a woman! The men, after proper remonstrance, were dismissed, and their places supplied by four women and three men, who worked harmoniously together. That was only five years ago, and now there are hundreds of female printers in Ohio; and one orphan girl has risen from type-setting to an editor's chair and a handsome competence.

Jealousy in America sometimes takes a more comical form. Coming home lately from a Female School of Design in another city, I expressed some disappointment at the character of the work and management. A young man in the room spoke of the impossibility of a woman's ever learning to design, in terms so contemptuous that I did not think it worth while to answer him. Making some inquiries, however, in private, I found that his master had often reproached him with *falling behind the women* at the school; so that personal pique had more to do with the whole thing than any real experience.*

---

* When I first began to lecture, many persons, sincerely interested in my success, objected to what they called the "antagonistic" tone occasionally adopted. They thought I ought to take for granted the cheerful co-opera-

VERIFY YOUR CREDENTIALS. 185

But, having made these remarks, I must recur to my previous statement, — that, in the main, no jealousy of cliques, no legal restrictions, prevent women from taking their proper place. A want of respect for woman, and a want of respect for labor, latent and unacknowledged in the public mind, must be

tion of the world, and that the woman's cause was the loser whenever the audience was reminded of actual difficulties in the way. But it would be hardly worth while for a woman to enter the desk, only to hedge it in with compromise and evasion. The simple truth is the "utmost skill" she needs to seek; and no reform built upon an inaccurate survey can be lasting. Only by telling our brothers openly what we think of their jealousy can we ever hope to shame them out of it. That the day of opposition is *not* passed; that the way of duty cannot, even in America, be trod in satin slippers, — the following extract, cut from a weekly paper while I am writing this note, will plainly show : —

"The Pennsylvania Medical Society has exhibited a narrow-mindedness altogether disgraceful to its members, by adopting a resolution recommending 'the members of the regular profession to withhold from the faculties and graduates of Female Medical Colleges all countenance and support; and that they cannot, consistently with sound *medical ethics*, consult or hold professional intercourse with their professors or alumni.' The Female Medical Colleges of Pennsylvania, it should be remembered, are strictly allopathic: so we are forced to conclude, that the objection to them is founded *solely* upon the fact that they afford the means of education to women. We echo the sentiment of the 'Philadelphia Sunday Dispatch:' 'Shame upon the men who, while prating about their respectability, would combine to rob women of the means of supporting themselves and their families! Such infinitesimal littleness cannot benefit them. The public are ever willing to aid the weak, and support them against the strong. The war against women cannot be sustained by the public voice: it will recoil upon and injure those who are so arbitrary and selfish as to endeavor to interfere with them.'" — *Antislavery Standard*, July, 1859.

"The medico-chirurgical school of Lisbon has granted the diploma of *pharmacienne* to Mesdames Marie Fajardo and Caroline de Matos, after a legal examination. These illustrious *pharmaceuticas* have a regular knowledge of their business, and passed a preliminary examination in 1859. 'The Gazette' does not say if they are *religieuses* charged with the management of a private pharmacy, or whether they are acting as civil *pharmaciennes*. In one of the hospitals of the city is a female dispenser, whose knowledge, accuracy, and care are said to be reliable and satisfactory."

overcome before she can do it. The overworked and ill-paid woman has seized every chance to slight her work; and an idea has gone abroad, that no slopwork will be fit for sale unless a man inspects it. So New York and Paris have man-tailors and man-milliners; and the poor, tempted, stricken girls are brought into contact, in the pursuit of bread, with the very men most likely to take advantage of every failure. Very sad stories could be told of work rejected day after day, on account of pretended faults, till the starving victim drops at the feet of the treacherous overseer, only to be trampled, in the end, under those of the whole town. Educated, respectable women should have the giving-out and the inspection of woman's work; but educated and respectable women will never stand in such a position till public opinion teaches them that all *labor* is honorable, and that no lady will ever sit with folded hands. How we rate an idle boy! how we bear with a dawdling girl! That father grows impatient whose son does not rise early, or show some desire for employment; but the same man keeps his daughters in Berlin wool and yellow novels, and looks to marriage as their salvation, even when he blushes to be told of it.

To prove this, let me show you that many employments have been open to a degree not generally acknowledged; and a safe foundation for this assertion will be found in the census of the United Kingdom and that of the United States.

It is a singular fact, that there are a great many

more women in England in business for themselves than employed as tenders or clerks; while, in America, the fact, at the present day, is directly the reverse.

It was not so in the time of the Revolution. Then, as in France, the men went to the war. Women of shrewdness and ability managed their husbands' affairs, — the shops and trades of the nation, — and grew so independent thereby, that even Mrs. John Adams had to rebuke her husband for the absurd inequalities of privilege which his new government sustained. In England, the deficient education of the lower classes makes it almost impossible for the women to make change quickly, or keep accounts; and we smile as we find the " Edinburgh Review " gravely contending that woman may master the rule of three; that, at least, they ought to have a chance to *try:* and we can afford to smile; for our public schools have taught us how much quicker most women can count than most men. While, therefore, the want of education has prevented a certain class of English women from becoming clerks or book-keepers, the national habits of thrift, and a certain respectable pride in a family shop or trade, have induced thousands of a superior class to assume, upon a father's or husband's death, the charge of his establishment, and so secure a competence for the heirs. This is what we could wish our women to do. We all know how frequently the whole social position of a family here changes with the death of its head. Let our women prevent this for the future, by cherishing a natural ambition to do for their children what the fathers of those children would have done.

The last census of the United Kingdom shows, that, while the female population has increased in such proportion that there are now *eight women* where there were *seven*, there are *eight working* women where there were only *six;* that is, there are more new workers than new women. There are 1,250,000 women earning their own bread as independently as any men. Of these, there are —

    385,000 employed in Textile manufactures,
    40,000 in Metal-works, and
    128,418 in Agriculture.

I hope these statements will not seem useless and superficial to you.

This hour cannot be better employed than in opening to you some of the mysteries of woman's work in England.

Among the 128,418 women employed in Agriculture, there are 64,000 dairy-women; not women who tend a single cow for a single family, but women of muscle, who wield large tubs and heavy presses, who turn cheeses and slap butter by the hundred-weight. Then there are market-gardeners, who not only raise their stock, but drive it to the town for sale; bee-mistresses and florists, of whom there are many among the Quakers; flax-producers, who not only raise the pretty blue-eyed flowers, but beat the silicious fibres apart; and they are followed by hay-makers, reapers, and hop-pickers, gracefully garlanding the group.

Naturally connected with this first interest of the soil is the second, or Mining. It is no longer considered fit for women to work in shafts, though the need of bread forces many to evade the law. The census, however, cannot touch them: the seven thousand women it reports as engaged in Mining are employed in dressing and sorting ore, and as washers and strainers of clay for the potteries, — heavy and disagreeable if not unfit work.

The next largest interest is that of the Fisheries. The Pilchard fishery employs many thousands of women. Jersey oysters alone employ over one thousand. Then come the —

> Herring,
> Cod,
> Whale, and
> Lobster fisheries.

The work in connection with the whale fishery consists chiefly in what is done after the cargo is landed. Apart from the Christie Johnstones, — the aristocrats of the trade, — the sea nurtures an heroic class, like Grace Darling, who stand aghast, as she did, when society rewards a deed of humanity, and cry out in expostulation, " Why, every girl on the coast would have done as I did!"

In natural connection with these come the —

> Kelp-burners, the
> Netters, and the
> Bathers,

or women who manage the bathing machines used on the coast. Then come two hundred thousand female servants; of which, largest in number, shortest in life, and, of course, the worst paid, are the general housemaids, or unhappy servants-of-all-work. Then come —

> Brewers,
> Custom-house and Police searchers,
> Matrons of jails,
> Lighthouse-keepers, and
> Pew-openers.

I cannot mention the Matrons of jails, without a sigh, when I remember, that at our common jail and at Charlestown there is no proper matron; and sickness, death, and childbirth meet only with such care as women detained as witnesses, or inebriates, can offer. Surely a Christian community should furnish Christian, womanly ministrations to its prisoners; and I would that some noble soul in an able body might be found to take up this work! Pew-opening has never been a trade in this community; but, as there are signs that it may become so, I advise our women to keep an eye upon it!

There are in the United Kingdom —

> 500,000 business-women,
> 94,000 shoemakers' wives,
> 27,000 victuallers' wives,
> 26,000 butcheresses,
> 14,000 milk-women,
> 10,000 beershop-keepers,
> 9,000 innkeepers, and
> 8,000 hack proprietors.

The difference between the employers and the employed is shown in the following numbers. There are —
> 29,000 shopkeepers, and only
> 1,742 shopwomen;

since the lower class of English women are seldom taught writing or accounts.

Telegraphic Reporters, Phonographers, and Railway-clerks, are on the increase. In reporting the Bright Festival at Manchester last year, the speed and accuracy of the young women were thought very remarkable. Six whole columns were transmitted at the rate of twenty-nine words a minute, almost without mistake, although the subject of the speeches was political, and so supposed to be beyond their comprehension!

Several railways employ women as clerks and ticket-sellers, and the results are more than satisfactory. Thus far the census; which has not been without its interest, since, in English parlance, shoemaker-wife means not merely the wife of a shoemaker, but a wife who shares her husband's labor, or has succeeded to it on his death. Butcher-wife also means a woman who can buy and sell stock, pickle meat, and perhaps drive a cart through the town.

Now for the results of some private letters. When I spoke of forty thousand Metal-workers, your minds did not revert, I trust, to those dens at Wiltenhall, where women have been struck with hammers, files, and even bars of iron glowing at a white heat.

Now, at least, let us visit a pleasanter scene. A man has forged and rolled out the sheet which is soon to pass for a hundred gross of Gillott's pens; but a woman cuts and bends and stamps, grinds, splits, polishes, and packs it, so that her sisters may have pleasure in the using.

It was at Birmingham that your gold chain was made. A man's strength drew out the precious wire; but hundreds of young girls cut it to the required length, shaped it on a metal die to the required pattern, soldered it invisibly over a jet of gas-light, ground the facets till they gleamed and polished the whole length to tempt the gazer's eye. Quiet, diligent, skilful, tidy, they sit; with polished slippers bobbing along the floor; not quite so healthy as those who labor on the pens, for the gas and solder do an unwholesome work. Others burnish the silver plate, sort needles, paint iron and papier-maché trays; and hundreds more are busy cutting and polishing screws, — a work mainly in their hands, because men cannot be trusted with the delicate manipulation.

There is a covered button, my brother, on your coat. Women cut the metal, the cloth cover, the paper stuffing, the silk lining; a child piles these in proper order; and, by one stroke of a magic press, a woman throws them out a finished button.

One young girl in London began life by designing for such buttons, till she found that she had a soul above them, and cheerfully entered an artistic career.

Nail-cutting and hook-and-eye making employ others; and, if we take a book into our hand, women follow us through all the stages of its manufacture. A woman cut and cleaned the rags, counted the sheets of paper, and set off the reams; a woman may have set the types; perhaps some worn-out seamstress wrote the verses, or a female physician composed the thesis: a woman *may* print, a woman certainly *will* fold it down and stitch it for the binder. A woman will engrave on wood its illustrations, or color in her own home its fine photographs or drawings: at the very last, her white hand will touch with gleams of gold its tinted edges or many-hued envelope.

It is women who pack cards and throw off damaged paper. I have not obtained any reliable account of English female card-makers; but there must be many. In an old Nuremberg rate-book are the names of "Elizabeth and Margaret," *Karten-mücherin,* reported in 1436 and 1438. Cards were invented in 1361. In about seventy years, therefore, the manufacture had passed into woman's hand. In my notes from the census, I find no mention of wood-engravers: but, in 1839, Charlotte Nesbit, Marianne Williams, Mary Byfield, Mary and Elizabeth Clint, held honorable positions among English wood-engravers; while, at the close of the last century, Elizabeth Blackwell executed botanical plates, and Angelica Kauffman engraved on steel, to the satisfaction of Sir Joshua Reynolds. In London, recently, one accomplished female engraver has turned her steel plates into a pleasant country-house, which she means to furnish with the proceeds of her delicate painting on glass.

A whole volume might be written concerning English female printers. Turning over some old books the other day in the Antiquarian Rooms at Worcester, I came upon Elizabeth Bathurst's " Truth Vindicated," printed and sold by Mary Hinde, at No. 2 in George's Yard, Lombard Street, 1774. A little farther along, I found Sophia Hume's " Letters to South Carolina," printed and sold by Luke Hinde, at the Bible in George's Yard, Lombard Street, 1752. Good Quaker books, both of them; and the titlepages told a pleasant story. Here, at the sign of the Bible, Luke Hinde carried on his work in 1752. When he died, his widow kept the establishment open, and taught her girls to stand at the forms; so, twenty-two years after (in 1774), the place goes on in her name. No change; only some dissenting wind has blown down the Old Bible, and a gilded number two shines in its stead. It is the history of half the businesswomen in England, and a very creditable history for Mary Hinde.

On those dishes of Liverpool ware are pretty pictures in gray ink. Women took them wet from the copperplate, and, laying them along the biscuit, carried it to the furnace; there the paper burns away: while others paint and gild, or, with hideous clatter of blood-stones, polish off the finer ware.

In the next street, hundreds of women make paper-bags and pill-boxes, without wasting a square inch of material.

Not long ago, two young girls, whose father's clerkship was ill paid, took to making artificial teeth, and succeeded so well as to obtain constant orders and a competence. More cheering still: a young servant, with strong elbows, took to French polishing, and gave desk and work-box and inlaid cabinet a gloss that no varnish of man could match. For two or three years she made contracts with upholsterers, and kept herself in profitable work: then Cupid pinched the strong elbows, and she slipped out of permanent reputation as a cabinetmaker's wife.

In brushmaking, women sort the hair, and set it in the holes. The delicate, cone-like arrangement of the badger's hair, in the modern shaving-brush, can be made only by a woman's hand; and she who has skill to do it well may ask her own wages.

Then there are glove-cleaners; women who strain silk, in fluting, across the old-fashioned work-bag or the parlor-organ front; women who shell pease and beans at so much a quart, and who make the thousands of baskets for the fruiterer's stall. Passing the white-lead factory at meal-times, you will see fifty women file away, whose duty it is to pile the lead for oxidation; and thousands, very different from these, sit making artificial flowers, many of them cheap enough, but others, from their exquisite grace and naturalness, bringing the artist's own price.

I have purposely dwelt on all these avocations. As

you have followed me, has it seemed to you that we wanted more avenues for manual labor? As many as you please. We are bound to inherit the whole earth. But it seems to me that what is most needed is, first, respect for woman as a laborer, and then respect for labor itself.

When men respect women as human beings, consequently as laborers, they will pay them as good wages as men; and then uncommon skill or power to work will be set free from the old forcing-pump and siphon, and we shall see what women can do. When men respect labor, — respect it so far, that they hold a woman honored when she seeks it, — then women of a higher rank will seek to invest their capital in mercantile experiments; will establish factories or workshops; will organize groups of struggling sisters; and the class that most needs to be helped, the idle rich, will find happiness and honor, will find help, in offering opportunities to the lowest.

What the lowest class of women need is active brains to plan and think for them. There are plenty of these active brains at the West End, tingling with neuralgia, hot with idleness, dizzy with waltzing. Offer a government testimonial to the first girl of rank who will carry her brains to a market, and you will see what a throng of aspirants we shall have; letting it be understood, mind you, that the public feeling sustains the government testimonial.

Let us ask, then, a few questions about the state of female labor in the United States. Our census is by no means so complete as that of Great Britain; and our statements will, therefore, be less accurate.

At the close of the Revolution, there were in New England, and perhaps farther south, many women conducting large business establishments, and few females employed as clerks, partly because we were still English, and had not lost English habits. Men went to the war or the General Court, and their wives soon learned to carry on the business upon which not only the family bread, but the fate of the nation, depended; while our common schools had not yet begun to fit women for book-keepers and clerks.

The Island of Nantucket was, at the close of the war, a good example of the whole country. Great destitution existed on the establishment of peace. The men began the whale fishery with redoubled energy: some fitted out and others manned the ships; while the women laid aside distaff and loom to attend to trade. A very interesting letter from Mrs. Eliza Barney to Mr. Higginson gives me many particulars. "Fifty years ago," she says, "all the dry-goods and groceries were kept by women, who went to Boston semi-annually to renew their stock. The heroine of 'Miriam Coffin' was one of the most influential of our commercial women. She not only traded in dry-goods and provisions, but fitted vessels for the merchant service. Since that time, I can recall near seventy women who have successfully engaged in commerce, brought up and educated large families, and retired with a competence. It was the influence of capitalists from the Continent that drove the Nantucket women out of the trade; and they only resumed it a few years since, when the California emigration made it necessary. Five dry-goods and a few large groceries are now carried on by women, as also one druggist's shop." Mrs. Gaskell, in her "Life of Charlotte Brontë," mentions a woman living as a druggist, I think, at Haworth; and I have always been surprised that this business was not left to women. Our Nantucket druggist is doing well. In Pennsylvania, the Quaker view of the duties and rights of women contributed to throw many into trade at the same period. One lady in Philadelphia transferred a large wholesale business to two nephews, and died wealthy. I saw a letter the other day, which gave an interesting account of two girls who got permission there to sell a little stock in their father's shop. One began with sixty-two cents, which she invested in a dozen tapes. The other had three dollars. In a few years, they bought their father out. The little tape-seller married, and carried her husband eight thousand dollars; while the single sister kept on till she accumulated twenty thousand dollars, and took a poor boy into partnership.

I have spoken of English female printers. The first paper ever issued in Rhode Island was printed by a brother of Dr. Franklin, at Newport. He died early, and his widow continued the work. She was aided by her two daughters, swift and correct compositors. She was made printer to the Colony, and, in 1745, printed an edition of the laws, in 346 folio pages. That she found time to do something else, you may judge from this advertisement: —

"The printer hereof prints linens, calicoes, silk, &c., in figures, in lively and durable colors, without the offensive smell which commonly attends linen printed here."

Margaret Draper printed the "Boston News Letter," and was so good a Tory that the English Government pensioned her when the war drove her away. Clementina Bird edited and printed the "Virginia Gazette," and Thomas Jefferson wrote for her paper. Penelope Russell also printed the "Censor," in Boston, in 1771.

When we record these things, and think how women are pressing into printing-offices in our time, it is pleasant to find a generous action to sustain them. At a recent Printers' Convention held in Springfield, Ill., the following resolution was adopted: —

"*Whereas*, The employment of females in printing-offices as compositors has, wherever adopted, been found a decided benefit as regards moral influence and steady work, and also as offering better wages to a deserving class; therefore, be it —

"*Resolved*, That this Association recommends to its members the employment of females whenever practicable."

Mrs. Barney tells us that failures were very uncommon in Nantucket while women managed the business; and some of the largest and safest fortunes in Boston were founded by women, one of whom, I remember, rode in her own chariot, and kept fifty thousand dollars in gold in the chimney corner, lest the banks should not be as cautious in their dealings as herself. While writing these pages, I have visited such a woman, still living in Prince Street, at the age of ninety-five. Her name is Hillman. She lived for sixty-four years in the same house, and made her property by a large grocery business, and speculations on a strip of real estate. Her father, Mr. William Haggo, was a nautical-instrument maker; and she has a very remarkable head, and as conservative a horror of modern changes — steam-bakeries, for instance — as any of you could wish.* Some of you will remember the two sisters Johnson, who, for more than half a century, kept a crockery-shop on Hanover Street, and separated about two years ago, — one sister to retire on her earnings; the other to rest in a quiet grave, at the age of fourscore. The spirit of modern improvement has since seized hold of the old shop.

It was one of the most distinguished of our female merchants — Martha Buckminster Curtis — who planted, in Framingham, the first potatoes ever set in New England; and you will start to hear that our dear and honored friend Ann Bent entered on her business career so long ago as 1784, at the age of six-

---

* I first saw Mrs. Hillman the day after the destruction of the steam-bakery at the North End. She was sitting up, reading the account of it, without glasses, and eloquent in behalf of the trade, and against innovations. Since the above passage was written, she has passed away.

teen. She first entered a crockery-ware and dry-goods firm; but, at the age of twenty-one, established herself in Washington, north of Summer Street, where we remember her. She soon became the centre of a happy home, where sisters, cousins, nieces, and young friends received her affectionate care. The intimacy which linked her name to that of Mary Ware is fresh in all our minds. What admirable health she contrived to keep we may judge from the fact, that she dined at one brother's table on Thanksgiving Day for over fifty years. She was the valued friend of Channing and Gannett; and her character magnified her office, ennobled her condition, gave dignity to labor, and won the love and respect of all the worthy. Less than two years ago, at the age of ninety, she left us; but I wished to mention both her and Miss Kinsley in this connection, because they were the first women in our society to confer a merchantable value upon taste.

Instead of importing largely themselves, they bought of the New-York importers the privilege of selection, and always took the prettiest and nicest pieces out of every case. As they paid for this privilege themselves, so they charged their customers for it, by asking a little more on each yard of goods than the common dealer.

I know nothing for which it is pleasanter to pay than for taste. When time is precious (and to all serious people it soon becomes so), it is a comfort to go to one counter, sure that in ten minutes you can purchase what it would take a whole morning to winnow from the countless shelves of the town.

Scientific pursuits cannot be said to be fairly opened to women here. The two ladies at work on the Coast Survey were employed by special favor, and probably on account of near relationship to the gentleman who had charge of the department of latitudes and longitudes. Their work is done at home. Some years ago, Congress made an appropriation for an American nautical almanac; and Lieut. Davis was appointed to take charge of it. Three ladies were at one time employed upon the lunar tables. Lieut. Davis told one of them that he preferred the women's work, because it was quite as accurate, and much more neat, than the men's. In 1854, Maria Mitchell was employed in computing for this almanac, with the same salary that would be given to a man. I may say, in this connection, that a great number of female clerks have been employed in Washington for many years. The work has generally been obtained by women who had lost a husband or a father in the service of his country; and, I am proud to say, such women have usually been paid the same wages as men. During Mr. Fillmore's administration, two women wrote for the Treasury, on salaries of twelve hundred and fifteen hundred dollars a year; but the succeeding administration reformed this abuse, and very few are now at work.

In 1845, there were employed in the Textile manufactures of the United States, 55,828 men and 75,710

VERIFY YOUR CREDENTIALS. 203

women. This proportion, or a still greater preponderance of female labor, — that is, from one-third to one-half, — appears in all the factory returns. As an *employed* class, women seem to be more in number than men: as *employers*, they are very few. The same census reports them as —

Makers of gloves,	Physicians,
Makers of glue, [leaf,	Picklers and preservers,
Workers in gold and silver	Saddle and harness makers,
Hair weavers,	Shoemakers,
Hat and cap makers,	Soda-room keepers,
Hose-weavers,	Snuff and cigar makers,
Workers in India-rubber,	Stock and suspender makers,
Lamp-makers,	Truss-makers,
Laundresses,	Typers and stereotypers,
Leechers,	Umbrella-makers,
Milliners,	Upholsterers,
Morocco-workers,	Card-makers, and
Nurses,	Grinders of watch crystals.
Paper-hangers,	7,000 women in all.

There is no mention of female wood-engravers, though we have had such for twenty-five years; and pupils from the Schools of Design have already achieved a certain success in this direction. To the enumeration of the census, I may add, from my own observation, —

Photographists and daguerrotypists,	Tobacco-packers,
	Paper-box makers,
Phonographers,	Embroiderers,
House and sign painters,	Fur-sewers; and, at the West,
Button-makers,	
Fruit-hawkers,	Reapers and hay-makers.

In a New-Haven clock factory, seven women are employed among seventy men, on half-wages; and the manufacturer takes great credit to himself for his liberality. At Waltham, also, a watch factory has been lately started, in which many women are employed.* In the census of the city of Boston for 1845, the various employments of women are thus given: —

Artificial-flower makers,	Comb-makers,
Boardinghouse-keepers,	Confectioners,
Bookbinders,	Corset-dealers,
Printers,	Corset-makers,
Blank-book makers,	Card-makers,
Bonnet-dealers,	Professed cooks,
Bonnet-makers,	Cork-cutters,
Workers in straw,	Domestics,
Shoe and boot makers,	Dress-makers,
Band and fancy box makers,	Match-makers,
Brush-makers,	Fringe and tassel makers,
Cap-makers,	Fur-sewers,
Clothiers,	Hair-cloth weavers, and
Collar-makers,	Map-colorers.

---

* I do not dwell upon this watch factory in the text, because, although fifty women are at work with one hundred and fifty men, they are only "tending machines;" so that, although employment is open, a career can hardly be said to be. The watches made at Waltham by machinery are said to be so superior to all others, that they are used by preference on the race-courses to time the horses. Men and women do not compete with each other there; but both are at service, with a steam-engine for their master.

For the first two months, the women earn two dollars and fifty cents *a week;* for the third, three dollars; and, after that, four dollars. The men earn from five shillings to two dollars a *day.* It seems that no special skill is required in the women, while the men in a few departments are still paid according to their ability. The steam-engine, it appears, has not yet learned how to cook dials! In this case, the operator must hold the dial, turning it evenly, as if he were a smoke-jack, which requires judgment and "faculty"!

I think you cannot fail to see, from this list, how very imperfect the enumeration is: not a single washerwoman nor charwoman, for one thing, upon it. Yet here you have the occupations of 4,970 women. Of these, 4,046 are servants, — a number which has, at least, doubled since then; and which leaves only 924 women for all other avocations.

In New York, Mr. Jobson, formerly surgeon-dentist to Victoria, offers to instruct women in the duties of a dentist. I do not know that he has a single practising pupil; but he asserts that some of the most distinguished dentists in Europe are women. A few years since, the town of Ashfield elected two women and three men to the duties of a School Committee, — duties for which women are greatly to be preferred. A letter from the senior lady shows that one of them at least never attempted to do the actual work to which she was called, considering it *out* of her sphere! Does any one in this audience suppose that those women felt incapable of the duty? We know better; but they were not of the stuff of which martyrs are made, and, deferring to popular views, set aside a sacred opportunity. They might have so done that work as to have secured the election of women for ever after.

The occupations of which the census takes no account may be classed as —

        Professions,
        Public Offices,
        Semi-professions, and
        Arts.

Under the Professions come —

   Physicians,
   Lawyers,
   Ministers,

of which there are increasing numbers.

Under Public Offices we find —

   Postmistresses,
   Registers of Deeds,
   The few calculators at Washington, and
   School-committee women at the West.

It is probably known to you all how largely the rural post-office duties are performed by women; petty politicians obtaining the appointment, and leaving wives and daughters to do the work. There are several Registers of Deeds; but I know only one, — Olive Rose, of Thomaston, Me. She was elected in 1853, by 469 votes against 205; was officially notified, and required to give bonds. Her emolument depends upon fees, and ranges between three and four hundred dollars per annum. She continues to perform the duties of her office, and, if an exquisitely clear handwriting is of service there, will probably never be displaced.

Under the head of Semi-professions come —

   Teachers,
   Librarians,
   Editors,
   Lecturers, and
   Matrons.

Under that of Artists, —

> Painters,
> Sculptors,
> Teachers of Drawing and the like,
> Designers,
> Engravers,
> Public Singers, and
> Actresses.

I am sorry to conclude these attempts at statistics with one reliable estimate, which holds, like a nutshell, the kernel of this question of female labor.

In 1850, there were engaged in shoemaking, in the town of Lynn, 3,729 males and 6,412 females, — nearly twice as many women as men; yet, in the monthly payment of wages, only half as much money was paid to women as to men. The three thousand men received seventy-five thousand dollars a month; and the six thousand women, thirty-seven thousand dollars: that is, the women's wages were, on the average, only one-quarter as much as those of the men.

If we inquire into details, we may find many exceptional causes at work, not perceptible at first sight: still this remarkable fact remains essentially unchanged.

In my first lecture, I showed you that women were starving, and that vice is a better paymaster than labor. I showed you the awful falsity of the cry, "Do not let women work: we will work for them. They are too tender, too delicate, to bide the rough usage of the world." I showed you that they were not only working hard, but had been working at hard and unwholesome work, not merely in this century, but in all centuries since the world began. I showed you how man himself has turned them back, when they have entered a well-paid career. Practically, the command of society to the uneducated class is, "Marry, stitch, die, or do worse."

Plenty of employments are open to them; but all are underpaid. They will never be better paid till women of rank begin to work for money, and so create a respect for woman's labor; and women of rank will never do this till American men feel what all American men profess,— a proper respect for Labor, as God's own demand upon every human soul,— and so teach American women to feel it. How often have I heard that every woman willing to work may find employment! The terrible reverses of 1837 taught many men in this country that they were "out of luck:" how absurd, then, this statement with regard to women! One reason why so many young women are attracted to the Catholic Church is, that the Catholic Church is a good economist, and does not tolerate an idle member. In Catholic countries,— nay, in Protestant,— the gray hood of the Sister of Charity is as sacred as a crown.

When I think how happy human life might be, if men and women worked freely together, I lose patience. Such marriages as I can dream of,— where, household duties thriftily managed and speedily discharged, the wife assumes some honorable trust, or finds a noble task for her delicate hands; while the husband follows his under separate auspices! Occupied with real service to men and each other, how happily would they meet at night to discuss the hours they had lived apart, to help each other's work by each other's wit, and to draw vital refreshment from the caresses of their children! It is your distrust, O men! that prevents your having such homes as poets fancy. You will not help women to form them. The sturdy pine pushes through the tightest soil, and will grow, though nothing more genial than a November sky bid it welcome; but tender anemones — wind-flowers, as we call them — must be coaxed through the loose loam sifted from thousands of autumn leaves, and tremble to the faintest air. Yet are anemones fairer than the pine, and their lovely blossoming a fit reward for Nature's pains. Follow Nature, and offer the encouragement which those you love best daily need. Do it for your own sakes; for proper employment will diffuse serenity over the anxious faces you are too apt to see. Do not fancy that the conventions of society can ever prevail over the will, it may be the freak, of Nature. That stepdame is absolute. She set Hercules spinning, and sent Joan of Arc to Orleans. She taught Mrs. John Stuart Mill political economy, and Monsieur Malignon netting and lace-work. She enables women to bear immense burdens, heat, cold, and frost; she sets them in the thick of the battle even; while in South Carolina, and in the heart of Africa, or among the Indians of the Rocky Mountains, old men croon over forsaken babes till the milk flows in to their withered breasts.*

Women want work for all the reasons that men want it. When they see this, and begin to do it faithfully, you will respect their work, and pay them for it. We are all taught that we are the children of God; only Mohammedans deny their women that rank: yet we are left without duties, as if such a thing were possible, — left without work that offers any adequate *end* as a stimulus to diligence or ambition; and, until "Work" becomes man's cry of inspiration, woman will never train herself to do her work well.

It was Margaret Fuller, I think, who wrote of the Polish heroine, the Countess Emily Plater, "*She* is the figure I want for my frontispiece. Short was her career. Like the Maid of Orleans, she only lived long enough to *verify her credentials*, and then passed from a scene on which she was probably a premature apparition." Ah! that is what all women should do, — verify their credentials! "Say what you please," said a young girl to her lover, as they passed out of a Woman's Convention; "a woman that *can* speak like Lucretia Mott, *ought* to speak." And men themselves cannot escape from this conviction. The duty of women, therefore, is to inspire it by doing whatever they undertake worthily and well; patient in waiting for opportunities, prompt to seize, conscientious to profit by them.

---

* Livingstone's "Africa." Paul Kane's "Travels in the North-west."

The Sorbonne, which still excludes woman from its courses and colleges, has formed a separate course, and now institutes examinations, and distributes diplomas for women. The Committee consists of three of the Inspectors of the University, two Catholic priests, one Protestant clergyman, and three ladies.

A daughter of the greatest living French poet passed the examination lately for the mere honor of it. Another girl, the daughter of one of the highest public functionaries, passed the examinations; going through the winter twilight every morning at five, that she might not only be permitted to found a school on her estate, but secure the right to teach in it. Aware that her rank would befriend her, she concealed her name that she might owe nothing to favor. That is the right spirit. When a majority, or even a plurality, of women are capable of it, farewell to lecturers and lectures, to conventions, special pleadings, and the like! The whole harvest will be open, and the laborers will come, bringing their sheaves with them.

In receiving lately a letter from a distinguished French author,—Madame Sirault,—I was struck by the following sentence: "Every career from which woman is steadily repulsed by man is, by this fact alone, marked with the seal of death. The very repulse stigmatizes it. Man may not be conscious of what he does; but the career which is too vile for a woman to enter has outlived all chance of reform, and must perish with its abuses."

And, heroic as this statement may seem to you, it is a simple statement of fact. Can man demand of woman a higher purity, a more ideal Christian grace, than the letter of the Scripture, than the spirit of Christ, demands of man himself? — "Be ye therefore perfect, as your Father in heaven is also perfect."

That was the clear command laid upon the simple fishermen, upon Luke the physician and Matthew the publican, as well as upon Mary and Martha. The world's eyes are slowly opening to the need of a pure life in men; and it helps to show men what they ought to be, when women knock at the doors of their workshops, and insist on entering.

"What!" says the soldier, "must my sister follow me to the field to take this blood-stained hand; to see me decked in the spoils of fallen men; or hunting unprotected women like a brute beast, till they fall senseless on the bodies of those they loved?"

"Shut her out!" cries the minister of state. "Shall my *sister* see these hands, dripping with blood-money, bribed by a slave power or a party interest, signing papers that condemn children yet unborn to the miseries of hopeless war?"

"Shut her out!" cries the advocate. "I am preparing to defend this man for luring helpless innocence to the brink of hell, for building up a fortune on dollars wrung from starving women, for putting a bullet through his brother because he did not live a life purer than his own."

"Turn her out!" cries the judge. "She will see

that my scales are loaded. She heard that railroad company offer me a bribe. She caught a whisper just now from the husband of yonder outraged woman. She will hear the liquor dealer's counsel, and see the golden lure that South Carolina offers when the fugitive stands at the bar. Turn her out!"

"Turn her out!" says the physician. "Shall she hear me jeer at what she deems holy? Would you have her grow shameless also?"

"Shut her out," says the trader, "while I mark my goods! This spool of cotton is short fifty yards: mark it two hundred. This yard of muslin was made at Manchester: sew on the Paris tack. This shawl was woven in France: label it Cashmere. Color that cheese with annatto, weigh down that butter with salt, dilute that rose-water from the spring, grate up turnip to mix with that horseradish; but turn that woman out!"

"Turn her out!" cries the priest, last of all. "Polemics and theology have no charms for her. She will ask me why I do not do justly and love mercy. Turn her out!"

"Turn her out!" and, in the shudder which creeps over him while he speaks, man sees not only how tender and strong is his love for the sister that hung on the same maternal bosom; but he sees also what the gospel without and the gospel within demand of the *son* no less than the daughter of God.

Farewell to war, to statecraft, to legal tricks, to shifts of trade; farewell to bribery, to desecration, to idle controversy, — when woman enters in to man's labor!

You feel the doom falling, and strive to put it off. Not because God has made woman of a diviner nature; not because he has made her more precious, to be kept from the rough handling of the world, — does it shrink from her pure gaze. No; but because God himself, in balancing the world's forces, has blended her moral nature with her mental, purposely to check her brother's aggressiveness, and moderate his lust of gain. So has he given to man a cooler temper, a grander deliberateness, a strength equal to every strain, which shall repair the fault of her warm impulses, her "nimble" action, her unfitness, casual or universal, for long-sustained effort. But what can either of you do alone? Impulse, tenderness, and moral promptings, grow into tawdry sentimentalism, when shut out from their fit arena, when untrained to emulate a brother's active life. Coolness, forethought, and strength grow into cunning, rapacity, and tyranny, when uninfluenced by that gentler element of your nature which God has placed by your side. Helpsmeet for each other you were ordained: why hinder and obstruct each other's pathway?

From this moment, put aside ignoble jealousy, inert sympathy, and stupid indifference to your own moral position. Only by heartily accepting the sweet juices and flavors of her life can you secure fragrant blossoms and precious fruit to your own. The words are just as true when I turn to counsel her. If ever this earth grows liker heaven, it will be when the broad and generous sympathies prophesied by this new movement take practical shape, and there are —

> "Everywhere
> Two heads in council, two beside the hearth,
> Two in the tangled business of the world,
> Two in the liberal offices of life,
> Two plummets dropped for one, to sound the abyss
> Of science, and the secrets of the mind:
> Musician, painter, sculptor, critic, more:
> And everywhere the broad and bounteous Earth
> Shall bear a double growth of its best souls."

I have often spoken, not only in this lecture, but in almost every one I have ever given, of the great need of conscientious, painstaking woman's work. During the last year, Baron Tœrmer has been borne by torchlight to his last home, and the mediæval artist has been mourned as a personal friend by many a crowned head. The torches of the priests who bore him to his grave very likely startled to the window our two young countrywomen, who are pursuing sculpture in the Eternal City. Little did they guess, that, in the city of Florence, there was living at that moment a woman as able, as renowned, though, for certain reasons, not so well known to them, as the great artist just departed. I will close this lecture with a brief sketch of Félicie de Fauveau, for whose woman's work no apology will ever need to be made.

Entering Florence by the Porta Romana, you find, in the Via della Fornace, a dark-green door, which opens in to a paved court, once the entrance to a convent. Beyond stretches a cool, quiet garden; and all manner of birdcages and dovecotes remind you of Rosa Bonheur's fondness for pets. Through that quiet garden, hedged with laurel and cypress, you might have walked, but a little time ago, with a shrewd, sagacious, life-loving French woman, an aristocrat and a Legitimist, whose eyes had looked upon the guillotine, and who was proud of having suffered for her faith and country. She would lead you to her small parlor, furnished with ancient hangings, carved chairs, and gold-grounded Pre-Raphaelite pictures of great value. Here she would introduce you to her daughter, Félicie de Fauveau.

A forehead low and broad; soft, brown eyes; an aquiline nose; a well-cut, well-closed mouth; a flexible, fine figure; a velvet skirt and jacket of the color of the "dead leaf;" a velvet cap of the same, drawn over blonde hair, cut square across the forehead, as in the picture of Faust, — this is what you see when you look at the artist; this is what Ary Scheffer painted and valued so, that no gold would buy the portrait while he lived. Fire, air, and water are in that organization: the movements of the arms are angular; but the hands are soft, white, fine, and royal.

Born in Tuscany, she was early carried to Paris; whence she removed, when very young, to Limoux, Bayonne, and Besançon. A great taste for music and painting she inherited from her mother. Her studies were profound, and among them she pursued archæology and heraldry. At Besançon she painted in oils, but was not satisfied; and from the workmen who carved for the churches she got her first hint towards modelling. When her father died, she was ready to devote herself to the support of her family. When people told her it was unbecoming, she drew herself up: "Are you ignorant," she asked, "that an artist is a gentlewoman?"

Benvenuto Cellini was her prototype; and to her may be attributed that revival of a taste for mediæval art which, proceeding from Paris, has had, of late years, so great an influence on England.

Her first work was a group called "The Abbot." Encouraged by unlimited praise, she made a basso-relievo, — containing six figures, and representing Christina of Sweden in the fatal galley with Monaldeschi. This was in the last " Exposition des Beaux Arts," and received the gold medal from Charles X. in person.

Up to 1830, the young girl remained in Paris. Her mother was so accomplished, Félicie herself so witty and profound a talker, that a distinguished circle gathered round them; among them, Scheffer, Delaroche, Giraud. All manner of fine artistic experiments in modelling and drawing were improvised about their study-table. There she executed for Count Pourtalès a bronze lamp of singular beauty. A bivouac of archangels, armed as knights, were represented as resting round a watch-fire, where St. Michael stood sentinel; round the lamp, in golden letters, *Vaillant, veillant*, — " Brave, but cautious;" beneath, a stork's foot holds a pebble surrounded by beautiful aquatic plants. Many models were lost on the breaking-up of her Paris studio. She was incessantly occupied with commissions for private galleries; she was to have modelled two doors for the Louvre, and to have superintended the decoration of a baptistery, — when the Revolution broke up her calm and studious life. With the celebrated daughter of the Duras Family, she retired to La Vendée, and, virtuous and honored, made herself as active, politically, as the reckless women of the Fronde. To this day, the peasantry know her as the Demoiselle. For those who remember her, there will never be another. Finally came pursuit and capture. After a long search, the two women were dragged from the mouth of an oven. Félicie assisted her companion to escape; was watched more closely in consequence, and remained seven months in prison at Angers. In prison she designed a group representing the duel of the Lord of Jarnac before Henry II., and a monument to Louis de Bonnechose. At the close of the seven months, she returned to her studio at Paris. But very soon the appearance of the Duchesse de Berri in La Vendée restored hope to all Royalist hearts, and Félicie rushed to her side.

"My opinions are dearer to me than my art," she said, and proved it by heroic sacrifices. On the failure of this second attempt, she was exiled by the government. In the very teeth of the authorities, she returned to Paris, broke up her studio, and joined her mother in Florence, where they have ever since resided, clad, not without significance, in colors of the fallen leaf. No one but an artist can guess what loss is involved in the sudden and forcible breaking-up of an old studio. At the very moment when Félicie and her mother were all but starving in Florence, a man in Paris made an almost fabulous fortune by selling walking-sticks made from designs which she had sketched during the happy evenings of her girlhood. The Fauveaus would not accept a dollar from the party they had served; and Madame had as much pride as her daughter in establishing the new studio. Félicie wrote, " We have manna, but only on condition that we save none for the morrow."

In her studio you find no Pagan traces, only Christian art, — St. Dorothea lifting her lovely hands for the basket of fruit an angel brings; a Santa Reparata, perfect in terra-cotta; exquisite mirror-frames of wood, bronze, and silver. She has executed for Count Zichy an Hungarian costume, a collar, belt, sword, and spurs, of finest work. The Empress of Russia has ordered from her a silver bell. It is decorated by twenty figures, the servants of a mediæval household; who assemble at the call of three stewards, whose figures form the handle. Round the bell is blazoned, in Gothic letters, —

"De bon vouloir servir le maître."
"With good will to serve the master."

Beside the crowded labors of twenty-five years, Félicie has studied the merely mechanical portions of her art, and tried to discover some old artistic secrets.

To cast a statue whole, so as to require no after-touch of the chisel, has been her lifelong endeavor She finally succeeded in her St. Michael, though not till it had been recast seven times. It is probable her experiments led the way for those by which Crawford succeeded in casting his Beethoven. I cannot tell how many of you have heard of Félicie de Fauveau. The fact that her works are chiefly in private galleries and her own studio, screens her from observation. The higher dignitaries of the church and the princes of art are almost her only companions. She works constantly. About a year since, the death of her devoted mother drew the veil still closer round her daily life; but I retrace her story with honorable pride.

Félicie de Fauveau is not merely an artist. She is the first artist in the world, in her peculiar walk. As a worker in jewels, bronze, gold, and silver, as a designer of monuments and mediæval furniture, she stands without approach.

> "Witness that she who did these things was born
> To do them; claims her license in her work."

So let all women claim it.

III.

"THE OPENING OF THE GATES."

"If such a day never come, then I perceive much else will never come; heroic purity of heart and of eye, noble, pious valor to amend *us and the age of bronze and lacquer*, — how can they ever come?" — T. CARLYLE.

"TO destroy daughters is to make war upon Heaven's harmony. The more daughters you drown, the more daughters you will have; and never was it known that the drowning of daughters led to the birth of sons."

This passage from the treatise of Kwei Chunk Fu upon Infanticide may be translated so as to apply to every Christian nation. The Chinese are not the only people who drown daughters. England, France, and America, the three leading intelligences of the world, are busy at it this moment. The cold, pure wave of the Pacific is a sweeter draught than that social flood of corruption and depression which, like a hideous quicksand, buries your sisters out of your sight. "The more daughters you drown, the more daughters you will have." Most certainly; and if, instead of the word "daughters," you insert the words "weak and useless members of society," — which is what the Chinese mean by it, — you will see that Kwei Fu is right. Let women starve; let them sink into untold depths of horror, without one effort to save them; and, for every woman so lost, two shall be born to inherit her fate.

Nor need the careless and ignorant man of wealth fancy that his own daughters shall escape while he continues heartlessly indifferent, though he never actively wronged a human creature. When the spoiler is abroad, he does not pause to choose his victims. The fairest and most innocent may be the first struck down; for human passions find their fitting type in the persecuted beast of the forest. It is not the hunter alone who feels his teeth and talons, but the first human flesh his lawless members seize.

If these things are so, surely it is our duty to consider well this question of work, to suggest all possible modes of relief, and, while waiting for the final application of absolute principles, to help society forward by all partial measures of amelioration; for only partial can they be, so long as the present modes of thought and feeling continue. How little any one person can contribute toward the solution of our difficulties, I am well aware; yet I venture to make a few suggestions.

The "Edinburgh Review," whether prepared to recommend female preachers and lecturers or not, *does* propose women as teachers of Oratory; and says distinctly, that, for this purpose, they are to be preferred to men, as their voices are more penetrating, distinct, delicate, and correct than those of men. I think it was a matter of surprise to American audiences, when women first came forward as public speakers, that, in so large a number of cases, the parlor *tone* would reach to the extremity of a large hall. Women, too, were heard at a disadvantage, because popular curiosity compelled them to speak in the largest buildings. There are a great many women, and there are also a great many men, whose voices are wholly unfit for public exigencies; but, when you consider that women have been wholly untrained so far, how great do their natural advantages appear! Several female teachers of elocution in our midst prove that this is gradually perceived. These remarks should be extended so as to cover all instruction in the pronunciation of languages. There may be men capable of distinguishing the delicate shades of sound, so that a woman's voice can catch them; but such men are rare exceptions to the common incompetency. The French nasals cannot be distinguished accurately by a man's voice: the bass tone is too broad, and the treble wavers in trying to find the middle rest. Pursue the study of Italian for years with the best teacher that Boston can furnish; and, when you first hear a cultivated Italian woman speak, you will find that you have the whole thing to learn over again. So there was never any teacher of the French language equal to Rachel, whose nimble and fiery tongue never dropped an unmeaning accent nor tone; nor of the English like Fanny Kemble, who, despite certain "stage tricks," in vogue since the days of Garrick, shows us what delicate shades of meaning lie hidden in the vowel sounds, and what power a slight variation of a flexible voice confers upon a dull passage. The teaching of oratory and of language, then, should devolve upon woman.

"Why," asks Ernest Legouvé, — "why should not the immense variety of bureaucrative and administrative employments be given up to women?" Under this head would come the business inspection of hospitals, barracks, prisons, factories, and the like; and the decision of many sanitary questions. For all this, woman is far fitter than man. Her eye is quick; her common sense ready: she sees the consequence in the cause, and does not need to argue every disputed point. A shingle missing from the roof is a trifle to a man; but, the moment a woman sees it, her glance takes in the stained walls, the dripping curtains, wet carpets, sympathetic ceilings, damp beds, and very possibly the colds and illness, which this trifle involves. For this reason, she is a far fitter inspector of all small abuses than man.

Consider, then, Legouvé's proposition. The proprietor of the London Adelphi advertised, at the opening of the last season, that his box-openers, check-takers, and so on, would all be women. Throughout the whole range of public amusements, there is a wide field for the employment of girls, which this single step has thrown open.

Women are so steadily pressing in to the medical profession, that I have no need to direct your attention toward it; but I may say, that it is much to be wished that women should devote themselves to the specialities of that science. Until within a very few years, a Boston physician has been expected to understand all the ills that flesh is heir to; an eye-doctor or an ear-doctor or a lung-doctor must necessarily be a quack. Women are entering, in medicine, a very wide field. A few specially gifted may master every branch of practice; but many will undoubtedly fail, from the want of *inherited* habits of hard study, of *transmitted* power of investigation. I wish those who are in danger of this would apply strenuously to one branch of practice; and a great success in any one direction would do more for the general cause than a thousand competences earned by an ordinary career.

I do not suppose there is a city in the United States, — and, if not in the United States, then certainly not in the world, — where, if you asked the name of the first physician, you would be answered by that of a woman.* I do not complain of this: it is too soon to expect it. Colleges, schools of anatomy,

---

* I am happy to find, on the authority of the "London Athenæum," that this statement was, when I wrote it, untrue. "Germany," it says, on the 23d of July, 1859, — "Germany has lost one of her most famed and eminent female scholars. Frau Dr. Heidenreich, *née* Von Siebold, died at Darmstadt a fortnight ago. She was born in 1792, studied the science of midwifery at the Universities of Göttingen and Giessen, and took her doctor's degree in 1817; not, *honoris causâ*, by favor of the Faculty, but, like any other German student, by writing the customary Latin dissertation, as well as by bravely defending, in public disputation, a number of medical theses. After that, she took up her permanent abode at Darmstadt, indefatigable in the exercise of her special branch of science, and universally honored as one of its first living authorities."

"Universally honored as one of its first living authorities," that was what I was in search of; and French and German papers confirm the statement. Dr. Heidenreich came of a family highly distinguished in her speciality. It was ancient and noble: she was a baroness in her own right. All readers of

clinical courses, have not yet been thrown open; and success, so far, has been mastered mainly by original endowment. Genius has held the torch, and shown

---

English works on midwifery know the authority given to the name of Von Siebold. Her father founded the famous hospital at Berlin; and her brother, still living, stands high in medical fame, having written the best history of midwifery extant.

Rosa Bonheur, also, is as unquestionably at the head of her department as Sir Edmund Landseer. The three pictures Boston has had a chance to see this autumn ought to fill every woman's bosom with a glow of honest pride.

I can find no better place than this, perhaps, to introduce the following facts, to which my attention has been directed by the kindness of Miss Mary L. Booth, of New York.

In the History of Southold, N.Y., — one of the oldest towns in the United States, — it appears that women have practised there as "doctresses" and "midwives" from the first settlement of the country. From 1740 to the present time, — more than one hundred years, — the town of Southold has had a trustworthy female physician. The first of these, Elizabeth King, who practised from 1740 until her death in 1780, attended at the birth of more than *one thousand* children.

During this time, — from 1760 to 1775, — a Mrs. Peck was also known in the same town as an excellent midwife. The direct successor of Mrs. King was, however, a Mrs. Lucretia Lester, who practised from 1745 to 1779. Of her my authority says, "She was justly respected as nurse and doctress to the pains and infirmities incident to her fellow-mortals, *especially* her own sex;" a remark which shows she attended *both*. "She was, during thirty years, conspicuous as an angel of mercy; a woman whose price was beyond rubies. It is said she attended at the birth of *thirteen hundred* children, and, of that number, lost but two."

A Mrs. Susannah Brown practised from 1800 to 1840, and attended at the birth of *fourteen hundred* children. From the number of patients these women must have had, it would seem as if they were sustained by the whole neighborhood. The book just published speaks highly of them, as what Henry Ward Beecher would call a "means of grace," and pleads, from the precedent, for the education of women to medicine.

Southold is in Suffolk County, on Long Island; and was settled in the early part of the seventeenth century. It has now three churches, and less than five thousand inhabitants.

The instance of so creditable a practice being maintained for a whole century, by three women, stands alone, so far as I know, in this country. Mrs. King probably studied abroad, and taught her next successor, and possibly Mrs. Peck, who seems to have assisted both. That three of the four women named should have practised forty years each, seems very remarkable.

the way; but I want women to remember, that, in this department, all the teachings of nature and experience show that they are bound to excel men. Let them, therefore, take the best way to accomplish it.

At the School of Design in New York, the other day, I pressed upon the observation of the young wood-engravers the possibility of opening for themselves a new career by wood-carving. It is quite common, in old European museums, to see the stones of plums and peaches delicately carved by woman's hand, and set in frames of gold and jewels. Sometimes they are the work of departed saints or cloistered nuns; and a terrible waste of time they seem to our modern eyes. Properzia dei Rossi, — whose early history is so obscure, that no one knows the name of her parents; while the cities of Bologna and Modena still dispute the honor of her birth, — Properzia began her wonderful career by carving on peach-stones. One she decorated with thirty sacred figures, holding the stone so near the eye as to gain a microscopic power. On one still in the possession of the Grassi Family, at Bologna, she chiselled the passion of our Lord; where twelve figures, gracefully disposed, are said to glow with characteristic expression. Properzia died a maiden, according to Vasari and the best manuscript contemporaneous authority; and there seems to be no ground for the vile stories that have clustered round her name, other than the fact, that in her sculpture of Potiphar's wife, finished when she knew that she was dying, she ventured to cut her own likeness. It is not to the carving of cherry-stones, however, that I would direct the attention of young women, but to the Swiss carving of paper-knives, bread-plates, salad-spoons, ornamental figures, jewel-boxes, and so on. On account of the care required in transportation, these articles bring large prices; and I feel quite sure that many an idle girl might win a pleasant fame through such trifles. No one will dispute the assertion, who recalls the pranks of her young classmates at school. Do you remember the exquisite drawings which once decorated the kerchiefs, the linen collars and sleeves, of a certain schoolroom? The sun of the artist set early; but I have often thought that a free maiden career in the higher walks of art might have preserved her to us. The same fancy, displayed in wood-carving, would have challenged the attention of the world; and the cherry-stones also bore witness to her power. The only practical difficulty would spring from the want of highly seasoned wood; and that could be obviated by a little patience. Should any young girl be tempted by my words into this career, I hope she will not give away her carvings to indifferent friends, but carry them into the market at once, and let them bring their price, that she may know her own value, and that of the work.

Properzia also excelled in engraving: so did Elizabetta Sirani in 1660. Her engravings from Guido are still considered master-pieces. We have female engravers on wood and steel, and also female lithographers.

I want some woman to apply herself to this work, with such energy and determination as will place her at the head of it. Let her do this, and she could soon establish a workshop, and take men and women into her employ; standing responsible herself for the finish of every piece of work marked with her name. Let some idle woman of wealth offer the capital for such an experiment, and share some of its administrative duties. "Success" is the best argument. It would be possible to organize in Boston, at this moment, a shop of the best kind, where all the designing and engraving should be done by women. Why can it not be tried? Carvers on wood, and engravers then.

I have known several English barbers, — not women of the decorative art, like our sainted Harriet Ryan; but women actually capable of shaving a man! Why, then, does the "Englishwoman's Journal" inform us, that, in Normandy and Western Africa, there actually are female barbers?

I think there is room in Boston for an establishment of this kind; a place from which a woman could come to a sick-room to shave the heated head or cut the beard of the dying; a place where women's and children's wants could be attended to without necessary contact with men; and with the absolutely necessary cleanliness, of which there is not now a single instance in this city.

When I mentioned wood-carving to women, I was thinking, in part, of the immense annual demand for Christmas presents. In this connection, also, I should like to direct the attention of our rural women to the art of preserving and candying fruit. "But that is nothing new," you will say. "Did not your Massachusetts census for 1845 enumerate certain picklers and preservers?" Yes; but those women were merely in the employ of men carrying on large establishments. What I would suggest is a domestic manufacture to compete with French candies, and to occupy the minds of our farmers' wives and daughters, to the exclusion of shirt-fronts and shoe-binding.

Every one of us, probably, fills more than one little stocking, on Christmas night, with candied fruit. If we belong to the "first families," and wish to do the thing handsomely, this fruit has cost from seventy-five cents to a dollar a pound; we knowing, all the while, that better could be produced for half or two-thirds the money. Last year, I purchased one pound of the candy, and examined it with practical reference to this question. Plums, peaches, cherries, apples, and pears, all tasted alike, and had evidently been boiled in the same sirup. Apple and quince marmalades alone had any flavor. Now, our farmers' daughters could cook these fruits so as to preserve their flavor, could candy them and pack them into boxes, quite as well as the French *men;* and so a new and important domestic industry might arise. The experiment would be largely profitable as soon as all risk of mistake were over; and perishable fruit at a distance from market could be used in this way. A few years ago, we had a rare conserve from Constantinople and Smyrna, called fig-paste. Now we have a mixture of gum Arabic and flour, flavored with essences; made for the most part at Westboro', and called by the same name. Yes, we actually have fig-paste, spicy with wintergreen and black-birch! Now, what is to prevent our farmers' daughters from making this? — from putting up fruits in air-tight cans, and drying a great many kinds of vegetables that cannot be had now for love or money? Who can get Lima beans or dried sweet-corn, that does not dry them from his own garden?

Do not let our medical friends feel too indignant if I recommend to these same women the manufacture of pickles. The use of pickles, like the use of wine, may be a questionable thing; but, like liquors, they are a large article of trade: and, if we must have them, why not have them made of wholesome fruit, in good cider-vinegar, with a touch of the grandmotherly seasoning that we all remember, rather than of stinted gherkins, soured by vitriol and greened by copper? There are many sweet sauces, too, — made of fruit, stewed with vinegar, spice, and sugar, — which cannot be obtained in shops, and would meet a good market. How easy the whole matter is, may be guessed from this fact, that, sitting once at a Southern table, — the table of a genial grand-nephew of George Washington, who bore his name, — I was offered twenty-five kinds of candied fruit, all made by the delicate hands of his wife; and seven varieties in form and flavor, from the common tomato.

I looked through Boston in vain, the other day, to find a common dish-mop large enough to serve my purpose. There was no such thing to be found. Taking up one of the slender tassels offered me, I inquired into its history, and was informed that it was imported from France. The one I had been trying to replace had been made by some skilful Yankee hand for a Ladies' Fair. Now, what are our poor women doing, that they cannot compete with this French trumpery, and give us at least dish-mops fit for use?

As teachers of gymnastics, women are already somewhat employed. A wide field would be opened, if a teacher were attached to each of our public schools, — a step in physical education greatly needed.

No conservative is so prejudiced, I suppose, as to object to placing woman in all positions of moral supervision. Female assistants in jails, prisons, workhouses, insane asylums, and hospitals, are seen to be fit, and to have a harmonizing influence in every respect. How many more such assistants are needed, we may guess from the fact that our City Jail and Charlestown are still unsupplied. Women of a superior order are needed for such posts; and when will they be found? Not till labor is thoroughly respected; not till the popular voice says, "It is all very well to be a Miss Dix, and go from asylum to asylum, suggesting and improving; but it is just *as* well, quite *as* honorable, to work in *one* asylum, carrying out the wise ideas which a Miss Dix suggests, and securing the faithful trial of her experiments." Many men in Beacon Street would feel honored to call the moving philanthropist sister or friend; but few would like to acknowledge a daughter in the post of matron or superintendent. Why not? There is something " rotten in the State " where such inconsistencies exist. How thoroughly men accept such women, as soon as they are permitted to try their experiment, we may judge from the case of Florence Nightingale and her staff. The very men, whose scepticism kept the army suffering for months, would be the first to send them now; and the soldiers, who kissed her shadow where it fell, would fill the whole Commissariat with women. When her gentle but efficient hand broke in the doors of the storehouses at Scutari, a general huzza followed from the very men who were too timid to break the trammels of office. The woman's keen sympathy with the advancing spirit of her time, taught her what it was fit to do; and, if the rippling smiles of suffering men had not rewarded her when the bedding and stores were distributed, the warm encomiums of her Queen, whose heart she had so truly read, must have done it. Following out this train of reflection, I have often thought it would some day fall to women, and to women alone, to exercise the function of parish minister! I do not mean " parish preacher." I hold pulpit graces cheap by the side of that fatherly walk among his people, which has made the name of Charles Lowell sacred to the West Church. Go back to the history of the first church in every town: see how the minister knew the story of every heart in his parish; how he kept his eye on every lonely boy or orphan girl; how widowed mothers took his counsel about schools and rents; how forlorn old maids trusted to him to make all "things come round right;" how the lad, inclining to wild courses, found no better friend than he. How is it now? The minister has his Sunday sermons, his annual addresses before certain societies, his weekly association. In the old time, such things were done, yet not the other left undone. Now the lonely boy or orphan girl must seek out the minister, — and how likely this is to happen everybody knows; the mother must tell over the story of her widowhood, pained to see how "in course" it falls upon that wearied ear; the spinster must tell again how the boat floated empty and bottom upward to shore long years ago, and so no one was "spared to keep all right;" and the wild lad — alas! how many such do the clergy save now?

As I see such things, — and I do see them often, — as I realize that change in men and times, in manners and books, from which this change is inseparable, — I confess I see a new* sphere opening for women. It takes no remarkable gifts, in the common sense of those words; only a kindly heart, a thoughtful head, a tender, reverent care-taking, wholly apart from meddlesomeness. Not many are the ministers now who

---

* See Appendix, sketch of Mrs. Roberts, and other female preachers.

will pause to explain to Martha that she is careful and troubled about many things; and that really the visionary Mary, with her dreamy eyes, is choosing the good part. Not many can see Nathanael standing under the fig-tree, and remind him of it at the needful moment. But if, in every religious household, there were a deaconess, called by nature and God to her work, — one to whom the young felt a right to go with questions home could not answer; one pledged to secret counsel, with whom the restless and unhappy might confer, — it seems to me the wheels of life would move more smoothly.* How the unlikeliest

---

* I did not think, certainly, when I wrote the above passage, of Arthur Helps's "Companions of my Solitude;" but, taking up the book during a day of illness, I find a parallel passage in what he writes of the "sin of great cities." In speaking of the many excuses which ought to be made for fallen women, he says: "And then there is nobody into whose ear the poor girl can pour her troubles, *except she comes as a beggar*. This will be said to be a leaning, on my part, to the confessional. I cannot help this: I must speak the truth that is in me."

It seems to me, that the "narrow" church, against which so much is intimated in our times, is nowhere so narrow as in its human sympathies. Oh that our clergymen knew how many utterly *friendless* souls sit before them clothed in "purple and fine linen"! It is not to be taken for granted, that, because a woman has a home, a father and mother, and a genial, social circle, she has a *friend*, or even a counsellor. It is not the beggar-girl alone who needs a "Confessor" within our Protestant churches. Many of the most refined, the most noble, and the most wealthy, are hurried into unfit marriages, because they dare not live alone, and think the superficial confidences of common courtship only a prelude to something deeper which never comes.

Why should not the "Comforter" have come to our churches, with some special significance, before this? If stout-hearted Luther could say, "When I am assailed with heavy tribulations, I rush out among my pigs, rather than remain alone by myself," why should any of us blush to confess our need of help? Herein, it seems to me, lies the vital want of the modern church. Here and there, the rare personal gifts of a single pastor lessen the evil; but what we want, in every religious circle, is a friend to whom we can

persons are sometimes raised up to such a ministry, let the following story tell. In the dim and dreary precincts of the Seven Dials in London, years ago, two orphan girls were left lying on door-steps, fed by chance charity, to grow up as they might. One died; and the other was finally adopted by an old man, an atheist, who had been neighbor to her parents. She grew up an atheist also, and married, — saved by God's mercy from what had seemed her likeliest fate. Stepping into the passage of the Bloomsbury Mission Hall to shelter herself from the rain, one night, a shaft, winged by the Holy Spirit, struck to her empty heart.

---

go, without the smallest danger of being suspected of impertinence or egotism, under the sanction of the divine words, "Bear ye one another's burdens." The burdens of temptation *must* be borne alone; but the burdens of poverty, sickness, and grief, should be shared in every Christian church, without regard to the social condition of the sufferer. Oftentimes the rich man is poorer than the pauper. I know all the objections that will be raised. I *feel*, to this day, how I saw one clergyman shrink, years ago, from a tale which he ought to have heard from one agonized woman's lips; and how others, admirable in the usual pulpit and pastoral charge, will think themselves unfit for this. Under such circumstances, let a clergyman call upon those of his congregation who are willing to become the friends of the rest, to meet in his study. From the half-dozen who will have at once the *modesty* and the courage to come forward, let a man and a woman be chosen to act as a "Committee of Comfort." This might be done with the utmost quietness; the minister alone need know the names of those willing to serve; but if it were an understood thing, that every church had such officers, the blessing would be beyond belief.

In many cases, no actual help could be given, beyond patient listening, a mutual prayer, or tender soothing; but in every church there are souls that need these far more than eloquent preaching, — souls that ask for nothing, except some one to hear and consider *who is not in a hurry*, some one to appoint those to their true uses who stand idle in a waiting world. I claim such an institution for the sake of friendless *women;* but such substitutes for it as the world has hitherto had, have been by no means useless to *men*.

The next week, a lending library was to be opened in the district. Marian was first at the door. "Sir," said she, "will you lend me a Bible?"—"A Bible!" exclaimed the man. "We did not mean to *lend* Bibles; but I will get you one."

How long she read, how she was at first moved, none but God can know. But, whether from mental distress or from the sad vicissitudes of her needy career, she became very ill, and went to a public hospital. While there, she saw the sufferings of those who applied for its charity, and observed that the filthy state of their persons needed a friendly female hand. When she came out, she wrote to the missionary, and told him she wished to dedicate all her spare time to the lost and degraded of her own sex. "God's mercy," she writes, "has spared me from their fate: for me their misery will have no terrors. I will clean and wash them, and mend their linen. If they can get into a hospital, I will take care of their clothes." You may suppose the missionary did not lose sight of Marian, and you may guess how gladly she undertook to distribute Bibles; going, where none of the gentry could go, into dens of misery known only to the police-officers and herself. Spending her mornings in distributing Bibles, and giving the kind and pastoral counsel everywhere needed, she discovered, in the autumn of 1857, a new want, and devoted her afternoons to teaching the ignorant women about her to cut and make their children's clothes. Why *she* knew better than *they*, who shall tell? Then came the November panic and its wide-spread distresses; and, seeing how food was wasted from ignorance, she opened a soup-kitchen of her own. She used what is called vegetable stock: her wretched customers liked it, and she sold it all through the winter for a price which just paid the cost of cooking. Her noble work goes on. The stone which the builders of our modern society would have rejected, is now the head of the corner; and Seven Dials knows her as " Marian, the Bible-woman."

Another mission has been begun at St. Pancras, where, in one of the worst neighborhoods, the most profligate men have gathered together, between church hours, to hear a young lady read the " Pilgrim's Progress," and are thus softened and led to higher things. Would you shut those sacred lips because they are a woman's? Would you quote St. Paul to her, and blush for her career, if she were your own daughter? I will not believe it.

At the parish of St. Alkmunds, in Shrewsbury, the wife of the clergyman, Mrs. Whitman, began by modest reading from house to house; a work which has since been greatly blessed. Gently she won profligate men and women to give up their beer, and the temptations of the " tap;" signing herself the pledge which they alone needed.

A very important work could be done in this city by the establishment of a proper Training School for Servants. One reason why our house-work is so miserably done is, that it is never regarded as a profession, in which a certain degree of excellence must be attained, but rather as a "make-shift," by the aid of which a certain number of years can be got through. The only thorough servant I ever had was one who had been educated at such a school in Germany. Here would be an admirable field for some of the women who have money and time, but no object in life. Such a school must be carried on in connection with a good-sized boarding-house of a respectable kind; and beside the regular superintendents, who will, of course, be hired for the different departments, there must be committees of ladies who should see to the practical working of the institution in turn. This is necessary to secure that thorough working in every department which the best housekeeping demands. Only by intelligent, refined oversight can feathered "flirts" be hindered from taking the place of the tidy dusting cloth; only so will a girl learn to sweep each apartment separately, without dragging her accumulations from floor to floor; only so can soap-suds be kept off your oil-cloths, soiled hands from your doors, and dust from your shirt-fronts. I do not believe a better service could be done to the community than the establishment of such a school, especially in relation to cooking.* A good many

---

* I must suggest, in this connection, a thought which I have not had time to elaborate in the text. Very much needed in Boston is a restaurant for the lower classes, presided over by the highest skill and intelligence, where well-cooked, well-flavored, and *stimulating* food could be offered at all times; and where a judicious alternation of pea soup, baked beans, and very

such experiments have been successfully tried in England, but none so thorough as that I would propose in Boston.

With regard to the lowest class of employed women, such as are employed at home, we have, it seems to me, several distinct duties to perform.

In the first place, we need a public but self-supporting Laundry. By this I mean two large halls, with an adjacent area, built at the expense of the city, and properly superintended, where, for so much an hour, women of the lower class may wash, starch, dry, and iron the clothes they take home. A bleaching-ground would be desirable; but, if it could not be had, a steam drying-room would be the next best thing. Good starch, soap, and indigo should be for sale upon the premises at wholesale prices; it not being desirable that the city should make money out of the necessities of its poor. If such

---

simple dishes, with roast meat and broths, might secure daily nourishment for a very low price. There is a great deal of very cheap food, which an epicure might desire, but which the poor have never been taught to prepare. Hundreds of wretched families in Boston ought never to try to make a cup of tea for themselves. In hot weather, the shavings and wood necessary to boil the water are worth as much as the tea itself. Crime of all sorts, and especially intemperance, will retreat before a proper provision of nourishing and stimulating food for the lower classes. Gallons of oyster liquor are thrown away every day by dealers who sell the fish "solid," which would make the most nourishing of soups and stews; for no food replenishes the vital essences so rapidly as the oyster: hence its inseparable connection with all places of dissipation and vicious resort. If men would only make a good instead of an evil use of the few natural secrets they discover! With such a restaurant, — which should, of course, be self-supporting, — a capital training-school for cooks might easily be associated; and so it would become an infinite blessing, in the end, to the kind hearts and wise heads of those who should project it.

an establishment could be had, a great many women would be changed from paupers to decent citizens. They are tired of seeking washing; for, in their one close room, scented with boiling onions or rank meat, without a proper area for drying, and compelled to pay high prices for poor soap and starch, they cannot do decently the very work which philanthropy soon becomes unwilling to intrust to them, and for which they are compelled to charge higher than the best private laundry. The city could buy coal, wood, soap, starch, and indigo at manufacturers' and importers' prices, and so give them a fair chance for competition. I hope this project, long since partially adopted in many cities of the Old World, may find favor with my audience.

There is in Boston no place, strange as it may seem, where plain, neatly finished clothing can be bought ready-made. I can go down town, and buy embroidered merinos, Paris hats with ostrich feathers, and lace-trimmed, welted linen: but if I want a plain, cotton skirt for a child, whereof the calico was eight cents a yard; if I want a plain, cotton print made into a neatly fitting dress; if I want a boy's coarse apron, — such things are not to be had, or only so very badly made that no one will buy them. I do not want lace or embroidery or silk, or fine linen; but I do want my button-holes nicely turned and strong, my hems even, my gathers stroked, and, however plain and coarse, the whole finish of the garment such as a mistress of the needle only would approve, such as no lady need be ashamed to wear So do others. The reasons given to explain the non-existence of such a magazine in Boston are, first, That our women of the middle class are, for the most part, accustomed to cut and make their own clothes; second, That there is a prevalent but mistaken idea, that clothes made for sale cannot possibly fit. With regard to the first point, it may be said, that, as more and more avenues of labor are opened for women, this class perceives that it is not good economy for them to do their own sewing. Hands compelled to coarser or heavier labor cannot sew quick or well, and those training to more delicate manipulation lose practice by returning to it; so there will be a constantly increasing class of purchasers.

As to the impossibility of fitting, that is a vulgar mistake. The human frame is quite as much the result of law as Mr. Buckle's statistics. Any comely, healthy form is a good model for all other forms of the same height and breadth. Who ever heard of a French bonnet or a bridal trousseau that did not fit? yet these things are made by arbitrary rules. Our superintendent could find every measure she would ever need in one of the teeming houses on Sea Street. She must take her measures from life, not books. Nor would I have the sewing done with machines, unless those of the highest cost could be procured and ably superintended. The best machine is as yet a poor substitute for the supple, human hand; and many practical inconveniences must result from its use. It requires more skill and intelligence to manage man's simplest machine, than to control with a thought that complicated network of nerve, bone, and fibre which we have been accustomed to use.

Capital to start such an establishment as I refer to is all that is needed. How desirable the thing is, you can easily see. In the first place, if good common clothing could be so purchased, mothers need not keep a large stock on hand: an accident could be readily repaired. In the second, it would greatly simplify and expedite many a charitable task. The terrible suffering which followed the panic of November, 1857, you all remember. Purses, always open hitherto, were necessarily closed; no Sister of Charity was willing to tread on the heels of the sheriff: yet the need was greater than ever. Many persons who had dismissed their servants were found willing to give a rough, untrained girl her board; but who was to provide her with decent clothes? They could not be bought, and to make them was the work of time and strength. May I always remember to honor, as God will always surely bless, one woman possessed of wealth and beauty, who did clothe from head to foot with her own needle, in that dreadful winter, *three* "wild Irish girls," and took them successively into her own family; training them to habits of tolerable decency, until others, less self-sacrificing, were found ready to do their part!

No people in our community suffer such inconvenience, loss, and imposition, in having their clothes made, as our servant girls. If a plentiful supply of calico sacks and skirts or loose dresses could be anywhere found, few girls would ever employ a dressmaker.

I have spoken of Public Laundry Rooms, and a Ready-made Clothing Room. There is a class of women greatly to be benefited by the establishment of a Knitting Factory. It is well known to every person in this room, especially to physicians, that no knitting done by machinery can compete with that done by the human hand, in durability, warmth, or stimulative power. Invalids are now obliged to import the Shetland jackets, which are always badly shaped; or to hire, at our fancy stores, the making of delicate and very expensive fabrics. Men's socks and children's gloves may be purchased; but the first cost from seventy-five cents to a dollar a pair, and the last are of very inferior manufacture. We cannot give out knitting to advantage, because of the dirt and grease it is liable to accumulate where water is not plenty nor ventilation to be had; and very good knitters of socks have not skill and intelligence to manage the different sizes, or to shape the larger articles, such as drawers and under-jackets for the two sexes. Coarse crocheting would answer better than knitting for many articles.

Let a large, airy room be hired, well supplied with Cochituate. Let all sorts of material be kept on hand, and some coarse, warm kinds of Shetland yarn imported that are not now to be had. Let at least two superintendents be appointed from among the women, who work *best* for our fancy stores; let knitting-women be invited to use this room for twelve hours a day, or less, as they choose, — receiving daily pay for their daily needs; and in less than one year you would have an establishment, for which not merely Boston, but all New England, would be grateful. I should hope that neither this nor the Clothing Room would ever offer very expensive or highly ornamental articles for sale. There is no danger that the interests of the wealthy will suffer. What I desire is to provide for the needs of the lowest women and the comfort of the middle-class customer.

The young girls in Beacon Street have now something to do. I offer them the establishment of a Training School for Servants, of a public but self-supporting Laundry, of a Ready-made Clothes Room, and a Knitting Factory; all simple matters, entirely within their control, if they would but believe it.

A certain human faithlessness often interferes with the execution of such plans. If my young friends doubt, let them go and talk to Harriet Ryan about it. She will show them, how, having taken the first step toward duty, God always leads the way to the second. To cheer them still further, I will tell them — for I may never have a fitter opportunity — of the splendid success of the industrial schools in Ireland, established in 1850 by Ellen Woodlock, — a name destined to stand honorably by the side of Florence Nightingale; nay, worthy to precede it, in so far as preventive measures are always a greater good than remedial. Mrs. Ellen Woodlock has powers of statement, according to the " London Times," equal to her extraordinary powers of execution; and it is from her own account of the work that I select what I have to offer you.

In 1850, Mrs. Woodlock had placed her only child at school, and began to look for something to do. A lady, who had started an industrial school on a gift of $250 from a clergyman, asked for her help. She proposed to teach young girls to do plain sewing. Very soon, there were more seamstresses than customers; but God did not fail to open a way. One poor, half-blind creature — very poor and very earnest — failed in the plain sewing, and was put to make cabbage nets. She did it so well, that Mrs. Woodlock taught her to make silk nets for the hair. The nets took: other girls were taught; and Mrs. Woodlock went to all the shops in Cork, and coaxed the merchants to buy of her. She very soon began to make nets for exportation. Mrs. Woodlock's fashionable niece arrived from Dublin, with a new style of crocheted net. Her aunt had a dozen made directly; and, by showing these, got orders from all the merchants for the new style. One day, a merchant came into the school, and saw a little girl at work on a mohair net. He asked the price, and found that she would make him twelve for the same money that he had paid for one in London. So you may guess where his next orders went.

Mrs. Woodlock then made interest with the "buyers," or young men who go to London twice a year to purchase goods. They took over her patterns, and returned with orders so large that their principals at once entered into the business. Yellow nets were made for Germany. Many were sent to England and America; and orders came so thick that they had to share them with the convent schools. They paid out a hundred dollars weekly; and alacrity and intelligence beamed where there had been, at first, only hopeless suffering and imbecility. Of course, this point was not reached without much self-sacrifice. At first, the children made awkward work that would not sell. Then the lady patronesses got tired, and dropped off. Worn and worried, Mrs. Woodlock fell ill. If you ever undertake any of the schemes I have mentioned, you must be prepared for all these things: they will certainly happen. No one ever fought a revolutionary war, and established an independence, without one or two defeats like that at Bunker Hill.*
When they become historic, we call them victories. When Mrs. Woodlock found that she was human and

---

* This allusion was made before an American audience, to show that the defeats suffered in a noble cause are honored in time as victories. So strong is our popular delusion on this point, that few of the common people can be found willing to believe that we were actually defeated at Bunker Hill. It was our "first battle." All honor to all such!

liable to fall ill, she sent for some of the Sisters of Charity, and trained several, so that they could, on an emergency, fill her place well.

But Mrs. Woodlock did not stop here. She used to teach the Catechism in the parish church; and, one day, she gave notice that a new school would be opened in that neighborhood. The next morning, one hundred and fifty girls, between the ages of fifteen and twenty-five, presented themselves. Mrs. Woodlock asked every girl, who had ever earned any money before, to hold up her hand. Four girls did so. They had sold apples in the streets. One hundred and forty-six suffering creatures, who had no way to earn a cent! Think what a class it was! Do you remember what I told you, the other day, of eighteen hundred and eighty women in New York who had never been taught to support themselves? Ten of the best workers from the first school were taken to teach these girls; and, for a salary, the teacher received the first *perfect* dozen of nets made by each of her pupils. This plan was not costly, and worked well. There was no lack of faithfulness. Travellers came to see the schools. There was no time wasted in looking for orders: they had more than they could fill. Of course, they must keep these hands employed: so other manufactures must be tried. Mrs. Woodlock thought she would try fine shirt-fronts for the city dealers. What do you think the people said? That it could not be done in all Ireland; that there was nobody to wash and iron them properly; that they would have to be sent all the way to Glasgow to be boxed in card boxes! Well, the nuns undertook the first washing and ironing,—making apprentices, let us hope, of some of the older pupils; and Mrs. Woodlock found a starving band-box maker, whom she herself taught to make flat boxes. And look now at the blessing which always follows wise work. This flat-box maker has had to take apprentices, has opened another branch of her business in Limerick, and has put money into the Savings' Bank.

Mrs. Woodlock's account of her work would be a great help to any young persons engaged in philanthropic effort. She lays the very greatest stress upon her machinery,—her methods. Every industrial work ought to support itself: if it does not, it is a failure. All her schools earn their own bread, *in every sense;* and all reforming agencies must always stand second to any institution which does that. See how she carried this thought into her daily life. Mrs. Woodlock had a brother who was one of the Board of Poor-Law Guardians. Seeing the success of her work, he persuaded the other members to employ an embroidery mistress in the Union School for a few months.

When these children knew enough, Mrs. Woodlock took out six, and put them into her industrial school, till she was sure they could support themselves. Then she let them look up lodgings, and continued to give them work from the school. In a few weeks, they got on so well that they began to take their relations and friends out of that terrible poorhouse.

Three young girls took out their mother and cousin, and supported them. Eighty girls were brought off the parish by the first working of her schools. A house has also been opened for orphans, where they are trained to support themselves.

Now, my friends, the census, at the end of ten years, will report a great change in the industrial condition of Ireland; and the beginning of that change was Mrs. Woodlock's intelligent moral effort to benefit her countrywomen, — in the first place, to teach one little sufferer to make cabbage-nets. That element will enter into the statistics on which Mr. Buckle bids you so confidently rely. Do not believe him when he says that *moral* effort can never help anybody but yourself, because it will be balanced, in the long-run, by your neighbor's *immoral* effort. Two and two make four in all statistics, and always will while the world stands; but two and two and one make five, and not four, as he asserts; and the one which he forgets to enumerate is no other than the divine Centre of life and action, — God himself. I value Mr. Buckle's book. I see how clearly he thinks; how much he has read; and how much truer his historical attitude than any ever before assumed. But when a man separates goodness from knowledge; tells you that intelligence may reign alone; does not see that the two are now and for ever one, equal attributes of the divine nature, — then he makes a mistake which saps the very foundation of his own work, and writes fallacy on every page.

What he says is perfectly true of *mistaken, ignorant* moral effort. That does help yourself, and does *not* help anybody else. It helps you, because it develops your right-mindedness, — your generosity. It does not help anybody else. It *hinders* others who are clearer intellectually: they see and despise the mistakes, and are not inspired by the purpose. Had it been intelligent, they would have seen it to be divine.

Mrs. Woodlock's work was both intelligent and moral. What inspired the pupils was her moral force and disinterested love. They saw this, and were kindled by it; while the community at large respected the intelligence and common sense with which she laid her plans. Intelligence made these plans self-supporting; intelligence gave them solid pyramidal position in the world: but moral energy gave them their prestige, and will win its way by the side of intelligence into the very columns which Mr. Buckle's closing volume must quote.

Do not be disheartened, then, as to the ultimate profit to others of any kindly work you feel inclined to do. Let kindliness inspire, let intelligence direct, your efforts. God has made your success certain from the very foundations of the world.

I cannot close such inadequate survey of this field as I have felt it my duty to offer, without alluding to one other fact, and making one parting suggestion. It cannot but be realized, by all the women to whom I speak, how very casual is the communication between the laboring class in this community and their employers. Suppose a housekeeper wants additional service, how can she secure it? If she is not wealthy enough to hire regularly, her "chance" is a very poor one; and she must take the recommendation, in nine cases out of ten, of some one in the charwoman's own rank of life.

Suppose a maid of all work leaves a mistress alone early some busy Monday morning, where can her place be filled? How can any one be found who will work by the hour or the day, in a cleanly, respectable manner, till a new servant can be deliberately chosen? Nobody knows of a washer-woman who is out of work on Monday. The intelligence offices hold no women so distressed that they will go out for less than a week, and that on trial. Yet, somewhere in the city, there must be women pining and longing for that waiting work.

Suppose a sudden influx of visitors exhausts your household staff, and makes a waiting-maid a necessity where none was kept before; suppose a large group of relatives, passing quickly through the city, come for a plain family dinner at a moment when your personal superintendence is impossible, — where is the active, tidy girl who can be summoned, or the decent woman of experience who can order matters in your kitchen as well as you can yourself?

Somewhere they sit waiting — suffering, it may be — for the opportunity which never comes. The intelligence office will get them places; but places they are not at liberty to seek. They need what they call "a chance lift."

I am well aware that wealthy and long-established families may not suffer much from this cause. Old servants well married, or a variety of well-paid servants with wide connections in the neighborhood, or deserving objects of charity personally met and understood, often prevent such persons from feeling any inconvenience; but for young housekeepers, for new residents, for persons of small means and few connections, there is no help.

I need not enlarge on the subject. There is no kind of female labor of which it is easy to get a prompt and suitable supply. To obviate this difficulty, I think there should be a sort of "Labor Exchange;" and this is a project which all classes would be glad to have carried out. How shall it be done? That, of course, must be settled by those who have the task in charge; but, to explain what I mean, I will offer a few suggestions. In the first place, What are the defects in the intelligence-offices now in existence?* There are several. They take cogni-

---

* I cannot allude to the subject of Intelligence-offices without saying, that all such institutions ought to be brought, in some *new* and *effective* manner, under public supervision and control.

A private Intelligence-office, kept in the superintendent's own house, cannot be interfered with, unless it can be proved a nuisance; and how difficult it is to abate a nuisance I need not tell anybody who has ever tried the experiment.

The keeper of a General or Public Intelligence-office makes application for a license to the city government, sustained by a certain number of respectable vouchers, and pays, I believe, a yearly fee of one dollar.

This looks fair enough; and, if every officer of the city government, from the lowest police-officer to the mayor, were immaculate, it would be so; but we all know what the fact is. It is an open secret, that, in all our largest cities, the marts of vice are stocked from these places, and that they serve

zance of domestic servants alone. They are kept by ignorant or inexperienced persons, who often lose sight of the interests of both the employer and the employed in their own pecuniary loss or gain. These persons have necessarily little insight into character, and do not see how to bring the right persons together. They will send a slow, dawdling girl to an impatient, lively mistress; — a smart upstart to some meek, little wife, who has hardly learned the way to order her own house; and the natural misunderstandings will occur. Then the books of the office are irregularly kept, and closed to the applicant, so that you have no chance to select for yourself. Go down to an office, and ask for a servant; tell the keeper not to send a raw girl, not to send one without a recommendation, not to send a foreigner who cannot speak English; and go home. The odds are, that, while you are taking off your bonnet, there will be three rings at the bell. The

---

the purposes of bad men better than houses of professedly vicious resort. One of the most excellent and respectable women I know, who superintends one of these offices. told me herself that four women made assignations on her premises, and went out of her office to keep them, without her having power to prevent it. She proved the correctness of her suspicions by employing one of her vouchers to watch the result. If this happens under the eyes of the virtuous and vigilant, what *may* not happen when the head of the establishment is in the pay of interested parties? I do not know in what way this wickedness can be broken up; but, in the words of Dr. Gannett, " what *must* be done, can be." Is it not a terrible thought, that fashionable women and tender girls should supply themselves with servants from the very brink of that hell they believe they have never touched? Is it not a far more terrible thought, that an innocent stranger cannot seek her daily bread without running the risk of certain perdition? How real these possibilities are, there are those in this city able to testify.

Ought not the ministers at large, of all denominations, and our overseers of the poor, to unite in prompt and efficient action in this regard?

first girl will be a barefooted imp of Erin, just from the steerage. Some one at the office has been watching three days for just such a hand to be broken into a farm-kitchen. The second wears a flower-garden on her head, more flounces than you do, and has, of course, no recommendation. Some soda-room wants her; but you do not. The third is high Dutch, and, when you ask her for the coal-hod, brings you, in her despair, the bread-tray. Neither of these three is what you ordered or wanted.

Do you ask me the reason of this bad management, and whether I think it can be remedied? The reason of it is, that the superintendence of these offices is not treated like a profession. People neither fit themselves for it, nor are attracted to it by nature: they simply *do* it; and how they do it we feel. They want comprehensive insight, have no business ways, and these difficulties are only to be obviated by bringing a higher intelligence to bear upon the arrangements.

Let us have a place where all kinds of female work can be sought and found; an intelligent working committee first, who know what is wanted, and how to get it, and who, most important of all, shall not be too wise to accept diplomas from experience.

Let us have a committee of five; its quorum to be three. Let these persons hire a large, clean, airy room, and appoint an intelligent superintendent, — one who will be interested to have the experiment thoroughly successful. Let them line the walls, and screen off the room with frames, having glass covers, to lock and unlock. Let one frame be devoted to cooks; another, to laundresses; another, to washerwomen, window-washers, charwomen, seamstresses, dressmakers, copyists, translators, or what you will; and under the glass the notices should be posted. Each should contain the name, age, and residence of the applicant; the situation last held, and for how long; the full address of the reference; and the date of posting. The date should be printed and movable, and changed semi-weekly, on the personal application of the poster. Each woman should pay five cents for the privilege of posting; should lose this privilege from misconduct, from neglect to report herself, from proved falsehood. No date should be left unchanged more than a week, and the superintendent should be responsible for the strict observance of the regulations. No woman, not even a charwoman, should be allowed to use the posting privilege, unless she has a reference. "What!" you will say, "is that kind?" Yes, it is kind: the want of it is doubly cruel. A woman who needs work can afford to offer a day's free work to get a reference; and referees should be required to tell the simple truth. A lady who once recommended a dishonest or incapable servant without the proper qualification should be struck off the books, not allowed to testify again in that court.

With regard to all transient labor, it should be the duty of the superintendent to see that the references are reliable before posting, so that those who apply in haste need not be delayed.

If a dressmaker or charwoman inform the superintendent that she has worked for A, B, and C, let a printed circular, addressed to such persons, inquiring if they can recommend her, and to what degree, be placed in her hands. To this she should bring written answers before being allowed to post.

If the institution became popular, books would have to be kept, corresponding to these glass cases — one book for cooks, another for housemaids, and so on; but the cases should never be given up. There should always be as many as the room will hold. Ladies should pay a certain sum for each servant they obtain; and the servant should pay for every place she gets, at a rate proportioned to the wages received. In most intelligence offices, the servants get two places for the same fee, if they do not stay over a week in the place, and the lady gets two girls or more on the same condition. This works like a premium on change of place. The servant should prove to the Labor Exchange, that she did not leave her place of her own will, and the lady should show that incapacity or insubordination made it impossible to keep her.

It should be a cash business, and a fee should be paid for each application. Wanting a cook, you go down to the room, and consult the proper frame. Finding, perhaps, forty posters, you select one that reads like this: —

Matilda Haynes.
Irish.
Twenty-five years of age.
In the country four years.
Thoroughly understands plain cooking.
Expects two dollars.
Is willing to go out of town.
Lived last at No. 4, Pemberton Square.
Kept the place six months.
May refer to it.
Can be found at 24, High Street.

You first go to Pemberton Square. It is quite possible that this girl may not be what you want; but if she is, and your eye tells you that you can trust the judgment of her referee, you have only to go to High Street, and make your own terms. If you are already prejudiced in her favor, you will go prepared to make some concessions, so that the chance will be better for you both; and this process may be repeated without loss of time, till you are supplied.

You will see that this is quite a feasible plan, and has two advantages. One is, that you have access to the books, and can choose for yourself; the other is, that there would be no waiting-room for servants, where they should talk with, prejudice, and morally harm each other. You would also be saved the pain of rejecting servants to their faces, on the ground of "greenness," or bodily unfitness. Such an institution would offer this advantage over the present offices, that it would direct you to temporary laborers, and give you in a moment the addresses of some dozens. Such an institution would be a very great saver of time, and so a great blessing.

If, in the course of these lectures, any words that I have spoken have touched your hearts, or carried conviction to your minds, do not put aside, I beseech you, such impulse as they may have given. Remember that, however feebly the subject has been treated, however presumptuous may seem the attempt, the subject itself is the most important theme that is presented to this generation. In my first lecture I showed you, that while women, ever since the beginning of civilization, have been sharing the hardest, and doing the most unwholesome work, they have also done the *worst paid* in the world. I showed you that this poor pay, founded on a false estimate of woman's value as a human being, and consequently as a laborer, was filling your streets with criminals, with stricken souls and bodies, for whose blood society is responsible to God. Having proved thus, that women need new avenues of labor, I tried in my second lecture to show you, that, when she sought these, she had been met too often by the selfish opposition of man. I showed also that all such opposition proved, in the end, unavailing; that all the work she asks will inevitably be given. I showed you, from the censuses of Great Britain and America, how much labor is even now open to her; that it is not half so necessary to open new avenues of labor as to make work itself *respectable for women;* and I therefore entreated women to learn to work thoroughly and well, that men might respect their labor in the aggregate. " Woman's work " means nothing very honorable or conscientious now. Alter its significance till it indicates the best work in the world.

In my present lecture I have indicated some of the steps that might be taken to benefit the women in the heart of this city. To encourage you to take them, I have briefly pointed out Ellen Woodlock's remarkable success. Have I kindled any interest in your minds? Can you enter into such labors? Have you strength or time or enthusiasm to spare? In the ballads of Northern Europe, a loving sister trod out, with her bare feet, the nettles whose fibre, woven into clothing, might one day restore her brothers to human form.

Your feet are shod, your nettles are gathered: will you tread them out courageously, and so restore to your sisters the nature and the privileges of a blessed humanity?

Opportunity is a rare and sacred thing. God seldom offers it twice. In the English fields, the little Drosera, or sundew, lifts its tiny, crimson head. The delicate buds are clustered in a raceme, to the summit of which they climb one by one. The topmost bud waits only through the twelve hours of a single day to open. If the sun do not shine, it withers and drops, and gives way to the next aspirant.

So it is with the human heart and its purposes. One by one, they come to the point of blossoming. If the sunshine of faith and the serene heaven of resolution meet the ripe hour, all is well; but if you faint, repel, delay, they wither at the core, and your crown is stolen from you, — your privilege set aside. Esau has sold his birthright, and the pottage has lost its savor.

THE COURT;

OR,

WOMAN'S POSITION UNDER THE LAW.

IN THREE LECTURES,

DELIVERED IN BOSTON, JANUARY, 1861

I. — THE ORIENTAL ESTIMATE AND THE FRENCH LAW.
II. — THE ENGLISH COMMON LAW.
III. — THE UNITED-STATES LAW, AND SOME THOUGHTS ON HUMAN RIGHTS.

"Kind gentlemen, your pains
Are registered where every day I turn
The leaf to read them."
Macbeth.

"Some reasons of this double coronation
I have possessed you with, and think them strong."
"Why do you bend such solemn brows on *me?*
Have I commandment on the pulse of life?"
King John.

"According to the fair play of the world,
Let me have audience. I am sent to speak."
King John.

"Let this be copied out,
And keep it safe for our remembrance.
Return the precedent to these lords again."
King John.

THE COURT.

I.

THE ORIENTAL ESTIMATE AND THE FRENCH LAW.

> "It was not Zeus who uttered this decree,
> Or Justice, dwelling with the gods below:
> Nor did I think thy will such power possessed,
> That thou, a mortal, could o'errule the laws
> Unwritten and immovable of God."
> <div align="right"><i>Antigone:</i> SOPHOCLES.</div>

> "We seldom doubt that something in the large
> Smooth order of creation, though no more
> Than haply a man's footstep, has gone wrong."
> E. B. BROWNING.

> "The law of God, positive law and positive morality, sometimes *coincide*, sometimes do *not coincide*, and sometimes *conflict*." — JOHN AUSTIN: *Province of Jurisprudence Defined*.

"OF Law, no less can be said than that her seat is the bosom of God; her voice, the harmony of the spheres. All things in heaven and earth do her reverence; the greatest as needing her protection, the meanest as not afraid of her power."

In reading this magnificent and well-known sentence from Hooker, the imagination is easily kindled to a divine prescience. We accept the definition. Fair before us rise the graceful proportions of eternal order in society, upon which wait present peace and future progress; towards which those bow most reverently who live most purely and see most clearly. But alas! if the reader be a woman, her heart may well sink when the enthusiasm of the moment has passed; and she must ask, with a feeling somewhat akin to displeasure, " Of *what* law realized on earth, administered in courts, dealt out from legislatures or parliaments, from republics or autocrats, were these sublime words written?"

Where in the soft shadows of Oriental hareems, in the gloom of Hindoo caves, Egyptian pyramids, or Attic porches, sculptured by divinest art, and luminous with marbles of every hue; where in the porticos echoing to Roman stoicism, or the baths floating on Roman license; where in the saloons of French society, or by the hearths of good old England; where, alas! in the free States of America, whether North or South, — has a system of law prevailed that women could think of, without blasphemy, as sitting in the bosom of God, and so entitled to the reverence of man?

We outgrow all things. Always the new patch breaks the fabric of the old garment; always the new wine shatters the well-dried leathern pouch which held the vintage of our ancestors. But most of all do we outgrow, have we outgrown, our laws. They fall back, dead letters, into the abyss of that past from which we have emerged. We put new laws upon the statute-book, and do not pause to wipe out the old; finding our protection in the public feeling and the public progress, if not in the traditions of the elders.

This, and this only, saves old systems from violent demolition. Were the State of Connecticut at this moment to attempt to put in force such of the blue-laws as are technically unrepealed, she would be met by the open rebellion of her highest officer; and the chief-justice who should attempt to fine a bishop for kissing his wife on Sunday might shake hands cordially with the chief-justice who once ruled that a man might beat his wife with a stick no bigger than his thumb!

The laws which relate to woman are based, for the most part, on a very old and a very Oriental estimate of her nature, her powers, and her divinely ordained position. We shall see this, if we follow the course of legal enactments or religious prohibitions from the beginning. When the subject of Woman's Civil Rights first came to be considered, it was customary to quote from the scholars one of the sayings of Vishnu Sarma: "Every book of knowledge which is known to Oosana or to Vreehaspatee is by nature implanted in the understandings of women."

Nobody asked what sort of knowledge was known to these two deities; but most readers took it for granted that it was divine: and ordinary people asked why, if society began with this reverent faith, we had nothing better now than the practical scepticism of priest and lawyer. When the names of these two deities were translated into Venus and Mercury (that is, into *love* and *cunning*), the announcement seemed more in keeping with the subsequent revelations of Vishnu Sarma: —

"Women, at all times," he says, "have been inconstant, even among the Celestials."

"Woman's *virtue* is founded upon a modest countenance, precise behavior, rectitude, and a *deficiency of suitors*."

"In infancy, the father should guard her; in youth, her husband; in old age, her children: for at no time is a woman fit to be trusted with liberty."

"Infidelity, violence, deceit, envy, extreme avarice, a total want of good qualities, with impurity, are the innate faults of womankind."

These extracts will throw some light, perhaps, upon the knowledge of Oosana and Vreehaspatee, and will save modern women from any very strong desire to restore the "good old rule." After such a commentary on this seeming compliment, we shall not think it strange, that, in a country where dialect is the exponent of condition, the most ancient drama represents the Hindoo wife as addressing her lord and master in the dialect of a slave.

"It is proper," says an ancient Hindoo scripture, "for every woman, after her husband's death, to burn herself in the fire with his corpse." I quote this saying here only to advert to the power of public opinion, which has been strong enough for ages to compel this sacrifice. But for it, many a woman, who had been burnt during her whole conjugal life in the fires of tyranny, self-will, and arrogant dominion, might have hailed with joy the hour of her release.

Under it, such a woman went calmly to the new martyrdom.

An ancient Chinese writer tells us, that the newly married woman should be but an echo in the house. Her husband may strike her, starve her, nay, even *let her out!* Such was the spirit of most Oriental custom and law. It has crossed the Ural; so that Köhl, the German traveller, tells us that a Turk blushes and apologizes when he mentions his wife, as if he had been guilty of a needless impertinence. The same thing is reported of one of the Sclavic tribes, among whom it may have been borrowed from their Ottoman conquerors.

In the "London Quarterly" for October, 1860, we are told that the convent of Nuestra Senhora da Ajuda in Rio was long employed for the purpose of locking up ladies whose husbands were on their travels. This has been forbidden by the present emperor.

There were, however, singular exceptions to the prevailing estimate. In the Island of Cœlebes, where the government is republican in form, the president, and four out of six councillors, are not unfrequently women. In the diary of the Marquess of Hastings, we are told, that among the Garrows, a populous and independent clan in the hill country in the north-east of India, all property and authority descend in the female line. On the death of the mother, the bulk of the possessions goes to the favorite daughter, *so* designated, without regard to primogeniture in her lifetime. The widower has a stipend settled on him at the time of marriage, and a moderate portion is given to each daughter. The sons are expected to support themselves. A woman, called Muhar, is the chief of each clan. Her husband is called Muharree, and has a representative authority, but no right to her property. Should he incline to squander it, the clan will interfere in her behalf. When the Duke of Wellington fought the battle of Assaye, in 1803, against the Mahrattas, a woman, the Begum of Lumroom, belonging to the military tribe of Nairs, fought against him at the head of her cavalry. In this tribe the succession follows, according to the duke's report, the female line. This was on the coast of Malabar, south of Bombay, and in what we should call the south-western part of the Deccan. In spite of the difference in orthography, and the statement about the north-east, I think these stories may refer to the same clan. An orthography so variously rendered as the East Indian is a blind guide.

Quite evident is it that the proverbs of more western and later-born nations grew out of the estimate of Vishnu Sarma and his compeers. Look at them: —

"A rich man is never ugly in the eyes of a girl."
"A beautiful woman, smiling, tells of a purse gaping."
"Every woman would rather be handsome than good."
"A house full of daughters is a cellar full of sour beer."
"Three daughters and the mother are four devils for the father."

"A man of straw is worth a woman of gold."
"A rich wife is a source of quarrel."
"'Tis a poor roost where the hen crows."
"A happy couple is a husband deaf and a wife blind."

It is quite evident, I think, that men made these proverbs; and somewhat mortifying, not to *women only*, but to our common humanity, that they should have the run of society and the newspapers, in an age which has given birth to Florence Nightingale, Mary Patton, and Dorothea Dix, — women who have been born only to remind us that their counterparts appeared a thousand years ago.

Aristophanes and Juvenal, Boileau and Churchill, turn these slanderous proverbs into verse, if not into poetry; and, in examining the laws of more modern times, we shall constantly trace the effect of the old Oriental estimate. In all such examinations, we have four points to consider: —

1st, That estimate of woman on which her civil position is founded, and those rights of property which are granted or refused to her accordingly.

2d, Such laws as relate to marriage and divorce.

3d, Such laws or customs as keep woman out of office, off the jury, and refuse her all authorized legitimate interference in public affairs.

4th, Her right of suffrage.

Of these points, the discussion of such laws as relate to marriage and divorce is alone to be restricted by any considerations of prudence. It has never seemed to me a wise thing to open needlessly this discussion; and the opening of it by women is needless, while they are in no position to discuss it equally with men. In the marriage relation, whatever is the certain loss and misery of one sex is also the certain loss and misery of the other. Whatever inequality and injustice appertains to it will be best removed when the two sexes can consider it together, like two equal and competent powers.* I shall advert to the laws of marriage and divorce, only to point out mistakes or bad results not generally perceived, and make no attempt to treat them at length.

When we consider what sort of public opinion has educated woman, what estimate has lain at the bottom of all the laws passed concerning her, it does not seem strange, that, after living for ages in a false position, she should somewhat approximate to this estimate; so that we say with pain of the mass of women, that *they themselves* need a change quite as much as their circumstances. It is common, in treating of this subject, to dwell on the position of woman under the Roman law; but very little is gained by it. We can see by the literature of the nation what estimate was put upon woman, and what share she took in the degradation of society; but how far this was the consequence of bad law, what changes were wrought from the time of Justinian, not merely in law, but in moral soundness under the law, it is not easy to tell in a country which had neither printing-presses nor news-

---

* Of course, I do not mean to be understood here as objecting to any temperate and earnest attempt by men or women to *amend law*.

papers. We have only the judgment of a few men, themselves law-makers, to rely upon; and their opinions had a very limited circulation in their lifetime, and could not be tested by any cotemporaneous verdict. It is in vain that we listen to testimony when no competent witnesses appear on the "other side." Women, however, ought always to remember to whom they owe the changes made in Justinian's time. The life of Theodora is yet to be written. The scandalous anecdotes of a secret history must some day be balanced by the public testimony of Procopius, and some good be told of the woman whose first thought, when raised to empire, was for the companions of her previous infamy, and whose influence over her husband never faltered, and is visible in every modification of the laws relating to her sex. If we could realize the corruptness of the higher classes of society, we should not wonder at the emperor who chose his wife from the streets; and the fact itself tells a story which he who *heeds* need not misunderstand.*

---

* It will easily be conjectured that I do not feel competent to treat the great subject of Roman legislation for women, in the noble and extended manner which is at once, as it seems to me, necessary and possible. Perhaps I shall never become so.

It seems to me proper, however, that I should indicate my dissatisfaction with existing methods in the clearest manner, and drop a few hints, as I do in the text, as to the difficulties in the way.

Roman sepulchral inscriptions, of the era generally considered the most licentious, bear witness in the fullest manner to the existence of chastity and domestic virtue. A sepulchral inscription, it may be argued, is a poor witness to facts. I would suggest in reply, that a nation ceases to commemorate the virtue which has ceased to exist, or which it has, through a general depravity of manners, ceased to respect.

The laws which most directly affect us here in America are the laws of France and England: the laws of France, because they modify the code of Canada, Florida, and Louisiana; the laws of England, because in her common law, recognized all over the country by all the States, we find the basis of all that is objectionable in our legislation.

First, then, let us consider the estimate on which the French law is based, and then its property-laws. Civil position and the right of franchise can be disposed of in a few words the world over. "There is one thing which is not French," said Bonaparte, as he closed a cabinet council, while preparing his famous Code; "and that is, a woman who can do as she pleases."

The estimate of woman in France is of a double character.

It is *low*, because marriage among the upper classes is, at the best, only a well-made bargain.

It is *high*, because women have been encouraged to enter trade, both by law, which protects them in their capacity as merchants, and by the military character of the nation, which prevents men from entering business.

It is *low*, because throughout the provinces there are remnants of old feudal custom, which keep her in the position of a slave. The peasant's wife rarely sits at table: she crouches in the chimney-corner, eating from the stew-pan; while her husband sits at the table in state before his porringer. Yet, in another respect, this very woman helps to raise the estimate of her sex; for she works with her husband in the field, while a wealthier wife is often only a burden. Like him, she is exposed to all the changes of the weather. Pregnancy does not save her from the plough or the vintage. While her husband rests at noon, she must nurse her babe or prepare his meal.

In most countries, it is desirable to turn the thoughts of women away from love, and give them some healthier occupation. In France, it would be well to stimulate the affections, because covetousness, a desire of worldly position, or splendid wealth, is the main motive to a marriage. With us, love constitutes the whole life of many a woman; while it may be only an episode in that of her husband.

In France, even woman seldom loves, but marries to establish herself in life. It is against this greed that she needs to be cautioned, *not* against that emotion and sentiment which God meant should be both a safeguard and a blessing. *Love* must rescue woman from vanity, self-indulgence, and empty show. Only through its divine power will she come to perceive the true nature of that shameful bargain, by which she surrenders what is most precious to appease the thirst of society. If we would save and serve humanity *here*, we must let natural susceptibilities have their full play.

At the same time, the business freedom which women enjoy in France has led many women to reflect thoroughly and act vigorously. The reading world is deluged with books relating to woman, — her education, her labor, and her civil rights. Out of this condition of things spring a class who long to share the sorrow and responsibility as well as the joy of liberty. They will not accept the tenderness and pity of such men as Michelet, who veil a profound sensualism with the graces of an affected sentimentality. Sometimes, like George Sand, these women break loose from social ties, test the world for themselves, and, when they have squeezed the orange which looked so tempting, show to others the empty, bitter rind, and return gladly to the daily bread of Divine Ordinance. Once, in Rosa Bonheur, fresh and wise, energetic and vigorous, the French woman has challenged the attention of the civilized world. With no womanish weaknesses, frank, loyal, and endowed with a serious and reflective nature, this artist has asked no leave to be of church or society. "I have no patience," she once said, "with women who ask permission to think. Let women establish their claims by great and good works, and not by conventions." She took the whole world in her two brave woman's hands, *found* her inheritance, and resolved to enjoy it.

It is in France, too, that Clara Demars thinks out all the psychological relations of love and marriage, and reminds us of Mrs. John Stuart Mill, by saying that "truth will never reign over the world, nor between the sexes, until, by being set free, woman loses all temptation to dissimulate."

There, too, Flora Tristan provokes a smile by echoing in prose the rhythmic platitudes of **Mr.** Coventry Patmore, and claiming, not *equality*, but sovereignty and autocracy, for woman.

There Pauline Roland boldly claims that marriage shall never be tolerated, till man as well as woman is compelled to keep the law of chastity.

There Madame Moniot claims her civil rights from the lecturer's desk; and Désirée Gay, interesting herself practically in the question of woman's labor, rules the women of the national workshops.

When both sides of this picture are studied; when we look back, on the one hand, to Marie Antoinette and Madame Récamier, and, on the other, to Madame Roland, Madame de Staël, and Marie de Lamourous, — it is not strange that the fanciful protectorship of such men as Michelet should be balanced by a claim, made not only by Talleyrand, but Condorcet, for woman's full equality as a laborer and a citizen. And this varying and inconsistent estimate of woman, made evident in the social, industrial, and literary spheres of France, is strangely sustained by her legal enactments. The "Code Napoléon" is founded on the Roman, and is very similar to the English common law, so far as it concerns woman: but beside this law, which is called, in reference to married women, the *dotal*, there is another, called the *communal*; and, before marriage, parties may choose between these two. That contract once signed, they must abide by their choice ever after. If the dotal law is founded on Roman law and usage, and so came naturally enough to prevail in Southern France until the time of the Revolution; so the communal law prevailed at the North, and is founded on the German habits and laws, beneath which always lay the idea, that, if not technically a laborer, the wife, by care and industry, — the thrift of the housewife, — contributed to the acquisition of property.

It is very singular that all the nations of Continental Europe, with the exception of Spain, have rejected the dotal or Roman law. The objection to it seems to have arisen out of the fact, that it permits the wife's property to be settled *solely* on herself, and to be so secured against her husband's debts. In the community of estates, the property of each is liable for the debts of either. It was on this account, probably, that, while the "Code Napoléon" elucidated and defined the dotal system, it expressly provided for the right of choice in the parties, and declared, that, if no choice were made, they should be supposed to be living under the German or communal law.

The Dutch law is essentially the same. When the "Code Napoléon" came into force, there were not wanting French legislators to say, that woman was now better *protected* than ever before. But this *legal protection* is of a kind due only to minors and lunatics. This law, like our own, suspects, not only the *intelligence* of woman, but her integrity; and aims not to protect *her*, but *man*, against her weakness or fraud. In marriage, the husband administers for both, not only the common property, but her personal possessions. That is to say, by *pretending to protect it,* the law *takes away* from woman her personal property. It often happens, that a woman who has brought her husband a large property is compelled to shift in narrow ways, like a beggar or a miser, on account of his parsimony or personal ill-will.

The wife cannot give away the smallest article, not even such as have been gifts to her: and the 934th article of the " Code Napoléon " declares, "that the wife may not accept a gift without the consent of her husband; or, if he should refuse, without the approbation of a magistrate." She cannot pledge their common property, even though it were to set her husband free when imprisoned for debt; nor, in the event of his absence, to secure necessaries for his children, without the same magisterial authority. Commonly, this authority would be readily obtained; but it is easy to see that many cases might arise, when, from defeated purposes, personal enmity, or the influence of the husband against her, it would be all but impossible.

Even in case of bankruptcy, French legislators tell us, the rights of the wife are protected. But this very protection is insulting; for it treats the wife as if she must of necessity be either an inert instrument in the hands of her husband, or a dupe, whose weakness he might readily abuse. *Through* such protection, the dishonest merchant finds it easy to defraud his creditors.

Now, this "Code Napoléon" says that "the husband owes protection to his wife; and the wife, on her side, owes obedience to her husband:" but it goes on to secure the obedience by giving an unlimited right to the person of the wife, without in any way providing the promised protection.

"The wife must live with her husband, and follow him wherever he sees fit to go. As for him, he must receive her, and furnish her with necessaries according to her wealth and rank."

Now, this clause actually constrains no one but the wife; for what would be the condition of a woman who followed her husband against his will, and remained *under* his roof when he was determined that she should quit it? Under such circumstances, his recognition of her wealth and rank would be very apt to fall to the level of his own irritation.

The French code will interfere to protect a wife against the total loss of her property, if she can prove *some* loss already experienced, either from the improvidence or the bad conduct of her husband; but it keeps her powerless to protect herself against that first loss. Having thus, and for such reasons, obtained a separate jurisdiction over her property, she cannot alienate, mortgage, or acquire a title to new property, without her unworthy husband's consent in person or on paper. The guardianship of the children is left to the survivor of the marriage; but the mother's right in such case may be restrained by the father's and husband's will. He can appoint a trustee to be associated with her. As a business woman, even if separated in estate, the wife cannot make or dissolve a contract without the consent of her husband.

As a "public merchant" under the communal system, — that is, pledged in *her own name*, — she is free from this restraint. As a citizen of the French republic, she in that case supports, conjointly with her husband, all State charges. She is taxed as much as he; for their common income is diminished as much for one as for the other. She has no suffrage; but, on the other hand, she is not liable for military service. She has no rights; a state of things, which, if it be excusable when she is absorbed into her husband's personality, is only absurd when she fulfils all the functions of a citizen. Well may Legouvé exclaim, "that, if the household be woman's own sphere, she ought to be queen in it; and her own faculties should secure her this supremacy. Her opponents should be forced, on their own principles, to emancipate her as daughter, wife, and mother." The woman who owns an estate is, under this law, sole mistress of it. She signs the leases and makes the bargains. She pays the State tax, an additional rate to her own department, a town tax, and a tax on roads. It is with her that the local or general government treat, if they cut through her estate for public ends. Against them, if wronged, she herself carries suit. By her influence as a proprietor, she controls many votes; yet she is not permitted to cast one. She cannot *directly* control the position of the very representative who imposes her taxes. She is in the same position with regard to all the higher officers, who decide such questions as affect the value of her estate. As citizen, therefore, under the communal law, her position is uncertain and contradictory.

So much for the estimate of woman in France; and so much for the rights of property, of marriage, and of suffrage, founded upon that estimate. What is her *civil position?* what office or employment is open to her? Women are better off in France, it is again said, than ever before. As merchants, fair chances, barred by some contradictions and anomalies, await them; but whoever ponders their condition cannot fail to see, that here, as elsewhere, the protection afforded by the law is merely the vigilance of a police officer, which protects the criminal, not for *her own* sake, but for that of society, which her very existence is supposed to endanger.

The most desirable amelioration of her lot will be secured by the admission of her free personality. When society strikes out from the statute-book all distinctions of sex, and admits that she is a person capable of thinking and acting for herself, she will lay the foundation of a new civilization.

In France, we are told, women sometimes fill public functions. They may be postmistresses, and inspectors of schools; or they may take charge of the bureaus of wood or tobacco. They may also be inspectors of public asylums, — a right and a duty of very great importance. As a public functionary, woman fills few and inferior posts; but in these she exercises and possesses all the rights of a man, with one exception, — that exception, alas! the very keystone on which all human success must rest: I mean, the right of *promotion*. Do not smile, prompted by an unworthy apprehension of my meaning. It is *not* because women are more greedy or more ambitious than men that I call the right to promotion the keystone of their success. Only small and narrow natures can be content in a treadmill. If constant motion will not carry her over the top of the wheel, instinct prompts the reasoning creature to abate her efforts. No man of his own free will turns into a road which abuts upon a stone wall. The State turnpike is better, where the wayfarer may die by a sunstroke, or perish of a frost; where endless miles stretch over uncultivated wastes: better; for here, at least, the way is open, the sky overhead.

Before proceeding to speak of the English common law, it will perhaps be well to turn from the " Code Napoléon" to the law of Louisiana, in which the influence of the two forms of French law still shows itself. I do not consider the laws of Canada, because they are complicated, not only by the English common law, but by Canadian statutes, somewhat in the spirit of our own recent enactments, and by curious archæological remains of feudal law, — laws which would sound like the decrees of Haroun al Raschid, were I to tax your soberness by setting them before you. They are, let us be thankful, of small practical importance, as is the great body of all law.*

In Louisiana, according to the civil code of 1824, the partnership of gains arising during coverture exists by law in every marriage, without express stipulation to the contrary. But the parties may regulate their married obligations as they please, provided they do nothing immoral. The wife's property is "dotal." What she *brings*, her paraphernalia, is "extra-dotal." The dowry belongs to the husband during marriage; and he has the administration of the partnership, and may alienate his revenue, without his wife's consent: but he cannot convey the common estate. If, before marriage, he should stipulate that there should be no partnership, his wife preserves the entire control of her own property. Her heirs take her separate estate; even money received by her husband on her account. If there be no agreement as to the expenses, the wife contributes one-half of her income. Her landed estate, whether dotal or not, is not affected by his debts. She is a privileged creditor, and has the first mortgage on his property.

If the parties have agreed to the "partnership of gains," the common property is liable for the debts

---

* The great body of all law is of small practical importance, because, in spite of the five points of Calvinism and the long faces of many bearded philosophers, the majority of mankind not only *obey* the law, but transcend it, — do better than it requires. It is only the few who transgress; and thus many absurdities are never or very rarely dragged into the light of a "decision."

of either. On the death of either party, one-half of the property goes to the survivor; the other, to the heirs of the dead partner.

You will perceive that this law seems a loose mixture of the Roman or dotal system with the German communal law, based on the partnership of gains; but the common law takes it for granted that the partnership exists, where there is no express stipulation to the contrary. As a public trader, the wife may bind herself in whatever relates to her business, without her husband's consent, — may even make a will; and reference is made to the " Code Napoléon," in the same way, to all appearance, that we refer to the common law of England.

The estimate of woman upon which the " Code Napoléon" is founded has the same effect upon her earnings as the English common law. As, in marriage, the policy has been to keep her subordinate and inferior; to give her no privileges which should lead to independence: so, in business, the effect of the law is to keep the price of her work down, and give her as few escapes from household drudgery as may be; to offer her, in fact, no *temptation* to escape.

As polishers, burnishers, and copper-workers; as glove-makers, enamellers, and wire-drawers; as flax-beaters and soakers; as spinners, gauze-workers, and winders; as basket-makers, and temperers of steel; as knife-handlers, embroiderers, and wheel-turners; as velvet-makers, cockle-gatherers, and ivory-workers; as packers, knitters, satin-makers, and folders; as picture-colorers, and workers in wood; as casters, weighers, and varnishers; as shoe-makers, strap-makers, lace-makers, and cocoon-winders, — the French employ many women; and the estimate of the law is practically indicated, there as well as here, in the price of the labor done.

The highest wages marked upon my list are those paid to the workers in a porcelain factory, who received one franc and fifty centimes a day, or thirty cents. The lowest are those paid to cockle-gatherers and lace-makers; that is, from twenty to twenty-five centimes, or from four to five cents a day.

The fact that the poor lace-makers, who lose their eyesight and their lives bending over their bobbins, are paid the same wages as the loitering girls who pick up gay cockles on the beach, shows how little the price of the labor depends on the value of the work done, and tells the whole story in a breath. The wages of the needlewomen of Paris have been diminishing ever since 1847, and, according to the "Revue des Deux Mondes," now average only from twenty to twenty-five cents a day.

II.

THE ENGLISH COMMON LAW.

"And we, perusing o'er these notes,
May know wherefore we took the sacrament,
And keep our faiths firm and inviolable."

King John.

IN approaching the subject of English common law, we come nearer to our own special interests. Twenty years ago, I am safe, I think, in presuming that this law was the basis of all our legislation in regard to woman, if we except that in French or Spanish territory; and, in criticising its provisions, I shall criticise all that is objectionable, whether in the laws that have been changed, or in the laws that remain to be changed, in our own States.

If we were to examine the literature of England with reference to this subject, we should probably find from the beginning many protests against the present position of woman. It is never safe, for instance, to assume what poets may or may *not* have said. If Dryden could get so far as to say that there is "no sex in souls," one would think the gentle Chaucer and heavenly-minded Daniel doubtless discerned still deeper things; but of lawyers we may say with some truth, that their early protests were so quietly made as scarcely to be recognized, or were made for the most part by unread and anonymous writers.

In the "Lawe's Resolution of Woman's Rights," published in the year 1632, there seems to be a distinct recognition of the true nature of the law:—

"The next thing that I will show you," says the author, "is *this* particularity of law. In this consolidation which we call wedlock is a locking together. It is true, that man' and wife are one person; but understand in what manner. When a small brooke or little river incorporateth with Rhodanus, Humber, or the Thames, the poore rivulet looseth her name; it is carried and recarried with the new associate; it beareth no sway; it possesseth nothing during coverture. A woman, as soon as she is married, is called *covert*; in Latine, *nupta*, — that is, 'veiled;' as it were, clouded and overshadowed: she hath lost her streame. I may more truly, farre away, say to a married woman, Her new self is her superior; her companion, her master."

Still farther: "Eve, because she had helped to seduce her husband, had inflicted upon her a special bane. See here the reason of that which I touched before, — that women have no voice in Parliament. They make no laws, they consent to none, they abrogate none. All of them are understood either married or to be married, and their desires are to their husbands. I know no remedy, though some women can shift it well enough. The common lawe here shaketh hand with divinitye."

In this plain statement of the old black-letter book lies the root of the evil with which we contend: "All of them are married or to bee married, and their desires are to their husbands." Woman, single, widowed, or pursuing an independent vocation, never seems to have entered the head of the law, as a possible monster worth providing for. The world of that day believed in the *sea-serpent*, but not in her. This book, " The Lawe's Resolution of the Rights of Woman," was, so far as I know, first brought under our notice by Mrs. Bodichon's quotation, in her " Brief Summary of the English Law." Then a few copies found their way to this country, and into the hands of curious persons. People began to wonder who wrote the quaint old book. In pleading before our own Legislature in the spring of 1858, I was myself asked by the committee who was its author; and I think it but right to rescue from oblivion the probable name of this early friend to woman and justice. It is always difficult to trace an anonymous book, and, this time, more difficult than usual, as it was probably published *after* its author's death.

Sir John Doderidge, to whom my attention was directed by an eminent antiquarian, was an able lawyer, and an industrious compiler of law-books of a special kind. He was from Devonshire, and admitted as a barrister in 1603. He was successively appointed Solicitor-General, Judge of the Common Pleas and of the King's Bench. Among the works known to be his, yet not commonly included in the list of his works, are the " Lawyer's Light," published in 1629; and " The Complete Parson," with the laws relating to advowsons and livings, in 1670, — books of the same class, character, and appearance as the " Lawe's Resolution."

As he died in 1628, I was at first inclined to suspect the fairness of this inference: but a further examination showed that all his publications were *posthumous;* which accounts, perhaps, for the *candor* of their covert satire. A few particulars of his life and standing may be gained from the new Life of Lord Bacon, where Hepworth Dixon says that "the Solicitor-Generalship, vacant once more, is given, over Francis Bacon's head, to Sir John Doderidge, Serjeant of the Coif." In 1606, when Sir Francis Gawdy dies, "Coke goes up to the bench; and Doderidge, the Solicitor-General, ought, by the custom of the law, to follow Coke, leaving the post of Solicitor void: but Cecil raises Sir Henry Hobart, his obscure Attorney of the Court of Wards, over both Doderidge and Bacon's head, to the high place of Attorney-General." Since that day, Bentham and Catharine Macauley, Mary Wollstonecraft, and John Stuart Mill, have made the same complaint; sustaining it, however, by vigorous argument for woman's full emancipation, and a demand for the right of suffrage.

Let us look at this English law. So far as it affects *single* women, it is very simple.

A single woman has the same rights of property as a man; that is, she may get and keep, or dispose of, whatever she can. She has a right, like man, to the protection of the law, and has to pay the same taxes to the State.

"Duly qualified," she may *vote* on parish questions

and for parish officers; and "duly qualified," in England, means that she shall have a certain amount of property, and so a vested interest in the prosperity of her parish. If her parents die without a will, she shares equally with her brothers in the division of the personal property; but her eldest brother and his issue, even if female, will take the real estate as heirs-at-law. If she be an only child, she inherits both personal and real, and becomes immediately that most pitiable of creatures, an heiress.

The church and all state offices are closed to women. They find some employment in rural post-offices; but there is no important office they can hold, if we except that of sovereign. This is sometimes spoken of as an inconsistency; but if we reflect upon the position of a constitutional sovereign, whose speeches are the work of her minister, and whose actions indicate the average conscience of a cabinet council, we shall find her legally but very little more independent than other women technically classed with minors and idiots.

There have been a few women governors of prisons, overseers of the poor, and parish clerks; but public opinion still effectually bars most women from seeking or accepting office.

The office of Grand Chamberlain was filled by two women in 1822. That of Clerk of the Crown, in the Court of Queen's Bench, has been granted to a female; and, in a certain parish of Norfolk, a woman was recently appointed parish clerk, because, in a population of six hundred souls, no man could be found able to read and write!

In an action at law, it has been determined that an unmarried woman, having a freehold, might vote for members of Parliament. Mr. Higginson tells us that a certain Lady Packington returned two.

In all periods, there have been women who have held exceptional positions, under peculiar influence of wealth or rank or circumstances; and though this has not affected the position of other women, or given them any more freedom, yet it is valuable in itself, because it has kept the *possibility* of their employment always open, and acted like a practical protest against the law.

The Countess of Pembroke was hereditary Sheriff of Westmoreland, and exercised her office. In the reign of Queen Anne, Lady Rous did the same, " girt with a sword." Henry VIII. once granted a commission of inquiry, under the great seal, to Lady Anne Berkeley, who opened it at Gloucester, and passed sentence under it.

Some of the old legal writers averred, that a woman might serve in almost any of the great offices of the kingdom. Lately we find it stated that a woman may be elected as constable, since she can *hire a man* to serve for her; but she may *not* be elected overseer of the poor, because, in this case, substitution, if not impossible, would be difficult!

What were the peculiar political excitements which enabled Lady Packington to return two members of

Parliament, we are not told; but it is quite certain that women of twenty-one, duly qualified, cannot and do not vote for members of Parliament by virtue of that decision. In rural districts, where personal influence weighed a good deal, such a vote might be courteously winked at. A woman of property and standing, in Nova Scotia, has in this manner, for more than forty years, cast her annual vote, without rebuke or interruption; but, should any *number* of women act on this precedent, a legal restraint would doubtless be laid.

No single woman, having been seduced, has any remedy at common law; neither has her mother nor next friend. If her father can prove *service* rendered, he may sue for loss of service.

In what " bosom of divinitye " does this law rest? Here is a remedy for the loss of a few hours, but no penalty held up *in terrorem*, to warn man that he may not trifle with honor, womanly purity, and childish ignorance or innocence.

In the eye of this law, female chastity is only valuable for the work it can do. It must not be thought, however, that the English common law stands alone in this moral deformity. Under the French law, female chastity does not seem of any worth, even in consideration of the work it can do. In honest indignation, Legouvé exclaims, —

" Let a man, who has seduced a child of fifteen years by a promise of marriage, be brought before a magistrate. He has under the law a right to say, ' There is my signature, it is true; but I deny it. A debt of the heart is void before the law.'"

Thus everywhere, in practice and theory, in society and in law, for rich and poor, is public purity abandoned, — the bridle thrown upon the neck of all restive and depraved natures.

Manufacturers seduce their work-people; the heads of workshops refuse to employ girls who will not sell themselves, soul and body, to them; masters corrupt their servants. Out of 5,083 lost women counted by Duchâtelet at Paris in 1830, there were 285 domestic servants seduced, and afterwards dismissed by their employers. Commission-merchants, officers, students, deceive the poor girls from the province or the country, drag them to Paris, and leave them to perish. At all the great centres of industry, as at Rheims and at Lille, are societies organized to recruit the houses of sin in Paris.

This is well known to be true of all the large English towns; yet the law is powerless, and philanthropy interferes with no other result than that of driving these societies from one post to another.

Can women be expected to believe that the law would be powerless, if there were a sound public opinion behind it to sustain the law; if there were any *desire* on the part of the majority of men that it should be sustained? "Punish the young girl, if you will," continued Legouvé; "but punish also the man who has ruined her. She is already punished, — punished by desertion, punished by dishonor, punished by remorse, punished by nine months of suffering, punished by the charge of a child to be reared. Let him, then, be struck in his turn. If not, it is no longer public modesty that you defend: it is the 'lord paramount,' the vilest of the rights of the 'seigneur.'"

In the laws which regard single women, we object, then, —

1. To the withholding of the elective franchise.

2. To the law's preference of males, and the issue of males, in the division of estates.

3. We object to the estimate of woman which the law sustains, which shuts her out from all public employment, for many branches of which she is better fitted than man.

4. We object to that estimate of woman's chastity which makes its existence or non-existence of importance only as it affects the comfort or income of man.

We do not mean that the present *interpretation* of the common law does not *sometimes* show a more liberal estimate than the law itself, but rather that the existence of this law, unrepealed, *unchristianized*, is a forcible restraint upon the progress of society.

"A legal fiction," says Maine in his "Ancient Law," "signifies any assumption which conceals, or affects to conceal, the fact, that a rule of law has undergone alteration, its *letter* remaining unchanged, while its operation is modified." Such fictions may be useful in the infancy of society; but, like absurd formulas and embarrassing technicalities, they should give way before advancing common sense, before the diffusion of general intelligence and a common-school system, which is destined to qualify the humblest man for a full understanding of the law under which he lives.

We have now to consider the laws concerning *married women*. " On whatsoever branch of jurisprudence may lie the charge," says a late reviewer, " of working the heaviest sum of suffering, perhaps we shall not err in saying that the sharpest and cruellest pangs are those which have been inflicted by our marriage-laws." In making our abstracts, we have need to avoid the absurd complications which confuse, not only simple-minded people, but lawyers themselves; and, to avoid any charge of ignorance or mistake, we will, as far as possible, adopt the language of Mrs. Bodichon's " Summary," which has stood for six years before the English public without impeachment.

We shall not discuss the question, as to what constitutes fitness for marriage in the eye of the law. In Scotland and in England, the consent of the parties is said to be the " essence of marriage;" but, alas! in how many cases is this " consent " taken for granted only, it being, in fact, the most baseless of legal fictions!

In commenting on the English law as compared with the Scotch, the reviewer adds, " A code so unsatisfactory, so unsettled, and by every alteration coming so palpably near to their own system, is one which Scotchmen may be pardoned for declining further to consider, and which certainly they cannot be expected to recognize as the model to which their own should be conformed."

The rule of the English law was, at the institution of the Divorce Court, that the wife should have the same domicile as her husband, and that within English territory. A dishonest domicile barred her claim to divorce; and the husband who abandoned his wife, and fixed his residence abroad, effectually bound her to him. Justice has of late been done, because it was justice, heedless of the question of domicile.

There are in relation to this subject many provisions which wrong men and women alike; and, if there are any which especially wrong woman, they wrong man in a still higher degree through her. As an example of the former class, we may take the impossibility of release from a hopelessly insane partner, which makes the point of the wonderful story of "Jane Eyre."

Now, several things are quite evident to the eye of common sense: —

First, That the insane partner should be properly provided for during life, in the upper classes, by the sane partner; in the lower, by the parish or state.

Second, That as it is a sin against God and society to bring children into the world, born of a hopelessly insane parent; so, on the other hand, it is a sin against God and society to compel any man or woman to a life of hopeless celibacy.

Third, That, if the law does use this compulsion,

it is responsible for the vicious connections that inevitably grow out of it; "*car les mauvaises lois produisent les mauvaises mœurs.*" * I should not turn aside from my main point to consider this, even for a moment, if it were not a striking instance of the want of common *sense* which afflicts the common *law*, and if I had not in my own experience been made aware of its frightful results. Within the limits of one small parish in the city of Toronto, Canada West, I found four instances in which men of the middle class had taken the right of divorce into their own hands, and were illegally married a second time. These persons, if not markedly religious, were respectable, orderly members of society, living properly in their families, supporting the wives they had left, and justifying the course they had taken. Two of them had left England on account of the hopeless insanity of their wives, and two on account

---

* A curious instance of the immoral result of holding marriage sacramental, and indissoluble under all circumstances, comes within my personal experience while I am correcting these pages for the press, Oct. 11, 1861.

A young Catholic girl was divorced some years ago, immediately after marriage, on account of the bad conduct of her husband. She was received into the family of a brother-in-law, in every way highly respectable. For the last two years, she has been courted by an officer in the navy of the United States; but nowhere in New England could a Catholic priest be found willing to marry them. The church still holds her responsible to her first vows. The officer honestly desired to marry her; but the natural result of her ignorance and perplexity followed. Expecting to become a mother, and rejected by her family, she came to me for advice. As the officer is a Protestant, I recommended that they should be married by a minister of that faith. She again consulted her priest, and was told that it was less sinful for her to remain in her present relation to her lover than to receive a sacrament from unholy hands; the priest ignoring utterly the *legal* protection and maintenance which she might thus receive.

of their hopeless immorality; the latter, cases in which the law would have granted a divorce, but at an expense which the husband could not pay. When I first heard this account of one person, I resented it as a slander, and went to console the afflicted wife, who was overwhelmed by the supposed rumor.

The husband met me at the door, with an honest, unabashed, but distressed face. "Don't deny it to her," said he. "I never committed but one sin, and that was when I kept it from her. She was a sweet, pious creature; and I feared she would not consent."

This man told me that he sent six hundred dollars yearly to his insane wife; that this kept her better than he could afford to keep himself and his family: "but," said he, "her station was always higher than mine."

In the other cases, the men had told their stories, and the wives had consented to the arrangement. It is obvious, that, if a wife wished to withdraw from a husband in this manner, she could not do it, on account of property restrictions, and the common unfitness for self-support.*

In the marriage of a minor, the consent of the father, or of a guardian appointed by him, is neces-

---

* The only excuse for considering this point, in an essay pleading especially for women, is that the law bears unequally on the two sexes; pressing hardest on woman, on account of her pecuniary dependence, and general subordination to man.

A woman, every reader will understand, would find it impossible to free herself from her obligations, like the men referred to in the text; nor is it desirable that she should *free herself*, but that the law should free her.

sary, but *not* that of the *mother:* another indication of the estimate the law puts upon woman, as compared with man; and this estimate, whenever and wherever it shows itself, has the effect to depress every woman's desire to fit herself to be a good citizen; and, when she fails in citizenship, man must fail also, as is ably shown by De Tocqueville.

"A hundred times in the course of my life," he says, "I have seen weak men display public virtue because they had beside them wives who sustained them in this course, not by counselling this or that action in particular, but by exercising a fortifying influence on their views of duty and ambition. *Oftener still,* I have seen domestic influence operating to transform a man, naturally generous, noble, and unselfish, into a cowardly, vulgar, and ambitious self-seeker, who thought of his country's affairs only to see how they could be turned to his own private comfort or advancement; and this simply by daily contact with an honest woman, a faithful wife, a devoted mother, from whose mind the grand notion of public *duty* was entirely absent."*

A man and wife are one person in law: a *wife loses all her rights* as a single woman. Her husband is legally responsible for her acts: so she is said to live under his cover. A woman's body belongs to her husband. She is in his custody, and he can enforce his right by a writ of *habeas corpus.*

---

* National Rev., Apr. 1861, pp. 291, 292.

This last is one of the points in which the public feeling is so far before the law, that the latter could never be wholly enforced.

If a woman were unlawfully restrained of her liberty, her husband might take advantage of a *habeas corpus* to get possession of her; but it is not probable that any court, in England or this country, would *now* grant one to compel a wife to live with her husband against her will. Still, the estimate of the marriage relation which such laws sustain is so low, that one never can tell what will happen.

In the year 1858, a curious but *unintentional* satire on the judicial position of the husband occurred in one of the London courts. A delicate, much-abused woman, unmarried, but who had been, in her own phrase, "living for some time" with a man, brought an action against him for assault. Erysipelas had inflamed her wounds, and endangered her life.

"Had she died, sirrah," said the magistrate, addressing the criminal, "you must have taken your trial for murder. What have you to say in your defence?"

"I was in liquor, sir," pleaded the man. "I gave her some money to go to market. I told her to look sharp; but she was gone more than an hour, your worship: so, when she came back, I — I was in liquor, your honor."

The magistrate leaned over his desk, and, speaking in the most impressive manner, thus endeavored to cut short the defence: —

"This woman is not your slave, man. She is not accountable to you for every moment of her time. She is not," he continued with increasing fervor, but a growing embarrassment, — "she is not — she is not" —

He paused; but the throng of wretched women who crowded the court interpreted the pause aright, and were not likely to forget the lesson.

A suppressed titter ran through the court: for every married man knew that the words, "she is not your wife," were those which had sprung naturally to the worthy magistrate's lips; and must have passed them, had not honest shame prevented.

The man then attempted to defend himself on the ground of jealousy: but this was instantly set aside; the unmistakable impression left on the mind of the court-room being, that the illegality of the relation was wholly in the woman's favor.

Since the war, freed-women at Beaufort, S.C., have refused marriage for this very reason.

Women long ago understood this, and literary gossip gives us a late instance in a maiden aunt of Sir Charles Morgan. This woman, descended from Morgan the buccaneer, has more than once turned the scales of an Irish election. When she once arrested a robber on her own premises, and held him fast till the arrival of an officer, the gentlemen of the neighborhood advised her not to prosecute.

" It is well known," they argued, " that you refuse

to employ a single man on your premises, and you may be marked out for the revenge of the gang."

"Justice is justice," she exclaimed in reply; "and the villain shall go hang!"

It was quite natural that we should find this woman telling Lady Caroline Lamb that no *man* should ever have legal rights over her, or her property. A wife's money, jewels, and clothes become absolutely her husband's; and he may dispose of them as he pleases, whether he and his wife live together or not. Her chattels real — that is, estates held for a term of years — and presentations of church livings become absolutely his; but, if she survive him, she may resume them.

Under such a common law as this, it is not surprising to find something needed which is called *equity*. Therefore, if a wife, on her marriage, gives all her property to her husband, the said *equity* (Heaven save the mark!) will, under certain circumstances, oblige him to make a settlement upon her. That is, when the wife has an interest in property which can only be reached by the husband through a court of equity, that court will aid him to enjoy it, *only* on condition that such part as it thinks proper shall be settled on the wife.

The civil courts in England cannot compel a man to support his wife: *that* is left to the action of the church, and her own parish.

A husband has a freehold estate in his wife's lands as long as they both live.

Money earned by a married woman belongs absolutely to her husband.

By her husband's particular permission, she may make a will; but he may revoke his permission at any time before probate, — that is, before the will is exhibited and proved, — even if *after* the wife's death.

The custody of a child belongs to the father. The mother has no right of control. The father may dispose of it as he sees fit. If there be a legal separation, and no special order of the court, the custody of the children (except the nutriment of infants) belongs legally to the father.

Except the nutriment of infants! Here is a hint from the good God himself. Should we not think, that the first time these words were written down, and men were compelled to see the natural dependence of the child upon the mother, — to detect the obvious laws of nurture, natural and spiritual, — the right of a good mother to her child would have made itself clear?

Yet, to this day, there are many States of our own Union where a mother can better authenticate her right to a negro slave than to the young daughter who is bone of her bone, and flesh of her flesh!

If the direct influence of Christianity did not, in some measure, modify the influence of the law in social life, there would be no such thing as a mother's exercising maternal authority over a son. No matter how wise, how old, how experienced, she may be, she never possesses, in the eye of the law, the dignity of a boy who has just attained his majority. Sufficiently instructed in legal maxims, he can always resist her, under the influence of the most besotted or unprincipled of fathers.

The word of a married woman is not binding in law, and persons who give her credit have no remedy against her.

The moral results of such a law are sufficiently obvious, not only in England, but in our own country. The statute-book does not, cannot, stand absolved, because public opinion in the present day abhors and contemns the woman who assists her husband to defraud his creditors, or takes refuge from her own debts behind this disgraceful cover. Yet, if the law gives her husband her property, it ought surely to hold *him* responsible for her debts. And this is what society calls *protection!*

As a wife is always presumed to be under the control of her husband (numerous instances to the contrary notwithstanding), she is not considered guilty of any crime which she commits in his presence.

When a woman has consented to a proposal of marriage, she cannot give away the smallest thing. If she do so without her betrothed husband's consent, the gift is illegal; and, after marriage, he may avoid it as a fraud on him: a strong temptation to any woman, one would think, to give away her all. You see here what estimate the law puts on property, as an inducement to marriage. This provision evidently grew out of the exigencies of the time, when marriage among the Anglo-Saxons was a *pure* matter of bargain.

As a protection against the common law, it is usual to have some settlement of property made upon the wife; and, in respect to *this* property, the courts of equity regard her as a single woman. Such settlements are very intricate, and should be made by an experienced lawyer.

The wife's property belonging to the husband, should her scissors, thimble, or petticoats be stolen, the indictment must describe either of these articles as his!

Of divorce it is only necessary to say, that a divorce from the bonds of matrimony in England could be obtained only by act of Parliament; the right of investigation resting with the House of Lords alone. Until the passage of the New Divorce Bill, only three such divorces had ever been granted to a woman's petition. The expense of the most ordinary bill was between three and four thousand dollars.

Nor need we dwell long on such laws as relate to *widows*. You may be interested to hear, that, *after* her husband's death, the widow recovers her right to her own clothes and jewels; also that the law does not compel her to bury him, that being the duty of his legal representative.

The indignation which we might naturally feel at the suggestion that a wife *could* forsake her unburied dead, cools a little as the law goes on to state, that a husband *can*, of *course*, deprive a wife of all share in his personal estate. Very graciously, also, the widow is permitted to remain forty days in her husband's house, provided that she do not *re*-marry within tha time!

The result of a great deal of reading of a great many law-books is only this, — that we are more firmly convinced than ever, that the most necessary reform is a simple erasure from the statute-book of whatever recognizes distinctions of sex. You should make woman, in the eye of the law, what she has always been in the eye of God, — a responsible human being; and make laws which such beings, male or female, can obey.

Even Christian, in his edition of Blackstone, said long ago, that there was no reason why civil rights should be refused to single women. In every respect but this, the single woman is independent; but let her take to herself a husband, and the law steps in to protect her, and she finds herself in a position of what is called " reasonable restraint." He may give her, says Blackstone, *moderate correction;* he may adopt any act of coercion that does not endanger life; he may beat her, but not violently. She may, by her labor, support him: but she cannot prevent him from bestowing her earnings, should he happen to die, upon those who have most wronged her in life; his mistress, it may be, or his illegitimate children. Do you tell me that men of good feeling never act on such laws? Why, then, should men of good feeling be unwilling to wipe them from the statute-book?

For the most part, it is upon women of the lower class that the property-laws most hardly press. It was the suffering of this class, years ago, when the common law of Massachusetts was the same as that of England, that first roused my interest, and excited my indignation; but the story which the Hon. Mrs. Norton tells us shows that this class of women are not the *only* sufferers.

"I have learned the law piecemeal," she says, "by suffering all it could inflict. I forgave my husband's wickedness again and again, and found too late, that, in the eye of the law, practical Christianity, the forgiving unto seventy times seven, was a condonation which deprived me of all protection. My children were stolen from me, and put into the vilest custody, where one of them afterwards died for want of a mother's commonest care. My husband brought an action against his kindest friend, of whom he borrowed money and received office. The jury listened with disgust, and gave their verdict against him. Then I was told that I might *write* for my bread, *or* my family might support me. My children were kept away, as their residence with me would make him liable for my debts.

"When my mother died, and left me, through my brother, a small income, he balanced the first payment by arbitrarily stopping his own allowance. For the last three years, I have not received a farthing from him. He retains all my personal property which was left in his home, the gifts of the royal family on my marriage, articles bought with my own earnings, and presents from Lord Melbourne. He receives from my trustees the income which my father bequeathed to me, which the 'non-existent' wife must resign to the 'existent' husband.

"I have also the power of earning by literature; but even this power, the gift of God, not the legacy of man, bears fruit only for him. Let him *subpœna* my publishers, and enjoy his triumph: he has shown me that I was not meant to write novels and tales, but to rouse the nation against such men as he, and such laws as they sustain. Let him eat the bread I earn; but it shall be bought with the price of his own exposure. If law will not listen to me, to literature I will devote my power, and secure for others what I have not been able to secure for myself."

No wonder that provident parents circumvent such a common law by a settlement before marriage! There is no chance for a partnership of gains or losses in England.

As we have already said, all sexual laws ought to be wiped off the statute-book; but the Hungarian law which was in force until 1849, when the German law was introduced into Hungary, is a comment on the absurdity of the English.

"No countrywoman of mine," said a proud sister of Kossuth, "would ever submit to such a marriage settlement as is common in England." In Hungary, inherited property could not be devised by will, and all unmarried women were considered minors. As soon as she married, a woman came of age, and into the full control of her estates. She could make a will, and sign deeds; and was not responsible for her husband's debts or the family expenses. As a widow, she was guardian of her children, and administrator on her husband's property. So long as she bore his name, she could exercise all his political rights. She could vote in the county elections, and for deputies to the Diet. Trained up under such a law, what could the Hungarian woman think who found herself for the first time in the power of the English law?

Among the refugees whom the misfortunes of a leading Hungarian family drove to these shores was one woman of the highest natural gifts, the best social station. She was married to a man, handsome, accomplished, and reckless, but hardly patriotic enough to have need to fly with her. In the city of New York she opened a boarding-house of the highest class, by which she strove to support herself and her children. A fascinating hostess, a skilful manager, she succeeded, as might be expected. Soon her improvident husband followed her. At first, he did not attempt to annoy her; but, in time, some one was found cruel enough to expound to him the English common law. He stared, refused to believe; but finally entered his wife's house, seized her earnings, compelled her boarders to pay their money into his hands, stripped her of all power to pay her rent and provide for her family, and then took himself off, enraptured, doubtless, with his brief experience of English and American liberty. Stripped of peace, position, and property, the injured wife had no longer courage to struggle. In underhand ways, to evade the unjust law, her personal friends settled her upon a little farm, where her shattered hopes found a short repose.

A few years ago, an American woman of captivating address gained great reputation in Paris as a milliner. She had a profligate husband, whom she invited to tea every Sunday, supplying him at that time with a sum for his weekly expenses. In an evil day, seduced by promises of high patronage, she went to London. She was very successful; but in a few months her husband surprised her, seized all she possessed, and, turned adrift on the streets, she went back to a country where the law would protect her industry. Marriage has been sought only to legalize a theft, — to apply the words of Wendell Phillips, when "*union was robbery.*" A respectable servant, who had laid by a considerable sum, was sought in marriage by an apparently suitable person. On the day before the marriage, she put her bank-book into his hands. After the ceremony, he said to her, "I am not well in health, and do not feel equal to supporting a family: you had better go back to service." Naturally indignant, she responded, "Give me, then, my bank-book." — "I am too feeble to spare the money," he replied. She went back to service, and has never seen him since; but, of course, she has been often obliged to change her name and residence to protect herself from a long succession of extortions.

We see thus, that if a woman is able to conquer her fate, and to gain a livelihood in spite of a dissolute or incompetent husband, her home is not her own.

Her husband's folly may, at any moment, deprive her children of bread.

I have said that there was no woman so pitiable as an heiress. I said it advisedly. I thought of the long persecution she must bear from unwelcome suitors, — of all appreciation of her personality, ever so lovely or gifted or individual, sunk, as it must be, in the mire of her money.

Mrs. Reid says, justly, that this money is not so much her own as a perquisite attached to her person for the benefit of her *future husband;* the larger portion of which will eventually pass to his heirs, whether of her blood or not. If forced from ill treatment to leave his roof, the law will return her but a scanty pittance.

The nature of the law itself, and that estimate of woman on which it is based, are so identical, that we are compelled, as we turn over its pages, to treat these two points as one.

"For one-half the human race," said Mrs. Reid years ago, "the highest end of civilization is to *cling* like a weed upon a wall;" a curious instance of the power that the use of language has over a fact. There is nothing captivating in clinging like a "weed to a wall;" but most women are satisfied to hang like the "vine about the oak."

It is a great misfortune, that this estimate of woman not only governs the courts in their decisions, but enters into and moulds all the movements of society. Such an estimate leads to constant contradictions;

being, as it is, directly the opposite of the *fact* in so many cases, and of the Divine Will in all. In a book on woman recently published by a lawyer in England, I found a pithy paragraph to this point, concluding some observations on the comparative longevity of the sexes: " The wife," he says, "*fitly survives the husband*, both to take care of *his* premature infirmity, and to consummate the rearing of their offspring "! — a creative effort of the imagination which certainly entitles the writer to the laurels of the century.

One reason that the wages of women are kept down is, that, for the most part, women do not begin to labor early; do not devote themselves *in youth* to any trade or profession, so as to compete with men who have. The plodding and steady habits of the man of business, he has acquired in his early years; and they are developed by the fact, that he is sole master of what he can earn, and can dispose of it as he thinks proper: but his wife has been brought up in no such school, — has no such motive to industry. Should she toil on for ever, she cannot possess what she acquires, nor lay out the smallest part of it, without another's leave. Even when man says to her with the sanction of the church and in the presence of God, " With all my worldly goods I thee endow," it means only that she is invited to enjoy, not possess them. This estimate of her rights, her position, and her ability, made manifest in every law-book, in the church itself, and obvious in every social form, discourages her whenever she would devote herself to any lucrative employment; so that it is only in desertion and despair, for the most part, that she becomes a laborer. She is not always conscious of this discouragement. She quiets the Cerberus within by a three-times-repeated "It is not proper," without pausing to analyze the conventional instinct. Here we find the real significance of the proverb, "A man of straw is worth a woman of gold;" for the "man of straw" is, at least, worth such money as he may hereafter earn, which the "woman of gold" is not.

We hear a great deal about laws for the *protection* of women; but we cannot urge too often the remark of James Davis in his Prize Essay of 1854, "that all early legislation for woman was founded, not on her own rights, but on those of her husband and children, and the *State over her*."

When one remembers that the "seat of the law is the bosom of God," it strikes one strangely, that moral consequences to character have so little to do with what one may call "sexual legislation."

In speaking of the frequenting of disreputable houses, neither Montesquieu, nor Dr. Wood in his "History of Civil Law," finds a single word to say as to the moral degradation of the race, of the special degradation of woman involved in it, but both grow eloquent concerning the ruin of the State. It requires a sounder mode of thinking than most men possess to see the relation between the ruin of the State and their own bad habits, the loss of one man's purity. Thus the laws concerning adultery, or divorce for that cause, bring the heaviest penalties, social and legal, upon the head of an offending woman. The legal excuse for this positive injustice is the safety of the family and the State, — the great crime of imposing upon a family false representatives of its name and honor; but a woman's brain and conscience are too clear to rest in this masculine decision.

If a man cannot bring a false representative into *his own family*, he can carry it into his neighbor's, when his profligate life violates the social compact; and, as to his own family, his vices may injure it far more than the infidelity of his wife. At the worst, her misconduct will only bring into the shelter of his home a child who grows up protected socially by her fraud; but, if *he* choose to "spend his substance in riotous living," his wife and children may, while the law gives him exclusive right to their common property, be deserted, or driven from their homes, to make room for those who are the companions of his guilt. It is quite possible, it will be seen, therefore, to show another side to this matter, in no better light than that of expediency. One canton of Switzerland (the Canton Glarus) possesses laws in regard to such matters, in marked contrast to those of the whole civilized world. The consequence is, that the falsehood and crime so common elsewhere are here unknown.*

---

* "A man who is guilty of adultery is branded by public opinion as a forger or bigamist is elsewhere, and is not eligible to public office during the whole of his life; which, under such a government, is the greatest

"Perhaps it would be just," says Poynter on "Marriage and Divorce," in 1824, — "*perhaps* it would be just, that where the husband violates the matrimonial compact, and the property originally belonged to the wife, he should give back the whole of it. Courts, however, have never gone that length."

One would think, nevertheless, that husbands themselves might go that length, and that men who aspire to the credit of decency would be ashamed to eat the bread of her they have betrayed and wounded. How is it that they have deceived themselves from the beginning, and have fancied that God requires of woman a fidelity and purity that was not of the smallest consequence to themselves?

In the late debate in Parliament on the New Divorce Bill, when a member objected to the introduction of a clause equalizing the relief of divorce to both sexes, he asked, "If this clause were adopted, I should like to know how many married men there would be in this house?" He was answered by shouts of laughter.

Would these men have laughed, think you, if they had been asked how many *pure wives* could be found in their family circles? and, if *not*, would it have been because they were capable of estimating the value of womanly virtue? No: *he* cannot esti-

---

punishment that can be inflicted. A man who breaks his promise of betrothal, or who in any way betrays a woman to mortification and shame, is heaped with the same scorn that women receive elsewhere. The woman who is betrayed is censured; but the man is henceforth an outcast." — *Cottages of the Alps*, p. 288.

mate that who has never known the worth of manly purity. The spectres of illegitimacy and civil ruin are what would stare them in the face, and turn their very lips so white.

In France, says the "Westminster Review," fidelity on the part of the husband is considered a sort of imbecility. What is thought of it in England? Does this scene in Parliament, printed for all our girls to read, suggest any higher view?

"The frequenting of disreputable places," says Davis, "was once an indictable offence in a *man;* but that is now obsolete." Obsolete? and why? A lawyer once told me, that the most obscene publication he had ever read was a book upon divorce. I can well believe it. I thought I knew how corrupt modern society could be; but I did not know how unsoundness had darted to its very core, till I began to read law, and to understand the estimate which that puts upon woman and chastity.

When I think of these things, I wonder that this platform is not thronged with the ghosts of dead and ruined women, crowding here to second my appeal to beseech you to grant human justice, to require human virtue! And all this sin is sheltered under the plea of protection! "How many delicious morsels I should miss if it were not for *thy* care, O most excellent jackal!"

"Lawyers," says Johnson in 1777, — "lawyers often pay women the high compliment of supposing them proof against all temptations combined."

Certainly, whatever the *lawyers* may do, the *law itself* confidently expects of them a superhuman strength. It gives them no defence but immaculateness. It offers them no shelter but God's temple, no robe but spotless ermine; and then, turning the page, it says, " A *husband* is expected to be vigilant, and so prevent his own dishonor:" as if his *vigilance* and quick-wittedness could save the woman whom his *love* had not blessed.

Ah! these lawyers are but blind guides, after all. Centuries of discomfiture and defeat have not sufficed to teach them how little security is to be found in suspicion and scepticism. If I do not want my groceries stolen, I must leave my storeroom open. The very servant who would not scruple to pick my locks will know better than to pick that of her own heart. " A thorough-bred woman," says Mrs. Reid, "is good only so far as her husband suggests and allows;" and, so long as *this* is the standard, woman's duplicity may well match man's utmost expectation, and there is not a privilege of his open vice that she will not secure by stealth.

There was a time when all the women at the court of France blushed for one of their number who unluckily made use of a hard word in a *proper* place. In like manner, the woman who reads law blushes to find herself even tolerably sincere and modest. It is not expected of her. Why has she never done any of the bad things the law so confidently predicts?

All thinking people must see how easily we turn from the consolidated law of ages, with its false views, its untrue estimate of woman and duty, to the question of the right of suffrage.

In 1848 and 1850, we used to hear a great deal of three objections to conferring this right upon women: —

1st, Its incompatibility with household care and the duties of maternity.

2d, Its hardening effect on the character; politics not being fit for woman.

3d, The inexpediency of increasing competition in the already crowded fields of labor and office.

To these three points we gave short and summary answers: —

1st, There are a great many women who will never be mothers and housekeepers; and, if there were not, suffrage is no more incompatible with maternity and housekeeping than it is with mercantile life and the club-room.

2d, If it hardens women, it will harden men; and the politics which are not fit for her are not fit for him, nor will they become so till her presence gives men a motive to purify them.

3d, At the worst, competition could only go so far, that a man *and* a woman would earn as little together as the man now does alone. This would be better than the present condition of things; for they would then be equal partners, and no longer master and slave. Both would work, and neither need pine.

These answers, whether logical or not, have practically silenced the objections. We hear no more of *this* nonsense. But, on the other hand, a respectable daily says, " As to the abstract right of a woman to vote because she is a human being and pays taxes, there is no such abstract right in any human being, male or female: the extent of the elective franchise is, and must ever be, limited by considerations of expediency."

Then a distinguished review goes on to say, "that while the question of suffrage stands where it now does, so unsettled that every Congress and Parliament discuss it anew, we are glad that any thing should prevent the discussion as to conferring on woman a duty, the grounds of which are very vague and undetermined so far as regards men;" and a critic of Rosa Bonheur's magnificent pictures advises the "sad sisterhood of women's-rights advocates to visit the exhibition, and sigh to think how much one silent woman's hand outvalues for their cause the pathos and the jeers of their unlovely platform."

Such remarks as these are easily met. To the first objector, who declares, although the professed advocate of a republican government, that *there is no such thing* as any abstract right to vote, we reply, that in this particular discussion we don't care about *abstract rights:* what we want is our *own share* of the tangible acknowledged right which human governments confer. If in England this right depends on a property qualification, then we claim that there the property qualification shall endow woman as well as man with the right of suffrage. If in America it depends upon an inalienable right to life, liberty, and the pursuit of happiness, then we demand that our government recognize woman as so endowed, and receive her vote.

To the reviewer we say also, If the grounds of suffrage are vague and undetermined in *theory,* they may remain so, so far as our interference is concerned. What we ask to share is the steady right to vote, which has been actually granted, and never disputed, since our government was founded; and sufficiently pressed, we might add, that, if there is ever any chance of limiting the right of suffrage, we shall do all we can to secure its dependence on a certain amount of education, in preference to a certain amount of wealth.

As to the art critic, we thank him for calling us the " sad sisterhood." We should be sorry to be otherwise, when pleading for women *before* men; sorry to find matter for jesting in those purlieus of St. Giles and Five Points and the Black Sea, beating up remorselessly against these very doors, which lie at the very heart of our effort. As to the matter of going to see the Horse Fair and the Highland Cattle, it will probably be found to be a fact, that, in every city where those great pictures have been exhibited, " *women's-rights women*" have been their *earliest* visitors; and, standing before the canvas, have thanked God, with an earnestness the art critic never dreamt of, for that silent woman's hand, that glorious woman's life. It was not necessary for him to remind us of what Solomon had said so much better three thousand years ago; namely, that " speech is silvern, and silence is golden." Nathless, silver is still current in all markets; and, God willing, we are not ashamed to use it.

We intend to claim, in words, the right of suffrage; and why?

Turning from that wretched estimate of woman, and of man's duty toward woman, which the law-books have just offered us, we claim the right of suffrage, because only through its possession can women protect themselves; only through its exercise can both sexes have equality of right and power before the law. Whenever this happened, character would get its legitimate influence; and it is just possible that men might become rational and virtuous in private, if association with women compelled them to *seem so* in public.

It is noticeable, that every man disclaims at his own hearth, and in the presence of women, whatever there is of disgraceful appertaining to political or other public meetings. *Somebody* must be responsible for these things; and yet, if we are to believe witnesses, nobody ever does them. The bare fact of association must take all the blame.

The laws already existing prove conclusively to woman herself, that she has never had a real representative. What she seeks is to utter her own convictions, so that they shall redeem and save, not merely her own sex but the race.

That the right of suffrage would be a protection to

women, we see from this fact, that it would at once put an end to three classes of laws: —

I. Those that protect her from violence.

II. Those made to protect her from fraud.

III. Those that protect society from the passions of both sexes.

The moment woman began to exercise this right, I think we should see moral significance streaming from every statute. We should no longer hear that seduction was to be sued as "loss of service:" it would become loss of honor to *more* than one. We should no longer hear that consent or temptation excused it: we should find that God demanded chastity of both sexes, and had made man the guardian of his own virtue. We should find, that, if its punishment admitted of degrees, it should be *heaviest* where a man committed it in defiance or abuse of a positive trust.

Let us look at a single decision in the light of these principles. Let us take the case of Harris *versus* Butler, reported in the notes to Davis's Prize Essay.

A man named Harris had apprenticed his daughter to a milliner named Butler, paying as an entrance-fee a sum equivalent to a hundred and fifty dollars. After a short time, the girl was seduced by her mistress's husband. She became seriously ill, and was returned to her father, who lost not only his hundred and fifty dollars, but all the benefits of her apprenticeship, and was obliged to provide her with board, medicine, and nursing.

Why the father became liable for the care of his child under such circumstances does not appear. Common sense would suggest that the court might have required this at the hands of the Butlers; but, unfortunately, law has very little to do with common sense.

The father brought an action against Butler: but the defence urged, that he could only sue for "loss of service;" that her "services" were not his after she was apprenticed to Mrs. Butler; that Mrs. Butler and her husband were " one person in law;" and that, if Butler chose to deprive himself of her services for his own ends, the law had no remonstrance to make, no redress to afford.

The prosecution urged, that the "care of morals" was one of the duties involved in the very system of apprenticeship; but the court denied the claim, unless it were distinctly set forth on the articles signed.

This is but one case out of hundreds accessible to you all. The moment woman becomes a law-maker, such records will be wiped out of your life. They may make a certain sort of show in your law-books; but what have the unbending laws of God to do with this " one person in law," this plea for "loss of service"? At the eternal bar, no man will dare to echo that plea, no judge rehearse that verdict. Such law rests not in the "bosom of God;" its voice chimes not in keeping with the harmony of his countless spheres.

You object to seeing women in Parliament. English lords tell us that delicate matters have to be discussed there, with which women would hardly care to meddle. The natural growth of society opens the area of all proprieties. Delicate matters come to be discussed in most households; and it is reasonable to suppose that they would be more delicately and rationally discussed if they were sometimes *publicly* met. It is my opinion, that no subject is fit for discussion at all that cannot be discussed between men and women. It is separating the sexes in such cases, that opens the way to indecency. All great themes of human thought and human virtue, men and women ought to be trained to consider seriously together; and where better than in the Congress or the Parliament? Think only of the debate which I have quoted on the New Divorce Bill! Could such a scene have taken place in the presence of women? Recur to the trial of Queen Caroline; or to that of the Duke of York, when accused of conniving at the corrupt sale of military commissions by his mistress, Mrs. Clarke.

Under date of Feb. 16, 1809, Freemantle writes: "The scene which is going on in the House of Commons is so disgusting, and at the same time so alarming, that I hardly know how to describe it to you. Of course, while this ferment lasts (and God knows when it is to end), no attention will be paid to the business of the country."

In these instances, high-bred men showed a taste for low scandal; battening day after day on the same loathsome details, which the presence of a single woman must have checked. Here was a woman, too, this very Mrs. Clarke, somewhat debased and hardened, who had never a seat in Parliament, who had never dreamed of exercising the right of suffrage, yet was quite equal, as the evidence showed, to any political venality, striving in her way to outdo the very jobbers of Downing Street itself! Why *should* elections be scenes of tumult, or parliaments free fields for imbecile improprieties? Why should not a peeress feel herself as properly placed among her peers as the Queen seated at her Council?

We are not likely to withdraw our claim while it is sustained by such a man as John Stuart Mill, who, in his late essay on "Political Representation," advises this extension of the suffrage: "All householders, without distinction of sex," he says, "might be adopted into the constituency, on proving to the registrar's officer that they have fifty pounds a year, and can read, write, and calculate."

"The almost despotic power of husbands over wives," Mr. Mill adds in his "Essay on Liberty," "needs not to be enlarged upon here, because nothing more is needed for the complete removal of the evil than that wives should have the same rights, and should receive the protection of the law in the same manner, as all other persons; and because, on this subject, the defenders of established injustice do not avail themselves of the plea of liberty, but stand forth openly as the champions of power."

The dedication of this "Essay on Liberty" ought to be preserved in these pages; for it is full of historic significance: —

"To the beloved and deplored memory of her who was the inspirer, and in part the author, of all that has been best in my writings; the friend and wife, whose exalted sense of truth and right was my strongest excitement, and whose approbation was my chief reward, — I dedicate this volume.

"Like all that I have written for many years, it belongs as much to her as to me; but the work, as it stands, has had, in a very insufficient degree, the inestimable advantage of her revision; some of the most important portions having been reserved for a more careful re-examination, which they are now never destined to receive. Were I but capable of interpreting to the world one-half the great thoughts and noble feelings which are buried in her grave, I should be the medium of a greater benefit to it than is ever likely to arise from any thing that I can write, unprompted and unassisted by her all but unrivalled wisdom."

I said that this dedication ought, for many reasons, to be preserved in these pages. What is better fitted than such a tribute to check the jeering scepticism of the crowd as to the ability and purity of the sex? What could lay a better foundation for a better estimate on the part of the law? Necker, in his report to the French Government, publicly awarded to his wife the credit of the recent retrenchment in the expenses of the Government; Bowditch dedicated his translation of the "Mécanique Céleste" to the wife who aided him to prepare, and by her self-denial opened a way for him to publish it: but where, in the records of the past, shall we find such a tribute offered by such a man, as honorable in itself to the first political economist of our time as it is a gracious adornment to the name of the woman he loved? Does it not promise in itself the dawning of a brighter future for woman, when no " sad sisterhood " shall be needed either to proclaim woman's rights or redress her wrongs?*

---

* In reprinting for his collected works Mrs. Mill's article on " The Enfranchisement of Women," Mr. Mill more lately says, " All the more recent of these papers were the joint production of myself, and one whose loss, even in a merely intellectual point of view, can never be repaired or alleviated. But the following essay is hers in a peculiar sense; my share in it being little more than that of editor or amanuensis. Its authorship having been known at the time, and publicly attributed to her, it is proper to state, that she never regarded it as a complete discussion of the subject which it treats of; and, highly as I estimate it, I would rather it remained unacknowledged, than that it should be read with the idea, that even the faintest image can be found in it of a mind and heart, which, in their union of the rarest, and what are deemed the most conflicting excellences, were unparalleled in any human being that I have known or read of. While she was the light, life, and grace of every society in which she took part, the foundation of her character was a deep seriousness, resulting from the combination of the strongest and most sensitive feelings with the highest principles. All that excites admiration, when found separately, in others, seemed brought together in her, — a conscience at once healthy and tender; a generosity bounded only by a sense of justice, which often forgot its own claims, but never those of others; a heart so large and loving, that whoever was capable of making the smallest return of sympathy always received tenfold; and, in the intellectual department, a vigor and truth of imagination, a delicacy of perception, an accuracy and nicety of observation, only equalled by her profundity of speculative thought, and by a practical judgment and discernment next to infallible. So elevated was the general level of her faculties, that the highest poetry, philosophy, oratory, or art, seemed trivial by the side of her, and equal only to expressing some part of her mind; and there is no one of these modes of manifestation in which she could not easily have taken the highest rank, had not her inclination led her for the most part to content herself with being the inspirer, prompter, and unavowed co-adjutor, of others.

" The present paper was written to promote a cause which she had deeply at heart; and, though appealing only to the severest reason, was meant for the

THE ENGLISH COMMON LAW.   329

About two years since (1858), the Stockholm "Aftonblad," a Swedish newspaper, stated that "the authorities of the old university-town of Upsal had granted the right of suffrage to fifty women owning real estate, and to thirty-one doing business on their own account. The representative that their votes assisted in electing was to sit in the House of Burgesses."

This is the way the matter is to begin. By and by, the interests of labor and trade will force the authorities of Bristol and Manchester, Newcastle and Plymouth, to do the same thing; and, after women have gone on for some twenty years electing members of Parliament, no one of us will be surprised to find some women sitting in that body. "But," objects somebody, "if that ever happens, we shall have women on

---

general reader. The question, in her opinion, was in a stage in which no treatment but the most calmly argumentative could be useful; while many of the strongest arguments were necessarily omitted, as being unsuited for popular effect. Had she lived to write out all her thoughts on this great question, she would have produced something as far transcending in profundity the present essay, as, had she not placed a rigid restraint upon her feelings, she would have excelled it in fervid eloquence.

"Yet nothing that even she could have written on any single subject would have given an adequate idea of the depth and compass of her mind. As, during life, she detected, before any one else had seemed to perceive them, those changes of time and circumstances, which, ten or twelve years later, became subjects of general remark; so I venture to prophesy, that, if mankind continue to improve, their spiritual history for ages to come will be the progressive working out of her thoughts, and the realization of her conceptions."

Such tributes, borne by noble men to noble women, are so frequently hidden away in the heavy volumes which lie out of ordinary reach, that I take pleasure in bringing them to support my own plea; and I only wish I could as easily add to that in the text the charming acknowledgments of Alexis de Tocqueville to his wife.

juries, women pleading at the bar, women as attorneys, and so on." And this is exactly what we want. Women are very much *needed* on juries, and *female* criminals will never be tried by their peers until they are there. It is very seldom that a criminal case in which women are implicated is brought forward, when women could not be of immense service in clearing up evidence, and showing to the male jurors on the panel the absurdity or impossibility of some of the statements. The recent instance of Miss Shedden, who took up, at a moment's notice, a case which five well-feed lawyers of distinction declared themselves unprepared to defend, might be quoted in confirmation of our view. Mr. Russell said at the Liverpool Assizes lately, in a case which involved some peculiar evidence, " The evidence of women is, in some respects, superior to that of men. Their power of judging of minute details is better; and when there are more than two facts, and something be wanting, their intuitions supply the deficiency." And precisely the qualities which fit them to give evidence, fit them to sift and test it. Women often have occasion to smile, sometimes sadly, sometimes mischievously, at the verdicts passed upon their own sex. If women were to enter into the practice of law, or become lawmakers, an immense change would take place in all that relates to it. Absurd technicalities would be swept off its papers. One hundred words would no longer do duty for one. Simple, common-sense forms of expression would take the place of obsolete Latin and Norman-French. Daylight would be let into indictments, and flaws would soon be hard to find. No woman ever existed, whose patience would stand, in cases where meaning and law are evident, the absurd delays of chancery courts, or the still absurder "filing of objections," or "defining of terms," with which lawyers amuse a jury, and which Sir Leicester Dedlock, we are told, considered as the bulwarks of the English Constitution. This impatience of woman might not be very valuable, if she were to legislate alone; but, controlled by man's conservative caution, it will be of the greatest service.

We are perpetually met by the opposition extended to *any thing* that is new. It ought to be our object, therefore, to show, that for woman to claim and possess the right of suffrage is by no means a new thing. It is easy to show from the records of most nations, that women held and exercised political power so long as power was supposed to inhere *chiefly* in property, and so long as women, either single or in association, possessed property not represented by men. Thus the suppression of religious houses in England put an end to the representation of abbesses. "Truly, we think more of money than of love," said one of the St. Simoniens: "we have more consideration for bags of dollars than human dignity. We emancipate women in proportion as they are property-holders; but, in proportion as they are women, our laws declare them inferior to us." It was only when the republican idea had crept to a certain extent into monarchical governments themselves, that women gradually dropped a recognized public influence which had depended on rank and wealth. What men have to do is, not to reconcile themselves to a woman's right to vote, — a right acknowledged hundreds of years ago, which is still covertly acknowledged when woman means property, — but to reconcile themselves to the idea that woman is a human being, and that *humanity* has a right to vote. Wherever governments decide that every individual has a right to life, liberty, and the pursuit of happiness, they must admit the right of the individual woman to vote, or deny the fact of her humanity. There is the dilemma. In support of this statement, I should have shown you, that in France, as early as the reign of Louis XIV., the political rights of property were respected in the persons of women. At the present day, the remains of the old feudal and communal system still secure a kind of political influence to certain women in the provinces, and often confer upon their husbands a right of franchise. In the reign of Louis XIV., the women who hawked and vended fish took up the business of the "insolvent fishmongers," and managed so well, that they acquired wealth, married their children into the first families, and finally became an estate of the realm.

"Les Dames de la Halle," or "Dames of the Market," as they are called, have a corporate existence; and, if corporations have no souls, they ordinarily possess *franchises!* They have their queen, their laws, and a language peculiar to themselves. They take part in revolutions, and send deputations to the foot of the throne. Nor am I alluding now to long-past feudal or re-actionary crises. Louis Napoleon treats them as civilly as he does the clergy. When he was married, and when the young prince was born, they went to the Tuileries in their court-dress. Their princesses — and we are told that their blood-royal claims the higher privilege of beauty also — their princesses took the front rank in the procession, and offered bouquets to their imperial majesties. In response, Louis Napoleon gave to them what he gives to all corporations, — a very diplomatic speech.

I have told you what was granted at Upsal in 1858. It is a curious fact, that, just at the moment when this question of suffrage was first agitated by the women of the United States assembled in convention at Seneca Falls in 1848, Pauline Roland and Madame Moniot publicly claimed their civil rights in Paris. Pauline went herself to the ballot, and, when her vote was refused, published a protest after the fashion of our tax-payers. Very absurd English society found woman's first demand for the suffrage; yet what Englishmen refuse contemptuously to *give to* woman, certain men of the mean sort, yet calling themselves respectable, have not been ashamed in that very country to *borrow of* her. Even "Blackwood" helps out our argument, when it says, in November, 1854, "I believe, Eusebius, I speak of a notorious fact, when I say, that it is less than a century since, for election purposes, parties were unblushingly married in cases where *women* conveyed a right of freedom, a political franchise to their husbands, and parted, after the election, by shaking hands over a tombstone, as an act of dissolution of the contract, under cover of the words, 'Until death do us part.'"* The men who looked calmly on this profane and absurd fraud may well dread the moral influence of woman on elections. As to the historical argument for England, ladies of birth and quality, we are told, sat in council with the Saxon Witas. The Abbess Hilda *presided* in an ecclesiastical council. "In Wightfred's great council at Benconceld in 694," says Gurdon in his "Antiquities of Parliament," "the abbesses sat and deliberated; and five of them signed decrees of that council, with the king and bishops:" and that illuminated prebendary of Sarum, old Thomas Fuller, thus further chronicles the same event:—

"A great council (for so it is titled) was held at Becanceld (supposed to be Beckingham in Kent) by Withred, King of Kent, and Bertuald, Archbishop of Britain, so called therein (understand, him of Canterbury), wherein many things were concluded in favor of the church. Five Kentish abbesses —

---

* In an article in the "Edinburgh Weekly Journal" for Jan. 10, 1827, written by Sir Walter Scott, the following allusion is made to abuses which had crept into the army in the middle of the eighteenth century:—

"To sum up this catalogue of abuses, *commissions* were in some instances bestowed upon *young ladies*, when pensions could not be had. We know ourselves one fair dame who drew the pay of a captain in the —— dragoons, and was probably not much less fit for the service than some who at that period actually did duty."

namely, Mildred, Ethelred, Æte, Wilnolde, Heresinde — were not only present, but subscribed their names and crosses to the constitutions concluded therein; and we may observe, that their subscriptions are not only placed before and above all presbyters, but also above that of Botred, a bishop present in this great council. It seems it was the courtesy of England to allow the upper hand to the weaker sex, as in their sitting, so in their subscription."

King Edgar's charter to the Abbey of Crowland, in 961, was with consent of the nobles and *abbesses* who signed that charter. In Henry the Third's and King Edward the First's time, four abbesses were summoned to Parliament; namely, of Shaftesbury, of Winchester, of Berking, and of Wilton. In the thirty-fifth year of Edward the Third, were summoned — by writ of Parliament, to sit in person or by their proxies — Mary, Countess of Norfolk; Alienor, Countess of Ormond; Anna Despenser; Philippa, Countess of March; Johanna Fitzwater; Agneta, Countess of Pembroke; Mary de St. Paul; Mary de Roos; Matilda, Countess of Oxford; Catharine, Countess of Athol.

As to the offices which women can hold in Great Britain, we have already quoted something from Mr. Higginson, in speaking of the prohibitions of the law. Lady Packington's estate has probably, by this time, passed into male hands: so *she* elects no more members of Parliament. Those who have read the plea of Lady Alice Lille, when she was forbidden to speak by attorney, will find no great difficulty in imagining that a woman could manage a government debate.

Such women as have purchased or inherited East-India stock have always had the privilege of voting at the meetings of the company, and so have assisted to govern that unhappy country. In the provincial English towns, if I may judge from the indirect testimony of novels and newspapers, women appear to attend all stockholders' meetings; certainly those held by the banks. In the United States, they are notified, *but not expected to attend;* a cool kind of insult, which I wish some women might astonish them by retaliating. If any bank were established by, or had a majority of, female stockholders, it would be quite easy to notify men, without expecting *them* to attend; and the alternative of trusting their own property to the judgment of *women* might possibly open the eyes of men to the absurdity of the present custom.

As we withdraw our eyes from the past, it is natural to inquire, What late changes have taken place in Great Britain? and what is the strength of the reform tendency? I have often said, yet I must repeat it here, that nothing has ever promised such noble usefulness for woman, nothing has ever occurred to change the popular estimate of her character, in the same degree as the formation of that *out-of-door Parliament,*—the Association for the Advancement of Social Science. It offers a position of entire equality to woman. It encourages her to express herself in the presence and with the sympathy of the wisest men, and gives her an opportunity to speak to the actual Parliament through her own influence exerted on its best members. It has been well said (I think, by Mrs. Mill), that the very best opportunities of education will be opened to woman in vain, until she is practically invited to turn them to account. Here, in this association, is her first practical invitation in Great Britain. God grant that she may understand the responsibility it involves, and bear it well! But the formation of this association in 1857 was preceded by other steps. It was on the 13th of February, 1851, that a petition of women, agreed to by a public meeting at Sheffield, and claiming the elective franchise, was laid before the House of Lords by the Earl of Carlisle; and, in July of the same year, Mrs. Mill's admirable article on the "Enfranchisement of Women," now become commonplace on account of the extensive and thorough use that has been made of it, appeared in the "Westminster."

The examination of Florence Nightingale before a commission of inquiry bore witness no less to the surpassing ability of the woman than to the increasing value of such ability to all governments. In connection with it, one could not but smile at the distress felt by certain journals over a single mistake on the part of the lady as to the proper title of a subordinate officer.

In the month of March, 1856, the "London Times" published a petition to both Houses of Parliament in behalf of an amendment of the English property-laws. This petition was signed by many women whose names are well known and dear to us, — by the late

Anna Jameson, so well known to the world as an accomplished critic in literature and art; by the wife and sister of the poet Browning, — Elizabeth Browning, herself the first poet among women, so far; by Bessie Raynor Parkes and Matilda Hayes, the editors of the " Englishwoman's Journal," the establishment of which of itself constitutes an era in the progress of human thought; by Barbara Bodichon, the well-known artist; by Harriet Martineau, distinguished in political economy; by Mary Howitt, the womanly story-teller and ballad-maker; and Mrs. Gaskell, the author of " Mary Barton." The petition was supported in the House of Lords by Lord Brougham, and in the House of Commons by Sir Erskine Perry.

After the close of the session in April, 1857, a dinner was offered to Lord Brougham in acknowledgment of the distinguished ardor with which he had pressed this bill, — the Married Woman's Property Act of 1857. This bill did not apply to Ireland or Scotland, nor to pre-existing contracts; that is, to marriages solemnized before the first day of January, 1858. It was not passed; but a clause for the protection of the earnings and savings of married women was introduced into the New Divorce Bill, and has already proved a blessing to hundreds. This clause, however, operates *only* in cases of desertion, — a charge easily evaded.*

---

* " In the little brown duodecimo which contains the jottings of 'that famous lawyer, William Tothill, Esquire,' there is the following entry, of the date of James I.: —

The New Divorce Bill passed in 1858: the Divorce and Matrimonial Causes Act Amendment Bill passed in July, 1858; and since then, the Divorce Court Bill in August, 1859; both of these last having been made necessary by the first change in the law. It was in April, 1858, that Mr. Buckle delivered his lecture on " Civilization;" an important contribution to that estimate of woman, which is beginning to act powerfully on all legislation. The Law-Amendment Society also published a report, urging a thorough reform of the law.

In connection with the reforms effected in the mother-country, it may be well to state, that similar reforms are being effected in Canada. Legislators there turn for their precedents to England; but there can be no doubt that the agitation in the United States largely contributes towards these changes.

A Married Woman's Property Act passed the Council in May, 1858; but as these changes are still in progress, and a progress much interrupted by political fluctuations, it seems hardly worth while to enter into their details.

In one respect, the statutes of Canada are marked by a singular inconsistency. They record the only instance, within my knowledge, in which a government distinctly *forbids* women to vote; and almost

---

" 'Fleshward *contra* Jackson. Money given to a *feme covert* for her maintenance, because her husband is an unthrift. The husband pretends the money to be his; but the court ordered the money to be at her own disposal.' " — *London Quarterly*, July, 1861. A very ancient germ of a " Married Woman's Property Law."

the only instance of a government *conferring* that right, even to a limited extent. In the twelfth year of Victoria, the Canadian Government passed a statute in these words: " No woman is or *shall be* entitled to vote at any election for any electoral division whatever." What spasm of autocratic terror, what momentary rebellion against their liege lady, inspired this act, we are left uninformed. For the most part, in all countries, women wait to be told that they *may vote;* and their ineligibility is decided by the introduction of the word " male," or the popular construction of the word " citizen," which, it is quite evident, does not mean a woman. But it was in Canada also that a distinct electoral privilege was conferred by intention in 1850; an intention, however, which indicated no enlargement of views, nor desire of reform, nor recognition of woman at her human value: it was simply an intention on the part of the Protestants to secure a little more political power. Not *humane*, then, but interested motives dictated the omission of the word " male" in that section of the statutes which provides for the election of school trustees. It was desired thus to bring the influence of female property-holders and Protestants to check the Roman-Catholic demand for separate schools. Three things made it easy for Canadian women to vote under this provision : —

1st, The great degree of individual independence seen everywhere in English-born women, as compared with American.

THE ENGLISH COMMON LAW. 341

2d, The respect felt, in all countries where distinctions of rank exist, for the mere property-holder.

3d, The political excitement of the local Protestant Church, which sustained them to the uttermost.

They have voted for ten years; and a four-years' residence among them was sufficient to convince me, that no greater derangement to society would occur if the full right were conferred. In connection with English government and English colonies, I ought to speak of the government of Pitcairn's Island. It was the mutinous crew of his majesty's ship "Bounty" that settled Pitcairn's Island. Adams, the boatswain, was the father of the little community, and drew up the simple code of laws by which the islanders are still governed. On Christmas Day, a magistrate and councillor are elected for the ensuing year; men and women over sixteen being allowed to vote. The women assist in the cultivation of the ground, and take no inconsiderable share in the municipal debates. The fate of this experiment is not yet decided; so I have thought it worth while to preserve the statement. You will have already seen, that in England, as elsewhere, so long as the right of suffrage depended upon possession of property, upon hard pieces of eight, or broad acres of land, there was no dispute of woman's privilege. It is no new thing for woman to vote in England: it is a very *old* thing. It is only a question whether she shall vote upon the ground of her humanity.

III.

THE UNITED-STATES LAW, AND SOME THOUGHTS ON HUMAN RIGHTS.

"Men often think to bring about great results by violent and unprepared effort; but it is only in fair and forecast order, 'as the earth bringeth forth her bud,' that righteousness and praise may spring forth before the nations." — JOHN RUSKIN.

IN passing last to the United States of America, one is tempted to ask, with Anna Brewster when rehearsing the hardships of Helvetian women, " Can it be true, as the advocates of despotic government often say, that under no government are women so harshly treated, so stripped of all independent rights, as under a republic? In republican Helvetia, the Vaudois peasant woman leaves all household care, to stand, spring, summer, and autumn, in her vineyard; but not a bunch of grapes can she gather for the market, without her husband's leave. *He* may have loitered and smoked through every sunny day, while *she* has dug and dressed and watered; but she may not sell one grape to buy bread for her children."

And this is a picturesque statement of the English common law, on which the common law of the United States still rests in the main, and on which it has rested entirely until within the last ten years.

A few passages from Chancellor Kent will indicate, —

I. The estimate of woman formed by this law, and the property-laws built upon this estimate.

II. The laws which regulate divorce. We shall have to consider, —

III. Woman's general civil position; and, —

IV. The right of suffrage.

Fortunately for us, Chancellor Kent talks plain English. He tells us exactly what the law means, and sets it forth as if it were written to be understood; which is not exactly the case with all his predecessors.

As to the estimate of woman on which the laws are based, we have, in connection with what we have already quoted from English law-books, the following statement: —

"But as the husband is the guardian of the wife, and bound to protect and maintain her, the law has given him a reasonable superiority and control over her person; and he may even put gentle restraints upon her liberty, if her conduct be such as to require it. The husband is the best judge of the wants of the family, and the means of supplying them; and, if he shifts his domicile, the wife is bound to follow him." — *Kent's Commentaries*, vol. ii. p. 180.

The best comment on this is found, I think, in a story told by Mrs. Stowe, who says that she once saw a little hut perched on a barren ledge of the Alps, out of reach of human help, and without pasture; but a little below it were stretches of sweet Alpine grass, inviting to eye and foot, and capable of affording sustenance to goats and sheep. "How long have you lived here?" asked Mrs. Stowe of the old woman. "Above forty years." — "And what made you come so far up? Don't you like the meadow?" — "I don't know," was the reply: "it was the *man's notion*."

It is somewhat questionable, whether this man *would* be the best judge of the wants of his family, Chancellor Kent to the contrary notwithstanding; as also what might be his idea of "gentle restraint," in case the wife had refused "to shift her domicile." As to property, Kent proceeds: —

The general rule is, that the husband becomes entitled, on the marriage, to all the goods and chattels of the wife, and to the rents and profits of her lands; and he becomes liable to pay her debts and perform her contracts.

1. If the wife have an inheritance in land, he takes the rents and profits during their joint lives. He may sue in his own name for an injury to the profits of the land; but, if the husband himself chooses to commit waste, the wife has no redress at common law.

2. If the wife, at the time of her marriage, hath an estate for her life, the husband becomes seized of such an estate, and is entitled to the profits during marriage.

3. The husband also becomes possessed of the chattels real of the wife; and the law gives him power, *without her consent*, to sell, assign, mortgage, or otherwise dispose of, the same as he pleases. Such chattels real are liable to be sold on execution

for his debts (vol. ii. p. 133). If he survive his wife, the law gives him her chattels real by survivorship.

4. If debts are due to the wife before marriage, and are recovered by the husband afterward, the money becomes, in most cases, absolutely his own.

On the other hand, the husband is, —

1st, Obliged to provide for his wife out of his fortune, or her own that he has taken into his custody, of what the court calls "necessaries," — these again, of course, to be dependent on the "*man's notion*"! and, —

2d, Becomes liable for her frauds and torts during coverture, — the law understanding, as well as a merchant, that it is useless to "sue a broken bench."

The *indulgence* of the law toward the wife, we are then told, is founded on the idea of force exercised by the husband; a presumption only, which may be repelled. What this indulgence is, we may well be puzzled to guess, unless the phrase indicate that she is not to be prosecuted for theft, where *both* are guilty; and yet, if the presumption that he compelled her to steal be *repelled*, she *may* be prosecuted, and found guilty.

A wife cannot devise her lands by will; nor can she make a testament of chattels, except it be of those which she holds *en autre droit*, without the license of her husband. It is not strictly a will, then, only an appointment, which the husband is bound to allow (vol. ii. p. 170).

The laws are essentially the same in Pennsylvania,

Virginia, North Carolina, South Carolina, Kentucky, and New York; in the latter State, of course, only as applicable to marriages contracted before the passage of the new bill. It is the same in all the States, with one or two Western exceptions; because the passage of a new law never annuls *pre-existing* contracts. In consequence, practice becomes contradictory and intricate; and most lawyers not only *feel*, but *show*, a great dislike to new laws on that account.

In regard to marriage and divorce, Kent says that the English practice was, not to grant divorce for unfaithfulness on the part of the *husband;* and the early settlers of Massachusetts made the same distinction, creating a difference at the very outset in the moral responsibility of the two, fatal alike to happiness and civilization.

In 1840, the policy of South Carolina continued so strict, that there had been no instance, since the Revolution, of a divorce pronounced by a court of justice, or an act of the legislature.

In Massachusetts, the law was, that divorce could only be had for criminality. In Vermont, New Jersey, Kentucky, Mississippi, and Michigan, divorce from "bed and board" may be had for extreme cruelty; and, in Michigan, for wilful desertion for three years.

In Indiana, it is rendered for any cause, at the judgment of the court.

In Illinois, divorce may be had for the usual causes,

and for drunkenness or cruelty, or such other cause as the court shall think right; and, in such cases, the wife does not lose her dower. These differences in statute law indicate, one would think, a variety sufficient to test in time all the theories of reformers and experimentalists.

As to the consistency of the law, Poynter says, —

"It is singular to see a marriage *annulled* on account of the misspelling or suppressing of a name, which would be held *valid* against the lasting misery of the parties."

By cruelty is meant "reasonable apprehension of bodily hurt." Mere austerity of temper, petulance of manners, rudeness of language, a want of civil attention, even *occasional* sallies of passion, do not amount to that cruelty which the law can relieve. The wife must disarm her husband by the *weapons of kindness!*

I have shown you upon what estimate the general common law of the United States is based, as regards both property and divorce. It is needless to say that this estimate is very little to be preferred to that of older countries; but, when the reformers of our cause are tauntingly asked what good they have done, they may reply proudly, though they should point to the changes of legislation during the last ten years alone. Since 1850, the laws have been changed in at least nineteen States. The credit of this change should certainly rest with the men and women of this reform; for, in every State, its sympathizing friends helped to frame the new laws.

Whether justly or not, Rhode Island claims the honor of leading the way in such changes. In 1844, the Hon. Wilkins Updike introduced a bill into her legislature, securing to married women their property under certain regulations. The step was in the right direction. In 1847, Vermont passed similar enactments. In 1848-9, Connecticut, New York, and Texas followed; in 1850, Alabama; in 1853, New Hampshire. In 1855, Massachusetts passed an act of a still more comprehensive kind. It was essentially the same as that introduced into her Senate, in 1852, by the Hon. S. E. Sewall. It was not wholly satisfactory to those who prepared it, but was the best it was thought possible to pass.* In 1856 and 1857,

---

* A law, apparently favorable to all widows, passed the Massachusetts Legislature at the last session. It seems to me, however, to bear the marks of a law passed for a special case. I have made several applications in the proper quarters for information concerning it, but have received nothing in return.

CHAP. 164.— AN ACT CONCERNING THE PROVISIONS FOR WIDOWS IN CERTAIN CASES.

Be it enacted, &c., as follows: —

SECT. 1. — When a man dies, having lawfully disposed of his estate by will, and leaving a widow, she may, at any time within six months after the probate of the will, file in the probate-office, in writing, her waiver of the provisions made for her in the will; and shall, in such case, be entitled to such portion of his real and personal estate as she would have been entitled to if her husband had died intestate: *provided, however*, that, if the share of the personal estate to which she would thus become entitled shall exceed the sum of ten thousand dollars, she shall, in such case, be entitled to receive in her own right the said amount of ten thousand dollars, and to receive the income only of the excess of said share above said sum of ten thousand dollars during her natural life. If she makes no such waiver, she shall not be endowed of his lands, unless it plainly appears by the will to have been the intention of the testator that she should have such provisions in addition to her dower.

SECT. 2. — Upon application, made by the widow or any one interested in the estate, the judge of probate may appoint one or more trustees, to receive, hold, and manage, during the lifetime of the widow, the portion of the personal estate of her deceased

the Legislatures of Kentucky, Missouri, Indiana, Ohio, Rhode Island, and Maine, altered their property-laws, — Rhode Island advancing somewhat on her first step.* Wisconsin and Iowa have followed; and it is not likely that any new States, unless they should be slave States, will repeat the old barbarisms.

I have given Rhode Island the precedence she claims; but there are certain statutes of the State of Illinois, as early in date as January, 1829, which

---

husband, exceeding ten thousand dollars, of which she is entitled to receive under this act.

SECT. 3. — The twenty-fourth section of the ninety-second chapter of the General Statutes is hereby repealed.

Approved April 9, 1861.

In a case on trial in the Superior Court to-day (Oct. 3, 1861), Chief-Justice Allen ruled, that the law of 1855, allowing married women to do business on their own account, separate and apart from their husbands, did not exclude them from entering into business-partnerships with men other than their husbands.

* On the 7th of April, 1861, the Ohio Legislature passed a bill concerning the Rights and Liabilities of Married Women.

SECT. 1 conveys the impression, that all married women may control their rents and issues of real estate belonging to them at marriage, or separately received after.

SECT. 5, however, says "that this law shall not affect any rights which may have *become* vested in any person at the time of its taking effect;" which, of course, cuts off from its beneficial results all persons previously married.

It seems a perfectly simple matter to a woman to obviate the difficulties and disappointments which arise in this way.

Let parties married under the old law, but desiring to benefit by the new, go before a magistrate, and state their wish; and then let the decision in their favor be published in the regular way.

Such a method would not benefit parties at variance; but it would benefit a large class of women engaged, or desiring to engage, in independent business.

The Ohio law repeals a former law of 1857, which secured to all married women the control of the sale or the disposal of personal property exempt from execution: so its benefits are of a nature by no means unmixed.

deserve to be alluded to, on account of their unusual liberality.

If married, and over the age of eighteen years, a woman in Illinois may, *in spite* of her husband, devise her real estate, and bequeath her personal estate, to any one for ever.

The wife may administer on her deceased husband's estate, in preference to all others, if she apply within sixty days. On her husband's death, she inherits one-half of his real estate in fee-simple, absolute; and the whole of his personal estate, with her rights of dower in addition.

The wife has not *legally* the first title to the guardianship of her child on the demise of her husband; but she has it by a kind of *comity*, the consent of public opinion and the courts.

In reference to the wife's inheriting from the husband, my correspondent, the Hon. William H. Herndon, says, —

"You will perceive a difference in the two sections relating to the wife and husband as inheriting from one another, favorable to the wife apparently. In the twenty-second section you will find, that, in case of the wife's death without children, the husband inherits one-half of her real estate in fee-simple, absolute; but nothing is said about her personal. This is because the common law has already given him her personal estate on her marriage."

So we see that the State of Illinois did not quite divest itself of the barbarisms of the common law.

In a later letter, Mr. Herndon continues: —

"Our Illinois Legislature has this winter (1860–61) enacted a law, allowing women (married women) all their property, — real, personal, mixed, — free from all debt, contract, obligation, and control of their husbands. This law puts man and woman in the same position, as far as property-rights and their remedies are concerned. This is right, — just as it should be. For my life, I cannot see why there should be any distinction between men and women, when we speak of rights under government. A woman's rights are identical with a man's. Where he is limited, she should be; where she is limited, he should be."

In Rhode Island, the civil existence of the husband and wife is but one; and, though the letter of the law considers her property acquired by trade or inheritance as technically her own, still it is no longer under her single control. If, as a wife, she sells merchandise, the buyer becomes a debtor to her *husband and herself*. If she makes a purchase, her note is good for nothing, unless her husband's signature is affixed to it. He can dispose of the whole of her personal estate, unless the buyer has been previously notified by *her*, in writing, that the property is exclusively her own. Her real estate the husband cannot sell: but *even of this* she cannot dispose by will; so, perhaps, it might as well be sold. The absurdity becomes ludicrous, when we remember that the law makes her competent to devise any number of millions, so long as it is invested in bank-stock or merchandise.

In the State of Vermont, there are three peculiar provisions: —

First, If the husband abscond without making sufficient provision for his wife, she is *permitted* (*!*) to use her own property and earnings, or the earnings of her minor children, to secure a support. This *permission* indicates the tender mercies of the common law, and reminds us of the Helvetian peasant-woman.

Second, She is exempted from personal restraint during the pendency of a divorce suit.

Third, A mother and her illegitimate child may inherit from each other.

A married woman may devise her real estate, and it is exempt from attachment for the sole debts of her husband. She may have her husband's life insured, the insurance to be made payable to her or her children. If he should be put into the penitentiary, she may transact business as if she were a *feme sole*.

The laws of inheritance are liberal; and the common law prevails by statute, when not repugnant to any recorded statute.

In Connecticut, in 1855, all the real estate owned at the time of marriage, or subsequently inherited by the wife, rests absolutely in her. All her personal estate passes to her husband; but all that she may afterward receive remains in her right, her husband being only her legal trustee. Her earnings are subject to his trusteeship, and nothing more. She is the guardian of her own children; and the court always confirms this right, unless she is incapacitated. In case of divorce, the father is entitled to the children, unless objection is made. On the decease of the husband childless, one-half of his personal estate goes to the wife, and a life-interest in one-third of the real; or the whole, if it be needed for her support.

In New Hampshire, the common law prevails for the most part. What express enactments she passed in 1853 seem to refer rather to making the position of a deserted wife equivalent to that of a *feme sole* than any thing else.

As regards Massachusetts, it is common to say that the legislation of 1855 leaves very little to be desired, beside the right of suffrage; but a keen eye still detects more than one shortcoming. The custody of the wife's person still vests in the husband.

With reference to the guardianship of children, the custom is in advance of the law; while her power to make a will is so carefully guarded, that it might as well be surrendered.

A married woman in Massachusetts can make no contract to bind her, except one strictly relating to her trade, business, or property. She cannot, for instance, indorse a note, or be a surety for another person in any way.

In Maine, since 1857, a wife may hold the wages of her own labor.

In Ohio, at the same date, the law gave this right only *under conditions*. Long before any such changes took place, however, the current of public opinion often forced courts to decide against the common law, and in accordance with equity, — equity not technically, but divinely, considered.

Judge Graham, of the Court of Common Pleas in

Perry County, Penn., made such a decision in a suit where a wife claimed return of earnings loaned by her to her husband, and accumulated *after* marriage. The legal question brought before Judge Graham was, " Can a wife maintain a suit against her husband?" He decided that she could legally hold him to a contract of the kind under consideration; and a verdict was rendered for the woman, in the sum of $2,508.

In August, 1859, Mrs. Dorr put in a claim for $40,000 on her husband's estate, in the Court of Insolvency in Worcester County. The court objected to entertaining the claim until after the choice of an assignee. The hearing was never completed; some private adjustment taking its place. The claim was said to be the first of the kind in the Commonwealth.

We come now to the consideration of the Property Bill, passed in the spring of 1860 by the State of New York. Not only as the latest act of specific legislation, but as the most complete provision ever made by any government to outwit the common law, it demands our attention. After it was passed, a deficiency relating to the rights of guardianship was discovered, and a supplement was added. By these two acts, the "New-York Tribune" tells us that at least five thousand women in that State are redeemed from pauperism, and established in peaceful homes.

But the supplement bears on one important point, which should be alluded to. According to the common law, as I showed in referring to England, a daughter owes service *only* to her father. The mother, who bore and nursed her; who has trained her up, it may be by painful sacrifices, to habits of propriety and thrift, — has no claim upon her service, even in her minority. By conferring on the mother, in case of the father's decease, all the rights, remedies, privileges, and responsibilities in law appertaining to the father, the new act meets the difficulty.

Before quitting the subject, we cannot refrain from alluding to the fact, that, as early as 1849, the State of New York had passed a qualified measure in regard to property; and directing your attention to the manifest truth, that every imperfect act of legislation constitutes a new set of exceptions to general rules, and very undesirably complicates legal practice.

If reforms are not to be unpopular, they should be simple and complete.*

In commenting on the passage of these bills, advocated by Mrs. Stanton before the committees of the Assembly and the Senate, the " New-York Tribune " says, —

"Mrs. Stanton talked forcibly. It is needless for me to say that she talked earnestly of woman's sufferings, sweetly of her endurance, eloquently of her rights. When she talked of her right to be protected in the enjoyment of her property, of her right to be released from the bondage of an ill-assorted marriage, she was listened to with marked favor. She pleaded these demands with the feeling of a true woman;

---

* See note, page 349.

and she carried the conviction, that she was not asking more than policy, as well as justice, demanded should be conceded. When she claimed that her voice should be heard on the hustings, and her vote be received at the ballot-box, she was earnest and eloquent and *plausible;* but she must have felt that she was not convincing her audience, and she did not."

Here the single word *plausible* vitiates, as cunning reporters well know how to do, the whole effect of the sentence. Far more reasonably, the "Tribune" might have said she was earnest, eloquent, and *sensible;* and so have spurred its readers to thought instead of ridicule. His criticism, however, launches fairly our last subject of discussion. It is needless to say, that nowhere in the United States has woman the full power of suffrage.

In New Jersey, women formerly possessed, and often exercised, this right. By the Constitution, adopted July 2, 1776, the privilege of voting was accorded to all inhabitants, of full age and clear estate, who had resided for a certain time in the country, and who had fifty dollars in proclamation-money.

In 1790, a Quaker member of the Assembly had the act so drawn as to read "he or she." Until 1807, women often voted, especially in times of great political excitement; at such times, for the most part, "under influence," we may presume. Many voted in the presidential contest of 1800; and a newspaper of that period thanks them for unanimously supporting John Adams in opposition to Jefferson. So they were supposed, at times, to act independently. At an election in Hunterdon County in 1802, the ballots of some colored women elected a member of the legislature. Probably this fact, by stimulating the local prejudice against color, and the fading-out of all aristocratic distinctions, which left no property qualifications on the statute-book, led to a change; for, in 1807, an act was passed, limiting the right of suffrage to "free white male citizens of twenty-one years." *

In later times, committees of intelligent men, in Wisconsin, Michigan, and Ohio, have reported in favor of granting to women the right of suffrage; but the question was lost in the ballot which followed.

If the constitution prepared for Kansas should be accepted by the people, single women will be empowered to vote there. In Nebraska, the lower house passed a vote, conferring the privilege; but it was too late in the session for the question to come before the upper branch.

In 1858, a proposition to amend the Constitution of the State of Connecticut, so as to extend the franchise to women, received eighty-two votes in the House of Representatives. It was defeated by a majority of forty-five. In 1852, the Kentucky Legislature, in providing for the election of school-trustees, enacted that "any widow, having a child between six and eighteen years, may vote in person or by proxy."

A provision thus limited by public opinion and prejudice would probably have very little force. I

---

* See Appendix.

have understood that such a provision has taken effect in some parts of Michigan, and it has also been recommended to the State of Massachusetts. Very early in the history of our government, its inconsistencies became a matter of comment among women themselves. How could it be otherwise? How can she be said to have a right to *life*, who has never consented to the laws which may deprive her of it, who is steadily refused a trial by her peers, who has no voice in the election of her judges? How can she be said to have a right to *liberty*, whose person, if not yet in custody, almost inevitably becomes so on her maturity, who does not own her earnings, who can make no valid contract, and is taxed without representation? How can that woman be said to possess either the right or the reality of *happiness*, who is deprived of the custody of her own person, of the guardianship of her children, of the right to devise or share her property?

The government is tyrannical which leaves a single citizen in this predicament. What is to be said of a government which enforces it upon half its subjects?

It is not strange then, that, half in jest, half in earnest, the wife of John Adams wrote to him in 1776 to ask if it "were generous in American men to claim absolute power over wives at a moment when they were emancipating the whole earth." Nor was it strange, that, in a more serious mood, Hannah Corbin of Virginia should write to her brother, Richard Henry Lee, on the same subject.

The American Colonies were struggling against the mother-country, on the ground that taxation and representation should be inseparable.

The "National Intelligencer" has to confess, when it tells the story, that it was not strange if "strong-minded" women of that era, finding themselves *taxed*, should wonder why they could not vote.

Mr. Lee wrote from Chantilly in reply, March 17, 1778:—

"I do not see," he says, "that any thing prevents widows, having large property, from voting, notwithstanding it has never been the case either here or in England. Perhaps it was thought unbecoming for women to press into tumultuous assemblies. . . . Perhaps it was thought, that, as all those who vote for taxes must bear the tax, none would be imposed, except for the public good.

"For both the widow and the single woman," he continues, "I have the highest respect; and would, at any time, give my consent to secure to them the franchise, though I do not think it would increase their security.

"The Committee of Taxation," he adds, "are regularly chosen by the freeholders and housekeepers; and, in the choice of them, you have as legal a right to vote as any person."

Mr. Lee thinks, that, in a few minutes' conversation, he could "content" his sister upon the subject; but eighty years have passed away, and the question is still unsettled.

What he calls a "woman's security" is proved to be no security, even in the small matter of money; for men are constantly imposing taxes, the burden of which *they* are never to bear. As I have shown, in treating of labor, what position women hold toward the State in the matter of employment, I will not repeat the statement here. Let these pages bear no other burden than that of woman's civil rights, — "woman's rights," — a phrase which we *all* hate; which soils the lips that use it; which women speak with such unction as a slave might clank his chains!

Soil the lips? Not because it is a phrase which stirs the ridicule and the contempt of the weak-minded; not because *you* consider it only the second term of the Bloomer equation: but because the necessity to use it shows how little has yet been done; shows that men still dwell on distinctions of sex, in preference to identities of duty; that women are playthings still in the popular estimate, — creatures of the nursery and the drawing-room, but not angels of God, joint-heirs of immortality.

We have not laid a secure foundation for any statement on this subject, unless we have made it clear that "woman's rights" are identical with "human rights;" that what men do for women, they do in far *wider* measure for themselves; that no father, brother, or husband can have all the privileges ordained for him of God, till mother and sister and wife are set free to secure them according to instinctive individual bias.

The subject would have no interest for me, if it were but a selfish clamor of one class for advantages over another; but it does interest me, — interest beyond all earthly debate, — because, in its evolution, there unfolds also the highest interest of our common humanity.

That public opinion has been somewhat conquered, the reception given to women in the lyceum is alone sufficient to show. When a woman of good social standing struggles with convention on the one hand, and womanly affection on the other, she still stands *on the platform* somewhat as she *did at the stake;* but, on the other hand, the awakening public interest has nurtured a class of women who owe all that they have and are to the platform itself.

With no oppressive restrictions in their circumstances, — endowed with strong good sense and a vigorous talent, — they have won their way to the public esteem; and are stronger and healthier than most women, only because they have had an object for life and thought to grasp.

What will most help women in the matter of labor, and, through labor, to their "civil rights," is a new conception of the dignity of labor on the part of the educated classes, men as well as women.

Harriet Hosmer comes back from Rome to queen it over our men; Rosa Bonheur drives a tandem of Flemish horses through a square of canvas, and over the very necks of her critics: but we want women who shall turn the trades into fine arts. Do you smile at the expression? It is legitimate. France has already answered my demand. A finer statue than the "Moses" of Michael Angelo would be one womanly model of patient thoroughness. A finer picture than the glowing pencils of Titian and Claude ever fused into a canvas would be the prospective elevation of manual labor.

The fine arts are already obedient to woman's will. To *what* woman is it reserved to make the useful arts pay tribute? Dependent upon the "right to labor," as we have already seen, is "woman's civil equality." If all the fields of human labor are thrown absolutely open (and you admit that they ought to be); if women enter and grow wealthy therein; if every second woman, for instance, were an intelligent property-holder, — is it credible that she, or her husband for her, would remain contented in her present minority? Would she not want a seat in the legislature to protect her property, a vote to control appropriations and taxes? There are no revolutionists like the industrial classes.

It was the discontent of merchants and artisans which hunted Charles Stuart to the block, and paved the way for English freedom. It was the discontent of trade, a long-entertained moral disgust, culminating in indignant contempt at a Stamp Act, which secured American *independence*, — I wish we could say, American *freedom* as well. Create, then, a class of wealthy working women, you who are ambitious of a female franchise, and society will be forced to give you your desire.

Wendell Phillips says, that, when woman is once brought to the ballot-box, men will cry out, " Educate her!" in self-preservation. If this be true (and I am not sure that it is; for a great many popular elections are at this moment carried in the Middle and Southern States, to come no nearer home, by the *un*educated class, partly by the dram-shops indeed), — if this *be* true, however, it is a "poor rule which does not work both ways;" and we may go farther than Mr. Phillips, and say, he will also cry out, "Give her something to do!" that she may understand the interests of property, and be qualified to plead for them. Mr. Phillips plants himself upon the right of suffrage, and *goes back* to secure education and free labor, for State reasons. He has every right to do it; but, on the other hand, *we* may rest upon our undoubted right to education, and go *forward*, with safe, strong steps, to claim the right of suffrage. When a majority of women find the means of thorough education open, then a much greater number will seek actual employment, and immediately the interests of property will compel them to clamor for suffrage. Do not misunderstand me. It is not a nation of paid underlings, of ever so intelligent clerks and apprentices, men or women, that will control the springs of government, and overthrow institutions as well as prejudices, if they stand in their way: it is the heads of firms, the movers in great undertakings, the proprietors of mills, the builders of ships, the contractors for supplies, persons conversant with large interests, and quick to see their jeopardy, which, as women no less than men, must secure the elective right.

How I should rejoice to see a large Lowell mill wholly owned and managed by women! What is to make it possible? — only, that the unoccupied women of wealth and rank, at this moment in the Commonwealth, should combine to build or buy such a mill. Suppose it *well* managed, representing ultimately a million of dollars: do you believe it would long remain without political power? Just as the testy trade of Upsal demanded the franchise for its eighty-one women, so would the Lowell mill.

Every year, these ten years, our sturdy friend Dr. Hunt has sent up her protest to the city assessors. She has not quite had the heart, as I wish some woman had, to let them sell her household gods over her head, for non-payment of taxes; but the City Government sits as serene and patient under her inflictions as if she had never spoken. Her protests probably go back to the pulp of the paper-mill; and, but for the newspaper, we should never know that they were written. But five thousand female property-holders, calling their own caucus, and storming the City Hall with well-concerted words, would compel any government to listen; would compel committees to sit, and departments to act. Let it be your first duty, then, to add to the number of intelligent female workers.

Last summer, I heard one of our friends say, that the reason that men did not wish women to enter medical societies, and receive medical diplomas, was, that they were unwilling to be detected in their own double-dealing and malpractice. I should not be willing to indorse a statement so broadly made. Mean men may justify it: but the men I have known, the men who have been at once my inspiration and my strength, — these men were not mean; yet among them even the bravest doubted, at first, as to the expediency of our discussion.

These men have felt a tender reverence for moral purity in woman. They have seen laborers of the lower class fall as if smitten by a pestilence. They had not faith to save the world at such a cost. From the malpractice and guilty dread of mean men, then; from the sensitive horror of the noblest, let us learn, at least, that the duty woman owes the State is a *moral* duty. A full understanding of this will give her courage to press her claims. It is the power of conscience and love which she is to bring to bear on the ballot-box, and which is to mould, with her aid, questions and interests hitherto untouched by any higher impulse than the love of gain.

I cannot leave this statement of human rights, without claiming for woman one right of which men very commonly deprive her; in behalf of which society makes no clamor, and about which the most radical reformers say very little. I mean woman's right to find man in his proper place, as counsellor and friend.

As *father*, to find him interested, equally with his wife, in the spiritual custody and training of his daughters; giving thus some portion of each day to imbuing young womanly souls with manly strength.

As *brother*, to find in him wise respect for womanhood, and helpful free communion.

As *husband*, to find him, unless there is manifest interposition of Providence, always at the head of his family, always the support and counsellor of his wife, as she in turn is to be his; making his love her shelter, his strength her dependence, his experience her guide, his manliness the complement of her womanliness.

As a *son*, to find him always anxious and ready to minister, provident to think, patient to bear, and willing to act; never shirking, from idleness, the duty which an active mother does not shrink from bending, perhaps *breaking*, beneath.

Society sets man free from every conceivable family duty, without a word. On the other hand, it binds women down to them with cords of iron, and is pitiless if a single one be snapped. I do not ask society to require less of woman, but *more* of man. There is an immense amount of cant, intentional and unintentional, talked upon this subject. Last January, I heard one of our wisest and best public teachers speak upon the constitution of the family; and, when he had spoken whole pages of solid sense, he said this foolish thing, — that the life of the family rested in the mother; that, when *she* died, the children must scatter, the father could not hold them alone, but that the father might be faithless or dissipated, might abide in foreign countries, might wander for years a stranger, and still the family sacredness be unbroken. I do not believe it. I protest against such a view of the family, as a great public evil, and one which no public teacher should strengthen by any heedless or sentimental words.

No man has a right to ask any woman to be his wife, who means to sacrifice her life to his own love of business or pleasure or vagrancy; who does not mean to stand strong at her side till death. I speak for the heart of all womanhood when I say, that no good woman would ever accept such an offer, if she supposed she were to be idly left to fulfil its duties alone. If God had intended to rear women independent of manly influence, he would never have constituted the family. It is because every woman needs every man that its laws are absolute. If the physical legitimacy of the family depend upon the mother, the spiritual legitimacy depends upon the holy faithfulness of the father. When death or sickness or imperative duty takes her beloved ones from her, God sends to woman the Comforter, who helps her to bear and do her double duty. Yet even this angel is born of a voiceless sorrow. It was in recognition of this human need, as much as of the divine love, that Theodore Parker was accustomed to pray to Him who is *both* Father and Mother.

Do you object, that, under the present constitution of society, man cannot find time for this fidelity? When woman becomes an active worker, adding to the resources of the household, man is set free from a portion of his care. The future offers him ample time; the present, more than he uses. I wish I could see him as anxious to make acquaintance with his own young children as with the gay society of his neighborhood.

The actual guardianship of society is now thrown into woman's hands. It does not belong to her: it belongs to men *and* women.*

Individual men shrink from the idea of being " governed by their wives." From traditional indolence, however, and that sentimental respect which does not permit a man to sit in a woman's presence, the " world " has certainly come to be governed by " *its*

---

* This passage was originally prompted by some reflections on the changes which have occurred in domestic life in Boston.

Here the family, even among those of the highest social rank, had once a sacred simplicity pleasant to remember. Men were accustomed to take their three meals with their wives and children. The latest dinner-hour was two, P.M.; and suppers were unheard of. The evening party began at seven; and young girls went freely and uninvited from house to house, with their needle or their book.

How greatly all this is changed, my readers, many of them, feel still more deeply than I; and, with this change, the formation of " clubs " of various kinds has brought about others far more important.

A young married lady of rank and fashion was lately lamenting to me the isolation of husbands and wives, fathers and children, consequent upon club-life.

" But," she concluded with a sigh, " if my husband had no club, he would expect a hot supper for a friend two or three times a week; and how could I ever accomplish that ? "

This *indolence* of *women* lies at the bottom of many serious social evils. The woman who will not, health and fortune permitting, make herself responsible in such a case for any number of hot suppers, deserves to see her own happiness wither, her own hearth made desolate.

It is needless to add, that if women would educate themselves to be true and noble companions to their husbands, and resign on their own part all that is unsound, and therefore unbecoming, in fashionable life, hot suppers would cease to be a desideratum, and men would pass pleasant evenings without them.

wife." Worst of all, nobody punishes it even by a sneer.

The historical development of woman's social progress corresponds to the logical statement upon which I have insisted.

Nearly two centuries ago, Mary Astell would have established a college for women; but the bigotry of Bishop Burnet defeated her plans. The niece of a beneficed clergyman, she had not the courage to press her schemes against the open opposition of the church. Many other efforts, like hers, to secure and make use of education, led the way to a recognition of a decided bias in the individual: so when, a century later, Mary Wollstonecraft was born, the way was open for the assertion of the right to labor. This assertion is hardly indicated in her most celebrated work; but it gives pungency and effect to the dreariest pages of her novels.

In Australia, when a female child is born, the natives break her finger-joints; an artificial distinction, which *they* seem to think more decisive and enduring than God's own limit of sex.

Mary Wollstonecraft saw, that civilized society, enslaved by tradition and custom, imposed conditions quite as arbitrary, and, to all practical purposes, broke *every* joint in a woman's body; leaving her helpless, to depend on the strength and skill and affection of man.

A passionate and thriftless father, who spent more than three daughters could earn, and whom she nevertheless protected to her dying day, did not give her a very high idea of the security of such dependence. The response to her appeal was heard in a myriad of distinguished voices, and seen in the consecutive, chosen, and persevering labors of Harriet Martineau in political economy, of Anna Jameson in artistic criticism, of Mary Carpenter in the reformation of criminals, of Florence Nightingale in sanitary reform, of Caroline Chisholm in emigration, of Mrs. Griffith in marine botany (a special study, which she may almost be said to have created), of Janet Taylor in practical philanthropy among seamen, and nautical astronomy.

This selection of duty shows the advance of the movement. Formerly a woman might be literary in a general sense: now she had the oversight of the field, and might choose the place and kind of her work.

All this prepared the way for the advent of Margaret Fuller, and brought about the condition of which she was the exponent. She caught the rumor which floated in subtle discord all around her. Her quick insight detected every true and living germ of thought in the confused social deposits and exhalations. Out of the discord, she wrought a quaint and scholarly music; out of the refuse, she enriched a fragrant garden: and this song, this outgrowth, had an essential music and beauty, and were caught at once to the popular heart.

That the division of labor was already taking place,

was obvious enough to her: so she claimed, in advance, the right of suffrage. Society was already prepared to make this claim, but only discovered its readiness as it listened to her enthusiastic song. Like Deborah, our friend struck her cymbals; and, when the heart of the people shouted consent, they " made her a judge over them."

Although it was doubtless owing to many older causes, it seemed as if her statement of the " great lawsuit" in 1844 led to the first Woman's Convention at Seneca Falls in 1848; and, in 1850, the National Woman's-rights Association began the yearly work in which it has ever since persevered.

Man, as well as woman, has been forced to respect this work, moved by the moral destitution in the lowest, and the profane inanity in the highest, ranks of life, which is the result of our social depravity.

Profane inanity, I repeat; for every helpless woman is a living, intolerable blasphemy against the Most High. Not more a blasphemy than every helpless man; but society neither expects, defends, nor provides for, helpless *men*. It is only the helpless woman who is expected and approved.

Often do we hear it said, that no law forbids American women to *work*.

Neither, it has been responded, is there any *law* which forbids Chinese women to *walk;* but the careful ligatures, so closely pressed by unsuspecting mothers about those tender feet, do not do their work more surely than the inevitable restrictions of society.

In summing up this constantly accruing list of influences and changes, I must again direct your attention to the fact, that, from the earliest dawn of modern civilization, women have been, in some nations at least, invested with political power.

The mock-marriage, by which the woman's entailed suffrage served a fraudulent purpose; the abbesses called to Parliament in right of abbey-lands, the permission accorded to the eighty-one women of Upsal, the position of the French "Dames de la Halle," the female stockholders in the East-India Company, that one persistent female property-holder in Nova Scotia, the fifty-dollar proclamation-money in New Jersey,— all indicate that there never *has* been, and never *will* be, any serious difficulty about woman's voting in any age or any country where the right to vote depends upon the possession of property, and where she herself professes to desire it.

Understand, then, that the abstract right to vote is not the question for you to consider: that was settled some hundreds of years ago.

The practical question for American men to put to themselves is, whether their own democratic experiment is a failure. Will you go back to the property basis for your own franchise? or do you still profess to believe, that man — as man, as child of God — has a right to reign, which does not depend upon broad doubloons or broad acres? And, if man has this right upon a simple human ground, how can you deny it to woman?

Will you say that she is not human,—that she has no soul?

Even Mahomet did better than that. Some one once asked him if the marriage-tie were immortal, and if a husband might claim his wife in the next world:—

"If the man be the superior being," he replied, "he can claim his wife or not, as he chooses; but, if the woman be the superior, the decision must rest with her."

And what Mahomet thus prophesied of the world to come is clearly true of the world that is. There is no such thing as cheating either God or humanity.

Let him who aspires to rule *make himself superior* in understanding and moral purpose, and he *will* rule.

No possibilities, visible or invisible, need daunt him; but, let him be false by one hair's breadth, and he carries his doom in his own bosom as certainly as the flawed crystal at the approach of frost.

You are, then, to base your demand for woman's civil rights upon her simple humanity,—the value of the soul itself.

If you deny this foundation for her, you deny it for yourselves, and the Declaration of Independence is only an impertinent pretence.

It may not be easy to push this truth home, and force your friends and neighbors to consider it; but, once convinced in your own minds, you cannot escape from the responsibility.

Wendell Phillips once told us of an old catechism, printed, I think, at Venice in 1563, which contained the following question and answer: —

Q. How shall I show my obedience to God?
A. By never doing any thing which is disagreeable to my neighbor.

Is it possible that this catechism is still in general use?

Fashionable morality is of so loose a sort, that to do any thing disagreeable to one's neighbor is still, in the estimation of most people, the unpardonable sin. People who are capable of hesitating on that account need not be greatly anxious about their responsibility.

Our cause does not need them; resting, not on timid self-deceivers, but on immutable truth, and the hallowed recognition of woman herself.

Society still cries, like King John in the play, —

> "If not, fill up the measure of her will;
> Yes, in some measure, satisfy her so,
> That we shall stop her *exclamation!*"

And woman, serener than Constance, may whisper back, —

> "Wherefore, since law is perfect wrong,
> Why should the law forbid my tongue to cry?"

TEN YEARS:

AN APPENDIX.

"The only respect in which all men continue for ever to be equal, is that of the equal right which every man has to defend himself; but this involves a source of much inequality in respect to the things which any one may have a right to defend." — ADAM FERGUSON.

TEN YEARS:

AN APPENDIX.

" To go on working, I consider the only thing to do; and, when friends urge this after every fresh effort, their doing so in itself contains a kind of verdict." — FELIX MENDELSSOHN BARTHOLDY.

THERE are some items of interest, that have come under my observation, for the first time, during the last few years, which I have not found it possible to add to the preceding lectures without destroying their symmetry. I therefore offer them in an Appendix. They are not placed here because they are unimportant, but simply that the later progress of public opinion may be set forth by itself.

For the last five years, the women of the United States have held few public discussions. They have done wisely. Circumstances have proved their friend. Nothing ever had done, nothing ever will do again, so great a service to woman, in so short a time, as this dreadful war, out of which we are so slowly emerging. Respect for woman came only with the absolute need of her; and so many women of distinguished ability made themselves of service to the government, that we had no single woman to honor as England had honored Florence Nightingale. With us, her name was *legion*. But with the prospect of peace comes the old duty of agitation; and we find ourselves again summoned to our work, and again anxiously awaiting its results, — *anxiously*, for the public work of women is an object which still attracts the gaze of the curious; and the smallest indiscretion on the part of a single woman has a retrograde effect, which very few seem able to measure.

Our reform is unlike all others; for it must begin in the family, at the very heart of society. If it be not kindly, temperately, and thoughtfully conducted, men everywhere will be able to justify their remonstrances. Let us rather justify *ourselves*. My last report to any convention was made to those called in Boston in 1859 and 1860. Between that time and 1863, I printed five volumes, which are nothing but reports upon the various interests significant to our cause. During the last four years, I have watched the development of American industry in its relation to women, and have, through the newspapers, aroused public feeling in their behalf. My labor is naturally classed under the three heads of Education, Labor, and Law. A proper education must prepare woman for labor, skilled or manual: and the experience of a laborer should introduce her to citizenship; for it provides her with rights to protect, privileges to secure, and property to be taxed. If she be a laborer, she must have an interest in the laws which control labor.

In considering our position in these three respects,

it is impossible to offer a digest of all that has occurred during the last six years. What I have to say will refer chiefly to the events of the last two.

EDUCATION.

The most important educational movement of the last two years has been the formation of an American Association for the Promotion of Social Science, with four departments, and two women on its Board of Directors. Subsequently, the Boston Association was organized, with seven departments, and seven women on its Board of Directors; one woman being assigned to each department, including that of law. Any woman in the United States can become a member of the American association. If the opportunities it offers are not seized, it will be the fault of women themselves.

During the past winter, the Lowell Institute in Boston, in connection with the government of the Massachusetts Technological Institute, took a step which deserves public mention. They advertised classes for both sexes, under the most eligible professors, for instruction in French, mathematics, and natural science. As the training was to be thorough, the number of pupils was limited, and the *women* who applied would have filled the seats many times over. These classes have been wholly free, and have added to the obligation which the free Art School for women had already conferred.

On the 25th of June, 1865, the Ripley College, at Poultney, Vt., celebrated its Commencement. Seventeen young ladies were graduated. Ralph Waldo Emerson delivered the literary address, and two days were devoted to the examination of incoming pupils. Feeling very little satisfaction in the success of colleges intended for the separate sexes, I take more pleasure in speaking of the Baker University, in Kansas, which was chartered by the Legislature of that State in 1857, as a university for both sexes. It has now been in active operation for seven years. A little more than a year ago, Miss Martha Baldwin, a graduate of the Baldwin University at Berea, Ohio, was appointed to the chair of Greek and Latin. She is but twenty-one years of age, but was elected by the government to make the address for the faculty at the opening of the Commencement exercises, and seems to have given entire satisfaction during the year.

Howard University was chartered at the last session of Congress, for the education of all classes of students, without distinction of sex, race, or color. It has purchased three acres of land in a pleasant part of Washington, and is now ready to receive about twenty-five students. Rev. Dr. Boynton, chaplain of the House of Representatives, is President of the Board of Trustees.

St. Lawrence University, Canton, N.Y., a university still very young, graduates both men and women, on precisely the same conditions. Civil engineering and political economy are the only optional studies with the women. It reports one theological student. Lombard University, Galesburg, Ill., does the same; but I know nothing of its standard of scholarship. It is only within the last year that I have been able to visit the most conspicuous colleges in this country in which women are taught with men. I consider the system of mixed classes an immense advantage, as it secures the standard of scholarship, prevents all foolish hazing, and places personal character and moral deportment in their right relations to classic study. It prevents also such instruction in the classics as must necessarily deprave the estimate of woman.

OBERLIN.

About all that I knew of Antioch, before I went West, was this, — that it was a college for the instruction of both sexes. I would like to have my readers know more of Antioch than I did, and to feel, without seeing it, the same intense interest that warms me now. They have heard of Oberlin, I suppose, — heard of it as a sort of fanatical way-station between the district school and Harvard University, where men, women, and "colored people" are all taught together. If I should show them what Oberlin has actually *done*, I think they may see more plainly what it is possible for Antioch to do: so I shall begin with some account of this college, which has " saved the North-west."

It is no idle boast: and, when I had stayed a week

at Antioch, and was thoroughly roused to a sense of its immense importance; when I had seen how admirably fitted was Dr. Hosmer for the work given him to do, — I decided this in my own mind; namely, that if any one thing had stood in the way of Antioch hitherto, if any thing had prevented her complete work, it was the Eastern prejudice, the idea that men and women could not be educated together. And, as they had been trying this experiment at Oberlin for thirty-two years, I thought I would go there, and see how it had worked. If I had known then, what I know now, that out of the bosom of Oberlin twenty-two colleges had sprung, and that, of the twenty-two, ten are at this moment officered by her own graduates, I think I might have spared myself the trouble. Here are their names; for you will care more for Oberlin, if you get some glimpse of the work she has done, before I tell you the details of her story. I have put an asterisk against the names of the colleges whose presidents are graduates of Oberlin. All of those named receive pupils of both sexes.

Ohio. — Baldwin University, Berea, three colleges and one university, 326 pupils, 1846; Heidelberg College, Tiffin; Antioch College, Yellow Springs; Mount Union College, Alliance; Otterbein College, Westerville, a Gallery of Fine Arts forming, 360 students.

Michigan. — *Olivet College, 308 pupils; *Hillsdale College, 609 pupils; *Albion College; *Adrian College, with an endowment of $300,000.

Wisconsin. — Madison University; *Ripon College, 87 pupils.

Illinois. — Wheaton College, 219 pupils; Lombard University.

Indiana. — *Union Christian College, Mecom, 115 graduates.

Minnesota. — *Northfield College.

New York. — Genesee College, Lima; Elmira College.

Kentucky. — Berea College.

Kansas. — State University, Lawrence; Lincoln College, Topeka; Baker University.

Iowa. — Grenell College; *Tabor College, 192 pupils.

To these we may add Oberlin herself, with 1,145 pupils for the term which has just closed, and the prospect of a college in Missouri, which her president has recently been solicited to organize. Wherever I have obtained the catalogues of 1866, I have recorded the present number of students in these colleges. To those I have not marked, it will be fair to allow an average of 210 students. Those are not high schools, be it understood, but colleges in the proper sense. There is no doubt, that Oberlin, as the principal educational influence in Ohio, imposed upon Antioch and all other " Christian " colleges the necessity of educating both sexes.

In 1832, Oberlin was a little religious colony, born into a complete wilderness out of the Presbyterian Church. The plan of the colony involved a school, for which a tract of five hundred acres was given. The sale of the remainder of a tract of six thousand acres furnished a small fund with which to begin teaching. A year later, the students of Lane Seminary determined to hold an antislavery prayer meeting. The trustees forbade it. "You are right," said old Dr. Beecher, when the mutinous lads appealed to him,—"you are right; but we are too weak to hold Lane Seminary on anti-slavery principles. Go and make it possible for us." They went—Theodore Weld and Henry B. Stanton among them—to speak the truth at Oberlin. Arthur Tappan called from the Broadway Tabernacle the man who had been in the front of the great awakening which has swept through the land, instinct in every fibre of his being with the spirit of aggressive Christian work. "Go," he wrote to President Finney,—"go and teach the young men whom Lane refuses." One hundred thousand dollars was pledged by the merchants. Oberlin studied in summer that her pupils might teach all winter. So, promising to return to New York for the winter seasons, President Finney found his way, one muddy spring morning, to Oberlin. What he found there was two frame-houses in the midst of the forest, and half a dozen log-cabins. He found also his sixty students.

Very soon they had no end of difficulties to contend with. A jealous college, that had wanted Dr. Finney for its president, did its best to break down Oberlin. The crash of 1837 came; and Arthur Tappan, and the rest who had not paid out capital, ceased to pay interest. It was necessary to raise $50,000, and President Finney went to England and did it. Every man's hand was against them. The cross-roads were ornamented with pictures of fugitive slaves, pursued by lions and tigers, and running in the direction of Oberlin. But when Oberlin became a station on the underground railroad, and the slave-hunters actually came there after their chattels, the case altered. The neighborhood took part with the college, as if by miraculous conversion, and the offensive pictures disappeared. Then a thousand scholarships were instituted, at $100 each. Some were perpetual; some for six, eight, or ten years. On the interest of this investment the college now lives. The scholarships, as they fall in, increase its means. It costs $15,000 per annum, and $15 is the student's yearly fee. He rents his scholarship of a broker in the town. The college is managed with exquisite economy, and the most perfect attention to essential neatness.

For twenty years the college sent out into the West five hundred anti-slavery pupils yearly, to take the post of teachers, ministers, editors, and lawyers. They were heretics, so they were pushed farther and farther West. For the last fifteen years, it has sent out a thousand yearly. In all, twenty-five thousand men and women have gone out from her bosom, who have eaten and drank and recited at the same board with the colored man. Through all her pecuniary troubles, her original teachers have stayed by her, have given up all else for her sake; and President Finney has never been without a colored student at his table. There are two large churches in the town; for a population of four thousand persons has grown up to supply the wants of the college, which has the great advantage of still retaining the services of those who originally created it. Last year, Dr. Finney, now nearly eighty years old, resigned his position as president, but still remains at the head of the Theological School. I had always thought Oberlin bigoted to evangelical ways. I did not find it so. I was made as welcome to cross-question classes as if I had been an ordained graduate of their own. All theological teaching is done by discussion; and the fact that the colleges which have grown up under her graduates are of all persuasions, from the Methodist to the Christian, will show that doctrine is not urged. In all the recitation-rooms, questions were freely asked by both sexes; and this questioning is encouraged by all the professors but one, a young man from Yale. "Yes," said President Fairchild, himself a graduate of Oberlin, when I had pointed this out; "yes, that is what remains of New-England stiffness. Six months will convert him: we shall let him take his own time." I have never seen any thing like the enthusiasm this college inspires in those who labor for it. Would that I could see a man bred at Harvard with the same patient fire in his soul as President Finney! As I knelt by his side morning and evening, I felt that under his ministry the very *stones* must cry out. The twenty-five thousand men sent out from Oberlin did not go out as citizens merely, but as *teachers*. I was not surprised to find, that, a few months before the Proclamation of Emancipation, a letter had gone to Washington, from President Finney, entreating Mr.

AN APPENDIX. 387

Lincoln to "recognize the hand of the Lord in this matter." In Oberlin, it is believed to have substantially modified the proclamation. Oberlin sent eight hundred and fifty men into the field during the rebellion. Professor Peck, our minister to Hayti, is the man who was once imprisoned by slave-hunters in Cleveland jail. An indignant mass-meeting was held in that city. Six hundred sabbath-school children went from Oberlin to greet their imprisoned superintendent, and the prosecuting attorney thought it best to give up the case. Professor Monroe, married to a daughter of President Finney, is our consul at Rio, and is well known as a controlling political power in Ohio. One of the faculty headed the first Oberlin regiment; a graduate of the Theological School, the second; Colonel Cooper, of the third, who went through with Sherman, is still doing antislavery work in Arkansas; and the present Governor of Ohio, Major-General Cox, also married to a daughter of Mr. Finney, has a record so brilliant, that it demands a volume in itself.

During the war, the college realized one unexpected advantage from the presence of women. The female pupils kept the college working! In the original constitution of Oberlin, it was stated that its main object was "to diffuse pure religion throughout the Mississippi Valley, and to elevate the female character." To both these objects it has been religiously faithful. In the Ladies' Library Room I saw a picture of Camp Dennison. It was drawn by one of the graduates;

was sent from camp to college, with the inscription beneath, "From the boys at Camp Dennison to the girls of '61, — the dearest girls in all the world." It was not put out of sight, but proudly shown to me. I have never been in any educational institution where the interests of the *pupils* so evidently rule. The vacation comes in winter, that the pupils may pass it in teaching; but the professors do not then take a vacation. They open a winter school, where students who are behindhand may make up deficiencies. I do not mean that all the pupils go through the entire college course: many cannot afford it. They stay as long as they can, and go reluctantly away.

They follow the fashions at Oberlin: the Continental pronunciation took possession of the Greek and Latin class-rooms last year. They employ undergraduates to teach the preparatory students at thirty cents an hour. The common or town school has 830 pupils, 180 of whom are colored. In the college, the colored pupils are 5 to 100, and the female pupils 40 out of 50. There are scarcely any rules. The few that are printed are enforced as friendly advice. President Finney says he has often known a year to pass without an opportunity for a presidential admonition. The management of the girls seems to me admirable. The teachers *feel* no doubt of their method; therefore they show none. Once a fortnight the lady principal meets the ladies, and talks with them privately on all questions of womanly habits and manners. The splendid endowment of Vassar

College could not give to Oberlin a woman better suited to this purpose than Mrs. Dascomb. Once a week there is a religious meeting.

The college has just now the brightest prospects. Its old buildings were far less convenient than those at Antioch; but at a late Commencement an appeal was made, and by a spasmodic response, like that which recently gave us $30,000 for Meadville, the graduates subscribed as much for a new "Ladies' Hall." The contracts were made before the war, the expenses managed with scrupulous prudence; and now a beautiful brick building, 121 feet by 121, is opened. It has a library, reading-room, and parlors; and a dining-hall, to which the male students are admitted, and where truly excellent board is given for three dollars a week. The kitchen would do anybody's heart good. On every floor is a wood and water room, where the wood and ashes go up and down on a dumb-waiter, where water is carried up in a well-protected pipe, and slops may be thrown into a sink. Two excellent new buildings for recitations will be ready for the spring term. Some idea of the admirable tact and prudence which have prevailed at Oberlin may be gleaned from the following anecdote: Thirty-three years passed before a colored *teacher* was employed in the Preparatory School. "We knew," said President Fairchild, "that we must not try the experiment till it was sure to be a magnificent success." In 1865, Oberlin had in Miss Fanny Jackson a pupil worthy of the experiment. She had been a slave in the District of Columbia, and so puny, that, at an early age, she was sold to her own aunt, a freedwoman, for a trivial sum. She was sent here, and with fear and trembling now yielded to the wish of the president. That no one might be compelled to enter her class, *two* advanced classes in English grammar were organized, one under the present wife of Dr. Finney. On the first day, an over-grown lad came to the president, and said, " My father would not like it very well if he knew I was taught by a woman,—but a woman and a negro!" " Stay in the class three days to please me," said the president; and, at the end of that time, the boy refused to be removed. After a day's absence from illness, Miss Jackson was received with cheers; and, when her class had to be subdivided, the heart-burnings of those who had to leave it were pitiable. She is now teaching in the Colored High School in Philadelphia, where she will remain till she has paid the price of her freedom. The brilliancy of her classical teaching is considered very remarkable in Philadelphia.

It remains only to consider the double system. Everybody at Oberlin was loud in its praise; no one would teach now in any other sort of college. The presence of women secured discipline. There was no chance for hazing or any other antiquated folly. Pupils and teachers who had gone from Oberlin to Vassar both missed the pleasant excitement of the old life.

" But," said President Finney, when I turned from all the rest to him, " it must not be forgotten that we have had great advantages. We came here for a religious reason; our pupils *came* for years. It is only lately that they have been *sent*. I expect that some difficulties may arise, but none worse than would arise in a neighborhood-school. It is God's way to rear us." The old man showed me, with great emotion, a confession, signed by three young girls, and read at college prayers in 1837. They had been walking, and met one of the students with an improvised sledge; without thinking, they jumped on and took a drive. There were no rules against it; but, when they came home, they remembered how much depended on their prudence as members of an antislavery institution, and wrote the confession of their own accord. One of these lovely women is now the wife of President Fairchild.

I record with pride the history of Oberlin, the first college which undertook to teach resident pupils of both sexes. I feel that it has been a great success. I am ashamed of the half-denominational prejudice which kept me from taking a warmer interest in it, in advance; and I greet its new life under President Fairchild, a graduate of the institution, with the warmest feelings of hope and admiration.

It has just received $25,000 from the executors of the estate of the Rev. Charles Avery, of Pittsburg, who left $150,000 in trust, to be devoted, according to the best judgment of the directors, to the "education and elevation of the colored people in the United States and Canadas." The conditions are, that the college shall never make any discrimination, on account of color, against colored students, and that it shall furnish free tuition to fifty of its most needy colored students who may apply for it; preference being given to twenty to be nominated by the American Missionary Association.

ANTIOCH.

The road to Antioch is hard to find: indeed, it would seem as if the trustees had specially secluded it, — made interest, perhaps, with the railroads to prevent the cars from stopping there, for the special protection of the young people! From Cincinnati, we wind along the lovely banks of the little Miami, through nurseries and hillside terraces, through groves of oak and sycamore, and birch-trees stretching out white, bewildered arms. Pigs are quietly grazing in the woods, as if it were their nature to "chew the cud;" there are groups of tiny powder-houses, made small, the people say, because they are "expected to blow up once a fortnight"! Heavy loads of corn and hay wind along the terraced roads; a gay-looking negro on horseback takes off his hat; two children are pulling a boat across the Miami; there are no houses along the shore, only safe-looking spits of sand jut out here and there; and, at last, having come the ten miles from Xenia in a private carriage, we roll on to Antioch Plain. I had heard that the college was on high land; so I was a little disappointed to find it on a table among the hills, which did not command any marvellous extent of country. As for the college, it has evidently made its toilet for posterity. I could not get a glimpse of its two fine towers and broad front, till I wandered down to the railroad track, and looked at it from the vicinity of a lime-kiln and a sorghum-mill. For some unknown reason, it turned its back on the village in the beginning, and pranks its beauty in full sight of that cursive population which travels by steam.

Yellow Springs is a pretty little place to live in, — an economical one, certainly, for there isn't a thing in it to buy; and, when we have looked at two or three little churches and Judge Mills's pretty park, we are quite content to go through the grounds of the Yellow Springs House, look down on the glen from the quaint, long, low southern piazza of the Neff House, and finally get home as we may, by log-bridges, and banks of moss, over which the walking-fern is striding. Ten miles of hedge, made of the Osage orange, surround the Neff Place, which a wealthy family in Cincinnati refuse to sell; but which is destined, in the far future, for a large hotel. In the little glen, — where a beautiful cascade falls, and tortuous rapids sputter and foam, and tiny fish dart up and down, and great graceful trees bend to shelter us, — we may find all the beauty of the White-Mountain passes. Two or three miles off, there are persimmons in the woods, and fossils under the soil; and, on Saturdays, pleasant parties go with Mr. Orton or Professor Clarke to find them. The "Yellow Spring," which gives the town its name, is of course largely impregnated with iron. It is imprisoned in a stone tank, which it colors brown; and it changes a rusty iron ladle to gold. It is a tonic; and, not far from the spot where it bubbles up, there is a pretty summer-house, where those who come to drink may sit and rest. As we walked toward it, a little brown rabbit skipped across the grass. From every high point in the glen, there are lovely views of the college and town.

Dr. Hosmer has just introduced a change into the Sunday-morning service at the chapel. He has taken the service-book of James Freeman Clarke, and, between reading and chanting, devised a matin service of great beauty. No musical professors could have done greater credit to the first performance than the students themselves. It made the bare, whitewashed walls of the chapel seem as sacred as a grand cathedral.

I did not look into the books at Antioch. Those at Oberlin I thoroughly investigated; and the strict economy the figures showed would distinguish honorably any institution in any land. But, as far as I can judge from oral testimony, the fees of the students and the interest of the endowment fund here amount to $13,000, and do not *quite* provide for the annual expenses. There is, therefore, no fund for *repairs*, none for *scientific instruments*, none for the *library;* and, while the president and professors feel that a further endowment will sometime be needed,

— nay, is needed *now*, — yet they also feel that they must show what work Antioch can do, before they ask further sympathy. Still, there are some few things which the wise prudence of the trustees, the thoughtfulness of loving friends, the surplus of full purses, can, in a quiet way, provide.

The pupils at Antioch make no complaint of their commons this year; yet it is undeniable that they should be better than they are. The commons are provided at Oberlin and Antioch in the same way; that is, by a family entirely disconnected with the college. At Oberlin, the table presents an attractive appearance. It would be grateful to any hungry person, and board is furnished at $3 a week. At Antioch, a pleasant and friendly woman has charge of things; but no great variety seems to be offered, and the board is $3.50 per week. Both these prices seem to me, after investigating Western markets, *starvation prices;* but it is evident, that, on this point, we have something to learn from Oberlin. If the president and faculty of Antioch should visit Oberlin, where they would be most kindly received, they would see, perhaps, that the difficulty lies in the cooking-apparatus. Oberlin offers a first-rate kitchen; Antioch, one very far behind what most of the pupils would find at home. I suppose no one will deny, that, when the average social standing of the students in these Western colleges is considered, it is desirable that they should find at the college-table a standard of cooking and serving which is a little in advance of that to which they have been used. The food may be plain and without variety, but it should be thoroughly nice and inviting of its kind. The ladies of any one of our city churches might undertake to furnish the kitchen at Antioch, and they could not have a better model than the kitchen at Oberlin. To advance the standard over previous experience, is, I think, a necessary part of education here.

Still farther, cisterns should be built in the upper stories of the dormitories, into which the waste-water may run from the roofs. Pipes leading downward from this should supply one sink on each story, and this sink should also carry away the waste-water from the rooms. A large "dumb waiter" — I use the word for want of a better — should be provided in each dormitory to carry up wood, and carry down ashes and dry dirt. I have already shown that this is done at Oberlin; and, if cisterns are not possible, then reservoirs and a forcing-pump should take their place.

There are but two dormitories, — one for men, and one for women; and when we consider, that, beside studying, the pupils have to help themselves by sawing wood and other manual labor, it will be acknowledged, that to bring their own wood and water up two or three flights of stairs is more than we can ask of them.

The library and scientific apparatus are very deficient for present needs. In the scientific department, some means of protecting the apparatus already obtained is greatly wanted. Microscopes are needed for scientific investigation. In the library, a translation of the " Mécanique Céleste," modern scientific books generally, Smith's " Bible Dictionary," and the leading works on English literature, are required. Trench, Müller, Taine, have not yet found their way to Yellow Springs.*

It seems to me, that, before Antioch, there now opens a great career. If her trustees and her faculty will but keep faith in her methods, surely we are bound to help them to the utmost. The personal friends of Dr. Hosmer also, who realize the nobility of that enthusiasm which made him willing to accept such a post while "looking towards sunset," ought, I think, to make the position as easy as possible, by anticipating these practical wants. Five hundred dollars would supply the most necessary books to the library.

But, if Oberlin does such noble work, what need of Antioch? Why should we strive to sustain an institution at such a continual cost, if one already established is competent to do its work? Let us get a glimpse of what Antioch can do, and then we shall be better able to answer these questions. In the first place, we are in possession of buildings worth now $180,000, and of twenty acres of land, worth $10,000. The land was a donation, in the beginning, from Judge Mills, the great man of the village, who perhaps fancied that a growing college would increase

---

* These have been supplied since my return to Boston.

the value of his real estate; and for this property, worth now nearly $200,000, we gave $50,000. For its proper appropriation we are responsible; and I think we have work enough to do, though Oberlin has saved the North-west, and though her new halls should be crowded thrice over.

In the first place, Antioch is to be a missionary station. No one who has not travelled through the West can imagine the thirst of the people for spiritual food. I think those who know least about it are the Western ministers themselves. I always found them sceptical about it, when I spoke to them; and I could not very well say, what I was sometimes compelled to feel, " It is because you could never satisfy this want, that it does not show itself to you." To Dr. Hosmer, however, with his warm, genial soul, with a temper conciliatory and discreet, the people are willing to speak. Beside the daily college prayers, there are services in the chapel on Sunday at half-past eight in the morning, and at three in the afternoon. During the last year, the audiences at the Sunday preaching had dwindled to a score: since Dr. Hosmer's arrival, it averages about two hundred and fifty; and, of course, townspeople, who come to the chapel regularly, grow in sympathy with the college and its purposes. Dr. Hosmer has promised to supply the Christian pulpit in Yellow Springs for eight Sundays, which gives Mr. McConnell liberty to do missionary work for the same time. The little town of Troy has some difficulty in keeping a minister. Dr. Hosmer promises him four Sundays, that he may go away, and so add to his substance. He goes also himself to the Universalist church in Columbus; and at Cleveland, where about twenty Unitarian families are hoping sometime to have a church, he promises them an occasional service if they will pay the expenses of transit. Professor Hosmer, whose preaching is thoroughly appreciated in the neighborhood, has also preached in Marietta; and either he or his father stands ready to supply Mr. Mayo's pulpit when that gentleman undertakes the missionary work, which has already made him one of the most useful of the Western clergy.

Who are the people that have this college in charge? What sort of pupils are likely to benefit by the education we offer? If we know a little about them, perhaps it will kindle a warmer interest. Beside the two Hosmers whom we know, there is Dr. Craig, Professor Weston and his wife, Professor Clarke, and Mr. Orton, with four teachers under him in the preparatory department. Dr. Craig was the man whom Horace Mann thought it constituted an era in his life to know. For fifteen years he was the minister of the church at Blooming Grove, Orange County, N.Y., a church which has existed for more than a hundred years without a creed, and which is governed by seven deacons and seven deaconesses. Professor Weston and his wife divide the classical department between them, having both taken the degree of A.M. at Oberlin.

Professor Clarke is the son of the famous Methodist minister in Chicago. He was professor of mathematics in Michigan University, and went abroad for two years to fit himself more thoroughly for his work. The war called him home; he raised a company, was made major, and, being taken prisoner, was thrown into Libby. There, he says, one of our Boston boys saved his life by sharing his supplies with him. He was removed to Macon, and, while sharing all the horrible experience of the stockade, succeeded in digging a tunnel, through which he would have escaped; but some other prisoners doing the same thing, and the escape of one being sure to lead to the detection of all, he waited honorably for the second tunnel to be completed. Meanwhile he was removed to Charleston, and put under Gilmore's fire, where, at last, his exchange was effected. When Professor Clarke left Michigan University to come to Antioch, he made a sacrifice born of the true missionary spirit. May we share his spirit sufficiently to strengthen his hands in the new work! Mr. Orton is most admirably fitted to his department, and has an excellent corps of teachers under him. Among them is one, the daughter of a mechanic, that went from Worcester to assist in building the college, who got her own education at Antioch by alternate years of study and teaching, having to earn one year what she spent the next. A more exquisite model school than that connected with the college, I never saw.

Among the older pupils of Antioch is the Christian

minister of Yellow Springs, the Mr. McConnell of whom I spoke, who may be called, if you prefer it, a brigadier-general. He was born humbly, in Ohio, had only the rudest schooling, was a Christian minister before he was twenty, and married before he was twenty-one. He was preaching in Troy when the first gun was fired at Sumter. He raised a company at once, and got a lieutenant's commission. In actual service, he was soon made a captain. He kept with General Grant throughout his Western campaign, and returned from Pittsburg Landing the colonel of his regiment; then re-enlisted for the war, went back to the front, kept with the Western army, and, at the close of the war, was mustered out a brigadier-general. He did signal service in many battles, but especially before Nashville, where his brigade, assisted by a negro brigade, broke Hood's centre by a very gallant charge. He went to Atlanta with Sherman, and could never weary of telling me how the Sanitary and Educational Commission followed the army with their fostering care, ever present, it seemed to him, like the blood which supplies with food the minutest nervous fibre of the human frame. When he returned, the people would have carried him into Congress; but he declined. Then they offered to make him a judge of probate, with a salary of $2,500 a year; but he told them he had chosen the pulpit for his field: and now, preaching in Yellow Springs, he comes into the college classes, and, hoping to take his degree, keeps faithfully all the college rules.

Still another pupil, now thirty years old, raised a company for the war. He was at the fall of Vicksburg, had not been at school since he was ten years old, but made $1,800 by buying and selling grain, and brought it here to carry him through college. When I cross-examined him in Greek history, I found he had read Grote! The teacher of the village school at Yellow Springs has had a more vexatious experience. He had finished his third year at Antioch, when he went into the army. He became an aid to three Western generals successively, and was with Grant when Lee surrendered. He saved $800 of his pay to carry him through his last college year, but had only been home a few days when a burglar stole it! He has taken the village school for $900 this year, studies hard; and the faculty have voted, that, when he can stand a certain examination, he shall take his degree.

It is for such students that Antioch is open. One-third of her present pupils are women. Pleasant levees are held once a fortnight at the president's house, where the two sexes mingle gracefully. The girls have a literary society, which they call the Crescent; the young men, two societies, the Star and the Adelphian. The Star and the Crescent have fitted up one room under the gambrel very tastefully. The Adelphians rival them. The folding-doors in the hall of the latter society open into a pretty alcove, where a good library is beginning. These two rooms are the only glimpse of tasteful, home-like comfort that one gets in any public room at Antioch. I attended the meetings of the three societies. Before the Crescents, I heard a graceful little essay on "A Rail-fence," from a girl of fifteen. From the Stars, I heard a discussion of Roman funerals. The Adelphians discussed the possibility of obeying an unrighteous law, very much as I have heard their elders do in Congress. Each society had a censor, who took notes of papers and discussions, and quietly criticised each performance when it ended. It was noticeable, that the performances of the women, making due allowance for age and opportunity, were far more graceful and able than those of the men, and a most valuable help to the latter. Coming home one night from the Adelphians, I found at Dr. Hosmer's a Southern refugee, who is educating her children at Antioch.

Sometime before the war, Mrs. Palmer and her husband went to East Tennessee from New York, carrying with them $50,000. I think they must have opened a store; for she spoke of having on hand a valuable stock of millinery and medicines. Being Northerners, they were constantly threatened, and at last consented to barricade their house. Three times the rebels stole their horse, a colt only two years old; and three times Mrs. Palmer's perseverance got it back. At last they surrounded the house at night, firing on the peaceable inmates; and Mr. Palmer, attempting to escape over the roof, got three bullets in his arm. The next day the party came back, robbed the house, and burned up the stores. The medicine was a great loss: there was no more within reach for rebel or loyalist. Mrs. Palmer succeeded in hiding her meat and meal. For eight days she and her family hid in the rocks, only venturing back to the house at night to cook and eat a little food. One night, when the poor wife was so employed, her feverish, half-delirious husband followed her, and, in some way, attracted the attention of the enemy. A terrible battle followed, and Mr. Palmer lay on the kitchen floor with eight wounds in his body. When the malice of the rebels was spent, Mrs. Palmer went out with her children, and called the cattle. By keeping them between her and the house, she succeeded in getting her husband into the woods. A Union man finally received and fed him; but it was many days before his wounds could be dressed. She then escaped with her children and the colt, on which they rode by turns. She had picked up some of the ends of her burnt millinery, which she used to barter for food as they went along. She came at last to an old school-house, where she lay down; and here she nursed her children through the measles. Here, after many weeks, her husband came to see her, but was taken prisoner as he crept away, and was sent to Libby. She saw many terrible things while she lingered here: one of her neighbors had his bowels cut out while he was still alive! When she started afresh, she had seven hundred miles to travel before she reached Bardstown. One of her five children ultimately died of the fatigue and hunger.

"How did you get food?" I asked.

"I prayed for it," she answered; "and I always felt sure of enough for the hour."

"Who would shelter you?" I continued.

"I never lay out but one night," she answered. "I used to tell them, wherever I went, that the Union soldiers must win in the end; that I was going to them, and would report whoever used me ill. So they would let me lie on the kitchen floor." At Bardstown, Morgan's men destroyed her last thing; and then a United-States sutler found her, and carried her to Louisville.

The children of many such women will hereafter seek Antioch. Let them find there a generous provision.

VASSAR COLLEGE.

Mr. Vassar's magnificent donation is drawing interest at last; and, though I do not feel as much confidence in any institution founded for women alone as I do in mixed colleges, we ought all to be grateful for the advanced standard lifted at Poughkeepsie.

Malt has always been a beneficent agent in the civilization of mankind. Ever since Mr. Thrale looked kindly on old Sam Johnson, brewers have seemed to have a generous pride in conquering human selfishness, and leaving something better than a family of children to interest posterity. Mr. John Guy, of Liverpool, a wealthy brewer without children, founded there the great "Guy's Hospital." He was the great-uncle of Matthew Vassar, also a great brewer in Poughkeepsie, N.Y. By and by, Matthew Vassar found his property close upon a million; and, as he had no children, he began to think what he should do with it. He had a good many poor relations, and those who were industrious and deserving he did not forget. One of them, a young niece, supported herself by school-teaching. He built her a school-house, and did what he thought right to ease her way. At last, sinking in a decline, she came home to die. As she lay on the sofa, day after day, she watched him walking back and forth, and talking over his plans. Now and then she would say gently, "Uncle Matthew, do something for women." After she was gone, Matthew Vassar went to see Guy's Hospital. His connections advised him not to give away his money. His Baptist friends in Edinburgh and Liverpool laughed at the idea of a college for women, which had already entered his mind. He came home, and tried to plan a hospital; he got up, and went to bed with the idea uppermost; but all the time he seemed to hear the voice of his niece, "Do something for women, Uncle Matthew." Mr. Vassar has two houses: one, in the heart of Poughkeepsie, which is opposite the brewery, and, with a long range of comfortable outbuildings, looks as steadfast and English as ever Mr. Thrale's own house could do; the other, a modest little country box, set on a hill among extensive grounds, and commanding, from various points, lovely views of the town and river. The peculiarity of this place is, that it is ornamented with all manner of punchinellos cut in dull gray limestone, and leering or grinning from every corner of the park. I did not find out who was responsible for this grim joke. In 1860, Mr. Vassar, with the humility and common sense which belong to his character, obtained a charter, and called together thirty trustees. To them he transferred more than half his actual property. When the opening of the war occasioned the failure of the contractors, he did not draw back, but gladly gave the additional $150,000 which the increased expense demanded.

The building is planned after the palace of the Tuilleries, having at each end the chateau roof and mansard windows. It is 500 feet long, and 170 deep. The only drawback to its architectural effect is the entrance, which should have been a magnificent double stairway, but is, for the present, only an ordinary private door. This building stands in the midst of two hundred acres of lovely sloping and swelling land. To the right, and quite visible at the porter's lodge, is the gymnasium and hippodrome under one roof; to the left, the graceful observatory, which is also the home of Miss Mitchell and her father.

In the two wings of the building with chateau roofs are five private dwellings, rented for a moderate sum to the resident professors. In the centre, just behind the entrance, are the dining-hall, the chapel, the art-gallery, and the library; also the large drawing-rooms, where pupils and teachers receive their friends, and the parlor and office of president and principal. Connecting this centre with each wing, on four floors, run long corridors with sunshine and bright windows on one side, and clusters of students' rooms and recitation-rooms on the other. The rooms are in pretty groups of four. Three bedrooms open into one study, the latter made pleasant and home-like by the united treasures of the occupants. The music-rooms are "deadened," so that the noise hardly strays beyond the walls; and the cabinet, where the students in natural history prepare specimens, is full of cases to preserve the work. The best that I can say of the building will hardly do justice to the intention of the founder, which no one can comprehend who has seen only such institutions as Harvard and Yale. There is no occasion here to wish for any thing which may perhaps come when the college is rich enough. Mr. Vassar's intention was and is to have the endowment perfect. The building is fire-proof, every partition wall being of solid brick. There are four pairs of fire-walls, into which iron doors run on rollers; and between these are fire-proof stairways, always safe, even if the wood work should catch fire. There is the physiological cabinet, with every thing for the use of the professor, including various manikins and wax preparations. The library, chiefly of books of reference, holds three thousand volumes, to be increased at the rate of five hundred per annum, and is also used as a reading-room, where newspapers and reviews may always be found. The art-gallery, purchased at an extra cost of $20,000, is such as no college in the country possesses.

It consists of good copies in oil, fine water-colors, including six real Turners, large portfolios of original sketches, and a perfect library of works on art and engravings, — in all, about a thousand volumes. Besides the five hundred pictures, this gallery contains a few busts and casts; among them, Palmer's Sappho in marble, an ancient wrought brazen shield, and specimens of ancient stained glass. The chapel seats seven hundred persons, and might hold a thousand. Over the altar is a beautiful copy of the Dresden Madonna, by Miss Church, of New York. There is also a fine organ.

The music-rooms accommodate a "conservatory" on the Charles Auchester plan, as well as separate pupils. Thirty-two pianos are in use.

The building on the outside is laid with brick in black cement, and has dark stone trimmings, which prevent its glaring on the eye like a new brick building. To the right is the riding-school, one hundred feet by sixty, where thirty horses are kept; and, in the same building, a gymnastic hall, thirty feet by seventy.

The observatory, eighty feet long and fifty high, rests on the rock, as well as the great pier. It contains a telescope made by Fitz, whose focal length is seventeen feet, and its object-glass is twelve and a half inches. There is also a smaller instrument, for the constant use of pupils, and, on the roof, a good comet-seeker. There is a beautiful transit circle, made by James, of Philadelphia, which Miss Mitchell considers invaluable of its kind; and a very perfect sidereal clock and chronograph, from the Bonds of Boston.

Between the observatory and the riding-school, four hundred feet from the main building, is the gas and boiler building, from which the college is lighted and warmed. Beside these, twenty miles of water-pipe travel up and down the corridors to supply culinary and domestic needs. Let us follow them into the kitchen, and we shall find there every possible convenience of a good hotel, to the steam-filled table on which the food is carved.

And now, the building once ready for its inmates, was Mr. Vassar rewarded for the sacrifice he had made? for all the time and thought bestowed on the outfit? No one had supposed that the school would be full when it opened in September, 1865; but there were 353 pupils on hand the first day, and the work of organizing was no trifle. When I looked at the teachers and principals in this institution, many of whom I had known before visiting it, it seemed to me that each one had been providentially fitting for the very work Mr. Vassar now offered. Of the thirty persons employed, I saw no one that I should have desired to change. Maria Mitchell, Hannah Lyman, and the admirable resident physician, Alida Avery, are now too well known to need any praise of mine. These persons are all of the faculty; and their names indicate how liberal all the decisions of the faculty must be. I visited the institution at the beginning of the second year, in October, 1866. It had already outrun its bounds. There was talk of still another dormitory. Four hundred pupils, well born, well bred, in good health, with more than ordinary education (for the tests are severe), and with ample means, had come to meet those teachers. They had come, between the ages of seventeen and twenty-two, at the very time when society holds out every attraction. Vassar is no charity school. Its necessary fees amount to four hundred dollars; and a girl should have six hundred to feel happy and at ease. It paid every bill the first year, but had nothing left for repairs and additions. To create a fund for this purpose, the fees have been increased to the above-named sum. When the first rush of pupils occurred, Mr. Vassar was almost dismayed. "God sometimes gives great thoughts to very little men," he said, and trembled; but, when the year came to a close, he lifted his hands in serene gratitude. I arrived at night; and the procession filing past me to enter the handsome dining-hall, supported by light pillars, about which were circular stands for the urns, occupied seven minutes. When I saw more than four hundred young women seated in groups of twenty, saw them bow their handsome heads in silent grace, — a suggestion which came, I think, from Miss Mitchell's Quaker father, — I felt excited with happiness. After tea, I walked round and through the groups of tables; and the bright faces smiled back at me either consciousness or question. When they left the dining-hall, they went to the chapel, where Miss Lyman offers an evening prayer, and, no gentlemen being present, talks to the ladies in reference to all matters of decorum; a practice I hope to see followed at Antioch. After breakfast the next morning, I went to President Raymond's short matin service, and then walked over to the observatory. There I saw the graceful figures of the girls bending to the instrument, as they recorded the spots on the sun. I saw the daily diagrams in which they had recorded the position of these spots for the last year, and other diagrams of lunar eclipses. "Women make better observers than men," said old Mr. Mitchell. "They have more patience, more accuracy. I had been observing thirty years, when Maria took it up, and I thought, mebbe, 'twas only Maria; but it is just the same with these girls. They do better than I did." I don't wonder Miss Mitchell is proud of her seventeen mathematical astronomers. She is a tender daughter, as well as a capable "observer;" and she would not come to Vassar without her father. All the girls come to the white-haired old man with their joys and troubles; and I saw a letter from an old pupil to Miss Mitchell when I was there, which contained this audacious sentence, left to tell its own story: "Was it not good of God to put it into Mr. Vassar's heart to spend his whole fortune in making your father's last years perfectly happy?" In the art gallery I found, one morning, twenty-five pupils copying; and, in the musical conservatory, one hundred and seventy-five. The gymnasium was not quite ready for use; so I went down to see the girls rowing on the pretty lake.

After school hours, the floral clubs were busy in the grounds. I cannot say any thing better of Professor Tenney's pupils, than that they work over their specimens as enthusiastically as boys. In chemical analysis, under Professor Farrar, the girls are greatly interested. The curriculum is such as we find adopted at all colleges, except that far more time is devoted to science than is usual at Yale or Harvard, and room is left for music. Riding, driving, rowing, &c., are extras, only allowed in the time allotted to out-door exercise. The resident physician, Dr. Avery, in whom the college is conscious that it possesses a great treasure, gives a regular course of physiological lectures.

Matthew Vassar was seventy-six years old on the 29th of April, and that day is a perpetual festival for the pupils. Could you see him meet the scholars in the grounds, you would think them all his children. I had interviews with the president, trustees, and the teachers; but was most attracted toward this noble old man. He told me that he meant to go on endowing the college until he died. "Then," he said, "I shall leave nothing for executors to quarrel about: money will be safe in brick and stone." He asked me to talk with him about a culinary and household college for the proper training of housewives, which he still wishes to erect. His last gift to the college was its magnificent cabinet of stones and fossils; one of the best, Professor Dana thinks, that he ever saw. Beside the beautiful specimens shown under glass, there are, in drawers beneath the glass cases, similar specimens which may be handled.

In furnishing Vassar College, no one has had to think what any thing would cost. When shall we have an institution for wealthy persons, of both sexes, with an outfit as splendid? It is a sight which Oberlin has earned the right to see.

LAWRENCE UNIVERSITY, KANSAS.

But a still more interesting story is that connected with the establishment of the State University in Kansas. Its name will be seen on the list of colleges which owe their existence to Oberlin. This university is one of those whose *character* was determined by the excitement the success of Oberlin had aroused; but its *existence* was due to two ladies from Western New York. It will have been seen, by some details in the body of this work, that an attempt was made to secure for woman a share in the noble State endowment at "Ann Arbor," Michigan, but without success. I will tell a part of the story in the language of Miss Mary Chapin, then of Milwaukie, the lady who, with the assistance of her sister, carried the work out in Kansas.

"Some years ago," she says, "the Legislature of Michigan decided that girls might be admitted as pupils to the State University. The faculty of that institution consulted the 'wise men of the East' on the subject, and excluded women on the ground of expediency. If it were necessary to make it a mixed school, in order to admit them, perhaps they acted wisely. It is no more just and wise to give the charge of endowed schools for girls to men, than it would be to put Harvard and Yale into the hands of women. Girls need incentives to study, even more than facilities for it. The fact, that the real education of the boy begins where that of the woman ends, is not so depressing as the 'hard work and low wages' which await her as a teacher. In 1863, Kansas accepted the grant of land from Congress for the endowment of a State University. The citizens of Lawrence secured its location in that city, by the gift of forty acres for a site. The college was not organized; and it seemed the time and place to decide whether women should enter endowed schools on equal terms with men, as pupils and teachers. Many of the most influential men of Kansas thought it both just and expedient to give women an equal share of the benefits of the university, and voted for such a result. To obviate the objection which closed the Michigan University to women, a bill was drawn up, organizing a double school; that for girls to be taught by women. Some objection was made to this unusual provision, and the time was too short to urge its necessity: so the bill merely reads, that it *may* be taught by women. The date of this law is February, 1864. A school-building was finished last summer (1866), and the college opened in September. The regents elected a president and three professors at the outset, one of the latter being a lady. There is some danger that the two schools will become one, by an act of the Legislature. If this occurs, nothing important is gained; but, if the present organization continues, woman may here show what a true feminine culture implies: for, while woman differs widely from man, like him she needs *development through her own work.*"

I have altered none of the statements in this admirable letter. It will be seen that Miss Chapin went to Kansas, desiring to accomplish two things: she not only wanted education, but position and *compensation*, for women, from the State fund. I want these also; but I only ask for the first, for I am certain the rest will follow. Neither do I think it wise to insist that women shall be taught only by women, until universities have done the necessary work of preparation. In all the colleges mentioned on the Oberlin list, women are employed as teachers: there are already a good number of professors of Greek and mathematics. Nor is the welfare of *women* alone a sufficient motive for me. I am satisfied, that humanity and civilization gain, in the mixed college, more than either sex can lose. It remains for me to give a few of the personal details which Miss Chapin's modesty has omitted. When she first thought it her duty to press this matter, she knew that she must be in Lawrence, in order to do the "talking" which must precede an act of legislation in America. She corresponded with Governor Robinson, in reference to a day-school in Lawrence, and started with her sister to take charge of it. On their way, they were startled by the terrible

AN APPENDIX.   417

news of the Kansas raid. They hesitated for a little; but, thank God, in spite of raids, the work of the world goes on. Miss Mary went on herself in September, and, after a week's residence, decided to defer the opening of her school. In December, both sisters went, and began their daily teaching, and the gentle agitation which was to yield the great result. They also tried, at the East, to raise money to realize at once, on a small scale, their ideal of a practical course of study for women, especially of a scientific school. "Science," says Miss Chapin, "has not yet been applied to the arts of domestic life. The ordering of home, as a centre of comfort and culture, has yet to be considered. Architecture has much to do with civilization. The laws of health and the means of social progress lie entirely in woman's province. Horticulture will do more for her than calisthenics. She is ready to do useful work, but has no means. A very wasteful economy denies her this, to lavish thousands on her folly and ostentation."

I cannot detail all the obstacles which Miss Chapin's effort encountered. Mr. Charles Chadwick, of Lawrence, drew up the bill; General Dietzler and Governor Robinson pushed it. At the last moment, the original bill was carried off in the pocket of an opposing member; but the wit and quick memory of a woman saved it.

It has been mentioned, that, after its passage, a lady was elected professor, with a salary of $1,600, and the same for her assistant. It is almost needless to say, this was Miss Caroline Chapin. She has not yet accepted the position. The two sisters are at the head of a high school in Quincy, Ill., which has this peculiarity: there is attached to it a school in modelling, under the charge of a professed sculptor.

In the first part of this volume, I have intimated that a new effort has been made, sustained by the pleading of Theodore Tilton, to open Michigan University to female students. At the moment when these pages go to press, it seems uncertain whether this resolution will prevail with the present Legislature, or whether a motion for a university for women, under the same regents, will supersede it. The Greek professor has practically solved the difficulty, by admitting his own daughter to his classes, without asking the faculty. This example was set him, years ago, by Mr. Magill, in the Boston Latin School.

As these pages go to press, an anonymous statement appears, to the effect that there have passed examinations for the University of Cambridge, England, — Junior boys, 1,126; Junior girls, 118; Senior boys, 212; Senior girls, 84. It would seem that the conditions of the opening of this university are hardly understood. If I am right, these examinations confer a certain rank on the female scholars, but do not admit them afterward to the university.

SCHOOL FOR NURSES.

The most interesting educational movement, at this moment, in that country, is Miss Nightingale's

"Training-school for Nurses," which has been in operation for three years in Liverpool. It was founded, after a correspondence with her, in strict conformity to her counsel. As a training-school, it may be said to be self-supporting; but it is also a beneficent institution, and, in that regard, is sustained by donations. A most admirable system of district nursing is provided, under its auspices, for the whole city of Liverpool, all of whose suffering sick become, in this way, the recipients of intelligent care, and of valuable instruction in cooking and all sanitary matters. It is too tempting an experiment to dwell upon, unless we could follow it into its details. Its report occupies a hundred and one pages.

It seems worth while to look into this report, and examine in detail its method of dealing with sickness among the poor. When Miss Nightingale drew especial attention to the want of such schools in England in 1861, some ladies and gentlemen in Liverpool came together, and entered into correspondence with her. Out of that correspondence grew the Liverpool school. The Liverpool Infirmary, the most considerable hospital in that city, entered into the plan, and offered its wards for the instruction of the nurses. The society proposed to itself three objects: —

1. To provide thoroughly trained nurses for hospitals.

2. To provide district or missionary nurses for the poor.

3. To provide trained nurses for private families.

Nowhere are hospital and private nurses so badly trained as in England; and Miss Nightingale well says that half the symptoms which are considered symptoms of disease are, in reality, indications of a want of air, light, warmth, quiet, or cleanliness, which properly instructed nurses would know how to supply. A want of punctuality in administering food, and of watchful care in detecting its effects upon the patient, create other classes of symptoms. The beer-drinking habits of the people lead to much intoxication; and we ourselves have seen ladies of quality lying on a sick-bed, where they suffered for the attention which a thoroughly stupefied nurse was incapable of giving. No amount of wealth, as Miss Nightingale testifies, can secure such nurses as wealthy patients often need, and for which a thorough hospital-training is required. The society strengthens her appeal by extracts from Dr. Howson's paper, read at the meeting of the Social Science Association in 1858.

The Liverpool school has erected a building, to carry out its purpose, eighty-five feet by forty. It has three stories, each of them eleven feet high; and, by a single glance at the plans which accompany the pamphlet, one sees that the arrangements for bathing and ventilation are what those of our new city hospital ought to be. One lady superintendent, with three servants, has charge of this building. It has thirty-one nurses under training. By the wages which they earn in the second and third years, the expenses of this Home are nearly paid, leaving a margin of about three hundred pounds to be supplied by donations. It is expected to be a self-supporting institution, except so far as it becomes a benevolent charity, by supplying to the poor, food and nursing. When the institution was ready to begin its work, the lady superintendent having been some months in training at St. John's College and the London Hospital, where the nurses educated by the Nightingale Fund are to be found, took possession of her building. Her head-nurses had been thoroughly educated. Pupils then offered: they were engaged for three years, the first year to be strictly probationary. Each head-nurse was to take charge of an entire ward of the hospital, to be responsible for the medicines and stimulants, always assisted by one pupil. Each pupil went first for two months to a surgical ward; then for two to the medical; then four at the surgical, and four again at the medical, — one course helping the other, and both filling the entire year under a thoroughly trained head. For the next two years, the pupil is employed without such superintendence wherever need is; and, for each of the three years, receives, in addition to board and lodgings, seventy dollars. At the Home there is a good library, and evening classes are held for the disengaged pupils. A superannuation fund has been started, to encourage respectable women to enter the Home. At the end of the third year, the Home has twenty-eight pupils under training, fourteen hospital nurses, fourteen district or gratuitous nurses, and ten employed in private families.

This gives an idea of the training process; but our chief interest lies in the district nursing. As soon as the Home had nurses it felt willing to trust, one of the experiments recommended by Miss Nightingale was tried. The wife of a Scripture-reader undertook to prepare sago, necessaries, &c.; the clergyman of the parish furnished a list of patients, and a central lodging for the nurse. The Home sent her out, supplied with cushions, blankets, and bed-rests. She went into the families, showed them what to do, and helped with her own hands. At the end of the first week, she came back, crying and begging to be relieved; she thought she never could bear the sight of the misery she encountered. But, in a short time, she was so strengthened by seeing the results of her labor, that she positively refused to take employment among the rich. It is easy to see what great advantages wait on this form of charity. As instruction is precisely what she comes to give, the poor cannot resent this from the nurse; she fears no imposition, for she is in the house at all hours of the day and night; her little gifts do not wound, but cheer like neighborly kindnesses. It is Miss Nightingale's idea, that such nursing is a far greater good than the establishment of hospitals. In six months, this nurse found two cases where the prolonged sickness of the wife had made drunkards of two otherwise steady husbands, and brought their families to the brink of ruin. The wives were cured, the husbands reformed, the families saved. A leaf from her report of cases will show what she did.

1. *Asthma and bed-sores.* — Lying on a floor; so thin, had to lift her on a sheet. Dirt, bad air: two children. Husband said he "was forsaken by God and man." Our nurse goes in, washes her, changes linen; lends bedstead and bedding, and air-cushions; cleans and whitewashes. The woman now sits up, and the man is again hopeful.

2. *Internal cancer.* — Nurse attended to the surgical operation, and administration of subsequent remedies. The woman is now at work.

3. *Paralysis.* — Nurse attended; gave instruction and food. Recovery complete.

4. A girl — as the doctor said — in a consumption. Hospital refused her as incurable. Beef-tea, wine, sago, and cod-liver oil supplied; and, in one month, she could walk to the nurse's lodging.

Out of all this success, the perfect plan developed. It had been proved, that the poor were willing to be taught *how* to nurse, and to keep their houses clean; that intense distress might be mitigated, and coming poverty arrested. It was also proved, that the nurse so employed could notify the health commissioners of incipient epidemics, and obtain for ignorant tenants, in return, necessary whitewashing, drainage, &c.

The city of Liverpool was now divided into eighteen districts, each of which, for practical convenience, was made to correspond to two church cures. The Home undertook to furnish a nurse to each district, provided it would elect for itself a lady superintendent, and raise a subscription for food, medicines, and necessaries. As soon as the superintendent is found, meetings are held to interest the district; each district having an average population of twenty-four thousand and over. A central lodging is then to be supplied for the nurse, and the district must furnish, for loan and use, the following articles: —

One iron bedstead, six pairs of sheets, six blankets, cushions, bed-gowns, shirts, flannels, wine, meat, sago, bread, coals, arrow-root, preserves, and vinegar.

If any thing excites one's envy in the current expenses, it is the amount of coals required. To think of warming forty people for one year for twenty-six pounds!

The superintendent is supplied with a map of the district, forms of recommendation, rules for patients and nurses, and slates and pencils to be hung at the head-board, to receive the directions of the doctor, and the inquiries of the nurse. In seven of the districts, the lady superintendents furnish the supplies at their own cost! How gladly ought any wealthy woman to avail herself of so sure a method! A strong woman is hired for scrubbing; and very often the first thing a nurse does is to demand whitewashing and repairs of the Board of Health. In each district, a person is provided to cook the necessary food; the nurse giving notice, through the superintendent, of her wants. The nurse herself confers with the doctors, waits on the surgeons, changes and cleanses the patient, and administers poultices, blisters, leeches, enemas, and the like. One Liverpool lady defrays the whole cost of washing the loaned linen for the eighteen districts! A registry of it is kept by the nurse.

We need not be surprised to find that this admirable plan has such marked success, that all the Liverpool charities are eager to play into its hands. Each district superintendent is appointed locally; but the Home has an out-door inspector, who looks after the district nurses. The superintendents make quarterly reports to the Home, and hold meetings of conference by themselves.

There is, at the seaside town of Southport, a hospital, which furnishes sea-bathing to invalids.

The Committee of Central Relief for the city of Liverpool are so delighted with this nursing charity, that they have already offered butcher's meat, three weeks of seaside bathing at Southport, and coals and money to any convalescing patient when deemed needful. The workingmen's dining-rooms offer, on proper application, warm dinners to convalescents; and the Home, through its inspector, superintendents, and nurses, makes sure there is no waste nor misuse.

The statistics for 1864 were as follows: —

Apparently cured	936
Partially restored	456
Relieved before death	488
Still hopeful	180
Hopeless	9
Dismissed	289
Total	2,358

Such a record as this makes one wish to emigrate to the land where such things are done. The rapid increase of the charity may be judged from the fact, that, in the previous year, only one thousand seven hundred and seventy-six patients were *treated*, and only six hundred and seventy-two were *cured*. This report comes to us with a letter and notes from Miss Nightingale. It is prepared with the most beautiful modesty. The names of the paid officers are given; but we cannot tell from its pages whose were the kind hearts and clear heads which first responded to Miss Nightingale's call. Nowhere has benevolent action accomplished so much as in Great Britain. Such a work as this may well challenge the gratitude and admiration of the world.

The "Arnott Scholarship" of Queen's College, London, — founded by Mrs. Arnott in 1865, for the promotion of the study of natural philosophy, and the highest scholarship open to women in England — has just been gained by Miss Matilda Ballard, a young lady of seventeen, daughter of Dr. W. R. Ballard, a native of New York, and, for some years, the leading American dentist in London. The prize, the money value of which is not far from two hundred dollars, consists of one year's free instruction and perpetual free admission to certain lectures, always interesting and instructive.

The ladies' classes at Oxford have proved a great success, and the committee have just issued a programme for the present term. The course of instruction includes Latin, French, Arithmetic, Euclid, German, &c. The Rev. W. C. Sedgwick, M.A.,

Fellow and Tutor of Merton College, has undertaken to deliver a course of lectures on the Italian Republics of the Middle Ages.

On the 26th of October, 1864, a Working-women's College was opened in London, with an address from Miss F. R. Malleson. It is governed by a council of teachers. In addition to the ordinary branches, it offers instruction in botany, physiology, and drawing. Its fee is four shillings a year; and the Coffee and Reading Room, about which its social life centres, is open every evening from seven to eleven.

In France, the Imperial Geographical Society, which is, in a certain sense, a college, has lately admitted to membership Madame Dora d'Istra as the successor to Madame Pfeiffer. Madame d'Istra had distinguished herself by researches in the Morea.

In Calcutta, Miss Mary Carpenter has been starting schools for Hindoo women, free from all religious character or sectarian denomination.

DEACONESSES' INSTITUTIONS.

This seems the proper place also to insert some details about schools like those at Kaiserworth, which I could not procure in an authentic form in 1858. The Kaiserworth school opened under Dr. Fliedner, in 1822, with "one table, two beds, a chair, and one discharged prisoner"! In 1852, the King of Prussia laid the foundation of a home for the aged deaconesses who have served as teachers and nurses.

The school at Strasburg, under Pastor Härber,

began, in 1842, with one sister from a higher rank of life. It undertakes to train servants, and is chiefly under women's control. Assistance is also given to clergymen in seeking out cases of temporal and spiritual distress, in detecting imposture, in attending the sick in their own houses, in teaching the poor how to nurse and how to cook, in promoting the attendance of children at school, in co-operating with charitable institutions to superintend sewing and mending schools, in influencing, for good, factory girls and servants; and, in the hospital at Mühausen, the women taught here make up bandages and prescriptions, cook for the poor and sick, receive the patients, and do out-door visiting. At Basle, there is a Deaconess House, under the charge of a daughter of a Basle manufacturer. It looks after the laboring classes, and provides for the sick.

The house opened at St. Loup, under Pastor Germond, in 1842, takes charge of sick children. At Geneva, a deaconess has had charge for six years; through whom five hundred servants get their places, and with whom they find homes when out of health or work. In 1859, twenty-one were nursed in the institution.

A house in the Faubourg St. Antoine, Paris, was proposed by M. Vermeil, in 1830. In 1840, Mademoiselle Malvesin offered to conduct it; her letter to Vermeil, and his to her, crossing each other. Holland and Sweden have opened several of these schools. In our own country, the Rev. Mr. Passevant, a Lutheran minister of Pittsburg, Pa., is establishing hospitals in every State, under the care of women. They are supported by contributions in all the city churches, except the Catholic. These hospitals are under the care of a sisterhood, who cannot, *as yet*, compete with the Sisters of Charity. It seems to me, that Mr. Passevant has erred in a most noble work, by drawing his sisters from the *uncultivated* classes. Such a work should bear the right stamp in the beginning. In Western Pennsylvania, also, Bishop Kerfoot has begun the noble work of endowing his whole diocese with suitable high schools for girls, where they may obtain at home, for one hundred dollars annually, what it would cost five times as much to procure at a distance.

MEDICAL EDUCATION.

As regards medical education, we know of two colleges, or, rather, of one college and one hospital, in Boston, where education is given. There is one in Springfield, and one in Philadelphia. We should be glad to get more statistics of this kind; for Cleveland, where Dr. Zakrzewska took her degree, is no longer open to female students, and Geneva is contenting herself with the honor of having graduated Dr. Blackwell. Nine women were graduated at the New-York Medical School for Women, in February of this year. Professor Willis then stated that there are three hundred female physicians in the country, earning incomes of from ten to twenty thousand dollars.

There is a female medical society in London. This society wishes to open the way for thorough medical instruction, which will entitle its graduates to a degree from Apothecaries' Hall; and it offered lectures from competent persons, in 1864, upon obstetrics and general medical science. Madame Aillot's Hospital of the Maternity, in Paris, still offers its great advantages to women; of which two of our countrywomen, Miss Helen Morton and Miss Lucy E. Sewall, have taken creditable advantage. They are both of them Massachusetts girls. Miss Morton is retained in Paris, and Miss Sewall is the resident physician of the Hospital for Women and Children, in Boston.

At present, to obtain thorough instruction in any branch, women are obliged to pay exorbitant prices, and receive, as the results of their training, but half-wages. In Boston, Dr. Zakrzewska has again unsuccessfully asked permission to become a member of the Massachusetts Medical Society. Many physicians, however, extend the fellowship which the institution denies, and the "Medical Journal" expresses itself courteously on this point. Efforts, sustained by the influential name of the Hon. Charles G. Loring, are at this moment making to secure the advantages of the Harvard-College lectures to women intending to become physicians.*

In 1863, there existed in St. Petersburg a stringent regulation, which prohibited women from following

---

* The application is declined, as we go to press, on the ground that no provision has been made at Cambridge for women.

the university courses. A Miss K., who had a decided taste for medicine, without the means to pay for instruction, applied for such instruction to the authorities of Orenburg. Orenburg is partly in Europe and partly in Asia, and its territory includes the Cossack races of the Ural. These people have a superstitious prejudice against male physicians, and are chiefly attended in illness by sorceresses. Miss K. offered to put her medical knowledge at the service of the Cossacks, and received permission to attend the Academy of Medicine. The Cossacks promised her an annual stipend of twenty-eight roubles; but, when she passed the half-yearly examination as well as the male students, they sent her three hundred roubles as a token of good-will!

In France, a Mademoiselle Reugger, from Algeria, lately passed a brilliant examination, and received the degree of Bachelor of Letters. She appealed to the Dean of the Faculty at Montpellier for permission to follow the regular course, and was refused on account of her sex. She then turned to the Minister of Public Instruction, who granted it, on condition that she should pledge herself to practise only in Algeria, where the Arabs, like the Cossacks, refuse the attendance of male physicians. Unlike our Russian friend, she refused to give the pledge. She threw herself upon her rights, and appealed in person to the emperor. This was in December last, and I have not been able to find his decision. It was doubtless given in her behalf; for Louis Napoleon will always yield, as a favor, what he would stubbornly refuse as a right.

A female medical mission is to be despatched to Delhi, for the same reason. The physicians sent out are,—

1. To attend native ladies in the Zenanas.
2. To set on foot a dispensary for women only.
3. To train native women as nurses.

Of the medical profession, it should be stated, for the encouragement of women, that there are over three hundred graduates from the several medical colleges for women; and that there is scarcely a village throughout the country but has its woman physician, of greater or less skill. In New-York City, there are many successful physicians beside the Drs. Blackwell. Dr. Lozier has a practice of $15,000, and owns two fine houses, earned by her own perseverance. In Orange, N.J., Dr. Fowler is very popular, and has a paying practice of $5,000 a year. In Philadelphia is Dr. Hannah Longshore, with a practice worth $10,000 per annum; then there are Drs. Preston, Tressel, Sartain, Cleveland, and Myres, with incomes ranging from $5,000 to $2,000. In Utica, N.Y., Dr. Pamela Bronson is a successful physician. In Albion is Dr. Vail; in Weedsport, Dr. Harriet E. Seeley. In Rochester, Dr. Sarah Dolley numbers among her patrons many persons of wealth and fashion, who, but a few years ago, ridiculed the idea of a "female physician." Mrs. Dolley's practice brings her fully $3,000 a year.

AN APPENDIX. 433

Dr. Gleason of Elmira, Dr. Ivison of Ithaca, and Dr. Green, late of Clifton Springs, who has opened a water-cure somewhere in Western New York, all have a large amount of practice, and prescribe with the greatest acceptance for those who favor hydropathic treatment.

At Milwaukee, in the autumn of 1866, I found Dr. Ross. She is one of the consulting physicians of the Passevant Hospital and of the Orphans' Home. She has practised with steadily increasing reputation for ten years. She understands what is due to her position, and has had a hard struggle with the empirical women of the medical profession that crowd the great thoroughfares of the West. But she would neither lower her fees nor abate her requirements to compete with this class. She came of the best surgical blood. Her grandmother was Mercy Warren, married to Darling Huntress, of Newbury, and first cousin to General Warren, of Bunker's Hill. Our famous Boston surgeons of the same family might be proud of her reputation. She has established her practice and her character, and would agree with all that I have stated in the body of this book in regard to the great need of medical societies to guard the position of well-educated physicians, which is now at the mercy of a worthless college diploma. Dr. Ross goes to the Paris Exposition of this year (1867), as an agent for the State of Wisconsin. She deserves the honor; and the State has done itself credit by the choice. The professional position of the physicians at the

New-England Hospital for Women and Children in Boston, is also a matter for general congratulation.

The English Female Medical Society reports (June, 1866) twenty students and good results.

The physicians of this country have been occupied this winter in discussing the discovery, by one of their number, of the active infectant in fever and ague. It has been found in the dust-like spores of a marsh plant, the Pamella. In Paris, at the same time, a woman of rank claims to have discovered the cause of cholera, in a microscopic insect, developed in low and filthy localities. Her details were so minute, that the Academy of Science, which began by laughing at the introduction of the matter, has been compelled to listen; and the subject is now under investigation.

THE PULPIT.

A very interesting account has lately been published of Amélie von Braum, an educated Swedish lady, the daughter of an army officer. She began to preach in 1843, at Carlshamm, where she lived, in the lowest dens of vice and misery. She carried with her a clean cloth and lighted candles, which give a festive impulse to the Swedish mind; and her serious words produced an extraordinary effect. In 1856 she removed to Stockholm, and was earnestly entreated to go to Dalecadin, and instruct the people. From that time, she has acted as an itinerant evangelist, preaching in summer in the open air. People listen to her for hours in rapt attention.

In Sweden, there is also Mamsell Berg,* a brave young woman, who thought herself moved by the Holy Spirit to teach the young Laps. She could not get away from the thought that she ought to do it. A clergyman, to whom she spoke upon the matter, counselled her wisely: "Endeavor to shake off the feeling; if you cannot, then accept it as a vocation from God, and try it for six months." She said, "If I go, it shall not be for six months, but for three years." She went; and the three years became seven. She seems also to have been a noble and beautiful creature. She gathered the children around her, under the most difficult circumstances, expending her little property in putting up a schoolhouse for them, and laying in sacks of potatoes, that she might feed the half-famishing; learning herself the Laplandish language, teaching them the Swedish, and discoursing to them about the love of God.

In spite of the bitter words of warning which John Ruskin has thought it his duty to speak to such women as enter upon theological studies, a good many women in Great Britain and this country have engaged in what is properly the work of the Christian ministry. The only ordained minister whose work has come under our notice since the marriage of Antoinette Blackwell is the Rev. Olympia Brown,

---

* I believe I am indebted for some of these items to Miss Howitt's book, but I have not yet seen it.

settled over the Universalist Society at Weymouth Landing, Mass., and lately called to Newburgh in New York. Her ministry has been highly successful, and is to be mentioned here chiefly on account of a legal decision to which it has given rise. The church at Weymouth Landing made an appeal to the Legislature, last winter, as to the legality of marriages solemnized by her. The Legislature gave the same general construction to the masculine relatives in the enactment which the English law gave to the old Latin word in the charter of Apothecaries' Hall; deciding that marriages so solemnized are legal, and no further legislation necessary.

Mention, too, should be made of Rev. Lydia A. Jenkins, who has been a successful preacher among the Universalists for the last eight or ten years, and is now settled at Binghamton, N.Y.

Very recently, during the illness of her husband, the minister at Bethesda Chapel, Newcastle, England, a Mrs. Booth occupied the pulpit, to the great interest and profit of the congregation. Among the Methodists and " Christians,"* as well as among the Quakers, women have always been received as preachers. In October, 1866, I found a Mrs. Timmins settled as the pastor of Ebenezer Church, three miles from Yellow Springs, Ohio, where she had been for three years. Ann Rexford is mentioned as an effective preacher among the Christians. Her preaching attracted large

---

* This word distinguishes a peculiar Unitarian Church, something like the Methodist.

crowds in the State of New Jersey, some thirty years ago.

But the most remarkable record, if we except those to be found among the Quakers, of any single woman's work in the ministry, is that of Abigail Hoag Roberts, who was the settled minister of a church built for her at Milford, N.J., and who died in 1841, at the age of forty-nine.

With her ministry is interlinked that of two other women, — that of Nancy Gore Cram, of Weare, N.H., and a Mrs. Hedges. Mrs. Cram began life as a Free-will Baptist, and undertook a mission to the Oneida Indians. The spiritual destitution of Central New York in the year 1812 affected her profoundly. Not a preacher of her own denomination in New Hampshire could be induced to go there. Disappointed in them, she hurried to Woodstock, Vt., and laid the case before a conference of "Christian" elders and ministers, then in session. They understood her better. She hurried back to the field she had left; and, when the ministers followed her, they were astonished at her work. A church was built for her at Ballston Spa. She is described as a delicate, blue-eyed woman, with dark hair, dressing plainly in black silk, with her hair in a silk net; her whole appearance and manner befitting her work. She died in 1816, suddenly, in the fortieth year of her age. Mrs. Roberts was one of her converts, — a woman who was a constant preacher, from June, 1814, to the June of 1841, in which she died, and, for many years, a settled pastor over the church at Milford, where a monument has been erected to her. More than once she defended the unity of God in public discussion with the clergy, whom she brought to ignominious defeat. She travelled through the three States of New York, New Jersey, and Pennsylvania, where her name is still a household word. More than once, she was threatened by her own sex with "tar and feathers." She seems to have been, like Ann Hutchinson, a witty woman. "If you feel called to preach," said one minister to her, "why do you not go to the heathen?" — "So far as I can judge," she answered, "I am in the midst of them." She had a large family of children, and was distinguished for her household skill. She was quite famed for delicate clear-starching, and, on one occasion, wove with a hand-shuttle twenty-four yards of woollen cloth between early morning and nine o'clock at night. Many people sought her for information. Disliking one woman's vulgarity, she said to her, "If you believe in the Holy Ghost, why not use the *language* that the Holy Ghost uses?" She was a great sufferer in her latter years, but continued to preach at the Milford church, where she had four hundred communicants, and a congregation, at times, of twelve hundred persons, even after she was compelled to lean upon a staff. The Rev. Eli Fay preached her funeral sermon, and bore testimony to her great ability. The life from which I have drawn these particulars was written by her son, and printed at Irvington, N.J.

Her colleague, Mrs. Hedges, died before her; but a singular anecdote is related of her. She was exercised with some doubts as to the separate existence of the soul, and besought God in prayer to satisfy her mind. It seemed to her, after retiring to rest, that her soul left her body, passed through locked doors, and found several unusual adjustments of furniture in the house, and at last returned to the pale form upon the bed. She rose happy, but, on trying to prove her vision, found every thing in its usual place. A thorough inquiry in the household, however, showed that the changes she had observed had actually occurred in the night, and continued for some time. Her experience was the not uncommon one of the Seeress of Prevorst.

It will be remembered, that, in the first edition of "Woman's Right to Labor," I proposed a deaconess in every church; and I found, the other day, a little record in reference to the old church at Amsterdam, in Holland, which I copy here: —

"In the church at Amsterdam, there were about three hundred communicants; and they had for pastors two admirable men, Smith and Robertson, and four ruling elders, as well as one aged woman as deaconess, who served them many years, though she was sixty years old when she was chosen. She filled her office honorably, and was an honor to the congregation. She sat commonly in a convenient place in the church, with a little birchen rod in her hand, and held the little children in much awe, so that they disturbed not the assembly. She diligently visited the sick and the infirm, especially women, and called on younger sisters, in case of need, to watch over them at night, and to give other assistance that might be required; and, if they were poor, she made collections for them, among those who were in a condition to give, or informed the deacons of the case. She was obeyed as a mother in Israel, and a true handmaid of the Lord."

With the exception of "keeping the little children in much awe," which might or might not have been desirable, these are precisely the functions which I desire to see formally renewed. The church at Blooming Grove, Orange County, N.Y., has existed, for more than a hundred years, without a creed, and is governed by seven deacons and seven deacon*esses*.

The following resolution was introduced by the Rev. S. J. May, at the Unitarian Conference which met at Syracuse, N.Y., in the first week of October 1866:—

"Whereas women were among the first, the most steadfast, and the most fearless disciples of Jesus Christ; whereas women have been, in all ages, the most ready to embrace the religion of the gospel, and the most constant and devoted members of the Christian Church; and whereas, in several denominations, women have been among the most effective preachers of Christianity: therefore, *Resolved,* That we, Liberal Christians, should do well to encourage those women among us who are moved by the Holy Spirit to devote themselves to the ministry, and should assist them to prepare themselves in the same manner, and to the same extent, as we deem necessary for young men."

The convention, having just passed a resolution to admit female delegates to the session of 1868, rather shrank from this second vote. Yet of what use to receive delegates, unless they feel free to join in discussion? and what woman, likely to be sent as a delegate by any Unitarian church, will ever address the convention until it *more* than welcomes the above resolution? To the local conferences, women are already being elected, and will do great good if they can get courage to accept their membership practically, and to speak when they have any thing to say.

It would not be quite honest nor fair to those women who seek to enter the pulpit, if I did not here record my own experience in connection with it.

I know very well where my natural sphere of work lay, and could I have had a theological education in my youth, or had even the paths of the ministry at large been open to women, I have every reason to believe that I should be at this moment a settled minister. As it was, it never entered my head that the thing was possible; and except that I taught steadily in Sabbath schools, and visited as steadily among the city poor, I never turned toward ministerial work. In the first year of my marriage, now twenty-two years ago, my husband was settled in the city of Baltimore, as minister at large to the degraded population, which has a special character (or want of character) in a large city, in a slaveholding State. I say *has*, for I cannot yet speak in the past tense. He had daily schools of girls and women, and nightly schools of boys and men. The latter were of all ages from six to forty, and had been gathered together by a great personal effort. In this state of things, my husband was taken ill. It fell to me, in the first place, not only to nurse him, but to take charge of his night-school. The ladies could do very well without me in the day-school; but there was no clergyman, nor leading man of character and culture, who could be depended upon to take the *general* charge of the men and boys, among whom were some desperate characters. I went first in a very stormy night; and my Irish servant took her knitting, and sat upon the steps of the platform while I addressed them. It happened that not a single teacher braved the storm; and the school, when I called the roll, responded to the number of eighty. I told them that I knew how dearly they loved my husband, that he was very ill, and that the only way in which they could help him was to behave so well that he need feel no anxiety about his work. They responded at once to this appeal, and I carried home the best possible account. As Sunday drew near, — this night-school having been held on Monday, — my husband grew more ill and more anxious. He thought of the large, mixed congregation, which met him every week, and for which no provision had been made. We were on an outpost of our faith; we could not have summoned assistance in season, nor without an expense we could not well bear. I thought the matter over; said to myself that it was only like a large Sunday school; that the fashionable ladies, who often dropped in to hear the preaching, would certainly stay away, knowing my husband to be ill: so I told him quietly that I had made arrangements for the Sunday service. He was too weak to make inquiries, but was comforted at once. He was sick several weeks, —

long enough for me to relinquish reading, and take to exhortation in pure despair; but he did not find a small congregation when he resumed his place, and that was my reward. Perhaps no such step was ever taken more simply, or with less idea of its natural consequences. When I came back to Boston, radical country ministers took pains to ask me to their pulpits. I shall not soon forget the first time I preached to a large Unitarian audience, with a good mixture of city people. It was at South Hingham; the church was crowded; the country covered with a crystalline mantle of snow, over which a clear moon glimmered. The beauty of that night is a permanent possession. So it went on, till I became, I believe in the winter of 1859 and 1860, the superintendent of the Sunday school at Indiana-place Chapel, in Boston, where I remained for five years. This broke up my preaching, for I could not leave town on Sundays; but it led to my addressing various Sunday-school gatherings, and my being asked to address Sunday schools when away from home in the summer. My addressing a Sunday school in Greenfield in the summer of 1865, while the pastor of the church was absent with his regiment, led, by his kind sympathy, to my preaching in the summer of 1866 in the regular Unitarian churches at Rowe and Warwick, as well as doing irregular service in many other places. The church at Florence had always shown me a generous appreciation; and I was often asked to preach for Theodore Parker's people at the Music Hall and the Melodeon. I always declined to speak for this last society, not because I do not sympathize with their purposes in the main, but because I would not consent to be advertised for a religious and especially a devotional service in the city which I make my home. There may be women who, in the present state of things, can do this innocently and properly; but *I* cannot go into the pulpit myself, except in the regular sequence of my work, and at the call of duty. The gaping crowd of curious people who would come to look at a woman in the pulpit, would disturb the sphere in which it is alone possible for me to work. It was the custom of the Music-Hall society to advertise for every Sunday, and they declined to relinquish this advertisement on my account. The delivering a course of lectures in Hollis-street Vestry in connection with the Suffolk Sunday-school Union, in April, 1866, showed me that there was a work of criticism to be done, — and necessary to be done, — which I could do: so in going West to examine the condition of certain colleges, in October, 1866, I gave it to be understood, that, if I were in any Western city over Sunday, I should prefer to preach for the Unitarian minister — giving him a "labor of love" — to addressing an audience at an evening lecture. This interfered with my pecuniary advantage; but I believed it was in my power to enter some pulpits that would not be offered to all women, and I desired to do what I could to create a demand for the preaching of women. In this way, I preached for Robert Collyer in Chicago, for Carlton Staples in Milwaukee, for Mr. Hunting in Quincy, and in the chapels of Oberlin and Antioch Colleges. I took the whole service, accepting no assistance in the reading or the prayer; for it is not well that a woman who fills the pulpit should seem to shrink from any service there, and sensitive women will always find their self-possession impaired by any second influence. I received the kindest sympathy and appreciation from the churches I have mentioned; and, in every instance but one, I received the usual fee for my service, voluntarily tendered. I think at least twenty other churches would have been open to me, could I have gone to them.

I do not offer this explanation of the manner in which I have been led into the pulpit, stupidly, in ignorance of the charge of egotism and folly that may be made against me by those who read it. I have borne harder things than that charge, for the truth's sake; and I hope that the real motive of this statement will be transparent to honest and gentle hearts.

I long to see women preparing for this work, for there are very few men in the field; and, if there were more than enough, the pulpit is still an eminently fit place for a woman. The encouragement I have received, will show young women what is open to them. With a few words of counsel to those who may desire to speak in churches, I leave the subject. The dress of a woman in the pulpit should be such as will attract absolutely no attention; yet it should be thoroughly graceful and lady-like. A black silk well made, with collar and cuffs of fine linen, is the best, with no ornament whatever save the needful brooch. Peculiarity should be avoided. When we are trying to win souls for heaven, we must not lose them, because of a "dress reform," which may wait patiently, until more important things are achieved.

Again, if the woman who enters the pulpit is a temperance, an antislavery, or a woman's-rights lecturer, it will be better for her to give lectures on these subjects in the week. In the pulpit, she should subordinate these subjects to theological reform, moral appeal, and that attempt to stimulate religious interest and faith in which most men fail. Nor would I have her, whatever her station in society, refuse the fee, small or large, which shall be tendered her. If she has no need of it, her "poor" will have; and it is important to let the ministry of women fall into the same social and congregational relations as that of men.

There has been a great change in public feeling since the day, not twelve years since, when I heard Dr. Parkman refuse Lucretia Mott permission to speak in the old Federal-street Church.

Among historical instances of the theological influence of woman, that of the Countess Matilda stands pre-eminent; but a book by Capefigue, recently published at Paris, shows, that Madame de Krudener was the first to conceive the idea of the Holy Alliance, and her influence over the Emperor Alexander was sufficient to induce him to propose what his allies had no power to decline. Her purpose was finally accomplished, by her engaging the emperor in prayer. She was finally exiled, and died, I believe, in the Crimea. It was pretended that her preaching was dangerous; but, as she spoke only in French, that could hardly be true.

ART SCHOOLS.

An art school, which started some years ago in Boston, in private hands, finally surrendered its casts, lithographs, and so forth, to the teachers of the Free Art School of the Lowell Institute. The female classes of this school are always crowded, and are doing a great deal of good. Artists are accustomed to say very disparaging things of the school at the Cooper Institute; but I visited it in December, 1866, and found a very great improvement within a few years. Under Dr. Rimmer, a most admirable lecturer on anatomy, there has been an infusion of new life. The drawings from casts looked better than I have ever seen them. They have a good master in color, and the drawing and engraving on wood by the pupils find a ready market. Two of them, Miss Roundtree and Miss Curtis, are said to have a high reputation. I was delighted to find a large class coloring photographs; for heretofore it has been almost impossible for women to receive decent instruction in this art. The classes are all full; and three times the number of pupils might be received, if there were more light in the large rooms. It is to be hoped Mr. Cooper may some time divide them, and put in gas.

I have taken advantage of the residence in this country of a well-known member of the Royal Academy, Mrs. Elizabeth Murray, to ascertain what circumstances led to the formation of the Society of Female Artists, in London. To Mrs. Grote, the wife of the historian, and Mrs. Murray herself, this society owed its existence, somewhere in the winter of 1854 and 1855. There is no objection to it, so far as I know, except one apparent on its catalogues, the present preponderance of distinguished amateur artists on the Board of Direction. I insert here Mrs. Murray's letter in reply to my inquiries. The best artists, such as Rosa Bonheur and Mrs. Murray herself, exhibit with this society.

My dear Mrs. Dall, — On my return to England, after an absence of many years, I found that women labored under very disheartening conditions; their professional occupations consisting chiefly of teaching, music and singing, literature and the fine arts. In the latter department, they came more under my own personal observation; and I found, that, although they were countenanced by men individually, collectively they were persecuted by men, seldom being permitted membership with any public body, or, when admitted, were not allowed the full privileges accorded to men.

For instance: At the Royal Academy of London, women are not admitted at all to membership. On the walls of that exhibition may be seen the works of women, which rank among the best; but here their privilege ends. They assist in bringing their quota of the entrance fees, the main source of income of the academy, while they are debarred from all privileges and emoluments.

The two water-color societies profess to admit women as

members, which they do to a very limited extent; but even here they are subject to the same restrictions. Under these circumstances, the project occurred to me of founding a separate and independent society, which should include only the works of female artists, in order to give to those excluded from other societies, opportunities of asserting their own powers.

The first step was to get up an exhibition to excite public sympathy in favor of the scheme. This was a most difficult undertaking, as opposition was met with, not only from men, but from the very women whose interests were at stake; those who were strong in the profession fearing to lose caste, and the weaker ones being afraid to act independently.

After much perseverance and explanation, several large-minded persons of the more moneyed and influential ranks in society came forward, and assisted, by their cordial co-operation, in establishing a temporary committee. Money was freely contributed; and the society had a fair start, opening to the public a very creditable exhibition of the works of female artists.

Finding that, for the future, I must necessarily be absent from England, I retired from the Committee of Direction.

The society has continued in a more or less prosperous condition up to the present time, although my plan of establishing an adequate school of art has not been carried out. Much private good has been the result; and I think the class of women for whom the society was founded, have been raised in position.   Believe me, dear madam,

Very truly yours,

(Signed)   ELIZABETH MURRAY.

13, Pemberton Square, Dec. 22, 1866.

In Paris, Rosa Bonheur is now the directress, under the government, of the École Impériale de Dessein, established exclusively for young women.

LABOR.*

The advance of women, as regards all sorts of labor, in the United States, has been such as might be expected by watchful eyes; and yet reports on the general question will not read very differently from those published ten years ago. In New York, women are still reported as making shirts at seventy-five cents a dozen, and overalls at fifty cents. These women have two Protective Unions of their own, not connected with the Workingmen's Union; and most of them have, naturally enough, sympathized with the eight-hour movement, not foreseeing, apparently, that the necessary first result of that movement would be a decrease of wages, proportioned to the limitation of time. Ever since the beginning of the war, women have been employed in the public departments, North and South. It has been a matter of necessity, rather than of choice. The same causes combined to drive women into field-labor and printing-offices. All through Minnesota and the surrounding regions, women voluntarily assumed the whole charge of the farms, in order to send their husbands to the field. A very interesting account has been recently published of a farm in Dongola, Ill., consisting of two thousand acres, managed by a highly educated woman,

---

* I wish to say in advance, that while the statistics in "The College" and "The Market" are based on a gold value, and are wholly reliable, I place no reliance on those furnished in this Appendix. The varying price of gold, and of the cost of provision and clothing, at the time the tables are made, are nowhere given, and are important elements in a sound calculation.

whose husband was a cavalry officer. It was a great pecuniary success. In New Hampshire, last summer, I was shown open-air graperies, wholly managed by women, in several different localities; and was very happy to be told that my own influence had largely contributed to the experiment. In England, field-labor is now recommended to women by Lord Houghton, better known as Mr. Monckton Milnes, who considers it a healthful resource against the terrible abuses of factory life. At a meeting of the British Association, last fall, he produced a well-written letter from a woman engaged in brick-making. This letter claimed that brick-making paid three times better than factory labor, and ten times better than domestic service. In addition to persons heretofore mentioned, in this country, as employing women in out-door work, I would name Mr. Knox, the great fruit-grower, who, on his place near Pittsburg, Pa., employs two or three hundred. I have seen it stated, that, during the last four years, twenty thousand women have entered printing-offices. I do not know the basis of this calculation; but, judging from my local statistics, I should think it must be nearly correct.

To the Committee of the Massachusetts Legislature on the eight-hour movement, the following towns report concerning the wages and labor of women, in 1866 : —

BOSTON. — Glass Company, wages from $4.00 to $8.00 a week. Domestics, from $1.50 to $3.00 per week. Seamstresses, $1.00 a day. Makers of fancy goods, 40 to 50 cents a day.

BROOKLINE. — Washerwomen, $1.00 a day.

CHARLESTOWN and NEW BEDFORD are ashamed to name the wages, but humbly confess that they are very low.

CHICOPEE pays women 90 per cent the wages of men.

CONCORD pays from 8 to 10 cents an hour.

FAIRHAVEN gives to female photographers one-third the wages of men.

HADLEY pays three-fourths; to domestics, one-third; seamstresses, one-quarter to one-third.

HOLYOKE, in its paper-mills, offers one-third to one-half.

LANCASTER pays for pocket-book making from 50 to 75 cents a day.

LEE pays in the paper-mills one-half the wages of men.

LOWELL. — The Manufacturing Company averages 90 cents a day. The Baldwin Mills pay 60 to 75 cents a day.

NEWTON pays its washerwomen 75 cents a day, or 10 cents an hour.

NORTH BECKET pays to women one-third the wages of men.

NORTHAMPTON pays $5.00 a week.

SALISBURY, for sewing hats, $1.00 a day.

SOUTH READING, on rattan and shoe work, $5.00 to $10.00 a week.

SOUTH YARMOUTH, half the wages of men, or less.

TAUNTON, one-third to two-thirds the wages of men.

WALPOLE pays two-thirds the wages of men.

WAREHAM pays to its domestics from 18 to 30 cents a day; to seamstresses, 50 cents to $1.00.

WILMINGTON pays two-thirds the wages of men.

WINCHESTER pays dressmakers $1.00 a day; washerwomen, 12 cents an hour.

WOBURN keeps its women to work from 11 to 13 hours, and pays them two-thirds the wages of men.

On the better side of the question, FALL RIVER testifies that women, in competition, earn nearly as much as men.

LAWRENCE, from the Pacific Mills, that the women are *liberally* paid. We should like to see the figures. The Washington Mills pay from $1.00 to $2.00 a day.

STONEHAM gives them $1.50 per week.

WALTHAM reports the wages of the watch-factory as very *remunerative*. In 1860, I reported this factory as paying from $2.50 to $4.00 a week. Here, also, we should prefer figures to a general statement.

BOSTON has now many manufactories of paper collars. Each girl is expected to turn out 1,800 daily. The wages are $7.00 a week. In the paper-box factory, more than 200 girls are employed; but I cannot ascertain their wages, and therefore suppose them to be low. I know individuals who earn here $6.00 a week; but that must be *above* the average.

The best-looking body of factory operatives that I have ever seen are those employed in the silk and ribbon mills on Boston Neck, lately under the charge of Mr. J. H. Stephenson, and those at the Florence Silk Mills in Northampton, owned by Mr. S. L. Hill. The classes, libraries, and privileges appertaining to these mills make them the best examples I know; and this is shown in the faces and bearing of the women.

We are always referred to political economy, when we speak of the low wages of women; but a little investigation will show that other causes co-operate with those, which can be but gradually reached, to determine their rates.

1. The wilfulness of women themselves, which, when I see them in positions I have helped to open to them, fills me with shame and indignation.

2. The unfair competition, proceeding from the

voluntary labor, in mechanical ways, of women well to do.

For the first, we cannot greatly blame the women whom employers choose for their *good looks*, for expecting to earn their wages through them, rather than by the proper discharge of their duties. Their conduct is not the less shameful on that account; but I seem to see that only time and death and ruin will educate them.

For the second, we must strive to develop a public sentiment, which, while it continues to hold labor honorable, will stamp with ignominy any women who, in comfortable country homes, compete with the workwomen of great cities. There are thousands of wealthy farmers' wives to-day, who just as much drive other women to sin and death as if they led them with their own hands to the houses in which they are ultimately compelled to take refuge. Still further, it has come to be known to me, that in Boston, and I am told in New York also, wealthy women, who do not even do their own sewing, have the control of the finer kinds of fancy work, dealing with the stores which sell such work, under various disguises. I cannot prove these words, but they will strike conviction to the hearts of the women themselves, and I wish them to have some significance for men; for, if these women had the pocket-money which their taste and position require, they would never dream of such competition. One thing these men should know, that such women are generally known to their employers, and their domestic relations are judged accordingly.

The recent investigations into factory labor in England concern rather the condition than the wages of the women. At *flower-making*, 11,000 girls are employed from fourteen to eighteen hours daily. In *hardware* shops and factories, they work, from six years of age, fourteen hours daily. In *glass* factories, 5,000 women are employed, from nine years of age and upwards, eighteen hours daily. In *tobacco* factories, 7,000 women are employed, under conditions of great physical suffering. As *knitters*, from six years old, they work fourteen hours daily for 1s. 3d. a week!

This terrible state of things is partly owing to competition with the labor of French machinery. A great deal of ignorant prejudice against machines is one of its results. In Sheffield, *files* are still made by *hand;* while here, in America, we make *watches* by *machinery!* The disposition of the whole community, both here and in Great Britain, towards this labor question, is kindly. It has become a momentous social problem. During the fifteen years that my attention has been riveted to this subject, I have seen a great change in public feeling.

I have received the Sixth Annual Report of the Society for the Employment of Women, of which the Earl of Shaftesbury is President, and Mr. Gladstone a Vice-President. This society has trained some hair-dressers, clerks, glass-engravers, book-keepers, and telegraph operators; but its greatest service consists in the constant issue of tracts, to influence developing public opinion. Such an association should be started in New York.

I should have been glad to inaugurate in Boston, during the last six years, several important industrial movements. The war checked the enthusiasm I had succeeded in rousing; and I have not been able to pause in my special work of collecting and observing facts to stimulate it afresh, or to solicit personally the necessary means. How easy it would be for a few wealthy women to test these experiments!

I would first establish a mending-school; and, having taught women how to darn and patch in a proper manner, I would scatter them through the country, to open shops of their own. As it is, I do not know a city, in which a place exists to which a housekeeper could send a week's wash, sure that it would be returned with every button-hole, button, hem, gusset, and stay in proper condition. These mending-shops should take on apprentices, who should be sent to the house to do every sort of repairing with a needle.

I would open another school to train women to every kind of trivial service, now clumsily or inadequately performed by men. If, for instance, you now send to an upholsterer to have an old window-blind or blind-fixture repaired, his apprentice will replace the entire thing at a proportionate cost, leaving the old screw-holes to gape at the gazer. I would train women to wash, repair, and replace in part, and to carry in their pockets little vials of white or red lead to fill the gaping holes. Full employment could be found for such apprentices.

At Milwaukee, in October, 1866, I found a young woman well established as a hair-dresser. She belonged to a superior class of society, and encountered great opposition in carrying out her plan. " People would treat her much better," said a resident clergyman to me, in detailing her struggles, " if she were the willing mistress of a rich man." She had no taste for teaching, but I found in her a cultivated and pleasant companion. Since the war began, a good many women have been employed as clerks in the public offices at Washington. There is now some talk of their removal. If this should occur, it would be in consequence of unfit appointments, and the habits and annoyances which demoralized women have imposed upon the departments. The proper place to begin removals is obviously with the corrupt men, who have pensioned their mistresses out of the public coffers.

In Chicago, I found Fanny Paine, a girl of thirteen, acting as paymaster to the Eagle Works Manufacturing Company. She will, in one year, pay out a quarter of a million of dollars. She keeps the time-sheets, pay-roll, and account-book of each of the four hundred men employed. She receives about five thousand dollars a week from the bank, and makes the proper balances with the cashier, after paying her men. She knows every man, earns six hundred and twenty-five dollars per annum, and is represented as perfectly robust. It gave me no pleasure to find so young a girl in a position so exposed. I would have her uncommon faculties mature in quiet. The "London Athenæum" lately said, " A phenomenon worthy of consideration is the increasing number of female players on stringed instruments in France. At the examination of the conservatory this year, Mademoiselle Boulay gained a first, Mademoiselle Castellan a second prize. The violoncello has its professional students among the gentler sex. Madame Viardot is about to turn her experience to account, by editing a classical selection of music."

A very dear friend of mine, — Charlotte Hill, of West Gouldsborough, in Maine, — born a farmer's daughter, too deaf to teach, and too delicate to sew, had an intense love for music. She taught herself the violin. She then made a profession for herself by offering to play it at rustic parties; and one year, in the pursuit of this profession, she travelled more than eight hundred miles, and laid by three hundred dollars. This money was not spent on jewelry, but on the best books that our best publishers could furnish. It takes a genius to do a thing like that, — trust in one's self, and a far deeper trust in God; but there are multitudes of women whom suggestion and sympathy would lead into such thriving ways.

I have heard recently of a young girl in Shirley, who supports herself and her father by gunning. She not only sends game to market, but prepares the breasts of birds for ornamental purposes. She has bought her own house by her profits.

When I was at Florence, Mass., in the summer of 1865, I drove over to the famous button-factory at Easthampton. This great industry was founded by a woman; and, as I had often heard mythical stories about it, I wished to get at the facts. I found Samuel Williston, a very good specimen of a fine old English gentleman. He is a man between sixty and seventy, with hair and beard as white as snow. I found him in a blue coat with bright buttons, a buff waistcoat, and white pants, and very willing to tell his wife's story, if it would "encourage other women."

" My wife's father," he went on to say, " was a Mr. Graves. He was a poor man, with a large family of children. His wife and daughters used to go over to Northampton to get knitting from the stores. One day, all the knitting had been given out; and Mrs. Graves showed her disappointment so plainly that the shopman asked her to take some buttons to cover. In those days, all our buttons came from England, where they were made by hand; but our tailor had got out, and wanted some for coats and vests in a hurry. Mrs. Graves made about a gross, all her daughters helping, and did it so well that the work was continued. Then my wife took it up. She got some of the work from her mother. That was in 1825–26, — forty years ago. I had invested in merino sheep. I had ninety ewes and a large farm; but I was a young man, and found it hard to get along. It looked as though this business would help. My wife wanted to control the work. She hired girls to help her, and took all the orders that came. J. D. Whitney and Hayden & Whitney sold all she could make. When she had had the business a year, I went to Boston, Providence, Hartford, New Haven, New York, — in short, I went *all round*, — with samples. I got my orders at first hand, and from that the business began.

"When we heard that machine-made buttons had been introduced into England, we sent over to buy the right to make them, and Mr. Hayden introduced them here.

"Every man must have his small beginnings," added Mr. Williston, with an embarrassed blush; "but, when a man has such a wife as mine, he is lucky."

It is said that nearly a million of dollars is invested in this button business at Easthampton. The Willistons are Congregational Christians; and the "Round Table" stated lately, that the wealth thus accumulated, besides being of great local value in developing the resources of the State, had established one seminary, built three churches, and assisted colleges and schools without number.

It is very rare that the labor of women becomes consolidated into capital; but there is no reason why it should not. The mother of James Freeman Clarke, whose name I use here in compliance with her own expressed desire, was a wonderful illustration of what common sense and determination will accomplish. The petted darling of a wealthy family, Madame Clarke found herself summoned, by her husband's illness and early death, to retrieve, almost unaided, the fortunes of six children. The first money which she could lay aside, at the head of a boarding-house, lifted the mortgage from a small property which she knew she was to inherit, and which she felt sure would increase in value. For this property she ultimately received her own price, being, to the great amazement of applicants, her own "man of business" in all negotiations. The small sum it yielded she put out at interest in new States, where money was scarce, and multiplied it tenfold before she died, not by careless speculation, but by investing it wisely in the heart of the great cities of Chicago and Milwaukee, by buying what she saw with her own eyes to be valuable. " I want women to know how to manage their own concerns as I did," she would say. " It only takes a little common sense. Women ought not to give up their property to men, or even ask their advice about it. The best men will prop up their shaky plans with a woman's money; but women should watch men, see where shrewd men put their money, and do as they *do*, not as they *say*."

I am sorry that the purpose of this volume does not permit me to show how this noble woman used the money she made for the profit, the religious advancement, and the bodily comfort of those who seemed to need its aid.

One other woman, whose name I am not permitted to mention, deserves to be spoken of in this connection. She was an orphan, and began life as a factory girl with twelve cents and a half. Her father had never dreamed of any need to educate a daughter. She took a sister into the factory with her; and, while one worked, the other went to school, — my friend opening a dressmaker's shop, at times, to speed the process. While in the mills, she secured, by a wise firmness, many privileges for the girls. She married, and, after the death of an only child, sought to make herself happy, by being of use; and opened, for the girls whose wages had been reduced, a Protective Union shoe-store, taking all that one man and eight apprentices could make daily. At last, she borrowed a hundred dollars, and went to Lynn, — the first woman that ever bought goods there. She soon controlled the prices of the trade, opened a second store, and finally bought out the Union.

Part of her store she devoted to fancy goods, and, for seven years and a half, did all the buying in Boston. She then went to Philadelphia, leaving the stores in her husband's charge, and took her degree at Pennsylvania College. After this, she lectured on Physiology throughout New England, being often profitably employed by the corporations to lecture to the girls. By this time, she owned her horse and carriage, her house, and twenty thousand dollars, beside having a good practice in a country town. Circumstances then carried her to California, where, in three years and a half, she made thirteen thousand dollars, partly by her profession, and partly by buying up Government vouchers, in which the men at the Navy Yard were paid. She gave gold, and received greenbacks. Before she left the State, one of its most eminent physicians came to her to know by what secret she cured patients whom he had given up. She showed him the errors of his own practice; and, when she returned to New England, left, with perfect faith, her patients in his hands.

If this woman were not still living, I should wish to record the details of her life; but they suggest so much, that I have not thought it right to suppress them altogether.

Mr. Thayer and two ladies have lately attempted, in Boston, at No. 28, Ash Street, a small experiment in the way of a lodging-house for girls. This was first suggested to the ladies, by the misfortunes of a young woman who came under their notice. They tried to hire a house, but found it cheaper to buy; Mr. Thayer being responsible for half the expense, and each of the ladies for one-quarter. The house was furnished at the cost of friends. It has gas and water in nearly every room, and shelters 29 girls. They pay for light, rent, lodging, and fire, repairs and service, $1.50 per week, and $1.25. There are two single beds in most of the rooms. The matron keeps an exact account of her expenditure; and each week the stores are weighed by one of the ladies, the waste being charged, as well as the marketing, to the girls.

The board, so managed, costs each girl $1.75 a week. Some of the girls wash for themselves in the evening, and a woman is hired for the house once a week. They take care of their own rooms. The matron employs a cook. There are only two rules, — that every girl shall be in at 10 P.M., and that a week's notice shall be given when any inmate desires to leave. No supervision is exercised except of the stores and the matron's accounts. The house was opened Dec. 15, 1866, and is a success according to its plan.

Grateful as I am to see this attempt made, I cannot feel that this plan should be followed for the future. Girls do not wish to receive charity, nor can any experiment be thoroughly successful, which does not pay, in the long-run, a fair percentage on the cost of house and furniture. Now, $4.00 a week is, in my estimation, only the fair cost price of the style of board and living which these girls receive; and it could not be kept at that under average management.

I do not know the cost of the house, but it would certainly rent for $600. The taxes upon it would be, at least, $120.

Now, let us suppose that 30 girls occupy it, each paying the highest rent, of $1.50 per week, which is $45 a month. In 13 months, they would pay $585; — a sum less than the rent alone; the house and water taxes, light, lodging, fire, repairs, and service, being thrown in gratis. I am sure my estimate of the rent and taxes is beneath the real value of both; and it is evident, that no efforts to benefit this class, on a large scale, will succeed, unless made to pay better: companies will undertake only profitable work. I want to see girls unite to furnish themselves, in a still more modest way, with what they need; and I wish to see a system of cooking-houses established, which shall simplify the whole matter.

In New York, a Working-women's Home is about to be established, the plan of which was long since submitted to the public. A building has been purchased on Elizabeth Street, which will afford accommodations for four hundred persons. For this, $100,000 has been paid, and $25,000 more will be expended in fitting it up. Half the amount has already been raised; and the managers are making strong efforts to collect the remainder. Of its objects, the "Evening Post" says,—

"In this Home will be found clean, well-ventilated rooms, wholesome food, and facilities for education and self-improvement. Girls exposed to the temptations of a city life will be surrounded by both moral and Christian influences.

"The institution is intended to benefit a class of women who now find it impossible, with their slender means, to procure comfortable homes, and are forced to live where moral purity, as well as health, is endangered.

"It is well known that families and boarding-house keepers almost always object to female boarders, and that many thousands of sewing-women find it difficult to obtain quarters. Artificial flower-makers, book-folders, hoop-skirt manufacturers, packers of confectionery, &c., are compelled, if deprived of parental shelter, to accept such homes and accommodations as their very limited resources will command.

"It is not intended to make this a charitable institution; but the prices will be made so moderate as to be within the means of those who are to be benefited by it, while, at the same time, the establishment will be self-sustaining."

Mr. Halliday says of it, —

"The whole expense of first purchase, alterations, and furniture, will be about $140,000. Messrs. Peter Cooper, James Lenox, James Brown, Stewart Brown, William H. Aspinwall, E. J. Woolsey, and Mrs. C. L. Spencer, have, unsolicited, each contributed one thousand dollars. Twenty thousand dollars has been appropriated on condition that we obtained a like amount in donations. We expect to have accommodations for nearly five hundred, and the charge for board and washing will be from three dollars and a quarter to three and a half per week.

"There will be parlors, reading room and free library, and ample bathing rooms. None of good reputation will be refused admission; no others can become members of the family."

It is hoped to open the institution by the first of June.

A Young Women's Christian Association was organized in Boston in May, 1866, under the auspices of Mrs. Henry F. Durant. Furnished rooms have been provided at 27, Chauncy Street, where young women can obtain information in regard to employment, boarding-houses, and so on. The applications average one hundred a month; and the association seeks to establish a home, where there will be a restaurant for furnishing meals, at cost, to *young women only*, a free reading and library room, evening schools, rooms for social purposes, and temporary lodging-rooms. This is a most dèsirable thing to do; but it will not be of permanent benefit, if it puts into a false position any girls capable of self-support. The funds of wise and kind people must start all such movements; but, to be useful, they must be, not only in appearance, but in reality, self-supporting.

During the summer of 1866, Octavia Hill, of London, a grand-daughter of the celebrated Dr. Southwood Smith, reports that, after conferring with John Ruskin, she had hired houses for poor tenants. She put them into good order, and kept them in it. She would allow, in her tenants, neither overcrowding nor arrears of rent. She had no middle-men. The experiment was wholly successful, and paid at once five per cent.

Mr. Ruskin's lodging-houses, as they are called, are the best that have ever been established in London. They furnish the cheapest and cleanest lodgings for the poor, yet pay a good dividend. They are entirely in the hands of Miss Hill, as Mr. Ruskin himself is more skilful to remedy any social excrescence than patient to bear with it. He forgets, I think, what he once wrote concerning the soul that denies itself an encounter with pain.

I have mentioned, in the body of this book, the great number of women who have entered printing-offices since 1860. I have thought that it might help women in some other departments of labor, to understand how some of these changes were effected, and in what manner advantages have been secured, which might easily have been lost. In a town that I know of, a weekly religious paper was printed by eight women. The most experienced acted as foreman; and when, in the second year of the war, strikes began in the printing-offices, a friend directed her attention to the fact, and showed her how to meet a strike should it come, as it did, into her own town. As soon as she heard of it, she consulted with the rest of the hands. Seeing a possible though by no means a certain advantage, they agreed to be bound by her action in such an event. At last, the hands employed on the daily evening paper of the town struck, and the publisher knew not what to do. The girl went to him, told him she would bring seven able hands with her, and was accepted at once. He was mean enough to offer half-pay, which she peremptorily refused. The eight women entered the office on full pay. They had not been there a week, before every body rejoiced in the change. There was no swearing and no drinking, but a quiet work-room. At the end of a month, the disappointed men offered to return: their services were declined, but the publisher was mean enough to go to his foreman. "My men are ready to come back," said he: "I have no fault to find with *you*, but I can no longer give you full wages." — "Do as you please," replied the girl: "you cannot have us for any less;" and, as the whole seven said amen, the publisher had nothing to do but to keep them. The advantage that flowed from union and good sense in this case are evident, and could easily be imitated in many directions. During the past winter, Miss Stebbens, of Chickasaw County, Iowa, has been appointed notary public; such appointments being still so rare as to make the fact worth recording.

LAW.

The "British Medical Journal" was lately reported to have said that more English women seek for admission to the bar than for entrance into medical practice. If this be true, it is in marked contrast to the state of things in this country. Some women have studied law here; many have written in lawyers' offices; but, so far as I know, not one has desired to be admitted to the bar: and, in England itself, so far as I know, Miss Shedden remains the single example of a woman pleading in a court of law.

The number of laws passed the last six years, affecting the condition of women, has been very small.

The New-York Assembly in February, 1865, passed a law putting the legal evidence of a married woman on the same basis as if she were a *feme sole*. The Massachusetts Legislature have legalized marriage ceremonies performed by an ordained woman; and in January, 1866, Mr. Peckham, of Worcester, moved for a joint special committee "to consider in what way a more just and equal compensation shall be awarded to female labor." On the 4th of April, just past, Samuel E. Sewall and others petitioned for leave to appoint women on school committees. It is difficult to conceive on what ground such petitioners had leave to withdraw. These things are only valuable as indicating that public attention is still alive.

In Richmond, Va., recently, a charge of stealing was sustained against a woman, who was afterwards acquitted, by appeal, on the ground that no married woman could own her own clothing, and the consequent flaw in the indictment. In consequence, a bill to secure the rights of property to a married woman, as if she were a *feme sole*, has been offered in the House, to the horror of members who gravely assert that there can be no marriages, if a man does not own his wife's wardrobe!

In Missouri, the new Constitution confers on women the right to make a will; and the Legislature is considering the subject of introducing women to the State University.

In England, a curious decision has recently been made, in the case of a clergyman, of the Church of England, who left his children to the guardianship of his wife, without expressing any opinion as to their religious education. Joint guardian with the wife was a brother clergyman, who brings action to have it decided by the Court where the children shall attend church. The mother, and a son of thirteen, desire to attend a dissenting chapel; but Sir J. Stuart, Vice-Chancellor, decided that the *father's* religious faith must decide the matter for the children! Such absurdity will do more than any argument to secure the future freedom of woman. The family history of Madame de Bedout, recently dead at Paris, furnishes, also, a remarkable illustration of the absurdity of the old laws.

The will of Francis Jackson, of Boston, has been recently brought before our courts to obtain instructions as to its construction. Mr. Jackson's bequest for the purpose of creating an antislavery sentiment has been sustained; but the decision reads, February, 1867: —

"The gift in the sixth article, to create a trust, unrestricted in point of time, to secure the passage of laws granting to women different rights from those belonging to them under the existing Constitution and laws, does not constitute a legal charity, and is therefore void, and is remitted to the testator's heirs-at-law."

The gift in question was intended to aid the publication of such books as the reader now holds in his hand.

A very important convention came together at Leipsic, in September, 1865. One hundred and fifty women assembled, pledged to assert the right to labor, and to bridge the gulf between the compensations of the two sexes. Madame Louise Otto Peters opened the conference in an able speech. She stated that there were five millions of women in Germany, who could each earn, if allowed, three thalers a week. A thousand women might find employment as chemists, on salaries of one hundred and fifty thalers a year, exclusive of board and lodging. Another thousand might be employed as boot-closers. The foundation of industrial and commercial schools was urged. The weak point of the speech, as reported, appeared to be, that it took no cognizance of the fact, that an influx of five millions of laborers must necessarily lower the current rate of wages she proposed I mention this convention in a legal connection, believing that it was intended to remove some local legal barriers.

A petition from sixty women of Potter County, Penn., has just been presented to the Legislature of that State, praying for the passage of an act to enable widows, on the death of a husband, to control the property acquired by joint labor, in the same manner as the husband does on the death of the wife.

When Freeman Clarke was Comptroller of the United-States Currency, he decided that a woman, not being a *citizen*, could not be a bank director. I consider this logical and satisfactory. I wish more decisions of this kind could be made. If the position that woman is not a citizen were pushed to its extreme, it would become untenable, her property could not be taxed, and the necessary remedy would be applied. One bank remonstrated against the comptroller's decision, desiring to retain the services of women "hitherto satisfactory." I see, by a Washington paper, that another national bank desires leave to diminish the number of its directors; so many of its shares being held by women, that nine men could not be found to fill the office.

Now, let some bright women buy up, through a broker, all the shares of such a bank, elect their own president and directors, and see what the Government can do. The absurdity of such a position, practically, is evident to all who know how business is done in our country towns.

SUFFRAGE.

Dr. Hunt and a few other women have continued their annual protests, without intermission. In somewhat the same way have petitions recently been sent to Congress in behalf of universal suffrage. We had no expectation that any favorable reception would await such petitions; but it was a duty to put them on record, if we could do it without perplexing public business. What fate they met in Congress, you have so recently heard, that I have no occasion to record it. Minnesota, New York, and other States, have petitioned their Legislatures to the same effect.

On the 7th of February, 1867, the House of Representatives in Kansas decided, in concurrence with the Senate, to amend a resolution for the amendment of the Constitution, by striking out the words "white" and "male," and making intelligence the basis of suffrage after 1870. This action has been since rescinded in some way, only the word "*white*" being stricken out. In Congress, Mr. Noel, of Missouri, offered a series of resolutions in favor of extending suffrage to women, and authorizing the calling of a convention to amend the Constitution in the State of Missouri. The acting Vice-President, the Speaker of the Senate, in recording his protest against the

Suffrage Bill of the District of Columbia, said, " Make it *intelligent* suffrage, and I will not only vote for that, but for *women* also."

At the recent election of officers for the Philadelphia Mercantile Library, the female stockholders were admitted to the ballot.

The " New-York Express " says: —

" The exercise of the elective franchise for women was practically illustrated in the election of officers for the Mercantile Library, Philadelphia, on Tuesday. A poll was opened for the female stockholders, who, to the number of a hundred and fifty-six, cast their votes. Both sexes voted together; and the proceedings were conducted with the utmost propriety, there being no confusion or disorder, as is too often the case where men vote alone. The ladies walked up, and deposited their ballots with as much *sang froid* as if they were accustomed to the privilege. As illustrating how the thing *might be done*, this voting at the library election should be noted."

Some doubts having been expressed as to the fact of women having voted in New Jersey, first published by me, on information given by Thomas Garratt, in my lectures upon Law, I append here a history of the Constitution of New Jersey in that regard, which has been gathered by Lucy Stone and Antoinette Blackwell, as well as an account of my own recent interview with a member of the House of 1807, which finally repealed the obnoxious clause.

During the recent important discussion in the Senate upon the proposition to extend the ballot to the women·of the District of Columbia, New Jersey was alluded to as a precedent. The precedent being disputed, the following statement was published in the "Newark Daily Advertiser:"—

"In 1709 a provincial law confined the privilege of voting to 'male freeholders having one hundred acres of land in their own right, or fifty pounds current money of the province in real and personal estate;' and, during the whole of the colonial period, these qualifications continued unchanged.

"But on the 2d of July, 1776 (two days before the Declaration of Independence), the Provincial Congress of New Jersey, at Burlington, adopted a Constitution, which remained in force until 1844, of which sect. 4 is as follows: 'Qualifications of Electors for Members of Legislatures. *All inhabitants of this colony*, of full age, who are worth fifty pounds proclamation-money, clear estate in the same, and have resided within the county in which they claim a vote for twelve months immediately preceding the election, shall be entitled to vote for representatives in Council and Assembly, and also for all other public officers that shall be elected by the people of the county at large.'

"Sect. 7 provides that the Council and Assembly jointly shall elect *some fit person within the colony* to be Governor. This Constitution remained in force until 1844.

"Thus, by a deliberate change of the terms 'male freeholder' to 'all inhabitants,' suffrage and ability to hold the highest office in the State were conferred both on women and negroes.

"In 1790, a committee of the Legislature reported a bill regulating elections, in which the words '*he or she*' are applied to voters; thus giving legislative indorsement to the alleged meaning of the Constitution.

"In 1797 the Legislature passed an act to regulate elections, containing the following provisions:—

"Sect. 9. 'Every voter shall openly, and in full view, deliver *his or her ballot*, which shall be a single written ticket, containing the names of the person or persons for whom *he or she votes*,' &c.

'Sect. 11. 'All free inhabitants of full age, who are worth fifty pounds proclamation-money, and have resided within the county in which they claim a vote for twelve months immediately preceding the election, shall be entitled to vote for all public officers which shall be elected by virtue of this act; and no person shall be entitled to vote in any other township or precinct than that in which he or she doth actually reside at the time of the election.'

"Mr. William A. Whitehead, of Newark, in a paper upon this subject, read by him in 1858 before the New-Jersey Historical Society, states that, in this same year (1797), women voted, at an election in Elizabethtown, for members of the Legislature. 'The candidates between whom the greatest rivalry existed were John Condit and William Crane, the heads of what were known, a year or two later, as the "Federal Republican" and "Federal Aristocratic" parties, the former the candidate of Newark and the northern portions of the county, the latter that of Elizabethtown and the adjoining country, for Council. Under the impression that the candidates would poll nearly the same number of votes, the Elizabethtown leaders thought, that, by a bold *coup d'état*, they might secure the success of Mr. Crane. At a late hour of the day, and, as I have been informed, just before the close of the poll, a number of females were brought up, and, under the provisions of the existing laws, allowed to vote. But the manœuvre was unsuccessful; the majority for Mr. Condit in the county being ninety-three, notwithstanding.'

"The 'Newark Sentinel,' about the same time, states that 'no less than seventy-five women were polled at the late election in a neighboring borough.' In the presidential election of 1800, between Adams and Jefferson, 'females voted very generally throughout the State; and such continued to be the case until the passage of the act (1807) excluding them from the polls. At first, the law had been so construed as to admit single women only: but, as the practice extended, the construction of the privilege became broader, and was made to include females eighteen years old, married or single, and even *women of color;* at a contested election in Hunterdon County in 1802, the votes of two or three such actually electing a member of the Legislature.

"That women voted at a very early period, we are informed by the venerable Mr. Cyrus Jones, of East Orange, who was born in 1770, and is now ninety-seven years old. He says that 'old maids, widows, and unmarried women very frequently voted, but married women very seldom;' that 'the right was recognized, and very little said or thought about it in any way.'

"In the spring of 1807, a special election was held in Essex County, to decide upon the location of a court-house and jail; Newark and its vicinity struggling to retain the county buildings, Elizabethtown and its neighborhood striving to remove them to 'Day's Hill.'

"The question excited intense interest, as the value of every man's property was thought to be involved. Not only was every legal voter, man or woman, white or black, brought out; but, on both sides, gross frauds were practised. The property qualification was generally disregarded; aliens, and boys and girls not of full age, participated; and many of both sexes 'voted early, and voted often.' In Aquackanonk Township, thought to contain about three hundred legal voters, over eighteen hundred votes were polled, all but seven in the interest of Newark.

"It does not appear that either *women or negroes* were more especially implicated in these frauds than the white men. But the affair caused great scandal, and they seem to have been made the scapegoats.

"When the Legislature assembled, they set aside the election as fraudulent; yet Newark retained the buildings. Then they passed an act (Nov. 15, 1807), restricting the suffrage to white male adult citizens twenty-one years of age, residents in the county for the twelve months preceding, and worth fifty pounds proclamation-money. But they went on, and provided that all such whose names appeared on the last duplicate of State or county taxes should be considered worth fifty pounds; thus virtually abolishing the property qualification.

"In 1820, the same provisions were repeated, and maintained until 1844, when the present State Constitution was substituted.

"Thus it appears, that, from 1776 to 1807, — a period of thirty-one years, — the right of women and negroes to vote was *admitted and exercised;* then from 1807 to 1844 — by an arbitrary act of the Legislature, which does not seem to have been ever contested — the constitutional right was *suspended*, and both women and negroes excluded from the polls for thirty-seven years more. The extension of suffrage, in the State Constitution of 1776, to 'all inhabitants' possessing the prescribed qualifications, was doubtless due to the Quaker influence, then strong in West Jersey, and then, as now, in favor of the equal rights of women.

"Since 1844, under the present Constitution, suffrage is conferred upon 'every white male citizen of the United States, of the age of twenty-one years, who shall have been a resident of this State one year, and of the county in which he claims a vote five months next before the election,' excepting paupers, idiots, insane persons, and criminals.

"This Constitution is subject to amendment by a majority of both Houses of two successive Legislatures, when such amendment is afterward ratified by the people at a special election.

"Lucy Stone,
H. B. Blackwell."

In a recent visit to Perth Amboy, a friend directed my attention to a figure in a broad-brimmed hat, very much like that which used to adorn the cover of Poor Richard's Almanac. "That man is ninety-five years old," said he. "He spent his youth in preventing the New-Jersey people from running their slaves off South. A prospective emancipation act had been passed, which made the young negroes a poor investment; but our friend Parker, there, looked after them without any fee. We think he looks like Benjamin Franklin." The next day, I took a drive with Mr. Parker himself, and I found he possessed another claim on my interest. The original Constitution of New Jersey, adopted in 1776, left women free to vote, by leaving out the word "male." In 1790, when the Constitution was revised, a Quaker member, "Friend Hooper," rose to say that among his people the women were allowed their natural share of influence. At his instance, the matter was made clearer by the insertion of the words "he or she." In 1807, after an election contested with singular virulence, these words were expunged, and the word "male" inserted. I had never expected to see a member of the Legislature who repealed this phrase; but Friend Parker was there, and helped do it. He assured me that the women were not at that time anxious to retain the privilege; but that, if they had been, the Legislature was so irate, that the change would have taken place. Lads, both white and colored, and under age, had dressed in women's clothes, to swell the ballot, which was more than double what it should have been; the irritating question being the possible removal of the county buildings.

A few days since, I cut from the paper the following paragraph:—

"In the Kentucky House of Representatives, on Friday last, an address was received by the Speaker, from Mrs. ——, of New York, and read by the Clerk, asking the Legislature of the Southern States to grant suffrage to white women in the South, so as to give the Democratic party the advantage over the negro votes, if Congress passes a general negro-suffrage law. By following out this plan, Mrs. —— thinks the South can govern the country, as in the days of Jefferson."

I suppress the name, which was printed in full, in this paragraph, because it is the name of a woman I respect; and I earnestly hope the whole charge is false. If women seek to advance their own cause by mean and meretricious tricks,—such as those which have dishonored the policy of men,—may God for ever disappoint their hope! I would rather be defeated with the friends of liberty than crowned with its foes. It is because I believe woman strong enough to withstand the low and loose and degrading temptations of public life that I would lead her towards it. If she cannot enter it as an inspiration, may she be for ever shut out!

Mrs. Stanton and Miss Anthony, assisted by Lucy Stone and Antoinette Blackwell, have been busy in agitating all legal questions, and especially the right

of suffrage, ever since the formation of the Equal-
Rights Association, in New York, in May, 1866.
Wherever there is any prospect of a convention to
change a State Constitution, it would seem wise
to agitate the matter; but here, in Massachusetts,
almost every thing has been done that should be
to protect women, except to give them the right of
suffrage. That question we are too wise to agitate,
until the country recovers somewhat from the anxieties and perplexities of the war. We have no
desire to win from an unjust judge, for our importu-
nity's sake, a right which could never be useful,
unless it were accorded with the hearty sympathy of
the best part of the community. On March 16, 1867,
a motion was made in the Massachusetts House to
instruct the Judiciary Committee to report an amendment to the State Constitution, granting the right of
suffrage to women. The yeas and nays were taken,
and the motion was lost: yeas 44, nays 97.

In New York, Illinois, and Michigan, the question
is to be brought before the Constitutional Convention. Wisconsin is our banner State, both branches
of her government having concurred, April 4, 1867,
in a resolution to submit it to the people. In New
York, last year, Mrs. Stanton proposed herself as
a candidate for Congress, and received, I think, thirty
votes. It was so well understood that her election
was impossible, that her card excited neither ridicule nor discussion. No one cared to turn aside
from more pressing interests to consider it. It was

therefore a waste of strength. I saw, with pain, that some women did not shrink from employing last year a politician's trick, and sent to Democratic members of the Senate and House the petitions for the right of suffrage for women, with which they knew them to possess no sympathy. Had these petitions been sent to Republican members of either House, they might have been overlooked in the press of graver anxieties. Mischievously sent to men like Cowan, women must have known that the petition would be produced, if it was only to annoy and perplex our honest friends of the Republican party. In what would our influence upon politics be better than that of men, if we resort to such measures? During the past year, I drew up, and forwarded to the Hon. Charles Sumner, a petition for the right of suffrage, and afterwards sustained it by two or three letters. I think Mr. Sumner never brought it forward; but I gladly defer to his judgment as to that. It was my duty to keep the subject in mind, and see that we did not appear, even in the tumult left by civil war, to lose sight of our claim. I am glad to offer public thanks to the Hon. George Thompson, who, in the meeting of the Equal-Rights Association, held in Philadelphia on Jan. 17, 1867, defeated a resolution of thanks to Mr. Cowan, and condemnation to Mr. Sumner, on precisely these grounds. "To thank men like Cowan, who did not *desire* to enfranchise woman any more than the negro, was to stultify ourselves," he said. " To condemn Sumner, because he did not think *this* the time to push the claims of woman, was not honorable to the long-tried friend of human progress."

Abroad, such things look better. The clean hands of John Stuart Mill — which no noble woman need fear to touch — have presented to Parliament the petition of fifteen hundred women for the right of franchise. This petition is so moderate and sensible, that it deserves to be preserved.

"The humble petition of the undersigned showeth, —

"That it having been expressly laid down by high authorities, that the possession of property, in this country, carries with it the right to vote in the election of representatives in Parliament, it is an evident anomaly, that some holders of property are allowed to use this right, while others, forming no less a constituent part of the nation, and equally qualified by law to hold property, are not able to exercise this privilege; that the participation of women in the government is consistent with the principles of the British Constitution, inasmuch as women in these islands have always been held capable of sovereignty, and women are eligible for various public offices.

"Your petitioners, therefore, humbly pray your honorable House to consider the expediency of providing for the representation of all householders, without distinction of sex, who possess such property or rental qualification as your honorable House may determine. And your petitioners will ever pray.

"Mrs. W. B. CARPENTER, 56, Regent's Park Road, London, N.W.
C. M. CLARKSON, Hatfield Road, Wakefield.
FRANCES POWER COBBE, 26, Hereford Square, London, S.W.
ELIZABETH GARRETT, L.S.A., 20, Upper Berkeley Street, London, W.
MARY ANN GASKELL, Plymouth Grove, Manchester.
MATILDA M. HAYS, Great Malvern.
MARY HOWITT, West Hill Lodge, Highgate, N.

M. S. KINGLAKE, 50, Upper Brunswick Place, Brighton.
ISA CRAIG KNOX, 14, Clyde Terrace, New Cross, S.E.
S. J. LEWIN, Birkenhead.
HARRIET LUPTON, St. Asaph.
ELIZABETH MALLISON, Camp Cottage, Wimbledon.
HARRIET MARTINEAU, The Knoll, Ambleside.
JANE MARTINEAU, 21, Tariton Street, London, W.C.
JANE MOXON, 1, Cundall's Yard, Leeds.
Mrs. ELIZABETH PEASE NICHOL, Huntly Lodge, Edinburgh.
BESSIE R. PARKES, 15, Wimpole Street, London, W.
ELIZABETH PROCTOR, Polam Hall, Darlington.
C. STURCH, Cumberland Terrace, Regent's Park, London, N.W.
Mrs. THOMAS TAYLOR, Aston House, Oxfordshire.
SARAH UNWIN, Hale Lodge, Edgeware, Middlesex.
ANNA MARY HOWITT WATTS, 24, Grove Terrace, Highgate Road."

I append to the above petition a few of the fifteen hundred names, which will serve to give it identity, and interest in this country. We miss, among the names, many names of the beloved dead; and many would doubtless be there that we know, could it be signed by any save property-holders.

A very powerful influence was brought to sustain this petition in Parliament; and among its advocates were James Martineau, Herbert Spencer, Professor Huxley, and Goldwin Smith. Mr. Mill seems to have presented a second petition, headed by Lady Goldschmid, and signed by three thousand persons; and another was offered, at the same time, by Mr. Russell Gurney. On April 11, 1867, the subject of female suffrage was first discussed in the House of Commons without being greeted with a laugh. A petition presented by Mr. Duncan Maclaren, from Edinburgh, was signed by eight university professors, six doctors of law, eighteen clergymen, eight barristers, ten physicians, ten officers, and two thousand other persons. Two women are said to have been lately elected parish overseers: Mrs. Slocomb for Brittadon, and Mrs. Craig for Bratton Fleming. The step-daughter of John Stuart Mill, Miss Helen Taylor, contributed to the January number of the "Westminster" an article which worthily sustained the far more comprehensive statement of her mother in 1851. It would be difficult to imagine a paper, however, that would appeal more forcibly to the English people. There is in England a Woman-Suffrage Association, which proposes to circulate that article as a tract. Mrs. P. A. Taylor and Frances Power Cobbe are among its most active members. Mrs. Bodichon has recently brought out two pamphlets on this subject. They contain one instance, which is not familiar, of the inconvenience of withholding the franchise from English women. Owners of estates seek to further their own interest through the voting power of their tenantry, and frequently eject women from farms, to replace them by men who have a freehold. On one Suffolk farm, seven women have been ejected. Among the instances which Mrs. Bodichon adduces to show the need of female votes are the neglect of female education; the refusal of leases, or the ejection of old tenants; the want of proper public spirit, which women might be expected to infuse into affairs; and the condition of workhouses, and charitable appropriations in general. In Austria, information furnished to one of Mrs. Bodichon's papers seems to show that the women have the same electoral rights as men, only that in a few cases they are compelled to vote by proxy. They vote as nobles, in their corporate capacity as nuns, and as tax-payers or merchants; but I need not say that there is much uncertainty in the Austrian administration of such a law.

In connection with the name of Fredrika Bremer, I have mentioned the great changes in Swedish law, mainly due to her influence. An indirect right of suffrage was further granted to women in 1862; but in December, 1865, the Reform Bill gave the election of members of the Upper Chamber to municipal and county bodies. In the election of these bodies, women take part. They must be unmarried or widows, be twenty-five years old, and have more than four hundred rixdollars per annum.

Article 15 of the Italian electoral law provides "that the taxation paid by a widow, or by a wife separated from her husband, shall give a vote to whichever of her children or near relatives she may select."

A curious petition has been lately presented to the Hungarian Diet. It is signed by a number of widows and other women who are landed proprietors, and asks for them the same equality of political rights with the male inhabitants of the country, as they possessed in 1848. These ladies represent that they have much more difficulty in bringing up their children, and attending to the estates, than men; that they have to bear the same State burdens; that they are not allowed to take part in the communal elections;

and that, although many of them possess much more ground than the male electors, they have no political rights.

In 1848, these women were, for the first time, excluded from the franchise.

PROGRESS.

The real gain of a reform, starting from the heart of the family, must necessarily be very slow. I remember, that some years ago, when I printed my book on Labor, one of my kindest critics congratulated the public, that, of my nine lectures, I had published only these. He thought it was useless to contend for more book-learning for women, and the subject of civil rights still disgusted his sensitive ear. The common sense of the book on Labor ought to have shown him how I should treat the subject of education. He could not understand how the woman who gets an education which does not make her a "bread-winner," is essentially defrauded, nor how a woman, well paid for her labor, is essentially wronged, when she is denied the privilege of protecting it by her vote. There is, however, a surely growing sense of this, shown in the substantial advance of her civil rights.

1. In the early part of 1865, the people of Victoria, in Australia, assembled to elect a member of Parliament, were surprised to find the whole female population voting. Some quick-sighted woman had discovered that the letter of the new law permitted it; and their votes were accepted, and wisely given.

The "London Times," in the month of May, says, that, in a *country like Australia*, it can easily believe that such an extension of the franchise will be a *marked improvement*, and thinks that the precedent will stand!

2. The government of Moravia has also, within the past year, granted the municipal franchise to widows who pay taxes.

3. In January, 1864, the Court of Queen's Bench in Dublin, Ireland, restored to woman the *old right* of voting for town commissioners. The justice (Fitzgerald) desired to state that ladies were entitled to sit as town commissioners as well as to vote for them; and the chief-justice took pains to make it clear that there was nothing in either duty repugnant to womanly habits.

4. The inhabitants of Ain (or Aisne), in France, lately chose nine women into their municipal council.

5. At Bergères, the whole council consisted of women; and the mayor, not being prepared for such good fortune, resigned his office.

6. Our cause has found able advocates in John Stuart Mill, the "New-York Evening Post," and Theodore Tilton. If I were asked, whether, in connection with this gain, we have lost any ground, I should reply that we have decidedly lost it in connection with the daily press. I do not know any newspaper, if I except the "Boston Commonwealth," which will print a letter touching civil rights, from any woman, precisely as it is written. I think what we need

most is to purchase the right to a daily use of half a column of the " New-York Tribune."

RECORD AND OBITUARIES.

I have been accustomed to connect with reports of this kind some honorable mention of distinguished women obscure or recently dead. I cannot do this at any length, after a pause of so many years; but a few names must be mentioned, a few facts recorded.

I had occasion, some years ago, to commemorate the services of Maria Sybilla Merian, painter, engraver, linguist, and traveller, who published, at Amsterdam, two volumes of engravings of insects and sixty magnificent plates, illustrating the metamorphoses of the insects of Surinam. I did not, at that time, know that some of her statements had been held open to suspicion. In the first place, she asserted, that a certain fly, the Fulgoria Lantanaria, emitted so much light, that she could read her books by its aid; still further, that one of the large spiders, called Mygale, entered the nests of the humming-bird in Surinam, sucked its eggs, and snared the birds. To all the contention which arose over these statements, Madame Merian could oppose only her word. Men who knew that her statements in regard to Europe were indisputable decided that her word could not be taken in Asia. A very common folly; but two hundred years have passed, 1866 arrives, and her justification with it. An English traveller, named Bates, has recently rescued quite large finches from the Mygale, and poisoned himself with its saliva, in preparing them for his cabinet.

I do not know how many years Madam Baring, the mother of the great banker, has been dead. It is only recently that I have heard, that to her prudence, activity, and business habits, the family attribute the sure foundation of their fortunes. Matthew Baring came to Larkbeare, near Exeter, from Bremen. His wife superintended, in his day, the long rows of "burlers," or women who picked over the woollen cloth he made. Her sons, John and Francis, sought a wider field for the fortune their father left, but did not forget to erect a monument to their mother's industry.

About a year since, Eliza W. Farnham laid down her weary head. I did not know her, nor did I sympathize in her theories. They were sustained by her imagination rather than her reason; by her impulses rather than any practical judgment. No moral superiority can justly be conferred on either sex of a being possessed of intellect and conscience. God has conferred no such superiority; yet I gladly name Mrs. Farnham here as a woman whose life — a bitter disappointment to herself — was useful to all women, and whose books, published since her death, show a marvellous mental range.

During the last year, Madame Charles Lemonnier died in Paris. She devoted her life to the professional education of women. For six years she found it so difficult to raise the necessary funds, that she had to content herself with sending her pupils to institutions in Germany. In 1862 the Society for the Professional Instruction of Women was at last constituted, and opened a school in the Rue de Perle. Two other schools have since been opened, — one in the Rue de Val Sainte Catherine; the other, in the Rue Roche. The morning is occupied in these schools with general studies; the afternoon, with industrial drawing, wood-engraving, the making-up of garments, linen, &c. She died after initiating a thoroughly successful work.

In July, 1865, there died at Corfu a Dr. Barry, attached to the medical staff of the British army. He was remarkable for skill, firmness, decision, and great rapidity in difficult operations. He had entered the army in 1813, and had served in all quarters of the globe, with such distinction as to ensure promotion without interest. He was clever and agreeable, but excessively plain, weak in stature, and with a squeaking voice which provoked ridicule. He had an irritable temper, and answered some jesting on the topic by calling out the offender, and shooting him through the lungs. In 1840 he was made medical inspector, and transferred from the Cape to Malta. He went from Malta to Corfu; and, when the English Government ceded the Ionian Islands to Greece, resigned his position in the army, and remained at Corfu. There he died last summer, forbidding, with his latest breath, any interference with his remains.

The women who attended him regarded this request with the shameless indifference now so common; and unable to believe, that an officer, who had been forty-five years in the British service, had received a diploma, fought a duel, and been celebrated as a brilliant operator, was not only a woman, but at some period in her life a *mother*, they called in a medical commission to establish these facts. A sad, sad picture, which those of us who inquire into the fortunes of women can readily understand.

Last November deprived us of Mrs. Gaskell and Fredrika Bremer, of whom a fuller record will be found in the body of this work.

In Paris recently died Mrs. Severn Newton. She was the daughter of the artist Severn, the friend of Keats, who is now British Consul at Rome. About five years since, she married Charles Newton, Superintendent of Greek Antiquities at the British Museum. She was a person in whom power and delicacy were singularly blended. Ary Scheffer was accustomed to hold up her work as a model for his pupils. Her renderings of classic sculpture were so true that they were termed translations; and she had recently devoted herself to oil painting with great success. She died of brain fever at the early age of thirty-three, one of the most honored of female English artists.

The common sense of society accepts the need of education for women. It begs that they may be permitted to earn their bread; but let society once grant the suffrage to woman, and she will take care of her own interests. She will found colleges, distribute opportunities, and protect vocations.

Education must, in time, earn independence for most women. Independence, taxed and made a citizen of, will insist, in the course of years, upon its suffrage; but whoso will help to reverse the process, and grant suffrage, so that woman may herself indicate what education she wishes to receive, and what labor she wishes to perform, will speed the process by scores of years.

It was pleasant to see four hundred young women, of the highest health, the best breeding, of good social standing, and abundant means, blossoming like so many tulips, at Vassar, — we must add, also, of good ability, and more than average education; for only good scholars could pass the rigid examination required of those who enter. It was pleasant to see, that between the ages of seventeen and twenty-two, when society offers its greatest allurements, four hundred wealthy girls could be found, ready to devote themselves in seclusion, and without even the stimulus existing at Oberlin or Antioch, to higher things. And then, if the want of public sympathy makes it a painful work to be always pushing the interests of women, such teachers and officers as one finds at Vassar compensate one for any amount of struggle. Miss Hannah Lyman, who is now the principal; Miss Mitchell, the astronomer; Dr. Avery, the resident physician; and Miss Powell, the professor of gymnastics, — it is only necessary to name to Eastern ears: but, besides these women, Vassar employs twenty others, in whom it would be hard to find a fault, and some of whom, we were glad to see, had taken their degree at Oberlin. Going westward to Antioch, it was pleasant to find other women who had taken their degrees, and were now teaching Greek and Latin. One of the graduates, employed as a teacher of mathematics, had won her own education in the college by teaching one year, — sometimes in distant district-schools, — and studying the next. At Oberlin, the picture was still more inspiring: for Oberlin has, I suppose, more pupils than any college in the land, if we except Michigan University; and one-half of them are girls and women. The practical working of this college is beautiful to see. It has been fortunate in the magnificent faith communicated to it by Dr. Finney. Most of the women who were its early students, and stamped its character, so that no scandal dared invade its borders, are now the wives of its professors, and many of them are still engaged in teaching. Mrs. Dascomb, who is the wife of the professor of chemistry, has been with the college from the beginning: she is as fine a person for her position, as lady-principal, as Miss Lyman; yet how differently have the two been trained! Mrs. Dascomb, by isolation, persecution, contact with the rudest elements in Western life, yet keeping, through all, a noble faith in manhood and womanhood; Miss Lyman, starting from the most distinguished social circle in Northampton, holding a high place among what Dr. Holmes would call the "Brahmins" of Montreal, and finally polished by a European tour, and holding control with a power as imperceptible as it is firm. At Milwaukee, beside Dr. Ross, to whose ten years of successful practice I have alluded, I found another physician, in happy partnership with one of the *brothers* of the craft, a Dr. Glass. He has lately moved from Minnesota to Wisconsin, where he has been several years in partnership with Miss Fairchild, and testifies that he has never seen her superior as a practical physician. Here, also, a young lady, of one of the best families, has lately opened a hair-dresser's store. Dr. Ross gives her sweet sympathy and cheer; but, as a proof that the world still needs converting, she has had a good deal of that insolence to subdue which pains just as much as if it were *worth* minding. Any thing like the number of female lecturers which I heard of in Illinois, I had never imagined. The medical women are readily accepted in most places, even without proper vouchers; and it is astonishing, how far common sense contrives to supply the place of education. But the want of vouchers is a serious evil, which must soon be met. In Chicago I heard wonderful stories of the business capacity of certain women. One lady, very well known on Michigan Avenue, brought one hundred thousand dollars' worth of Chicago City bonds to Boston and New York, and safely sold them for her husband. A farmer's wife, from the centre of the State, came up, while I was there, to speculate in corn. She said her husband had lost money several years in succession, and now *she* was going to try. By her first speculation, she made five thousand dollars; and this she put into competent hands, for re-investment. It gained her twenty thousand dollars. The Chicago merchants thought that she would go on speculating until she lost it all; but I do not. I think our Pleasant-street Hospital has proved that women are more cautious than men, and are willing to bear a good deal of obloquy rather than permit rash ventures to be made.

In the country, everywhere, I heard charming anecdotes of the vigor and self-sacrifice women showed in the early settlement of the States.

It happened one spring, that, when the ice broke up on the Fox River, a terrible storm of wind and sleet and rain came with it. Not a man in the State, however great the emergency, would have thought that he could cross. In this state of things, a woman was taken in childbirth, some two or three miles from the ferry. Just as the ferry-woman was going to bed, in the "outer darkness" of that terrible storm, she heard her name shouted from the opposite bank. She listened, and a grievous story was shouted across. She went to the stable and saddled her mare, and, all alone, forded the stream: the floating ice, heaped into walls, struck the sides of the faithful beast, and tore the woman's skirt to tatters. Now and then a flash of lightning showed her what progress she had made. At last, she struggled to the bank, and gave the needful help. Nobody ever asked how she got back. On the grass about Elgin, a whole ship's load died of cholera, nearly forty years ago. All the neigborhood stood back in dread; but I saw one aged woman, who closed the eyes of nine, and received the foreign blessing, which she felt, although she could not understand. In Quincy, I found two ladies just establishing a high school for girls, whom I have previously mentioned as having pushed through the endowment, for women, of the State University at Lawrence, and having opened a class in modelling in clay, under Professor Volkers. At the Cooper Institute I found more women at work than ever before, and to better advantage. A large class had just been formed to color photographs on glass, porcelain, and paper. Under such circumstances, we need not be disheartened because an ignorant woman, in a man's costume, has found the way to attract some attention in Europe and some contempt from Tom Hughes. Neither need it dismay us that the "Boston Advertiser" thinks the Equal-Rights meetings, in New York, have not been largely attended. There are those who want the suffrage, who do not care to encourage women to offer themselves for Congress before public opinion can accept them, and who are sufficiently disgusted by what looks like a mannish coalition with Democrats, to keep away from public meetings.

Meanwhile, the women of Parma clamor for the right to vote for Victor Emanuel. A freedwoman, Charlotte Scott, proposes a monument, on behalf of her emancipated race, to President Lincoln; and the noble inspiration of Harriet Hosmer carries out the thought.

But the very things we turn from force the necessary issues on the world. Wise action would never have brought the recent debate in Congress; nor prudent measures have secured thirty votes for Mrs. Stanton, and nine senatorial ballots for female suffrage. Once agitated in these quarters, the matter draws nearer to a final test.

"Ride on! the prize is near."

L'ENVOI.

My Song, I do believe that there are few
Who will thy reasoning rightly understand,
To them so hard and dark is thy discourse.
Hence, peradventure, if it come to pass
That thou shouldst find thyself with persons who
Appear unskilled to comprehend thee well,
I pray thee, then, my young and well-beloved,
Be not discomforted; but say to them,
"Take note, at least, how *beautiful* I am!"
DANTE, from the "Banquet."

Art thou not beautiful, my new-born Song?
Then thou art piteous, and shalt go thy way.
Rime Apocrife, G. G.

American Women: Images and Realities
An Arno Press Collection

[Adams, Charles F., editor]. **Correspondence between John Adams and Mercy Warren Relating to Her "History of the American Revolution," July-August, 1807.** With a new appendix of specimen pages from the **"History."** 1878.

[Arling], Emanie Sachs. **"The Terrible Siren": Victoria Woodhull, (1838-1927).** 1928.

Beard, Mary Ritter. **Woman's Work in Municipalities.** 1915.

Blanc, Madame [Marie Therese de Solms]. **The Condition of Woman in the United States.** 1895.

Bradford, Gamaliel. **Wives.** 1925.

Branagan, Thomas. **The Excellency of the Female Character Vindicated.** 1808.

Breckinridge, Sophonisba P. **Women in the Twentieth Century.** 1933.

Campbell, Helen. **Women Wage-Earners.** 1893.

Coolidge, Mary Roberts. **Why Women Are So.** 1912.

Dall, Caroline H. **The College, the Market, and the Court.** 1867.

[D'Arusmont], Frances Wright. **Life, Letters and Lectures: 1834, 1844.** 1972.

Davis, Almond H. **The Female Preacher, or Memoir of Salome Lincoln.** 1843.

Ellington, George. **The Women of New York.** 1869.

Farnham, Eliza W[oodson]. **Life in Prairie Land.** 1846.

Gage, Matilda Joslyn. **Woman, Church and State.** [1900].

Gilman, Charlotte Perkins. **The Living of Charlotte Perkins Gilman.** 1935.

Groves, Ernest R. **The American Woman.** 1944.

Hale, [Sarah J.] **Manners; or, Happy Homes and Good Society All the Year Round.** 1868.

Higginson, Thomas Wentworth. **Women and the Alphabet.** 1900.

Howe, Julia Ward, editor. **Sex and Education.** 1874.

La Follette, Suzanne. **Concerning Women.** 1926.

Leslie, Eliza. **Miss Leslie's Behaviour Book: A Guide and Manual for Ladies.** 1859.

Livermore, Mary A. **My Story of the War.** 1889.

Logan, Mrs. John A. (Mary S.) **The Part Taken By Women in American History.** 1912.

McGuire, Judith W. (A Lady of Virginia). **Diary of a Southern Refugee, During the War.** 1867.

Mann, Herman. **The Female Review: Life of Deborah Sampson.** 1866.

Meyer, Annie Nathan, editor. **Woman's Work in America.** 1891.

Myerson, Abraham. **The Nervous Housewife.** 1927.

Parsons, Elsie Clews. **The Old-Fashioned Woman.** 1913.

Porter, Sarah Harvey. **The Life and Times of Anne Royall.** 1909.

Pruette, Lorine. **Women and Leisure: A Study of Social Waste.** 1924.

Salmon, Lucy Maynard. **Domestic Service.** 1897.

Sanger, William W. **The History of Prostitution.** 1859.

Smith, Julia E. **Abby Smith and Her Cows.** 1877.

Spencer, Anna Garlin. **Woman's Share in Social Culture.** 1913.

Sprague, William Forrest. **Women and the West.** 1940.

Stanton, Elizabeth Cady. **The Woman's Bible** Parts I and II. 1895/1898.

Stewart, Mrs. Eliza Daniel. **Memories of the Crusade.** 1889.

Todd, John. **Woman's Rights.** 1867. [Dodge, Mary A.] (Gail Hamilton, pseud.) **Woman's Wrongs.** 1868.

Van Rensselaer, Mrs. John King. **The Goede Vrouw of Mana-ha-ta.** 1898.

Velazquez, Loreta Janeta. **The Woman in Battle.** 1876.

Vietor, Agnes C., editor. **A Woman's Quest: The Life of Marie E. Zakrzewska, M.D.** 1924.

Woodbury, Helen L. Sumner. **Equal Suffrage.** 1909.

Young, Ann Eliza. **Wife No. 19.** 1875.

HQ1423 .D22 1972

WITHDRAWN
From Bertrand Library

DATE DUE

APR 28 1978			
MAY 5 1991			

GAYLORD · PRINTED IN U.S.A.